THE AUTHO

Jill Wallis was born in Southport but was brought up in St Asaph, North Wales. She studied history at UCNW, Bangor, graduating with first class honours in 1974. She went on to gain an MA for research into the operation of the World War II evacuation scheme.

Jill is a qualified archivist and worked for several years at the Head Office of British Petroleum in London. She has had two other books published: *Valiant FOR Peace. A History of the Fellowship of Reconciliation 1914-89*, and *Mother of World Peace: The Life of Muriel Lester*. She now works as a freelance editor and proofreader from her home on the Wirral, where she lives with her husband and two daughters.

ACKNOWLEDGEMENTS

I should like to thank everyone who has in some way or other contributed to this book - the former evacuees, teachers, billeting officers and host family members who have shared their memories of evacuation with me (a list of whom appears at the end of this book); library and records office staff across Merseyside and North Wales who have patiently helped me track down archives, books and photographs; local newspapers who printed my appeal for memories of evacuation, and particularly the Liverpool Daily Post who have allowed me to quote extracts from wartime issues of the paper. Thanks also to Radio Merseyside's 'A Team' for broadcasting details of my research. I am very grateful to everyone who has lent me material relating to evacuation - photographs, luggage labels, letters and other documents - all of it very precious. Special thanks go to Don Aird, Eric Jackson, Margaret Jones, Sue Ellis, Keith Ashley and Dave Kesterton, and to all my family and friends - who've had to put up with 'evacuation' talk for so long! Finally, to Andrew, Anna and Katy - many, many thanks for all your help and support in a million and one ways.

NORTH WALES and MERSEYSIDE
1939-1945

CONTENTS

Acknowledgements iii

Author's Preface vi

Introduction: Evacuation - Why? and How? ix

1. Preparing for a Local War 1
2. Farewell England: Croeso i Gymru 21
    The Market Place 40
    The Bud of the Nation? 49
3. The Phoney War: About Turn 56
    'I need a drink' 57
    'Take me home!' 60
    Visiting 63
    Upstairs Downstairs 68
    'He who gives a child a home...' 71
    'Let Them Remain' 72
4. 'Tact, Tolerance, Enterprise and Ingenuity' 84
    Wet Beds and Itchy Heads 84
    From Plimsolls to Clogs 106
    Schooling in Wartime 115
    Chapel - and more chapel! 143
    'We're in Germany!' 153
5. Preparing a New Scheme 165
6. Fleeing the Bombs 181
    Exodus 181
    No Vacancies 191
7. Minding the Children 212
8. More Comings and Goings 242
9. Home Again to Wales 259
10. The Verdict 270

Bibliography 277

List of Contributors 283

Index 285

PREFACE

In 1974, as a postgraduate history student, I was searching for a suitable topic of research - preferably social history, perhaps covering the period of the Second World War. As I was based in Bangor it seemed sensible to try and discover what records were available on the North Wales area for the war years. I was amazed to find there was a huge amount of paperwork - much of it dealing with the government's evacuation scheme. To be honest although I was vaguely aware that such a scheme existed I had absolutely no idea what it had involved - at that time very little had actually been written on the subject. Two years and a mountain of research notes later I began to realise just what an enormous task evacuation had been.

As a student I'd found evacuation a fascinating topic. Years on, married with two children of my own, I began to view it in a rather different light. Now I found myself wondering how on earth parents had been able to hand over their children into the care of strangers, and how those same strangers had coped with the awesome responsibility of looking after someone else's little ones - and in the middle of a war. Not to mention what it must have been like for the children themselves!

In 1999, the year of the 60th anniversary of the start of the evacuation scheme, I decided to try and bring my research up to date. Although a lot more had now been written about evacuation in general, the history of the Merseyside / North Wales experience had not been fully chronicled. My original research had been a study of North Wales as a reception area. Now I needed to look at how things had been organised on Merseyside and, especially, how the evacuees had viewed it all.

An appeal for memories, put out on local radio and through the local press, produced an astonishing response. Former evacuees wrote to me, phoned me, e-mailed me and even turned up on my doorstep. And they brought with them a wealth of memories - some happy, some sad, but almost all extremely vivid despite the fact that so many years had elapsed since those luggage-label days.

THE AUTHO

Jill Wallis was born in Southport but was brought up in St Asaph, North Wales. She studied history at UCNW, Bangor, graduating with first class honours in 1974. She went on to gain an MA for research into the operation of the World War II evacuation scheme.

Jill is a qualified archivist and worked for several years at the Head Office of British Petroleum in London. She has had two other books published: *Valiant FOR Peace. A History of the Fellowship of Reconciliation 1914-89*, and *Mother of World Peace: The Life of Muriel Lester*. She now works as a freelance editor and proofreader from her home on the Wirral, where she lives with her husband and two daughters.

ACKNOWLEDGEMENTS

I should like to thank everyone who has in some way or other contributed to this book - the former evacuees, teachers, billeting officers and host family members who have shared their memories of evacuation with me (a list of whom appears at the end of this book); library and records office staff across Merseyside and North Wales who have patiently helped me track down archives, books and photographs; local newspapers who printed my appeal for memories of evacuation, and particularly the Liverpool Daily Post who have allowed me to quote extracts from wartime issues of the paper. Thanks also to Radio Merseyside's 'A Team' for broadcasting details of my research. I am very grateful to everyone who has lent me material relating to evacuation - photographs, luggage labels, letters and other documents - all of it very precious. Special thanks go to Don Aird, Eric Jackson, Margaret Jones, Sue Ellis, Keith Ashley and Dave Kesterton, and to all my family and friends - who've had to put up with 'evacuation' talk for so long! Finally, to Andrew, Anna and Katy - many, many thanks for all your help and support in a million and one ways.

iii

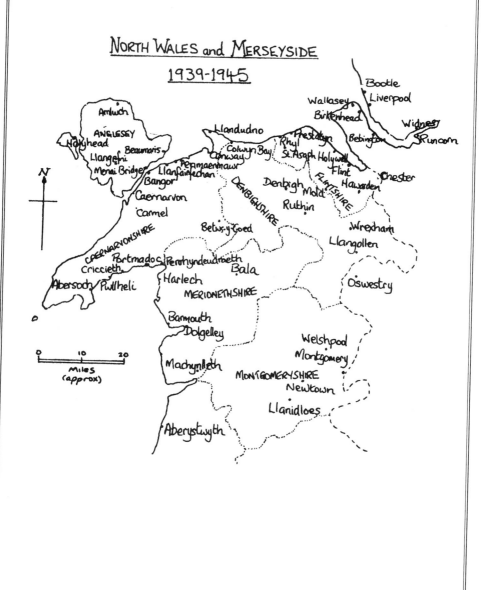

NORTH WALES and MERSEYSIDE
1939-1945

CONTENTS

Acknowledgements   iii

Author`s Preface   vi

Introduction: Evacuation - Why? and How?   ix

1. Preparing for a Local War   1
2. Farewell England: Croeso i Gymru   21
     The Market Place   40
     The Bud of the Nation?   49
3. The Phoney War: About Turn   56
     'I need a drink'   57
     'Take me home!'   60
     Visiting   63
     Upstairs Downstairs   68
     'He who gives a child a home...'   71
     'Let Them Remain'   72
4. 'Tact, Tolerance, Enterprise and Ingenuity'   84
     Wet Beds and Itchy Heads   84
     From Plimsolls to Clogs   106
     Schooling in Wartime   115
     Chapel - and more chapel!   143
     'We're in Germany!'   153
5. Preparing a New Scheme   165
6. Fleeing the Bombs   181
     Exodus   181
     No Vacancies   191
7. Minding the Children   212
8. More Comings and Goings   242
9. Home Again to Wales   259
10. The Verdict   270

Bibliography   277

List of Contributors   283

Index   285

PREFACE

In 1974, as a postgraduate history student, I was searching for a suitable topic of research - preferably social history, perhaps covering the period of the Second World War. As I was based in Bangor it seemed sensible to try and discover what records were available on the North Wales area for the war years. I was amazed to find there was a huge amount of paperwork - much of it dealing with the government's evacuation scheme. To be honest although I was vaguely aware that such a scheme existed I had absolutely no idea what it had involved - at that time very little had actually been written on the subject. Two years and a mountain of research notes later I began to realise just what an enormous task evacuation had been.

As a student I'd found evacuation a fascinating topic. Years on, married with two children of my own, I began to view it in a rather different light. Now I found myself wondering how on earth parents had been able to hand over their children into the care of strangers, and how those same strangers had coped with the awesome responsibility of looking after someone else's little ones - and in the middle of a war. Not to mention what it must have been like for the children themselves!

In 1999, the year of the 60th anniversary of the start of the evacuation scheme, I decided to try and bring my research up to date. Although a lot more had now been written about evacuation in general, the history of the Merseyside / North Wales experience had not been fully chronicled. My original research had been a study of North Wales as a reception area. Now I needed to look at how things had been organised on Merseyside and, especially, how the evacuees had viewed it all.

An appeal for memories, put out on local radio and through the local press, produced an astonishing response. Former evacuees wrote to me, phoned me, e-mailed me and even turned up on my doorstep. And they brought with them a wealth of memories - some happy, some sad, but almost all extremely vivid despite the fact that so many years had elapsed since those luggage-label days.

In the pages that follow I have tried to explain a little about how there came to be an evacuation scheme in the first place, and what preparations had been made in both Merseyside and North Wales before it was put into operation. (I have used 'North Wales' to describe the area stretching roughly from Anglesey down to Aberystwyth, including the Borders.) I have looked at the departure of the evacuees, their arrival at the various reception areas and, often, their speedy return home again, explaining some of the raeasons why so many did go back so quickly.

Chapter Four examines the problems encountered and how they were dealt with - matters of health, clothing, schooling, religion and the Welsh language. The government's new scheme is outlined, and 'Fleeing the Bombs' describes how many thousands again left Merseyside in late 1940 and early 1941, this time driven out by the ferocious blitz and into an increasingly overcrowded North Wales. 'Minding the Children' considers work done to safeguard the welfare of evacuees - the vigilance of those involved but sadly, too, occasional lapses. Then 'more comings and goings' take place in 1944 as most Merseysiders leave for home to make room for those escaping the 'V' bombs in the south. But this is not quite the end of the story - many evacuees had formed strong ties with Wales and down the years have often journeyed back there: 'Home Again to Wales' tells of some of the evacuee reunions which have taken place.

The final chapter offers a brief verdict on the whole evacuation experience: was it all a dream, or was it a nightmare? Was there really a welcome in the hillsides for Merseyside evacuees?

Jill Wallis

8th June, 1946

T O-DAY, AS WE CELEBRATE VICTORY, I send this personal message to you and all other boys and girls at school. For you have shared in the hardships and dangers of a total war and you have shared no less in the triumph of the Allied Nations.

I know you will always feel proud to belong to a country which was capable of such supreme effort; proud, too, of parents and elder brothers and sisters who by their courage, endurance and enterprise brought victory. May these qualities be yours as you grow up and join in the common effort to establish among the nations of the world unity and peace.

George R.I.

A Celebratory Greeting Card from the King George to all schoolchildren at the end of World War II. On the reverse of the the card is a list of dates of the major war events entitled 'My Family's War Record'. The only important dates that are missing are those of the mass evacuation from the cities of Britain.

Introduction - *Evacuation: Why? and How?*

On 1 November [1911] an Italian airman, flying over a Turkish military encampment at an oasis in Tripolitania, leaned out of his craft and dropped a few small bombs by hand. No serious damage was done, but a new, and in due course terrible era had been inaugurated, that of aerial bombardment...[1]

The idea of a government-organised scheme of mass 'evacuation'- moving vulnerable civilians away from danger zones - developed in response to the way warfare was changing in the twentieth century. As early as 1898 the Hague Convention had outlawed the dropping of bombs from balloons or (with a view to future inventions) from any other kinds of 'aerial vessels'. Yet a few years later at a second Hague meeting, in 1907, only twenty-seven of the forty-four countries present voted to retain this ban - though it was still agreed at this stage that civilians should not be regarded as legitimate targets! Soon the major powers began to compete in stockpiling first airships and then aeroplanes. In 1908, reporting to a government-appointed Committee on Aerial Navigation, Sir Hiriam Maxim (inventor of the Maxim gun) made a chilling prophecy when he said that: *'If a thousand tons of pure nitro-glycerine were dropped on to London in one night, it would make London look like a last year's buzzard's nest.'*[2] Somewhere along the line, the notion that civilians should not be involved seems to have gone by the wayside.

It was to be more than thirty years before Maxim's grim forecast was realised but less than ten before Britain experienced its first air raids. During the Great War of 1914-18, bombs, dropped by German Zeppelins and giant Gotha bombers, caused 4,820 civilian casualties, with 1,413 people killed. London had been the enemy's first and main target but in January 1916 the Midlands also came under attack. Not surprisingly, people panicked; Londoners crammed themselves into underground stations to escape the terrifying new menace. This was 'total war'- civilians in their homes, in a country which had not actually been invaded, were under attack - and the authorities were not slow to realise its implications.

Obviously, as aircraft technology developed - Britain already had 22,000 warplanes by November 1918 - 'aerial bombardment' would become a far greater feature of any future war and the reaction of the population could prove vital to the overall war effort. Never mind the distress of the people themselves, the nation simply could not afford to have its transport systems and production lines thrown into disarray by a panic-stricken public fleeing the cities; nor could she afford to have her fighting men distracted by fears for the safety of their families back home. Purely as a military expedient, then, the prospect of civilian attack made it necessary to develop civilian defence; and so a Civil Defence Strategy began to be developed, to counter the likely effects of air attack among sections of congested urban populations. The Evacuation Scheme was to become a key element in this strategy.

Before looking at the plans drawn up by the government in the twentieth century it is interesting to note that the actual idea of moving civilians away from war zones was not entirely new. During the Napoleonic Wars, when it had looked likely that Britain might be invaded by the French, quite detailed plans had been drawn up for moving some women and children (and livestock!) away from East Anglia and the south coast. In 1803 the Taylor family (including Jane Taylor, writer of 'Twinkle, Twinkle Little Star') were amongst those affected, having to move from Colchester to the comparative safety of Lavenham. Those who were planning the scheme in the twentieth century should perhaps have read Mrs Taylor's account; whilst travelling from Merseyside to North Wales in 1939 might not have been quite so primitive, there are aspects of this early flight to safety which may well have rung true with many a World War II evacuee! In the journey from Colchester:

> ...there were upwards of twenty and each woman had a child ... They were indeed of the lowliest sort but they were civil creatures ... But what we suffered from heat, smell and bad language during the day was nothing to what we suffered when night came on. The road bad, the waggon so loaded that we expected to break down and the horses so tired that they could scarcely go on. The drivers were frightened and you may be sure the passengers were so. (Mrs Taylor, 1803)[3]

What was different about the evacuation scheme in 1939 was of course the nature of the threat to civilians and the sheer scale of the planned operation. It was clear that the government had accepted the principle of mass evacuation as early as 1924 when preliminary discussions were held by a newly-formed sub-committee of the Committee of Imperial Defence. This sub-committee on 'Air Raid Precautions' (soon universally referred to as ARP) was chaired by Sir John Anderson - a man who would later play a key role in finalising the evacuation scheme but is perhaps best known for giving his name to a highly succesful air raid shelter. The committee's first report was published in 1925, and despite confining its discussions to London it did set down some important general principles, emphasising, for example, the need for persuasion rather than coercion in handling any removal of women and children. The committee mainly comprised representatives from the War Office and the Home Office though the Health Minister and the Chief Schools Inspector were also on hand to give advice. Even some insight into future difficulties was voiced when one member commented that some of the London children *'would not be the kind of children that would be welcomed too ardently, even by patriotic householders'*.[4] A specific Evacuation Sub-Committee was set up in 1931, benefiting from the presence of Wing Commander John Hodsoll, who had been involved in the evacuation of the British from Kabul during the 1929 Afghan revolt. It was already agreed that any scheme of evacuation should, if possible, be set in motion *before* a state of war was declared. Yet still it was only London which was the focus of attention, and an emphasis on secrecy made it virtually impossible to prepare detailed reception plans.

In 1932 Stanley Baldwin made his famous comment that 'The bomber will always get through.' He also maintained that *'The only defence is in offence - which means that you have to kill more women and children more quickly than the enemy if you want to save yourself'*[5] - a ruthless sentiment, but one which nevertheless recognised the inevitability of civilian involvement in any future war. It was Baldwin's National Government that revitalised evacuation plans, abandoned the secrecy, established an ARP Department at the Home Office and brought Sir John Anderson back into the picture. Ten years had passed since Anderson's first far-seeing report had been produced, yet there had been little concrete progress. Admittedly during the intervening period neither the Government nor the people had been much inclined to contemplate war of any kind. The Great War had, after all, been 'the war to end wars'. Popular 'pacifism' was running high - indicated by such activities as the Ponsonby Peace Letter, the Oxford Union Debate and the Peace Ballot and by organisations like the No More War Movement, the League of Nations Union and Dick Sheppard's Peace Pledge Union. Writers such as Aldington, Graves, Hemingway, Sherriff, Remarques, Sassoon and Vera Brittain had all highlighted the horrors of the 1914-18 war and had done much to generate an anti-war sentiment in the country at large.

Yet as the thirties progressed, there were ominous developments on the international scene. Hitler's voice was becoming ever more strident in Germany; Mussolini illustrated the possibilities of poison-gas warfare when he used this against the Abyssinians in 1936; the devestating potential of air attack was demonstrated first in Shanghai and then in Guernica. To make matters worse the Government discovered that German strike power had been seriously underestimated. Revised Air Staff estimates now projected that bombing raids would inflict enormous casualties and that areas other than London would be affected. The House of Commons began to grow restless over Civil Defence affairs, and questions increasingly centred on evacuation plans which had been strangely neglected in the Air Raid Precautions Act of 1937. On 24 May 1938 a House of Commons Committee on Evacuation was appointed under the chairmanship of Sir John Anderson, by this time Permanent Under-Secretary at the Home Office. Anderson was a civil servant *par excellence*, an extremely capable administrator but rather a 'cold fish'. The fact that Anderson was the driving force behind the evacuation plans may explain why the scheme was such a triumph of logistics but often failed on simple humanitarian grounds. Nevertheless, his presence did at least ensure that, not before time, a vigorous study of the whole issue of evacuation was now to be set in motion.

On 26 July 1938 the Anderson Committee presented its report, outlining what were in effect to be the five main principles of the Evacuation Scheme: Whilst production would have to be maintained in the large industrial towns it was vital that facilities be provided for evacuating substantial numbers of people from such areas. Evacuation was not to be compulsory, except where military reasons made it necessary for specific areas to be cleared of civilians. Arrangements for reception of the refugees was to be based on the principle of billeting in private houses, with powers of compulsion to be available to local authorities. The government was to bear the initial cost of evacuation but those who could afford it were then to contribute to the cost of their upkeep. Finally, to meet the needs of parents unable to make arrangements of their own, special schemes would be drawn up to enable schoolchildren to move out in groups from their schools in the charge of their teachers. The committee also emphasised the importance of establishing both central and local machinery to undertake the huge amount of detailed planning which such a programme of evacuation would entail, and to inform and educate the public. As a start local authorities were to make an immediate survey of all available accommodation.

Anderson's report was not actually published until 27 October 1938 by which time Chamberlain had returned seemingly victorious from his meeting with Hitler, clutching the famous scrap of paper and proclaiming 'Peace in our time'. The Munich Crisis had passed but in the frantic preparations beforehand, when war had seemed inevitable, some attempt had been made to apply the principles which the report outlined. On 29 September the government had made known plans for the voluntary assisted evacuation from London of 2 million persons, timed to begin with the evacuation of schoolchildren the following day. Only a few days earlier, at one of the hastily convened meetings to discuss contingency plans it had been suggested that children might *cycle* out of the danger areas - such was the rudimentary level of organisation![6]

On Merseyside, the evacuation of schoolchildren was discussed at a meeting of the Education Committee on 26 September 1938, at which the chairman, C.G.S. Gordon announced there were *'no arrangements for the total evacuation of the school population because we have no idea where they could go to'*.[7] Schools were certainly to be closed if war was declared - the committee felt children would be better off under parental control in such circumstances - but plans for evacuation were then hastily improvised, although no details of these have survived. Similar improvisations were drawn up in other parts of the country - in all it was thought that about one third of the population should be removed from various industrial centres in the Midlands, the North East and the North West (including Liverpool and Bootle). Fortunately for all concerned a cancellation was issued at the eleventh hour. One of the newly appointed Regional Commissioners admitted that had it been necessary to actually implement a scheme it would have been nothing short of chaotic.

Wales was not supposed to have featured officially in the evacuation plans drawn up in 1938,[8] but local authority records, certainly in the north, seem to indicate that they were involved. Several Welsh authorities received an urgent request from the Health Ministry on 16 September 1938 for an estimate of how much surplus accommodation was available, based on an 'Overcrowding Survey' made under the recent (1935) Housing Act. More than this, evidence suggests quite detailed schemes were actually drawn up to meet the possibility of certain areas being called upon to receive evacuees - hence this note dated 29 September 1938 from Miss Ellis Davies, Honorary Organiser of the WVS for Anglesey and Caernarvonshire:

The WVS have been asked by the Home Office to organise the scheme for the evacuation of schoolchildren from the towns likely to be bombed to safe zones in N. Wales ... Committees have been formed in all the towns and some of the larger villages in both counties [Anglesey and Caernarvon] and arrangements are to be made to house the children in some buildings such as Vestries, Memorial Halls etc., until the committee find permanent billets for them. The Education Authorities of the home town meet all expenses and teachers who accompany the children will carry on their education ... The scheme has the full approval of the Medical Officer of Health for the County and of Colonel Wynne Finch, the ARP Officer.[9]

The 'WVS' was a new civilian body which had been set up at a meeting of representatives of Britain's chief women's organisations at the Home Office in May 1938. Led by the Dowager Marchioness of Reading, 'The Women's Voluntary Services for Air Raid Precautions' were to take responsibilty for 'the enrolment of women for the ARP services of the Local Authorities, to help bring home to every household in the country what attack may mean and to make known to every household what it can do to protect itself and help the community'. Early in 1939 it was renamed the 'Women's Royal Voluntary Services for Civil Defence' and its role was considerably extended.[10]

As it transpired Miss Davies's scheme, and others', were made redundant by the Munich settlement - but they had given some firmer insight into what exactly 'Reception' might entail; and had shown how much was still to be done. Some of the assumptions underlying the Evacuation Scheme should perhaps also have been questioned following the experiences of 1938. In the first place, at most of the high level discussions of evacuation which had taken place over the last ten years or so the general consensus had been that it would be 'the lower orders' who were likely to panic in the event of air attack. Yet Wales alone had witnessed an influx of some 150,000 people in the tense summer months of 1938 - and it was not the masses who were running away but 'wealthy exiles from south-east England' who now, as they would again later, *settled into hotels on the Welsh coast with the intention of sitting out the war drinking gin, reading novels and playing cards'*.[11] The truth of the matter was that many of the ministers and civil servants had little real knowledge of Britain's working classes: on the one hand they thought them incapable of bearing a 'stiff upper lip' in the face of danger; on the other hand, with their own 'boarding-school mentality', they assumed these parents would readily give their children over to the care of strangers. They were to be proved wrong on both these counts. The essentially 'male, military, ministerial and middle-class' influence behind plans for evacuation would have some unfortunate consequences.

The evacuation plans also carried an underlying assumption that a vast army of volunteers would provide accommodation and run the scheme. Yet there were warning signs issuing on this score, too. In March 1938, following the fall of Austria, the Home Secretary, Samuel Hoare, had appealed for volunteers to undertake emergency work: he asked for a million to come forward - less than half this number did so.[12] Although Lady Reading later met with better results in her recruiting of women, overall the results were disappointing. Perhaps the memory was still too fresh of what had befallen those in a previous war who had rallied to the cry 'Your Country Needs You'?

In the inevitable 'post-mortems' held after the Munich crisis had passed, evacuation arrangements, indeed Civil Defence plans in general, came in for widespread criticism. On the grounds that reception of evacuees was mainly a matter for housing, education, health and poor law, responsibility for the scheme was transferred from the Home Office to the Ministry of Health and an Advisory Committee was appointed. This comprised representatives of the Association of Local Authorities, of Local Education Authorities and of the teaching profession, and finally undertook to translate Anderson's recommendations into specific plans.

By January 1939, though not without difficulty, the country had been divided into three zones: 'Evacuation', 'Neutral' and 'Reception' - a classification incidentally which obviously bemused some members of the public such as the woman who, travelling by train in January 1940 from Huyton and Kirby, then a 'neutral area' was heard to comment: *'Oh well, we're neutral now but things happen so quickly these days I expect we'll soon be at war with Germany too'.*[13] Many local authorities objected to their particular classifications but had to plan accordingly pending appeal. As far as the Merseyside area was concerned, the County Boroughs of Liverpool, Bootle, and Birkenhead, as well as parts of Crosby and Wallasey were identified as Evacuation areas, whilst the urban districts of Ellesmere Port and Runcorn, with the Borough of Bebington were, somewhat controversially, classed as Neutral.

Bearing in mind that accommodation in the designated reception areas was limited, it was decided that the evacuation scheme should be restricted to certain 'priority classes' which were defined as:

Schoolchildren removed as units under the charge of their teachers.
Younger children accompanied by their mothers or some other guardian.
Expectant mothers.
Adult blind and / or crippled persons.

However, as the government retained the idea that evacuation must be voluntary - not, it should be added, on any humanitarian grounds but simply in order to avoid any liability - it was very difficult to assess precisely how many would be involved. Given the shortage of building time, the likely expense - and the dubious desirability in any case - of using camps or hostels, the Anderson Committee's original solution, of resorting to private billets, was adopted. It was here that the voluntary nature of the scheme had to be abandoned. Perhaps the earlier lack of enthusiasm for 'volunteering' had been noted, or perhaps this was a recognition of 'human nature' plain and simple - whatever the reason, it was certainly recognised now that a policy of billeting on private households might just prove unpopular and that powers of coercion would have to be available to gurantee sufficient accommodation. Despite this, the Minister of Health, Walter Elliot, in broadcasting details of the scheme to the nation on the evening of 6 January, 1939, insisted that:

We want this to be a matter of real human relationship and affection - a willing host and a willing guest. The whole nation will have to feel itself as one if such a crisis really comes. And, remember, no one can say, 'My house will never be destroyed.' It may be for any one of us to ask as well as to give, this national hospitality.[14]

It was important to establish quickly just how much billeting space there was in those areas designated for reception, and early in January 1939 local authorities were asked to conduct a detailed survey. This was intended not just to discover the extent of unused space but also to 'test the water', to check out public reaction to the scheme by seeing exactly how many people would co-operate. As Walter Elliot recognised, it was obviously desirable that *'children should be accommodated where their presence would be willingly accepted'.*[15] It was at this stage that the Local Authorities of North Wales were obliged for the first time to seriously consider the role they would play in the Government's evacuation scheme, for the Ministry of Health explained: *'Broadly speaking, the areas in which the survey of houses with suitable accommodation will be conducted, are the areas which are not contiguous to obvious large targets and those which are less densely populated and, therefore, are more suitable for reception.'*[16] North Wales seemed to fit the bill very nicely.

From the aspect of security the area offered obvious advantages - it was a mountainous region, and this alone would present dangers to enemy aircraft, particularly if flying at night. In any case Wales was felt to be too westerly to suffer air attack from Germany (though, in the event, not only were there raids in Cardiff, Swansea and Pembroke docks but even some remote areas in the North were targetted or were hit when German planes 'offloaded' their bombs![17]). In addition it was a predominantly rural area, possessing few of the 'obvious large targets' likely to attract enemy attention. The western and southern parts of North Wales, and its coastal areas depended primarily on agriculture and the tourist trade, although there were scattered slate mines and stone-quarrying works, and also docks at Holyhead. Along the Flintshire coast were a number of important industries, principally iron and steel, and rayon, and there was coal-mining in the Wrexham area. Other small industrial concerns included chemicals, woollens, saw-milling and metal windows[18] but taking the region as a whole such pockets of industry were few and far between. Indeed, its economic condition on the eve of the Second World War was a cause for some concern.

Unemployment, high throughout Britain in the 1930s, had been particularly bad in Wales, reaching a peak in August 1932 when 42.8 per cent of insured Welsh males were unemployed. Even when things had begun to pick up in other parts of the country, the revival in Wales was slow; many people left to look for work in England or abroad. In 1936, Harlech and Portmadoc were included in the list of places to be given priority in the allocation of official contracts, being areas where the rate of unemployment among men aged over eighteen had averaged at least 25 per cent over the previous twelve months. The North Wales slate industry, hit by poor management relations, by a depression in the building trade, by foreign competition and by the use of new building materials, was experiencing a steady decline.[19]

But it was not only the industrial areas of Wales that were suffering. Low food prices and a fall-off in demand for wool, mutton, beef, butter and cheese - staples of the Welsh agricultural economy - meant that the rural population was equally depressed. There were some improvements in the late 1930s with the establishment of the Milk Marketing Board which gave Welsh farmers a secure market and a regular income, but this did not come soon enough to prevent a serious depopulation of rural areas - which would, incidentally, have interesting repercussions as far as evacuation was concerned. Many former evacuees speak of being billeted on 'old people' and it is easy to think that this was just the imagination of children to whom anyone over the age of thirty might be called 'old'! But in fact in Welsh rural counties the population *was* markedly older than it was in Britain as a whole. Depopulation of the country areas also meant that there was a notable shortage of farm labourers (a 33 per cent fall in such between 1930 and 1939) so that the prospect of tough young evacuee boys to 'help out' on the farms must have been very welcome to many farmers!

In June 1939, the Report of the Anti-Tuberculosis Service of Wales and Monmouth was published. This offered a comment on Welsh local government, in particular on the administration of the health service, and rural authorities were stigmatised as being backward, grossly negligent and inefficient. The principal author of the Report, Clement Davies, asked Caernarvonshire County Council members if they were not utterly ashamed of themselves.[20] This weak administration, along with financial constraints, meant that local authorities had failed to fulfil their duties in respect of health, housing and welfare. The countryside lacked the services of full-time medical officers or trained midwives, and there was little provision of milk and meals for schoolchildren. Housing services fared little better: efforts to disinfect contaminated house were 'woefully inadequate', in fact the housing stock in general was a cause for serious concern. The authorities had failed to take advantage of the Addison Act and, despite depopulation there was a severe shortage of adequate housing and some serious overcrowding. In 1939 the living conditions in one of the villages of Anglesey were declared to be *'worse than the native quarters of Shanghai'*.[21] Following publication of the Anti-Tuberculosis Report, it was urged in parliament that rural Wales should be designated a 'Special Area' in order to ensure its social services be brought up to the level of other parts of the UK.

So, whilst North Wales may have been perfectly suited in geographic terms as a place of refuge, in several other respects it was hardly well-placed in 1939 to cope with a massive influx of population, with all the demands that this would make on administration, health services, housing, and so on. There were also other considerations - *'It will at once be conceded'*, concluded the 1939 Report, *that, alongside the poverty and weakness of administration, 'much of the idealism of Wales [also] finds its birthplace in rural areas'.* This 'idealism' centred as it was around religion and language was destined to provide some additional elements to the evacuation scheme in North Wales. Religion, mainly Calvinistic Methodism at that date, still played an enormous part in the social life of the region, and the Welsh language was closely associated with this chapel culture. In fact, in many northern counties Welsh was still extensively used in the home and in the schools. In some of the rural districts of Caernarvonshire, Denbighshire, Anglesey and Merionethshire there were pockets where almost half the population could only speak Welsh.[22] It is interesting to bear this in mind in view of the fact that after the outbreak of war the Foreign Office, in response to offers from various South American countries to take evacuees, replied that large evacuations of British children were to be limited to English-speaking countries only![23]

As will be seen, all of these considerations - the relative poverty of the area, the weakness of the administration, issues of religion and language - were destined in various degrees to affect the 'evacuation experience' in North Wales. On the whole, the local councils administered the scheme far more successfully than the comments of the Tuberculosis Report may have led one to expect. But just how did they cope with organising a welcome in the hillsides?

NOTES

[1] Martin Gilbert, *A History of the Twentieth Century*, vol.one 1900-33, p.238

[2] Gilbert, op.cit. p.168

[3] Doris M. Armitage, *The Taylors and their Circle*, quoted *Liverpool Daily Post*, 7 September 1939. For details of a scheme in Dorset at this time, see M. Parsons, *I'll Take That One*, p.22

[4] Comment made in an exchange between H.M. Richards (Schools Inspector) and I.G. Gibbon (Assistant Secretary, Ministry of Health), cited in Ben Wicks, *No Time to Wave Goodbye*, p.11)

[5] Hansard, House of Commons Debate, vol.270, col.632, 10 Nov.1932

[6] See Travis L. Crosby *The Impact of Civilian Evacuation in the Second World War*, p.22

[7] Quoted in J.N. Sissons, *Planning Air Raid Precautions in the City of Liverpool 1935-40*, M.Phil, University of Liverpool, p.33. Liverpool schoolchildren were fitted by their teachers for gasmasks on 27 September; they were actually to have received them on 30 September but the Crisis ended just hours before distribution was due to begin.

[8] The official historian of the Evacuation Scheme, R.M.Titmuss, in his *History of the Second World War - Problems of Social Policy*, (London,1955), p.30, indicates that Wales and the South West counties were excluded from the 1938 scheme.

[9] Penmaenmawr UDC 'ARP Evacuation File 1'. See Wallis, *N. Wales 1939-45* for details.

[10] See T.H. O'Brien, *Civil Defence*, pp.128-9

[11] John Davies, *A History of Wales*, p.600

[12] See Ben Wicks, *No Time to Wave Goodbye*, p. 17

[13] Caernarvon Borough Evacuation Papers, Box 3 - Letters January and February 1940

[14] Quoted in the *Liverpool Daily Post*, 7 January 1939

[15] Ministry of Health Circular 1759 and E.V.1

[16] cited in *The Times*, 10 January 1939

[17] See Ivor Wynne Jones, *The Air War over Denbighshire and Flintshire 1939-45.*

[18] See M. P. Fogarty, *Prospects of the Industrial Areas of Great Britain, p.90*

[19] J. Lindsay, *A History of the North Wales Slate Industry*

[20] See Davies, *A History of Wales*, p.588

[21] cited in John Davies, op cit p.588, also *Liverpool Daily Post*, 14 March 1939

[22] The 1931 census shows the highest proportion of monoglot Welsh speakers was in Penllyn RD (Merioneths) - 493 per thousand speaking only Welsh, and in Lleyn RD (Caerns) - 483 per thousand.

23 cited Carlton Jackson, *Who Will Take Our Children?* p.72

1 - *Preparing for a Local War*

In view of the fact that the evacuation of 1939 was, and has since been, widely proclaimed 'a failure' it is interesting to look at just what preparations had been put in hand in the months leading up to September 1939.

The first task was to ascertain how many people would leave the cities, or in other words would need accommodation in reception areas, and to establish precisely where that accommodation was to be found. This was fundamental to all the planning details which would follow and, on the face of it, seemed relatively straightforward. Unfortunately it wasn't quite so simple. Whereas, for example, the Merseyside authorities knew that some 346,000 inhabitants were eligible for evacuation (106,000 schoolchildren and 240,000 mothers and babies, aged and infirm)[1] they had no way of knowing at this early stage exactly how many would actually wish to take advantage of the government's scheme, given that it was entirely voluntary. Those trying to set in hand detailed arrangements had little option but to work from these maximum figures and to seek out accommodation in reception areas accordingly.

In January 1939 all of the local authorities in North Wales received a circular from the Ministry of Health requesting full details concerning available accommodation. They also received several memoranda - EV1, EV2, EV3, and EV4 - the first batch of a long line of ministerial communiqués which by the end of the war had been issued to cover almost every conceivable aspect of the evacuation scheme. This particular series offered guidelines on prepararing an Accommodation Survey, giving advice on the choice of Visitors, details of the work entailed and ideas on the possible format of an advance letter to householders: the bureaucracy was about to be set in motion and so, too, was the propaganda machine.

A flurry of activity followed: sub-committees were set up, and officers - usually the Sanitary Inspector or the Borough Surveyor - were appointed to act as Chief Survey Officer. A suitable intoductory letter was drawn up - in some cases in Welsh - and a copy despatched to every housholder. The actual 'Visitors' were usually provided from local voluntary organisations, though acting under the auspices of the local council. Sometimes teachers were asked to participate - an early hint for them of all the extra work that evacuation was about to bring.

As billeting was to become such a controversial aspect of the evacuation scheme it is worth looking briefly at what exactly this survey entailed. Amongst other

1

duties the Visitors were required: to learn what the evacuation scheme involved and impart this knowledge to householders, dealing with them 'in a kind and tactful manner'; to record, on special forms, details of accommodation available for the reception of evacuated persons; and to note the *suitability* of such accommodation for housing unaccompanied children. So the exercise was really more than a mere measure of available space and could almost have developed into a full-scale social enquiry. Most local authorities did recognise the need for some care in the selection of personnel to undertake the survey but it was only in Amlwch UDC that a protest was made about simply using 'lady' volunteers. With some justification, the Medical Officer, who was concerned about evacuation in view of the primitive sanitary arrangements in his district, pointed out that a more professional eye would be doubly beneficial:

> *Lady visitors ... while they may be admirable, say, as members of a nursing committee on account of their social prestige, may not only be quite incapable of summing up the possibilities of a household from a billeting point of view, but ... may be regarded as unwelcome intruders into the privacy of their neighbours, especially if their qualifications are inadequate ... First decide that your sanitation is sufficient, with the aid of ministerial advice. If it is, in my opinion the most suitable visitors would be two: the Council's Surveyor or Medical Officer of Health and a lady trained in domestic science and for nursing. This would be efficient, avoid friction, and lead to practical results.*[2]

The survey in Amlwch was eventually made by county councillors. Even this was not ideal, but of course there was then simply no fund of paid social workers available to undertake this kind of work. The government's timetabling- requiring returns to be completed by 28th February- also left little time for detailed checking.

Surviving Registers of Accommodation show that note was taken of householders who were aged or invalid, and of homes in a poor condition or simply 'unsuitable' for the housing or care of evacuees - how effective this would be in weeding out 'undesirable' billets remains to be seen. Only on rare occasions at this stage did Visitors note a lack of co-operation or positive hostility from householders, though the Clerk of one council reported that a certain amount of 'refined coercion' had been employed in securing promises of billets! Great play had been made of 'the country's need', 'the danger to children remaining in exposed cities' and 'the Authority's expectation of every citizen doing his duty'.[3] The Government had tried to smooth the way with a broadcast on 6 January 1939 by Walter Elliot, the Minister of Health, on 'The Transfer of Population in Time of War' and had issued a series of leaflets on *What the Householder is Asked to Do* and *An Outline of the Government Scheme.*

Armed with their completed Registers, the local councils now set about making a provisional decision on the numbers that could be accommodated and duly despatched these figures, along with an indication of possible additional bedding requirements, to the Ministry. All those who had assisted or co-operated in this initial task were duly thanked and a series of Window Cards was produced to be exhibited by any householder who'd agreed to take in schoolchildren if the need arose. The local authorities in North Wales as well as the public at large now knew that in the event of war they would be called upon to perform an important task. At this stage, with the exception of an outcry (which will be looked at later) from the Welsh Nationalist Party, there seems to have been very little adverse reaction to the plans. So far, so good.

It was at this point that the numbers game now began in earnest. The survey returns enabled the Ministry to note what and where accommodation was available (interestingly, across the country as a whole, some 19 per cent had

Householders who in April 1939 agreed to take in evacuated schoolchildren had window cards to display proof of their involvement in this vital National Service.

already been privately reserved). The total for each county was made up of details on private houses; camps, hostels etc; hotels and boarding houses; and empty property. By far the largest figure related to private houses, convincing the government that it had been right to see billeting as the key to its needs. Nevertheless, to placate those who still opposed this solution it was agreed in February 1939 that a limited number of camps should be constructed and several Welsh authorities quickly submitted applications. It now fell to the Ministry to decide upon allocations for each receiving area. This was not a straightforward task by any means, complicated by transport limitations, but Hitler's seizure of Czechoslovakia in March added a new sense of urgency to the matter. By the end of the month not only had approximate numbers been calculated but detailed timetables had also been worked out. Underlining the gravity of it all, the Home Office also issued a circular to Receiving Areas in March, covering the topic of 'Provisional Local War Instructions'. This notified local authorities of the use of the code word LOWIN to precipitate Civil Defence action, in particular the start of the government's evacuation scheme.

The reception areas were now armed with enough information to develop their own plans - the District Councils were to concentrate on housing aspects, the County Councils on education, health and welfare, with the Ministry of Health (soon for Wales, the Welsh Board of Health) in overall control. A variety of committees were hastily elected comprising local council officials, teachers, ministers and representatives of the WVS, Toc H, and other voluntary organisations. It was about now that several North Wales authorities received a communication from C.F. Mott, Director of Education, and now also Evacuation Officer, for the City of Liverpool. Mott was faced with a difficult task. At the same time as the Welsh authorities had been trying to drum up local enthusiasm for the idea of welcoming evacuees, the authorities in Liverpool, Bootle, Crosby, Birkenhead and Wallasey, as in other designated evacuation areas, had been trying to persuade people to sign up to the government's scheme.

In the early months of 1939 a concerted effort was made to educate the public on the dangers involved in staying in the city. To some extent the groundwork had already been laid - recent newsreels had carried horrifying pictures from abroad showing civilians being caught up in bombing raids on Spanish cities and fleeing poison-gas attacks in Abyssinia. The *Liverpolitan* in November 1938 published a hard-hitting article entitled 'If Merseyside Were Bombed'. It featured photographs from Barcelona and painted a vivid picture of what war would likely bring to Liverpool, which, it explained, the Germans would

4

obviously recognise as a vital port:

> *The most competent authorities in Liverpool regard it as practically
> certain that all the important public buildings in the heart of the city would
> be laid in ruins by high explosive bombs, and that loss of life would be
> enormous. No sooner had the first flight of aeroplanes discharging high
> explosive bombs, passed over the City than they might be followed by
> another fleet, showering thousands of small incendiary bombs each capable
> of causing a conflagration, and Liverpool would be fortunate if this was not
> the prelude to a baptism of gas bombs which would spread death and
> suffering amongst all who failed to escape from the deadly vapours of
> mustard gas, phosgene, etc.*

As if this was not enough, the article then devoted a section specifically to 'educating' Merseyside mothers on what bombing would entail:

> *...It does not require the exercise of much imagination to previsualise the
> absolute chaos, the anguish and the hopeless and helpless plight of
> thousands especially in the congested districts of Bootle, the Scotland
> Division, Anfield and Dingle. ... The mother's instinct to protect her
> offspring would be strained to the point of frenzy. Where to go for safety
> and what to do! ... Panic has no conscience, no reason. It is Public Enemy
> No.1. We should have screaming mothers dashing aimlessly about with
> crying children in their arms ... And amidst the hysteria, the tumult and
> the conflict, Heaven help the little ones. Despite the best of parental
> intervention, the exertion of the most heroic efforts at self-sacrifice, it
> would be the children who would chiefly fall victims of the holocaust.*

In slightly less melodramatic but equally chilling terms, the *Liverpool Daily Post* also carried an article, on 15 March 1939, headed 'Picture of Next War'. This included a warning from Oliver Simmonds, MP (chairman of the Parliamentary ARP Committee) that unless thorough ARP methods were adopted Britain could expect to suffer very heavy casualties in any future war - specifically 300,000 air casualties *weekly* (100,000 dead, 200,000 injured). Citizens, in Merseyside as elsewhere, were told that they could help drastically reduce these projected casualty figures and avoid the fate of those featured on the news from Spain - by taking advantage of evacuation plans. Only in the light of such accounts can evacuees perhaps begin to understand how their parents could ever have agreed to part with them in 1939.

5

Anfield Rd C. .... School,

.... Infants' Dept. ....

Liverpool,

March, 1939.

Dear Sir or Madam,

I have to inform you that a scheme has been prepared for the evacuation of school children and certain other classes of the civilian population from the congested districts of the City in the event of an emergency. The Evacuation Scheme will not be compulsory, and I have arranged a meeting of parents to be held at this School on   Monday   March 13TH at   2 .   p.m., at which the scheme will be explained and applications received from those who wish to participate. At the meeting an endeavour will be made to answer any questions you may care to put.

I have much pleasure in inviting you to attend this meeting, and as the matter may be one of great importance to you, I hope you will make every effort to be present.

I have to add that the fact that a meeting has been arranged does not mean that there will be a crisis in the near future. It is necessary that everyone concerned must be as fully prepared as possible for all events. The plan is now being worked out in time of peace in order that in case of emergency it may be put into practice without a day's delay.

Drill Hall

Douglas Rd.

Yours faithfully,

Head Teacher.

In March 1939 parents in Merseyside danger zones were invited to meetings to hear details of the Government's Evacuation Scheme. (Letter courtesy Bert Jones)

6

In Liverpool, for example, it was explained that the scheme[4] was being administered by the Corporation through a co-ordinating committee of 16 headteachers representing schools and groups chosen for evacuation. Information was distributed through schools, churches, council offices and newspapers; public notices were put up and vans with loud hailers toured the most vulnerable areas, giving out details of the plans and of public addresses. Parents were invited to attend meetings on 13 March where the scheme would be explained and registration forms given out. Parents of children under five could obtain similar forms from Corporation Clinics, and forms for blind people wanting to register for evacuation were distributed through the Liverpool Workshops and Home Teaching Society for the Blind. Arrangements for the evacuation of what were described as 'adult non-effectives' were organised in Liverpool by a liaison committee of representatives from the local authority, maternity and child welfare workers, schools medical and nursing staff and some head teachers.[5]

Birkenhead's scheme was drawn up by the Director of Education, G.B. Dempsey - a logical choice as the area defined as the danger zone in Birkenhead (the area formed by a line drawn a mile distance from the River Mersey and the Docks) contained almost all the town's public elementary and secondary schools.[6] The Wallasey authorities also centred arrangements around local schools. For the benefit of those unable to attend the meetings, the *Wallasey News* published information on the plans to date and urged parents to return completed registration forms as soon as possible.

Yet in Wallasey's case, it was hard to avoid an underlying feeling that the whole scheme was a little ridiculous. When the zoning of the country had been announced in January, only part of Wallasey was classed as an Evacuation zone[7] and nearby Bebington had not been classed as an Evacuation Area at all, despite being on the banks of the Mersey, near to three aerodromes and to one of the largest shipbuilding yards in the world! As late as 29 July 1939, one local paper could claim that *'all this lends support to the view that high authority does not seriously anticipate the necessity for giving the order to evacuate'.*[8] In fact 'high authority' was doing all it could to sell its evacuation scheme to the public. Leah Manning, left-wing politician and prominent NUT member was one of those brought in by the Government to try and spread the evacuation message. She had been in Spain during the civil war, had witnessed first-hand the bombing of Guernica, and had organised the evacuation of 4,000 Basque children to Britain. She knew only too well the importance of *'creating the right psychological approach and an enlightened attitude'* to evacuation, and would later claim that the 1939 scheme had failed because this sort of preparation had not been

7

thorough enough. Leah toured the nation in the summer of 1939, discussing evacuation with education authority officials and teachers, and addressing groups of parents. She later wrote: *'The only thing that could stir me to anger were the mothers who said, "If we're going to be bombed, we'll all stay here and be bombed together." How many times at meetings of parents I tried to hearten the doubtful by telling them the story of the mothers of Bilbao.'*[9]

Clearly this was not an uncommon attitude, for despite all the 'hype', all the propaganda, the horror stories about bombing and the reassurances about the scheme, of the 340,000 or so eligible for evacuation from Liverpool, by early May 1939 only about 160,000 had expressed a wish to be evacuated.[10] As the scheme was voluntary it was not possible to force people into agreeing to leave. The problem was that should the other 180,000 subsequently ask to be removed to safety, the authorities were bound to act; it therefore seemed expedient to make contingency plans - or, as it was called, a supplementary scheme - to take account of this potentially larger exodus. But this was an added complication which both evacuating and receiving authorities could well have done without. They would certainly need to work together on this and other aspects of the scheme and with this in mind a series of County Conferences was convened, to be held in North Wales in the first week of May 1939.

In all the conferences, the majority of time seems to have been taken up discussing numbers and transport arrangements - both the initial transfer by train from the towns and subsequent distribution (usually by a combination of public and private means) within the reception areas. A few other issues were touched upon - but rarely discussed in sufficient detail. Sometimes potential problems were glossed over, sometimes delegates were positively misled. The conference in Caernarvon for example, which was expecting to receive some 24,500 evacuees from Liverpool, was addressed by the city's representative, H.W. Lowe. With hindsight his comments can at best be described as controversial. Above all, he asserted categorically that the people from Liverpool would go to the Welsh county in good order, the children clean and free from infectious disease! He also stated that most of the evacuees would be Protestant, though about one third would be Roman Catholic. No one seemed to attach much importance to this at the time - though, along with the condition of the children, it was destined to be a source of considerable irritation!

The conference held at Mold on 9 May was perhaps the most complicated of the county meetings as Flintshire was designated to receive evacuees from Wallasey and Birkenhead as well as from Liverpool. The agenda also looked more promising as health matters, rations and the settlement of disputes were due to have been discussed, but in the end here too these seem to have been overlooked. The failure to examine the health question more carefully at any of the conferences was indeed a serious omission. But given that the government itself seemed to be treating the scheme more as an exercise in logistics - stressing transport and billets - than as a dislocation of communities, it is hardly surprising that the authorities at the local level also failed to appreciate all the intensely human problems that were to be encountered.

Following the conferences, plans throughout North Wales began to mature and more attention was given to small but important practical details such as provision of blankets and the ordering and storing of the emergency rations which were to be given on arrival to each evacuee - those same brown carrier bags which many evacuees recall, containing a can of corned beef, a tin of evaporated milk, some biscuits (usually broken), sometimes some fruit and almost always a bar of chocolate which hardly ever made it intact to the billet!!

Although the government itself was pledged to meet bedding needs it soon became obvious that it would be unable to do so fully and that local authorities would have to try and augment supplies. This was a welcome predicament for parts of mid-Wales, where there were blanket-producing mills, but was a considerable headache for other authorities. Towards the end of May, for example, councils in Denbighshire were notified that the Ministry of Health would only be able to supply them with a quarter of their estimated requirements. The response of the County Clerk provides an interesting comment on the local situation and raises an issue, concerning the distribution of evacuees, which would return time and again:

> *I fear it will not be at all easy to obtain anything like sufficient supplies from local residents ... It appears to me that **the poorer people have been much more ready to take evacuees than their richer neighbours** and the former will not have any spare bedding. With regard to the richer people, they have, in many instances, promised to take relatives and friends from vulnerable areas and will have a call on their stocks.* [my emphasis]

Right up to the onset of evacuation there remained a serious shortage of blankets. As late as 28 August Caernarvon's WVS organiser was telegramming Liverpool on the matter, only to learn that they had no blankets at all in stock. Merseyside newspapers put out an appeal and two days before the scheme became operational Lord Wootton made a nationwide appeal over the radio.

9

This, along with a desperate search in reception areas, finally produced sufficient to meet the demand which was fortunately almost everywhere less than originally anticipated.

Procuring supplies to fill those little brown carrier bags made it necessary to appoint Food Supply officers in all the receiving areas. In fact a small army of recruits - ranging in rank from Chief Reception Officer to Messenger Boy - was needed to undertake all the various reception duties. At the parish level it was the Billeting Officer who was the key figure. He (or she) had to be someone who knew the area and the people well and was himself well known. As so many of the evacuees were to be children it seemed logical that school staff or headteachers should be asked to fill this role. In Llanidloes the task was given to two brothers known as the Guerra brothers. As Gwen Jones explained:

> *Living in the town at that time were two French brothers who had been schoolmasters and who had, over many years, brought a great number of boys on camping holidays to our area. They loved the place so much that they had a house built here, to which they eventually retired. Rene Guerra became the Evacuation Officer and was assisted by his brother. Their typical French berets became very well known to all our evacuees.*

The Guerras apparently dealt very sympathetically with all the newcomers to the area and doubtless did an excellent job - but one has to spare a thought for the poor confused children who having arrived goodness knows where were first met by Welsh-speaking locals and then handed over to the care of beret-sporting Frenchmen!!

Others appointed to perform this task were bank managers, council officials and of course local WVS organisers - often the same people who'd undertaken the accommodation surveys in January. Incidentally, aware that these surveys contained material of a delicate nature, the local authorities had been ordered to treat them as secret and keep them locked away until a crisis arose. Some officials chose to ignore these instructions and to make regular updates. Unfortunately, by no means all were as far-sighted and on the eve of evacuation many found themselves working with an obsolete set of figures, much of the accommodation formerly available having since been promised to relatives or private evacuees.

Looking at the correspondence which passed between the council clerks and those who were being invited to act as billeting officers casts an interesting light on what billeting work was thought to entail - and just to what extent the nature of the task was underestimated. It was widely held that the job would be complete 'in 2-3 hours' or that at most it would involve being taken away from normal duties for 'not more than a day'. It was a common fallacy, as Ruthin's Evacuation Officer confessed a few weeks after the first evacuees had arrived, *'to imagine that as soon as the evacuees had been lodged in their billets the work of the Evacuation staff had been completed; in actual fact it was only just commencing and I myself had not anticipated that there would be such a volume of work ...*[11]

If the authorities failed to appreciate the problems that billeting would pose, they failed also to appreciate the impact of evacuation on local education facilities. All those evacuees who were to enjoy a prolonged summer holiday in 1939 have to be thankful to a Board of Education which seemed oddly reluctant to face up to the implications of a large-scale transfer of schoolchildren from the towns to the countryside. One Clerk, trying to discover what he could report in respect of educational arrangements, had been told by his Director of Education that:

> *On the 20th March all the Education Officials in England and Wales were summoned by the Board of Education to a conference in London, where a full discussion took place with regard to the situation. It was reported then that no education officials in the country had received any information with regard to the question of evacuation ... all information was being sent to the County Councils but none to the Education Committees who would be responsible for making arrangements for educating the children. Some of the members present attacked the Board very savagely - in fact I have never been at such a meeting. However, the Board told us that communications would be addressed to [the committees] as soon as possible, but not a word has reached me to the present, and unless and until I hear something from the authorities in London I do not propose to take any action.*[12]

Clearly the Board of Education was in disarray and some local education officials were in a state of pique! The Board, perhaps preoccupied with general preparations for the raising of the school-leaving age, issued only two circulars on evacuation in the months leading up to the start of the scheme, the second of these, on 29 August, leaving (as it happened) no time at all for pre-evacuation planning. As for the Ministry of Health, its Memo EV4 showed that it simply assumed that children brought into a reception area would go to school in the

11

same way as native children - a comforting if somewhat naive assessment!

Happily, not all Local Education Authority (LEA) officials were quite so complacent. Having established details of surplus school accommodation, Flintshire's Director of Education made a full report to his committee on 12 July regarding arrangements for evacuated Elementary and Secondary schoolchildren from Liverpool, Birkenhead and Wallasey. Merionethshire Education committee not only appointed an evacuation sub-committee but also a special assistant to liaise with the Birkenhead officials and to prepare a scheme for the distribution of evacuee schoolchildren amongst the various local schools. Denbighshire's Director, J.C. Davies, had as early as May 1939, alerted C.F. Mott to likely difficulties, explaining that:

> All the Secondary Schools in this county are full and most of them already overcrowded. It will therefore be seen that few, if any, of the evacuated children can be accommodated at our secondary schools under normal conditions. In other words if they are to be admitted at all it must be by a system of double shifts. This applies to Llangollen, Wrexham, Denbigh and Colwyn Bay as far as secondary schools are concerned.

These districts had been allocated over 700 secondary schoolchildren which would seem ridiculous in view of the above comments but, not for the first time, Mott had to explain that his hands were pretty much tied by the Railway Companies - if convenient entraining stations were to be used in Liverpool, then destinations in North Wales were severely restricted.

Often the best approach seemed to be for headteachers of evacuating schools to meet directly with education officials in the reception areas. This was what took place in Beaumaris, for example, where the Borough Clerk met with the Headmaster and Chaplain of Liverpool Blue Coat School. Elsewhere on Anglesey elementary schoolchildren were expected and head teachers in the Aethwy district met with their Director and with the local Schools Inspector. In fact, as will become clear, it was often only the ingenuity of individual headteachers and their staff that prevented complete chaos in education services on the outbreak of war.

Whilst the matter of school accommodation was a problem for all receiving areas, North Wales had another difficulty to contend with here. At a meeting convened in Penmachno (Caerns) by the Women's Voluntary Aid Association it was pointed out that practically all the teaching in local schools was conducted in Welsh. What provision was being made, it was asked, regarding evacuated children who could only speak English? In this instance, the Council was saved from its predicament when its schedule of evacuees arrived, indicating that only pre-school children were to be expected in the area. *'So the query put forward'*, concluded the Clerk, with an almost audible sigh of relief, *'does not appear to arise.'* In truth, of course, the problem wasn't so easily solved - the children would not stay 'pre-school' for ever, and what of other Welsh-speaking areas where older children were to be billeted? Nowhere it seems was the language issue seriously discussed - though, as with other aspects, the authorities seemed frustratingly close to foreseeing and addressing potential difficulties.

In one matter, however, though not strictly concerning education, some education authorities did institute a sensible pre-evacuation measure in stressing the need to expedite immunisation of local schoolchildren in view of the possible influx of evacuees. Dr Enid Hughes, Medical Officer (MO) for Ruthin Borough, where a free immunisation scheme meant that a high proportion of local children were already immunised, was anxious to discover what steps were being taken in Liverpool, so that children coming into the area were not put at risk. Dr Hughes was not alone in her concern over what a contemporary medical journal described as *'the danger of serious disturbances of the epidemiological balances of the districts into which these town dwellers are introduced, arising from the difference between the immunity values of town and country populations'.*[13]

There was great discussion among medical authorities at this time of the threat in general to the health of the nation which a large-scale movement of poulation might pose. Yet it was only in July that the Ministry of Health began to express anxiety about the low level of infectious disease accommodation in reception areas! The Treasury were reluctant to sanction any expenditure and Mr Wrigley seemed content to take comfort from the fact that *'the aim of the evacuation scheme was to billet only the healthy child'* adding somewhat prophetically that *'any other arrangements would be to ask too much of the goodwill of householders in general'!*[14] It was not until late August that the Ministry managed to persuade the Treasury to sanction some additional expenditure which would enable Health Departments to authorise local authorities to incur *'such reasonable expenditure as is necessary for the reception of evacuated persons'.* Most local councils received the circular conveying this information on 28 August - a matter of days, as it transpired, before the first evacuees began to arrive.

Occasionally local authorities had attempted to devise some scheme of their own to deal with prospective health issues in the event of evacuation - as in Criccieth where local officials had tried to raise the matter with the Welsh Board of Health as early as June, only to be informed that this was a matter for the County Council to deal with. Merionethshire Council certainly seemed to have a draft scheme in hand in the late summer for the setting up of a County Isolation Hospital. Judging, however, from the flurry of activity to establish sick bays throughout North Wales in the wake of the first evacuation it seems that whatever tentative plans had been made proved wholly inadequate. With the government talking in terms of evacuating only healthy children and the Treasury baulking over expenditure, very little of the blame can really be laid at the door of the local authorities. Yet again it seemed that they had come close to addressing the problem in advance - but not close enough.

Not only was little attention paid to the health of those entering the area but there was surprisingly little thought given to the condition of those who were to receive evacuees. Again it was an issue which seems only to have been appreciated at the eleventh hour - on 28 August Deudraeth RDC received a letter from the Ministry of Health stating that *in view of the reference to housing conditions made in the Report of the Anti-Tuberculosis Service in Wales and Monmouth the Minister has decided to arrange for early visits by Housing Inspectors to Wales ... to ascertain the nature and extent of the problem that exists in your area'.*[15] Five days later 800 children arrived in Deudraeth! This failure to take account of the known high incidence of tuberculosis in many parts of North Wales was a serious omission, destined along with many other inadequacies, to be highlighted following the first ordered movement of population in 1939. Perhaps in the eyes of the planners, the risk of contracting TB was an acceptable alternative to death by bombing?

It may well be the case that attention would have been turned to other facets of reception had there not been quite such confusion on the central issue - of just how many evacuees were to be expected in any one area, and of what category. To start with, when Councils first received details of their expected contingency they often failed to bear any resemblance to the local circumstances which accomodation returns had indicated. A clear example of this is shown in a letter from Wrexham Borough Clerk to the County Council, June 1939 in which he writes:

As you know, I have now had precise particulars of the constitution of the evacuees we are expected to take and it is obvious that no regard has been

> *had to the survey. In particular, the number of mothers and young*
> *children under five contained in the return was approximately 250*
> *whereas I am informed that some 1200 are coming.*[16]

On the other hand, the Borough was only scheduled to receive 1,405 unaccompanied children although the canvass had revealed room for 3,584. Asked for an explanation, Liverpool had answered that there was a disproportion between the number of voluntary offers for unaccompanied children and the actual numbers allocated in most districts. Put in another way - no one particularly wants mothers and babies but someone has to have them! This of course explains why there was ultimately such a lot of trouble with this group of evacuees - many must have been billeted on householders who had clearly never wanted them in the first place.

Throughout May and June the North Wales authorities received a bewildering array of figures and undertook new surveys accordingly; in July there was a widespread revision of all the allocations. Local officials must have felt they'd become somehow involved in a bizarre game of roulette! In order to try and clarify the situation another large-scale conference was convened for 28 July. Held in Chester and attended by representatives of the Ministry and the Welsh Board of Health, Liverpool City Council, Birkenhead Corporation, North Wales County Councils and the Chester Blind Welfare Society, it aimed *'to clarify the position generally in regard to the numbers of evacuees ... and to make arrangements in regard to Public Health and Education duties'.*[17] Some progress was made here in respect of the 'special classes' of evacuees - expectant mothers, the adult blind and crippled, but at the end of the day it was again the vexed 'numbers game' that dominated proceedings. This time it was not so much the constant changing of numbers that caused an outcry but the realisation that some areas seemed to have managed to avoid taking any evacuees at all - and were consequently making 'financial killing' from so-called 'private arrangements'. Again Mott blamed the Transport Authorities, explaining that he was forced to evacuate into the larger and more accessible counties - to which the receiving areas responded, rather tersely, that the Government should be exercising control over the Transport Authorities, not vice versa! Tempers, it would seem, were becoming a touch frayed.

On 28 July 1939 all evacuating and receiving authorities were advised to review their positions to make sure that plans could be brought into operation at short notice.[18] The Welsh Board of Health had recently sent out inspectors to each of the North Wales districts to help iron out any problems. Each council had been sent a questionnaire beforehand asking for details on arrangements at the Railheads and Assembly Places, particulars of distribution, personnel, billeting and food supply, and a list of any remaining difficulties. The returns show that for the initial reception of the evacuees most areas planned to make use of schools, or church or village halls, some but not all intended to provide a welcoming meal or light refreshment, most had drawn their personnel from council or teaching staff or from the WVS.

Surprisingly the majority reported that no great difficulties remained - where there were still problems outstanding, these invariably revolved around accommodation. Some authorities feared they wouldn't be able to provide sufficient billets as much available housing was currently occupied by workers brought in for construction of military camps, like that at Kinmel in Flintshire. Elsewhere it was the presence of large numbers of summer visitors which caused concern. The Town Clerk of Colwyn Bay, which had additional problems created by the Government having requistioned a number of hotels and houses for its own use, dreaded to think *'what the accommodation situation will be here if a crisis were to arise at any time during the holiday period ... it will be impossible for us to take in the number allocated to us if the emergency takes place between say Easter and the middle of October'.*[19] Unfortunately Hitler failed to appreciate this need to confine his activities to 'off-peak' times!

Perhaps feeling the public needed a gentle reminder of its duties the Government, in August 1939, prepared and distributed another leaflet outlining the evacuation plan, and advised local authorities to contact householders to verify accommodation figures. The returns showed what many local officials must have feared - as in Bala where the Clerk had to report back to his council that some local people were taking in private evacuees for profit, thus placing the authorities in a difficult situation. Here it was decided to list all who, because they had private evacuees, were now refusing to take in official ones, and the Council could then prepare to exercise its compulsory billeting powers. Ominously other councils had also begun to set up Billeting Tribunals (to hear appeals against billeting notices) - even though the official line was that these should be established promptly *once a state of emergency had been declared.*

To make matters worse it was at this moment that the Government announced various amendments to its original zoning of the country. North Wales was affected by the decision to constitute the Boroughs of Runcorn and Widnes as Evacuation areas and the surrounding rural districts as Neutral, the powers-that-be having belatedly realised the risk posed by hundreds of tons of lethal phosgene and chlorine stored at the ICI works.[20] News of this reached the Welsh Counties on 30 August (bearing in mind that evacuation was actually set in motion the following day)! In addition to this a string of revisions was being issued by the Birkenhead authorities following an evacuation rehearsal in the town which had presumably brought home the seriousness of the situation and provoked a sudden upsurge in the numbers registering themselves for the scheme. Penllyn (Merioneths), Connah's Quay, Hawarden and Buckley were all warned on 30 August that Birkenhead was working on a new set of figures.

So how prepared was North Wales in late August 1939? Without doubt, sufficient attention had been given to evacuation planning to ensure that at least the immediate reception of the evacuees, within the limited aim of providing refuge for those fleeing from danger, should be accomplished with reasonable efficiency. But what of their after-care? As one District Clerk put it, '*The subsequent care of these children after arriving will give rise to a considerable amount of labour and thought but at the present moment I am only concerned with the recruitment of personnel for their reception ...*'[21] Here at least was recognition that troubles would not be over once the billeting was complete. Indeed, welfare matters had not been totally neglected in pre-evacuation discussions but for a variety of reasons concrete results had rarely been forthcoming. The Anderson Committee report had foreseen the likelihood of 'considerable friction' between inhabitants of reception areas and the incoming evacuees and had warned that '*such a situation will be fruitful of trouble unless special steps are taken to counteract the consequences of boredom and discontent*'.[22] Admittedly many areas had set up Tribunals for sorting out any problems but few seem to have taken more positive steps aimed at preventing rather than curing difficulties of this nature.

Ought the authorities have been prepared for considerable friction? Having looked at the extent of the technical preparations in North Wales we should perhaps just look briefly at the general atmosphere prevailing in the area in the midst of all these reception arrangements. As we have seen some of the local authorities did feel a sense of growing frustration in the face of constant revisions of detail; the Denbighshire Council felt a little aggrieved in general over the number of evacuees that North Wales had been allocated; Flintshire was unhappy that some of its seemingly vulnerable districts had not been excluded from 'reception area' status. Yet all were adamant that they would not be found wanting in the fulfilment of reception duties once these became necessary. The Lord Lieutenant of Merionethshire had expressed his opinion as early as January 1939 that the reception of evacuees should be his county's first concern.[23]

17

A somewhat different sentiment found expression in parts of Caernarvonshire at this time when the response of the Welsh Nationalist Party to the Government's Evacuation Scheme was made known. The first alarm bells had actually begun to sound amongst Nationalists back in 1938 following the sudden influx of English people into Wales at the time of the Munich crisis. The much-respected journalist, Edward Morgan Humphreys, had warned then of the need for vigilance in safeguarding the Welsh language and Welsh identity.[24]

Again, in January 1939, J. E. Jones, the Organising Secretary of the Welsh Nationalist Party, had openly criticised the Government for involving Wales in its evacuation plans. It was reported in the *North Wales Chronicle*, 13 January 1939 that Jones had declared:

> *The indiscriminate transfer of English people into Wales will place the Welsh language, and even the very existence of the Welsh nation, in jeopardy. The National welfare of the Welsh people should be a matter of first consideration by the authorities who are planning evacuation into our countryside. We, as Nationalists, demand that there should be no transfer of population into Wales that would endanger Welsh Nationality. If England cannot make its emergency plans without imperilling the life of our little nation let England renounce war and grant us self-government.*

This argument was elaborated upon the following month with the publication of *A Memorandum on the War-Time Evacuation of the Government* written by the Nationalist Party's feisty chairman, Saunders Lewis, and presented on behalf of the Party Executive to the relevant Government departments. Amongst other things, this declared that:

> *To treat Wales merely as an English 'reception area', to the evident endangerment of all Welsh social tradition and social unity, is to show towards Wales a spirit of militaristic totalitarianism contrary to all principles of democracy and to the rights of small nations.*[25]

Welsh Nationalists maintained their opposition to evacuation throughout the war but it would be unfair to portray this attitude as representative of the country as a whole, or even of the county of Caernarvonshire. It was very much a minority view, and one which some Welshmen found distinctly unacceptable. Veteran minister, Revd John Kelly, writing in the Welsh Methodist denominational weekly, the *New Watchman*, declared:

It is a grief to my soul that some of our leaders are opposed to allowing innocent English children to be sheltered in our land ... I cannot conceive anything more likely to cloud all glory as a good little nation than this attitude nor can I imagine anything that would glorify us more than to die if need be to defend little children.[26]

Other voices of protest were raised from time to time, for example from holiday resorts such as Criccieth and Llandudno, anxious at the thought that livelihoods would be put at risk if billeting of evacuees prevented hoteliers and guest-house owners from operating as usual. On the whole, however, the atmosphere in North Wales in advance of evacuation was not one of hostility. With few exceptions members of the public were willing, even eager, to volunteer their services, their cars, their equipment and their homes. As Gwen Jones explained:

It was the responsibilty of the Mayor to organise the proper reception of these young children into the various homes in the town [Llanidloes] and surrounding countryside. As one of his employees I was very much involved in these arrangements. I can well remember the overwhelming support of the whole community, who quickly responded to requests for accommodation and there was a home available very soon for every child expected to arrive.

One Beaumaris couple, it appeared, could hardly wait for the scheme to start. 'My wife and I', remarked the gentleman, *'have been wishing for sons for 50 years and now the National Government is going to provide us with two fine boys.'*[27]

Everything seemed set then for a warm welcome.

NOTES

1 see *Liverpool Daily Post* 'Evacuation Plans', 7 March 1939

2 Amlwch UDC Council meeting, reported in the *North Wales Chronicle*, 10 February 1939

3 Extract from a report by George A Davies, 10 Dec 1945 (Penmaenmawr UDC 'File - Evacuation General W3')

4 Interestingly described as *'an adaptation of one that was completed down to the last identification tag in the September crisis'* (*Liverpool Daily Post*, 7 March 1939)

5 Ibid.

6 All except Oxton C of E schools and 3 schools in Upton and Woodchurch - see *Liverpool Daily Post*, 13 March 1939

7 North of an irregular line running from Cliff Road to Martin's Lane and Maddock Road was deemed to be Neutral.

8 *Wallasey News*, 29 July 1939

9 Leah Manning, *A Life for Education*, p.145. The plight of Spanish evacuees is also portrayed in a novel by Luis de Castresana, *El otro arbol de Guernica* (I am grateful to Michele Davies for pointing this out to me, along with other details of Spain's evacuation scheme).

10 These figures were given by the Liverpool representative at the Anglesey Conference held in Llangefni on 8 May 1939. See Amlwch UDC Evacuation File 1939-41 (Llangefni RO). For Birkenhead the numbers as at 8 April 1939 were 13,829 schoolchildren (plus 837 teachers & helpers); 8,835 mothers with under-5s and 433 'Specials'- see Birkenhead Educ. Cttee B/308/4

11 Report of the Evacuation Officer, 10 Nov 1939, Ruthin Borough Council 'Minutes, Agendae and Reports' No. 60.

12 Letter 27 April 1939 from Education Offices to the Clerk to Denbs CC (Z1345)

13 *The Medical Officer*, 6 May 1939 'Epidemiological Aspects of ARP Evacuation Schemes', p.174, cited in Titmuss, op cit p.15

14 PRO ref. HO186/128/643/3

15 Deudraeth RDC Minute Book 1937-40, 28 August 1939 (Dolgellau RO)

16 Denbs. CC File 17/5 (Ruthin RO Z1345)

17 Conference Report, Flints.CC File FC/4/2/50

18 Ministry of Health Circular 1841

19 Letter, H.E. Braithwaite to William Jones 25 July 1939, Denbs. CC 'Government Evacuation Scheme, File 2

20 Hodsoll Papers 5/5 'The storage of Phosgene and Chlorine at Messrs ICI works at Runcorn and Widnes', cited Sissons, *Planning ARP in Liverpool*, p.118

21 Letter from Nant Conway RDC Clerk to WVS member, 21 July 1939; Letterbook 'Evacuation 1939-41'

22 Report of the Anderson Committee, July 1938 (copy in Caernarvon Borough ARP Box 55)

23 Merioneths.CC, ARP Committee meeting 27 Jam.1939, file Z/CM/5/2

24 See Edward Morgan Humphreys Manuscripts (UCNW, X 15745-16028)

25 *The Welsh Nationalist*, February 1939, p.3. See Wallis,G. (MA Thesis) for full text.

26 Quoted in Liverpool Daily Post, 10 March 1939

27 North Wales Chronicle 1 September 1939

2 - Farewell England : Croeso i Gymru

On 31 August 1939 local authorities all over England and Wales received a simple coded message - LOWIN. The Government's LOcal War INstructions were to be set in motion: the evacuation scheme was about to begin.

In the days leading up to evacuation many of the education offices and schools in the vulnerable areas had been inundated with parents undecided what to do for the best. Teachers were on hand to answer queries during rehearsals held at many Liverpool schools over the weekend of 26-27 August. The *Liverpool Daily Post* reporting on the events the following day had tried to reassure parents, explaining that some 3,000 teachers would be accompanying the 100,000 children for whom arrangements had been made, along with 5,000 volunteers who had been enrolled to act as escorts. Bootle also seemed well prepared: rehearsals had been taking place there over the previous few months and particulars for each child - including identity discs and a postcard for the children to send home the minute they reached their billet - were carefully stored in envelopes in readiness for the actual start of proceedings.

The Birkenhead authorities had run a full-scale rehearsal of evacuation on 28 August involving some 17,000 children. Everything would have gone very smoothly but for the 'harrassed parents'. As the *Birkenhead Advertiser* reported on 30 August 1939:

> *Harrassed parents, unable to decide whether or nor to let their children be evacuated were found to be the chief difficulty during the rehearsal of evacuating Birkenhead's 17,000 school children on Monday. Though many of the parents had stated as long as six months ago that they wished their children to be evacuated, they suddenly changed their minds on Monday and decided not to let them go away. On the other hand, there were those parents who at the last minute said that they wanted their children evacuated, thus adding to the general confusion.*

But who, in all honesty, could blame the parents for being in a dilemma? It was truly a heartbreaking decision to have to make - whether to let your child be taken off to an unknown place to be handed over to the care of unknown people, or whether to keep the family together and possibly subject them to poison-gas and bomb attack. The children themselves, at least those involved in the rehearsals, seemed to be taking everything in their stride. No doubt older ones knew what was happening but teachers and helpers explained again the purpose

21

of evacuation before the children set off, carrying their bags, gas masks, packed lunches and labels, as they would for the real thing, and marched to the railway stations. The would-be evacuees were generally well behaved and most took the matter quite seriously, apart from a small band of youngsters in Birkenhead *'who went along Conway Street swinging their gas mask boxes in time to "Old Soldiers Never Die" causing some amusement in what was otherwise a rather grim situation'.*[1] When evacuation proper occurred on 1st September there would again be a mixture of carnival atmosphere and funeral wake about the proceedings.

The practice runs in the Merseyside area had shown not only that parents were undecided but that many were, or seemed, unprepared in practical terms for their children's departure. They had been notified months earlier that the children would need to have with them, in addition to their gas masks and a day's provisions: a change of clothing, night wear, house shoes or plimsolls, spare stockings or socks, a toothbrush, a comb, a towel, some soap and a facecloth, a handkerchief and, if possible, a warm coat or mackintosh. Many parents had painstakingly gathered the items together over the summer, yet many had not - or could not. As the editor of one local newspaper commented at the time of the rehearsals:

> *The smallness of the bundles carried by some of the children would seem to suggest that there is an opportunity for voluntary assistance for mothers who are unable to provide their families with adequate equipment for their journey.* [2]

The 1930s had seen widespread unemployment in Liverpool and in it's wake, terrible poverty. Dock work, at best intermittent, had been badly hit by the fall-off in trade. In 1939 the percentage of people unemployed on Merseyside (18.8) was almost twice that of the national average (9.6).[3] At a time when it cost 'tuppence to cross the Mersey'[4] Helen Forrester was just arriving in Liverpool and found it 'a dismal place' full of shabby men in shabby cloth caps, shuffling from bin to bin in search of dog-ends and scraps of food. In the course of his *English Journey*, J.B. Priestley also noted the sad demise of the once-bustling seaport. Although some of the very worst of the city's infamous crowded, insanitary courtyards had been demolished by this time, there were still parts of Liverpool where people lived in dreadful squalor. The City Corporation had embarked on a vast scheme of slum clearance in the inter-war period, building some 22,000 new houses between 1925 and 1938.[5] In fact, by 1931 about one-eighth of Liverpool's population lived in 'corporation' houses - which, if fairly basic, still had sufficiently modern facilities to make evacuees notice how extremely primitive the living conditions were in the country! Many of the new estates, however, were located on the outskirts of the city. It was the area around the docks and city centre which contained some of the worst housing stock - dilapidated old properties converted into flats or bed-sits, and gloomy, rat-infested tenement blocks. This, of course, was the very area now deemed most at risk from enemy activity and from where many of Liverpool's evacuees would be drawn.

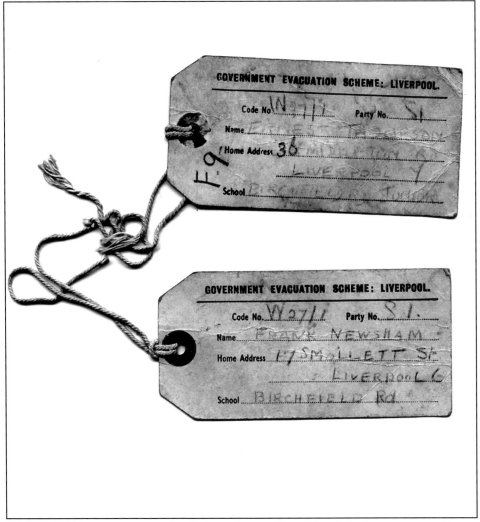

Luggage labels were very much a feature of evacuation. John Ackerley was amazed to find these at home in Prestatyn over fifty years after his mother had taken in two little evacuees from Liverpool. (Courtesy John Ackerley)

23

Despite their dire circumstances, most parents doubtless did the best they could - such as the Liverpool woman who explained that she had one roller towel at home for the use of her six children. When it came to packing their belongings she'd had *'to cut it into six pieces so that every child had a bit of towelling to go with ... nothing more than a facecloth really, just a strip.'*[6] Where poverty was at its most extreme, sleepwear and underwear were not seen as priority items. It would come as a shock to some foster parents, and even to some of Merseyside's own volunteer helpers, to discover that a number of the little girl evacuees had no knickers and that quite a lot of the children, come bedtime, simply took off their topmost layers of clothing. It was not unusual at this time to see streetloads of children running around with no shoes on: the fact that Liverpool was soon to be dubbed 'Plimsoll city' rather than 'Barefoot city' only proves what an effort was made - however inadequate this may have seemed. No doubt many would at least have sent their children away with clean clothes - but even this was probably not appreciated at the time, for as one Liverpool teacher explained:

> *...if you've only got a backyard in which three or four families dry their clothes, your clothes never looked snow white... [the foster parents] thought they were dirty and took them off and went and bought them new, which was rather sad for the kids because probably mother had taken great care to get their clothes together and patched all up.*[7]

It seems to have been quite widely acknowledged that some parents would experience difficulties. The Liverpool authorities, rather than insisting that children bring a suitcase or rucksack, had stipulated that belongings should be carried in a pillowslip. Somewhat belatedly, on 25 August, the Ministry of Health had given evacuating authorities permission to spend a meagre sum - not exceeding £1 for every 200 children - to buy boots and clothing, though the public were not to be informed of this arrangement! In the short time left to them, G.W. Molyneux, Liverpool's Public Assistance Officer, and his staff worked around the clock, trying to distribute as much clothing as they could - there was a great deal of need, but no time to check too closely on parental means. Molyneux later reported: *'We got £3000 and I spent it all ... if the children needed clothes they got them and no distinctions were made.'* [8] Lewis's Department Store in Liverpool, on the first day of evacuation, sent out a van full of baby clothes with instructions that they should just be put to use wherever they were needed.[9]

Apart from some concern over the children's belongings and a last-minute jiggling of numbers, it seemed that all was ready for the great exodus to get under way. Teachers had been called back prematurely from their summer holidays following an announcement over the wireless and had joined in the work of spreading the news to parents and others who had signed up for evacuation that departure was imminent.

As for the departure itself, few if any of the evacuees, even those who were little more than toddlers at the time, seem to have forgotten the day they waved goodbye - though not all understood quite what was going on. Six-year-old Ron Organ had run home and excitedly told his parents that he was about to be 'evaporated'! Some parents had clearly sat their children down and talked it all over beforehand; sadly others had made no attempt to explain what was afoot. Marjorie Lamb was only five at the time and had been vaguely aware that something strange was happening because her teacher had called round and her father had gone off to work one morning with tears in his eyes. When she'd seen a row of yellow buses at school she'd been quite excited because she usually got a yellow bus when she was going to visit her aunty. Even on the journey she still thought that was where she was going, but when no aunty came to greet her the idea began to dawn that for some reason her mother had sent her away:

> *Why the conspiracy of silence ... I will never understand. Perhaps it might not have been so bad if someone had just explained to us what was going on. Why had we been sent away, we were so young. I had terror in my heart when a few small words might have re-assured me.*

At the other extreme some parents had gone to quite a lot or trouble to ease their children's fears. Charles Crebbin recalls that:

> *In the summer of 1939, my parents took my 15 year-old brother and me to North Wales on holiday, where we stayed in the village of Dyserth. My parents knew that this was the general area to which Liverpool evacuees were planned to be sent in the event of war and their idea was that my brother and I should become familiar with the area ...*

Somewhat indignantly, many now remember that they were never consulted about whether they should be sent away but most were at least informed of their parent's decision and why it was felt to be the right thing to do. Gwenda McGarity had grandparents who lived in a little cottage between Caernarvon and Beddgelert. She could have been sent to live with them but as her whole school was being evacuated, including all the teachers, Gwenda's mother felt she should opt for the official scheme so as not to disrupt her daughter's education.

Sometimes the parents seemed to be at odds with each other over whether to let the children go. Pat Crick remembers that her mother wasn't keen on the idea but her father insisted as he thought it was for the best. Occasionally the children took matters into their own hands -Dorothy Berry recounts how:

> *I came home one day and announced to my father 'I'm going away to Wales.' I can remember standing in front of my father saying this; he reacted with good humour and I suppose amazement. I think my parents allowed me to be evacuated becaues I had actually made my own decision and there was no pressure, and also because they feared the worst living so close to Liverpool city centre.*

Younger children were often told that they were to have 'a special little holiday' or that the whole thing was just a practice - as Mrs E. Watson ruefully recalls: *'We were sent to Aberystwyth the day before war was declared "just*

Children at Mersey Park School, Birkenhead, prepare to set off, September 1939. (Photos courtesy Eric Jackson - the little girl is his sister, Dorothy)

26

for a trial run" and were there three and a half years!'. Alf Bryce was fed a similar line: *'My mam told me it was just an exercise and if things got better it wouldn't be for long ...'*

Many of the older ones regarded the whole thing as something of an adventure. Elsa Chatterton had her own little fantasy about evacuation. She was ten at the time *'... and I had begun to read stories of boarding school life. I thought it would be great to spend all day and all night along with my school friends'.* Margaret Ferguson, two years older remembers:

> *... the night before evacuation I had gone to bed visualising the 4 of us [she was being evacuated with a sister and two brothers] being in one bedsit, and me sitting darning socks!! I'd never darned a sock in my life!* [10]

The night before departure must have been a tense time in many homes. *'All I remember of that awful evening',* writes Edna Griffiths, *'was a mixture of excitement and of being scared till I felt sick.'* But when the actual morning of evacuation dawned, some parents found it very hard to cope. Edna continues:

> *Come the Friday morning and I was up and dressed without having to be asked. My mum was on her knees black-leading the grate (it was Friday after all!) and didn't even look up when I left, and never said a word. In a children's way I thought that perhaps she was glad I was going; it never occurred to me at the time that she was so upset she couldn't say anything. I ran to catch the train to school, my bundle under one arm, cardboard gas-mask container bumping against my hip, tears running down my face, and thinking just how sorry mum would be if she never saw me again.*

Other mums busied themselves with last-minute preparations. Rita Sandford recalls that all the parents were fussing and that her mother had had to dash off to Boots to get barley sugars in case she and her brother were travel sick. John Doyle's mother also had to make a last-minute dash to a chemist - in their case to purchase a bandage! As John explains:

> *My earliest memory of it all was being told we were going to be evacuated. That morning I put my fist through a glass window and cut my hand - I thought if there was something wrong with me I wouldn't have to go. However, my mum had other ideas ... my hand was bandaged and I was sent to school with my three sisters!*

27

The actual departure procedure was much the same in most areas: children were to assemble in their school yards and would then walk or be bussed to the railway station. Looking back on that morning, Beryl Traynor recalls:

> *We met at school carrying white pillowslips with our belongings and were issued with a brown stringed label - we'd been told to wear a coat with a suitable button hole or something to which it could be attached. We walked down the middle of the road to the station - the mums walked alongside on the pavement.*

Older children, or those from schools located fairly near to their entraining station, set off, like Beryl, on foot - 'a juvenile army on the march', crossing roads in a carefully planned manner using the 'wave' method in which the long crocodile of children stopped at the blow of a whistle, turned to face the road and on another command crossed all together in a line which took up a long length of road but involved children being on the carriageway for the shortest possible time. Where schools were some distance from the railway stations, double-decker buses were on hand, as Hilda Cooper recollects:

> *On my arrival in the playground three double decker buses were parked in the playground and teachers were handing out the labels. Mum had packed a case and given me a bag of sweets together with a ten shilling note in a small purse. This to me was a fortune. After the labels were pinned on to our overcoats Mum saw me on to the bus, told me to be a good girl, gave me a kiss, and along with other parents waved me off.*

As if saying goodbye once wasn't hard enough, Pat Crick remembers that, having seen them off at school, some mums dashed to the station ahead of the school party, for one final wave *'so it was doubly upsetting'*. The authorities, no doubt anticipating emotional scenes, had tried to establish some safety procedures. The *Birkenhead News* 2 September reporting on the previous day's evacuation of some 9,000 children from Woodside Station, explained that

> *Parents were not allowed inside the station and police officers were on duty to restrain any who found the parting too hard and attempted to follow the children.*

Inevitably there were tears all round though most parents tried to put on a brave face and many children responded accordingly. One railway official commented that *'The children might have been going on holiday. They gave three cheers when the train came in and the same thing happened when the train drew out.* '[11] Without doubt, the novelty of travelling on a steam train - a first for many of the children - did help soften the pain of leaving. Ice cream vendors on the platform did a roaring trade - police officers collecting the children's pennies and returning to the carriages with the ices.[12] Whether this was a good idea or not would soon become apparent once the train was in motion! On a similar note, Frank Jagger remembers:

> *Steam and smoke were everywhere and we waited for ages with the doors open for some reason. A neighbour of ours was the guard and gave my brother a huge bag of Pontefract cakes which made me sick. A first setback for us!*

With the now-familiar black and white photographs which captured the scenes at many stations as the evacuees prepared to leave, it is not always easy to picture what a .colourful occasion it really was; yet the evacuees themselves, tending to remember it in minute detail, recall not just buses but that they were *yellow double deckers*, that Dorothy Wharton's wellingtons which were tied to her rucksack and bounced up and down as she walked along were *little red wellies*, that the precious handbag which slipped from Margaret Jones's grasp, to be retrieved from the tracks by a kindly official, was *a little blue bag*, that it was *a bottle-green coat* (with inevitable pixie-hood) that Betty Aindow was wearing as she stood on the platform at Edge Hill! Perhaps least colourful were the dull cardboard boxes housing the gas masks, and those buff-coloured labels, forever-after the symbol of the evacuee, which gave the child's name and the school party's name and number. Of course the labels did serve a practical purpose but perhaps above all else this one item should have alerted evacuees to the fact that they were primarily regarded as little pieces of equipment to be transported from A to B! Margaret Ferguson writes:

> *One of the things I hated was arriving with a luggage label attached to me, showing my name. We also, for the first few months of the war, had to have sewn on our coat sleeve a large white diamond shaped piece of material (to identify who were evacuees).*[13]

The wearing of arm patches like this just for a minute conjures up pictures of the Jews in Germany, forced to display Star of David badges on their sleeves - though happily the 'labelling' of evacuees was purely for their own welfare and without sinister intent! As was explained in the *Flintshire Observer*, 7 September 1939:

Owing to the fact that the town has so few numbered houses and the Welsh names of roads and houses are so difficult to remember, we find that many of the child evacuees are getting lost when they go out. We ask earnestly for the co-operation of the residents in writing their house and road on the back of the label worn by the children. If they prefer they can sew it to the children's clothing.

Nevertheless, the universal donning of luggage labels by evacuees now seems symbolic of the whole thinking behind the evacuation scheme, in particular the failure to see it in *human* terms. That aside for the moment, however, the actual safe and swift removal of thousands of children and other evacuees (over one and a half million across the country) from would-be vulnerable areas was a remarkable feat, and would doubtless have gone down as such in history if the expected torrent of bombs had indeed immediately rained down on British towns.

As far as the Merseyside authorities were concerned, the departure of the evacuees had gone off remarkably smoothly. There seem to have been very few casualties - just one little Birkenhead boy who got his finger caught in a carriage door at Woodside Station (quickly mended on the spot by two first-aid men 'with bandages and words of consolation'[14]) and five-year-old Bobby Bardwell of Aspinall Street, Liverpool, who was taken to Bridgnorth Infirmary with slight concussion after falling out of the train at Cound.[15] As elsewhere in the country, the whole programme had been staggered over a number of days; by 5 September 25,000 children, teachers and mothers with young children had left Birkenhead and Wallasey; 95,000 had been evacuated from Liverpool (including 57,000 children and 31,000 mums with under-5s); and a further 13,000 left from Bootle and Crosby. In all, over 130,000 were evacuated from the Merseyside area at this time.[16] Although the numbers had fallen short of those expected (about 35% withdrew at the last minute), Liverpool still succeeded in despatching to safety over 60% of schoolchildren from its vulnerable areas. This represented a much better result than other evacuation areas, such as Birmingham (25%), Glasgow (42%) and London (49%).[17] By contrast the number of mothers who turned up for evacuation with their pre-school children was disappointingly low. One Liverpool teacher claimed at the time that this was because they thought they would lose their dole allowance![18]

When it came to leaving, Merseysiders by and large managed to faithfully observe the motto that had been adopted nationwide for the occasion - 'Chins up and Smile'. There were some wet eyes, of course but many, children and parents alike, put on a brave show. Those who had left on 1 and 2 September often remember it as quite a party occasion; but things were dramatically different for those departing on 3 September, the day war broke out:

While the fateful broadcast was in progress hundreds of schoolchildren were being evacuated from Lime Street but the parents who saw them off had no idea that war had actually begun. At about 11.30, however, just as the last children entered the station portals the newsboys ran across shouting the war news and the gaiety among the crowds ceased.[19]

Beryl Murray vividly remembers walking along a street of small terraced homes in Liverpool with her mother, on their way to school on the day of her evacuation:

As we passed one house there was a woman standing weeping at the open door and inside we could hear the voice of the Prime Minister. My mother asked the woman if war had been declared and she nodded. My stomach turned over and I looked up at my mother and saw her lip tremble, but she squeezed my hand and tried to reassure me by telling me, 'It won't last long.[20]

News that war had actually been declared also convinced many of those who had made private arrangements that this was a good moment to 'head for the hills'. Beryl Wade, who was to go and live with an aunty and uncle just outside Chester, describes how *'Mother packed a small bag for me and it was then that we discovered there was very little prospect of getting public transport that day. Most of it had already been commandeered for evacuation purposes.'* Eventually they managed to get a lift on a lorry across Liverpool, looking on in amazement at streets teeming with 'official' evacuees, through the tunnel and on to Birkenhead where Beryl and her parents were allowed on to one of the 'Special' trains which would pass through Chester.[21] The start of Sheila Rimmer's time as a private evacuee was even more fraught:

We set off for Aberystwyth where my mother's second cousin lived. We were all jammed into Dad's Morris 8. It was very hot and the traffic was terrible. We ran over a dog just outside Ruthin, I think, and it was very badly injured, so Dad had to kill it with a tyre wrench or something. It was a ghastly journey.[22]

In Liverpool Parish Church, Dr A.A. David, the Bishop of Liverpool, led prayers

31

for the country and the Empire, for the King and Cabinet, for the Forces of the Crown, and 'for the children this day streaming out of our city'.

With the children, teachers and helpers all aboard, the doors closed and whistles blown, the Evacuee Specials slowly pulled out of the stations. The question on everyone's mind was where exactly were they heading for? In general terms it had been announced in early March that Liverpool City, Bootle, Crosby, Birkenhead and Wallasey had been allocated reception areas 'in parts of Lancashire, Cheshire, Shropshire, Hereford & Glamorgan and in all of Anglesey, Brecknock, Caernarvonshire, Carmarthen, Denbighshire, Flintshire, Merionethshire, Pembroke and Radnor.' [23] As the months passed, other hints were given as to what areas were likely to act as hosts but for reasons now hard to credit, government policy was to urge local authorities to secrecy. It was felt expedient not to divulge precise details of where particular parties were to be billeted, yet clearly not all authorities adhered to this approach. Some parents did have an idea where their children were going, and some schools knew their precise destination in advance, but many - children, parents and teachers - were indeed heading off into the unknown. Worse still, in a few cases it seems the parents hadn't even realised their children were actually being evacuated on the day they left. Frank Smith comments:

> *My mother was waiting for me to come home from school. In the end she went to the school looking for me; there were a lot of other mothers doing the same. As the school was closed, mums had to wait for their children to write before they knew their whereabouts.* [24]

The headteacher of Morrison Junior School, Mossley Hill was clearly *au fait* with the plans for her school, but had no intention of agreeing to the area initially allocated! Helen Woodward, a former teacher at the school, remembers that:

> *Our headmistress firmly refused to accept the Education Officer's first arrangement to send our children all the way to the Teifi Valley in a non-corridor train! We were kept 'on hold' for a few days before then being allocated places at Bagillt in Flintshire.*

By contrast, Frank Jagger relates how:

> *Mr George Croft [our teacher at St Luke's, Birkenhead] told us, fifty years later, about that first train journey and how none of the teachers knew where the train would end up, Top Secret! It was only when they left Chester that the teachers were told that they were bound for Bala.*

September 1939 - hundreds of Birkenhead schoolchildren with their teachers detrain at Oswestry Station hoping for a welcome in the town and in the nearby Welsh border villages.(Photo by permission of the National Library of Wales)

Needless to say, there was a lot of speculation amongst the children. One little boy seeing the mountains through the window of the train thought they were heading for 'indian country'. Ron Organ had also devoted hours to watching American cowboy films, set amongst rolling tree-clad countryside. Seeing the hills and trees of North Wales, he, too, was convinced he was in America. Donald Parker was only four when he was evacuated with his older brother:

> *I had no idea what was happening or where we were going. But I can remember a policeman at the railway station in Liverpool asking us to bring him back a parrot. I think this was to cheer us up but at the time it gave us the impression that we were going to a tropical country!* [25]

One youngster felt sure they were heading for Austria (having misheard 'Oswestry'!); another little girl, on hearing Welsh spoken for the first time, whispered to her friend *'We're in Gemany!'* Talk about out of the frying pan into the fire!

For many of the children, it seemed as if they were travelling to the other end

33

Conway Street (Birkenhead) Girls arriving at Oswestry Station in September 1939. Notice the armbands as well as the labels. 'Big sister' in the middle has clearly been told not to let go of her brother's hand! (By permission of the National Library of Wales)

A group of Birkenhead children, complete with labels, luggage and gas masks have just received their brown carrier-bags full of emergency rations. All they need now is somewhere to stay! (By permission of the National Library of Wales)

of the world. Rita Holmes was crying when the train pulled away from the station. Her mother's parting words were 'Rita, don't let go of Nancy's hand' - so she held her hand all the way. She thought they'd never get there, but kept repeating to her sister 'We'll be there soon, we'll be there soon.' Hilda Cooper also found the journey something of a nightmare:

As the train pulled out of the station the crying started and some children were so upset that they were physically sick. I remember thinking 'Please make it go away. I don't want this adventure, I want my mum.' So for the first of many times in the next couple of years I said to myself 'Don't cry, just carry on the best way you can.' I remember trying desperately to comfort the girl sitting next to me , but nothing I said helped. Eventually a teacher calmed her down. The rest of us in that carriage became silent, too frightened to speak in case it would upset anyone.

Some of the evacuees, like Mrs A Jones, enjoyed the journey. Her mother had tied her 'comforter', a little toy dog, around her middle so that he wouldn't get lost - causing much hilarity amongst the other children. Some were quite enchanted by what they could glimpse through the windows. Ron Shaw has recollections of a train journey *'through lovely countryside and travelling along the coast - I think it must have been Conway - and going through tunnels which caused a great deal of excitement for a trainload of youngsters'.*

But most of the children found the journey terribly long and the teachers had their work cut out trying to keep them amused, pointing out things of interest along the way and organising sing songs. To their horror, some teachers found that their schools were travelling on non-corridor trains, which meant there were no toilets. Barbara Wilson remembers:

It was a long train journey [Birkenhead to Harlech] and there were no toilets on the train. The teachers realised the children couldn't have drinks so they gave out big bags of Taverners' fruit drops and they taught us to sing 'Men of Harlech'.

However much the teachers tried to keep the children's minds off possible calls of nature there were inevitable accidents. Other problems lurked unseen - the weather was warm, the children were bundled up in winter coats and the carriages soon became stifling - a perfect breeding place for bugs and lice! Many of the children had been given bars of chocolate, either as part of their 'emergency rations' or simply as a treat to lessen the pain of departure. They

35

also all had packed lunches, with jam a popular choice of sandwich filling. The description given here by Charles Crebbin no doubt applied to many another travelling evacuee:

> It seemed to take all day to get there; we left home in the morning and it was dark by the time we reached Prestatyn. I remember joining in with the other children in drawing pictures, with our fingers, on the grimy windows of the steam train, and I remember eating sandwiches ('jam butties') so I assume that, by the time we reached our destination, we were a sorry looking bunch of urchins.

With all the emphasis which had been put on sorting out the travel arrangements, the decision to place, for example, some 400 mothers with children under five years old on a non-corridor train travelling from Liverpool to Pwllheli, a distance of some 120 miles, seems beyond belief. The problem was, on the one hand not all the numbers expected had actually turned up to be evacuated; on the other, the declaration of war on 3 September, when evacuation was still in progress, meant train schedules had to take account of additional priorities, such as the mobilization of the Armed Forces. To try and avoid delay and congestion, it was decided that waiting trains should simply be filled - so some parties ended up on the wrong train, heading for the wrong place, to the confusion of those waiting to greet them! Nevertheless, with high expectations and a strong sense of duty, many had been working hard in the reception areas, preparing their welcome.

Croeso i Gymru!

As in Merseyside, receipt of the LOWIN message in North Wales had sparked off a period of intense activity for all who were involved in preparing the government's scheme. On receipt of the Evacuation Warning the machinery of reception was set in motion by the Chief Reception or Chief Billeting Officer who contacted his assistants, issued Warrants of Appointment and detailed final instructions, arming the Billeting Officers with the necessary accommodation lists and books of billeting forms.

Final details of billeting allowance had been sent to the authorites on the same day that the evacuation order was given. These showed that unaccompanied children were to be provided with food and lodging at the weekly rate of 10/6d where only one child was taken or 8/6d where more than one was accommodated. Mothers or other adults accompanying pre-school children were to be provided with lodgings only, at the rate of 5/- per adult and 3/- for each child under 14 (mothers could opt to keep school children with them too). Teachers were to be treated in the same way, i.e. housed for 5/-, making their own arrangements regarding meals, but volunteer helpers were to be given board and lodging for which householders would receive 21/-. To tide them over the first 48 hours the evacuees were to be issued with a bag of supplies to give to their hosts. These emergency rations were now taken from storage and volunteers set about the task of filling the carrier bags. Bedding was also prepared for despatch, and last-minute efforts were made to supplement supplies; First Aid posts were installed at the dispersal centres. Where they had not already been established, tribunals were set up; everyone who had a part to play was told when and where to report for duty. In Flint the reception 'team' was even given advice on the best attitude to adopt - a kindly but firm approach was recommended in what would clearly be an emotional situation:

> *It will be remembered that we shall be dealing in the first instance with children who have been parted from parents as well as homes, at a time of general stress and excitement. Whilst we shall naturally wish to extend to these children nothing but kindness it will be necessary to deal very firmly with them in order to maintain discipline.*[26]

When the trains finally pulled into the Welsh stations, they were often greeted with due pomp and circumstance, with the Chairman of the Council, or the Mayor in full regalia, extending a formal welcome to the newcomers. Perhaps this was not always fully appreciated at the time? More often than not, the weary little souls emerging from the carriages wanted nothing more than a drink, something to eat, a good night's sleep and lots of reassurance.

Precisely what did emerge from the trains sometimes came as rather a shock to the Reception Committees, not only because of their sorry state but because they frequently bore no resemblance - in terms of numbers or age - to what had been expected! Mostly there were fewer than had been allocated, sometimes barley half the scheduled figure as in Denbighshire where 17,721 arrived instead of the expected 31,615. In Caernarvon, which had awaited the arrival of 2,320 evacuees, 1199 arrived, and another North Wales area received less than 6,000 instead of 10,000.[27] Elsewhere the figures fell short by less drastic amounts whilst some parts actually received more evacuees than had been anticipated. This was especially the case on Anglesey where numbers were thrown into disarray by the last-minute change in the status of Runcorn and Widnes. The Director of Education for Anglesey reported what had occurred:

37

Cyngor Dosbarth Gwledig Gwyrfai.

At y Teuluoedd a'r Personau a gymerant i mewn Ffoaduriaid ar adeg o argyfwng.

CYFARWYDDIADAU A DARPARIADAU.

Dymuna Cyngor Gwyrfai ar ran y Gweinidog Iechyd a'r Cyngor ddatgan eu gwerthfawrogiad o'r cynorthwy parod a gaed gan breswylwyr y cylch, a chan y rhai fu yn cynorthwyo drwy ymweled â hwy.

Erbyn hyn cwblhawyd y trefniadau i symud mamau a phlant o ardaloedd per-yglus ar adeg o argyfwng, drwy yr Awdurdodau Lleol, a chan ddatgan ein diolch-garwch am y cydweithrediad gaed, dymunwn roddi isod fanylion o'r trefniadau fel y byddwch yn deall yn hollol beth fydd ei angen a beth i'w drefnu.

PWY DDAW.

Trefnir i tua 2500 o gylch Lerpwl ddod i Wyrfai. Yn gyntaf, daw yr hanner fydd yn blant ysgol yng ngofal athrawon ac eraill, gydag un person i ofalu am bob deg o blant. Wedyn daw y gweddill yn blant bychain yng ngofal eu mamau ac eraill. Ni threfnir i rai gwael neu anafus ddod i gylch Gwyrfai.

SUT Y DEUANT.

Trefnir iddynt ddod gyda moduron i'r gwahanol ardaloedd, a bydd Swyddog-ion cyfrifol yn trefnu gyda chynorthwy lleol i'w dwyn i'r tai lle y byddant i aros.

The Welsh language was widely used in homes and schools across North Wales in 1939. Here a leaflet in Welsh issued by Gwyrfai Council on 1 September, tells householders that 2500 evacuees are expected to arrive in the district and gives details of billeting allowances, schooling and other aspects of the scheme.

*... when the evacuation took place, the education committee had
knowledge of the intention to evacuate into Anglesey the Alsop and
Oulton High Schools, the Blue Coat School and 625 elementary
schoolchildren ... Instead of 625 elementary pupils 2,468 arrived ... In a
few days 3,405 schoolchildren, 300 teachers and helpers, 413 mothers
with 667 young children had arrived from Liverpool into Anglesey, as well
as some 500 elementary schoolchildren, 48 secondary schoolchildren and
an unknown number of adults outside the Government scheme.*

How the little island fared under this human bombardment will emerge in due
course. But Anglesey's experience was not unique. Pwllheli had not been
expecting any evacuees, but learnt, on 2 September, that 890 were heading
their way. In the event it was actually 492 that arrived. They didn't reach
Pwllheli until 8 pm but were all fed and billeted by 10.30 pm, an excellent piece
of organisation and much needed - these were the mothers with pre-school
children who had been despatched from Liverpool many hours earlier on a non-
corridor train!

The people of Conway were also a little surprised by their guest contingent.
Word had got around that 'the sailors are coming' and all the young ladies had
turned out in their Sunday best to greet the handsome young men in their smart
uniforms. Imagine the look of surprise on their faces when a group of rather
decrepit seamen from the Old Mariners' Home on Egremont Promenade
gingerly stepped on to Welsh soil. Mr Nickson, the former chiropodist at the
Home, still chuckles when he recounts the event!

Denbigh Borough received an unexpected additional quota of some 400
evacuees, and Wrexham, already a little alarmed to find that their 38 expectant
mothers carried with them some 31 children in addition to their unborn, found
themselves being asked to accommodate another group of mothers and children
who should have been bound for Colwyn Bay. In fact several train-loads of
evacuees had had to be diverted elsewhere because of Colwyn Bay's difficulties
- caused by the Government belatedly earmarking numerous properties for its
own use in this Welsh seaside town. (Eventually Colwyn Bay would become
home to the Ministry of Food; some 5,000 clerks being billeted there to
administer Britain's rationing system.)

Wrexham Borough officials had managed to sort something out for their
unexpected arrivals, reporting that *'a number of mothers had to be provided
with temporary accommodation overnight. Apart from this, however, a*

39

tremendous task was fulfilled both willingly and capably.'[28] This, indeed, was the typical initial reaction of the reception authorities - a little self-praise, a good deal of acknowledgement for all the voluntary assistance and considerable pride in the local show of hospitality. But just how well had the reception arrangements been handled, and what did the evacuees themselves make of it all?

The initial reception procedure followed a similar pattern in all areas. Where one station served as a Detraining Point for several different districts, the first task - made complicated where the numbers weren't as expected - was to separate the quotas for each district and to send off the groups to their respective Distribution Centres. Here, particulars of every evacuee were noted, they were sometimes given a medical examination, and usually given a drink and a snack or a meal before being issued with their emergency rations and allocated to their billets. All very civilized - in theory.

Even the final distribution of evacuees sounded fine on paper. In some areas precise details had been worked out in advance, evacuees had been already alloted to a specific billet and were either collected by the billetor or delivered by the Billeting Officer. As one former Billeting Officer explained, this gave him chance to choose the 'better' type of household, avoiding houses with known bad debtors, with drunkards, with 'women of easy virtue' or with those inclined to frequent public houses (often akin to a crime in many Welsh communities at this time).[29] Elsewhere it was decided that householders should be allowed to select their own evacuee/s either from the room where they were gathered or on the very doorstep of their new homes. This approach was adopted throughout the country and was no doubt seen as an excellent way to avoid any mis-matching, but it became one of the most hated aspects of the evacuation scheme and arguably caused some of the children lasting psychological effects.

The Market Place

Writing of the impending evacuation of schoolchildren, the *Liverpool Daily Post* on 1 September 1939 had explained reassuringly how '*some will live with farm workers, now busy with the corn harvest, others with bank managers, milk farmers and leading tradesmen. There will be no selection of children. As an official put it "it's all according to the luck of the draw".*' In reality, of course, a great deal of 'selection' did take place, and that could be fine - as long as you were selected quickly. The trouble began when you were left until last! But the evacuees and other onlookers can best describe, in their own words, what really happened when the trains came to a halt - the good experiences and the unhappy ones, not to mention the strange criteria that some of the householders used in choosing their evacuees!

...the evacuee train chugged into St Asaph. From the seemingly endless chain of carriage windows there issued a series of bobbing red caps. Scouts, Guides and St John's Ambulance helpers were everywhere offering to carry the luggage ... [St Francis Xavier College pupil]

I was twelve years of age in 1939 and a member of the local scout group. I, along with my contemporaries, knew the town and its inhabitants intimately and so were ideal as 'delivery' agents. The children arrived and were shepherded to the Boys Club where officials were ready to allocate them ... The last child to be lodged was called Doreen. I still remember her pale rather pinched face, riddled with anxiety, all alone and being escorted to goodness knows where by goodness knows who!! [John Manuel]

... My little brother had fallen asleep and had to be carried from the train by one of our minders. A fleet of vehicles was awaiting us to take us up the mountain to the village, where we were shepherded into a large hall. There were a lot of adults there and one of them began reading out names from a long sheet of paper. Gradually the hall began to empty ... at last we were taken by car (!) to a large modern house ... [Mrs F.M.Smith]

We arrived in Carnarvon and were taken to a large place (I rather think it was Central School) where large tables were laid out, it was like a party. A lady came down the row of children ... [and] said to me 'You're a very nice little girl aren't you?' to which I replied 'Yes'. I was nicely dressed, being an only child, and quite assured... [Dorothy Berry]

I clearly remember standing in the schoolyard whilst our future carers chose us. My friend and I were extremely lucky as the schoolmaster and his wife picked us - part of this could have been because my name was Jones. Some of the children were not so lucky. [Gwenda McGarrity]

I remember we arrived at the Church Hall and were issued with a carrier bag of tinned condensed milk, chocolate, that sort of thing. We (my sister and I) got chosen fairly quickly and were taken to quite a posh home - the lady seemed a bit 'toffee-nosed'. We were shown into the hall and the lady said 'Pick up the cases, Elsie.' My name is Elsie so I thought she was talking to me but it turned out 'Elsie' was the name of the maid! [Elsie Carvell]

41

Our evacuees came on 3 September 1939 - the day war broke out. My parents went to the Miners Institute to collect them ... 2 girls if possible because I was a girl. They came from St Werburg's School, Birkenhead. The day they arrived I was excited but I had to go to Sunday School. I drew a hopscotch on the road so that when they came and settled in we could start playing straight away and so make them feel welcome ...
[Lily Powell][30]

People came in cars to the station and took us to the Memorial Hall by the Castle. It was all pre-arranged that Mothers and children would go to the YHA. I rather upset the arrangements by going up to a young man with a nice face, offering him a sweet and asking 'Can I come home with you and can they (pointing to my brother ansd sister) come too?' He went home to check and it was all agreed. [Barbara Wilson]

As our names were called we had to go and meet the people to whom we had been allocated. My sister Edna and I were taken by Mr and Mrs Price. I well remember walking up Ifton Heath with Mr Price walking behind and as I turned round he was wiping tears from his eyes. [Vera Quinn][31]

I remember standing in the VP School yard when people were 'selecting' their evacuees and pulling at my mother's shirt, pestering and pestering 'please get a little girl' - but we came away without one. I remember it as a dull miserable day! [Jessie Wynne, whose family later took in many evacuees]

We had tea then I learnt why I had been chosen [the little girl of the household had been allowed to choose]. I was the only one with long hair! Very few girls had long hair in those days. [Joyce Light]

It seemed to me like the middle of the night and far, far from home. We must have been tired and filthy and it felt, in that church hall where we were assembled, as though we were up for auction - and as adults came along and selected children here and there, it felt to those who were left to last (I was one of them!) that no one wanted us. We heard adults asking for 'a little girl' or 'a brother and sister' etc - but no one seemed to ask for a lone little boy wearing glasses! At that time of course, as a 6 year old, I knew nothing of auctions; but very soon after, I recall the local vicar coming to the school and telling us a story about, I think, St Augustine who had seen a slave auction, in Rome, of captured Angle children. Seeing these fair-haired, blue-eyed children, St Augustine proclaimed 'They are not Angles they are Angels'. Immediately I realised that the disposition of evacuee children on that first night was exactly like a slave auction, and, since I had fair hair and blue eyes, I immediately cast myself in the role of 'Angel'! [Charles Crebbin]

I remember sitting around feeling very alone, puzzled by the gradual disappearance of my schoolmates and by what it was all about. Finally I was introduced to an 'old' lady (everyone there was very 'old' to me) and walked to her home nearby. I recall being given a big bag full of tins of things by the reception centre, which I thought were for me, but later found they were to help feed me! [D.W.Honey]

We arrived at the Village Hall. It was dark by this time. I remember long trestle tables laden with food. The local people were there choosing their evacuees. Because there were two of us - one girl and one boy - no one chose us straight away, but after a while we were taken by car to a beautiful farm. I remember the family were all sitting round having supper - we children were seated on a big settee beside the fire - the oil lamps were burning. But we were a bit tired and a bit weepy by now. We pretended to read comics but suddenly looked at each other and both started to cry. We were treated very kindly. [Rita Sandford]

I remember arriving at a school hall and sitting on school benches - I was wearing a little red coat with a fur collar, and my label of course. Our mother had said 'Stick together' but no one wanted me because I was too small to work on a farm - we got a few knockbacks because my sister insisted we must stay together. Eventually a little man called Mr Edwards said he'd take all 3 of us. [Dorothy Wharton]

The boys and girls of Lister Drive School arrived in [Llandegla] Village Hall. If I remember right there were 50 evacuees. It was a sad sight - they looked so bewildered, some crying, brothers and sisters comforting one another. They had their gas masks on their backs, a bag with their belongings, and a label fixed on their coats with their name on it. I was 12 years old. With watery eyes I watched our billeting officer sorting their billets. It wasn't an easy job as some families weren't to be parted.

[Betty Edwards][32]

43

*… my mother told us not to be separated. All the single children were
selected first by the younger couples and about four sets of sisters were
left; they had been told the same as my sister and I, to stay together.*
[Doris Coxon]

*My memories are of something that was akin to a cattle market, with our
Welsh hosts saying 'I'll have that one ' or 'Those two!' My sister and I
were the last children to be taken and we had come to the conclusion by
then that no one wanted us.* [Walter Hurst]

*We were all directed into the school where there were lots of people that
we did not know, mostly ladies, sitting on chairs around the edge of a
school hall. We were told to sit on chairs placed in the middle of the hall
… we were given a drink of milk and a biscuit. The women looked at us. I
wanted my mum. Why had she sent us away? … The hall slowly emptied.
I, my brother Gordon, and some other children had not been 'picked'. I
felt unwanted. This feeling stayed with me for many years. I know now
that it was a feeling of rejection. My mum had sent me away and I had not
been 'picked'.* [Marjorie Lamb]

*We were all assembled on 'The Green' [Beaumaris] - it was boiling hot
and we were tired and hungry. All the girls got sorted first - then it was
the boys' turn - but it was done in alphabetical order so of course we were
at the end. It got down towards the 'W's and I started to cry - there were
only a few of us left - an odd 'Y' or two - all the others had been collected
- some by horse and cart and a few by car. There didn't seem to be anyone
left to take us. My brother said 'Never mind - they might send us home!'
But then someone came and took our cases and we only had to walk round
the corner to our billet - a three-storey house belonging to Mr Williams,
the Council School headmaster. We probably got our tea before most of
the others in the end!!* [Bill Wilkinson]

*It was a large room, a community centre. We were all together, waiting.
Then there was only my twin brother and I. Years later I found out people
were only prepared to take one child, two children were a big problem,
especially being twins.* [Peter Sherlock]

*My parents agreed to take 2 evacuees and were allocated Nancy and
Josephine, each of the girls had a brother and initially refused to be parted
from them so my mother agreed that for one night the boys could share*

the bed with the sisters - 2 girls at the head of the bed and 2 brothers at
the foot! Next day the boys were persuaded to stay with a lady living 100
yards away. [Enid Harrison][33]

*We were sent to Wales, to a place in the middle of Anglesey. It was night
time when we arrived. We had been travelling all day on an old steam
train which didn't go very fast and were cold, tired and hungry. We were
taken to the village school where a lot of people came to look at us as if
we were puppies in a pet shop and having decided which children they
liked the look of, took them off to their homes. My brother and I along
with four other boys were the last to be chosen. The person who was to
take care of us was a little old lady dressed all in black from her head to
her toes. I was a little frightened of her .. but we had to go with her as it
was getting late and no one else wanted us.* [John Houston]

*We were paraded round the village school - like a prize show. Then those
that were left were marched out and up a nearby road where they were
placed, two in each home - the householders had no choice. We were
billeted on a 90-year old lady!* [Eric Jackson]

*We were paraded in a ring and people made their selection. Those not
chosen (I was one) were then put on another coach, taken a short journey,
and paraded again. I found it all very undignified and I was quite a
confident little girl ...* [Pat Crick]

*We were not selected in a hall, we were herded like cattle around the
streets, officials knocking on the doors of those who had put their names
down as wanting evacuees, that person then came out of his/her house and
chose whom they liked the look of. It was total chaos ... some children
were still being walked around the streets at midnight!*
[Margaret Ferguson][34]

*Red Cross people were there to meet us. They gave everyone a brown
carrier bag with string handles, three-quarters full of broken biscuits and a
tin of corned beef. We set off walking along Marine Terrace - I soon got
separated from my brother (it turned out he was at no.1). The teacher and
local authority officer knocked at each door and the people chose who they
wanted on the doorstep. I was selected by an elderly lady and taken up to
her parlour on the first floor ...* [Beryl Traynor]

The sad, and rather surprising, thing is that this same sort of cattle-market / pet shop selection procedure was used time and time again, not just in 1939 but in later evacuations, too. There doesn't appear to have been any official directive ordering this approach, yet it seems to have been spontaneously employed in reception areas across Britain. To some extent, especially in the more rural areas, it may simply have been regarded as a natural way to go about things, steeped as the countryside was in the tradition of the 'hiring fair'- in Wales the 'ffair cyflogi'- at which children (even as late as the 1930s in some places) were scrutinised prior to 'selection' as contracted farm labourers.[35]

In certain areas, however, even from the outset, there was no 'choosing' by foster parents - they were simply allocated one or more children by the billeting official; elsewhere there are signs that a market approach, if perhaps used initially, was subsequently discontinued. Joyce Light, for example, who explained above how she had been chosen for her long hair, was just settling down with her new young friend when she discovered she had to go elsewhere - *'It seemed that the villagers were not supposed to pick and choose, as we had already been allocated our places.'* This was in 1941, when many of the problems associated with the first evacuation had been sorted out. On the other hand, in some areas the selection procedure became, if anything, even more painful as accommodation grew increasingly scarce but private billeting was still seen as the best option for children. So, Hilda Cooper remembers her dreadful experience in the spring of 1941:

We duly arrived and were taken to a Church hall. Camp beds were on the upper floor and at this (collection) centre about twenty of us were billeted ... The people who looked after us were very kind and did try in many ways to help us through this time ... The days merged one into another except Friday, which was the day I dreaded. Each Friday prospective Foster Parents would call. The children were sent downstairs and a selection process would follow. Some would be picked and go to their temporary homes ... I came to dread the call to go downstairs. It took about three weeks for me to be picked. I remember thinking whilst standing in a row 'Would I be chosen this time?' With hindsight I suppose what I was experiencing was my very first introduction to rejection. I remember rationalising, for instance, was it the way I looked or my black straight hair cut in a fringe. I even thought it was my face and I used to look in the mirror to check. In the end there were about five of us left. I remember 'Aunty Sadie' saying 'Well I really wanted someone a little older' but in the event she chose me. My heart soared. She liked me!!

It wasn't just the children who viewed the proceedings with disbelief. One evacuated teacher, clearly rather shocked though trying to retain a sense of humour through it all, described what happened when he arrived in North Wales with his school party in September 1939:

> *The Billeting Officer drew me to one side and asked if I could recommend one nice, clean little girl as his wife would be pleased to take one evacuee ... I selected a victim ... the 'market' was then declared open. To [my fellow teacher] and I the procedure of adoption was just guesswork, as neither of us could understand a word that was being said. The local helper stood at the door, allowing the foster parents to enter the room one at a time. She was armed with a three-foot blackboard ruler which she held 'at the slope', considering this an appropriate attitude to adopt in a state of national emergency. When a new 'customer' was admitted the sound of high words and a scuffle came from the waiting room. Obviously there was a common desire to be first in the queue and 'bag' the cleanest looking child.* [Bryan G. Blades][36]

Even local people themselves were dismayed by some of the scenes they witnessed during the first days of evacuation, as the following letter shows (printed in the *North Wales Chronicle*, 8 September 1939):

> *Last Sunday evening I saw something I will never forget. A little crowd of homeless schoolboys evacuated from Liverpool sat huddled on the pavement in one of the most well-to-do roads in Bangor, outside the house of a married couple who refused to take them. The billeting officers had argued and begged 'You have 7 empty rooms and no responsibilities,' they pleaded. 'You are only taking one grown up. Can't you manage even two of these tired children?' 'No, I cannot,' snapped the woman and closed the door. While the billeting officers discussed what to do with the children the garden gate opened and the 'lady' of the house emerged, followed by her husband. They were going to Church! They stepped daintily through the pathetic little bundles, haversacks and gas masks and the children watched them, saying nothing. They passed by on the other side ...*

The writer goes on to explain how the Billeting Officers were determined to find homes for the children and finally succeeded with all except four for whom nowhere could be found:

> *... One of them, a pale-faced little lad who had brought his football boots*

47

*said wistfully; 'They don't seem to want us in this place.' Considering his
experience of being deposited on doorstep after doorstep, no one can
blame the little fellow for coming to this conclusion.*

Unlike the couple here, the majority of people involved in receiving the
evacuees had shown a natural compassion, recognising that the children in
particular were tired and frightened. Mrs Redmund was in her twenties when
evacuation began 'and I remember it so well,' she adds:

*Richard was a lovely little boy - a five-year old from Birkenhead - with big
dark eyes. He was just brought to the door - it was obvious he'd been
crying. He'd never been away from home before. Well, I took him inside
and the first thing he said was 'I don't like you, you won't take me home!'
He wouldn't eat any tea so I took him down to the playground to play on
the swings. He was quite happy then till we came in. Then he started to
cry again. He was so tired. In the end I half lay on the bed with him and he
finally fell asleep.*

This was really all that was needed - a little bit of loving ideally, but failing that
then at least a bite to eat, a bed and a welcome of sorts. Again we must
emphasise that most evacuees were received with great warmth, even those who
felt 'soiled' by the process of selection often go on to speak of the kindness of
the householders who then took them home; yet some, as we have seen, were
not only left feeling decidedly unwanted but clearly *were* unwanted. What,
then, had happened to the acclaimed Welsh sense of hospitality in these cases?

The answer, of course, is to be found in the condition in which some of the
evacuees arrived. At this stage the difficulties of billeting should not be
exaggerated; there were very few instances where compulsory powers had to be
used during the first few days of evacuation, but from then onwards they did
have to be applied as voluntary offers dwindled in the backlash from the
experience of September 1939. With no other war news to report in this 'bore
war' period the newspapers were full of tales of evacuation - and, although the
majority of evacuees were happily settled, there were occasional horror stories
and it was these, of course, that hit the headlines. Within days, if not hours, in
some areas the complaints began. A comment by the Rector of Overton in the
Church Magazine sums up the situation nicely:

*Before the children arrived, many were busy preparing to receive them,
feeling sorry for them and hoping to make them happy. But when the*

mothers and children arrived all were shocked at the condition of many of them and naturally wondered how they could be asked to receive them into their homes.[37]

The Bud of the Nation?

In March 1939, in a speech in the House of Commons, the Minister of Health, talking about prospective evacuees, declared *'...these are not scrofulous and verminous children ... they are the bud of the nation'*. These words must truly have haunted the Minister in the days that followed the first evacuation!

Mrs E. Jackson remembers the day the evacuees arrived in her area:

> *I was living in Tregarth, just outside Bangor, at the time. They were very rough - from the Dingle area of Liverpool, which had terrible poverty then. The mothers wore shawls and wrapped them round the babies. They looked as if they'd come straight off the streets. Some of the children didn't even have shoes on and they were filthy. They wouldn't sleep in the beds but curled up in the corner of the room - they were frightened of having a bath - I suppose they'd never had one before. They didn't know how to use a knife and fork. The mothers wouldn't stay because there were no so-and-so pubs. But some of the children stayed - and never went back!*

Some of the people in Aberystwyth, too, could hardly contain their initial surprise/horror as they watched the arrival of 900 mothers and young children from Liverpool and Birkenhead on 2 September. Reporting the scene a few days later, the *Cambrian News* commented that:

> *The weather made the proceedings difficult and many of the mothers had to struggle to carry a baby in arms and look after one or two small children at the same time. A most displeasing feature was the crowd of sightseers who regarded the arrival of the evacuees as something akin to a circus, and whose rude remarks must have caused great pain to a number who had been forced to leave their homes and come to Aberystwyth.*

Quite apart from all the travelling, which would have left even the smartest child looking somewhat grubby and dishevelled on arrival, given the conditions which prevailed in parts of Merseyside during the 1930s it is hardly surprising that some of the evacuees arriving in North Wales were in a deplorable state. As Jim McHugh writes:

49

When war broke out my sister and I were living in a bug-ridden, rat-infested slum in Scotland Road, Liverpool. One day we were playing on the cobbled streets of gaslit coach and dock warehouses, the next we awoke to life in Bethesda, surrounded by mountains and fields.

If the children were surprised by the countryside, imagine the surprise of the hosts when some of their evacuees turned out to be the very same 'scrofulous and verminous children' that the Minister of Health had guaranteed would *not* be arriving!

The situation would have been much less controversial if only those in authority had given the reception areas some prior warning of what might be expected. Instead, the Ministry had blandly declared in its Memo EV2 (January 1939) that: *'Any householder who raises a question as to the cleanliness of the children may be assured that schoolchildren are subject to regular medical inspection, that there is no greater danger of dirt or infection from these children than from any other representative group in the country and that the best possible arrangements will be made for their medical supervision.'* This was not only misleading but, in the light of a meeting held just two months later, was sheer hypocrisy. Here it was acknowledged that it would be quite impossible to arrange for the inspection of a million and a half children in order for them to be certified as healthy immediately before they were handed over to the reception areas. [38]

Furthermore, these same *'regular medical inspections'* had only the previous year revealed conditions which hardly justified the Minister's reassurances - or those more specifically from the Merseyside authorities to North Wales: the Schools Medical Officer's Report in 1938 showed that 24,130 elementary schoolchildren in the Liverpool County Borough were verminous - the percentage involved, 20.8 per cent, being the highest in the country! With one in five children already infected when the evacuees set out, how many more so would have been by the end of the journey? Responding to a barrage of criticism, Liverpool explained that it would not have been possible to examine all evacuees in the time available before departure:

The numbers concerned approximated the numbers attending a Wembley Cup Final. Quite clearly, to have examined, and cleansed where necessary, such enormous numbers of individuals would have taken so long that it would have caused a complete breakdown in the transport arrangements as planned. [39]

50

Faced with a seemingly impossible task, C.F. Mott had taken the decision to not even attempt it. Instead he'd opted to loan his 70-strong staff of school health visitors to the Maternity and Child Welfare Department which, in the last two weeks of August, was engaged in making home visits to the 4,000 expectant mothers registered for evacuation.[40]

Some of the complaints which were made about the state of certain evacuees were then probably quite justified - they were certainly not restrained! Yet it must not be forgotten that while some foster parents were quick to voice their disgust, the majority chose to simply accept the situation and apply themselves seriously to the task of 'cleaning up' their charges. Unfortunately there were also some who, through ignorance or neglect, failed to tackle the problem at all, to the horror of those parents who had sent their children away perfectly clean. Despite the outcry, it was only ever a percentage of the evacuees whose condition was truly deplorable but the fact that very few areas escaped from experiencing dirt, disease and vermin to one degree or another created the impression that this was the whole story.

In Caernarvonshire, of the 14 districts in the county which reported on the condition of the evacuees received, only 3 could state they'd had few complaints on the matter. Education arrangements were disrupted on Anglesey as many schools had to be used as cleansing stations; one District Medical Officer there, who had inspected every mother and infant arriving in his area from Liverpool, reported that the majority were unfit for admission to private billets, mostly because of their verminous condition. The Flintshire authorities had a similar tale to tell - Buckley UDC for example reported difficulties arising from the state of evacuees from Birkenhead:

> *...several occupiers of Buckley houses have called at my office to complain of the verminous condition of the children or that they are suffering from skin disease. In addition many of the children are apparently filthy and they are not observing the ordinary decencies in the houses where they are billeted. Regarding adult women, more than one complaint has come that they are not merely offensive in their behaviour but also that they are guilty of excessive drinking. In addition, a certain number of women are as filthy as the children who've come with them.*[41]

This sounds rather like an echo of the comment made by a Liverpool schoolteacher, recording for Mass Observation, who, watching a group of evacuees leaving Liverpool, had written:

51

I felt sorry for the receiving area or district - the mothers and children are a mixed crowd - black, white, yellow in various degrees, dirty, immoral and quarrelsome and drinking. Pity the poor billeting officer.[42]

The report of the Wrexham Medical Officer on 11 September 1939 showed that of the 800 children examined on arrival: 10 had impetigo, 14 had bronchitis, 49 had adenoid or tonsil problems, 2 had scarlet fever, 2 had chicken pox and 5 were suffering malnutrition. 35 per cent of the girls and 11 per cent of the boys were found to have head lice. Perhaps not surprisingly, Wrexham Education Committee voted to pass *'a severe censure on the Municipal Authorities of Liverpool and Merseyside for allowing children to be sent to Wrexham in a "filthy condition"'.*[43]

Other authorities said they were receiving daily complaints about the verminous condition of the evacuees; householders in Flintshire claimed to have had to burn their bedding and demanded that the evacuation scheme be brought to a halt; billeting officers in parts of Denbighshire were being warned that there would be no further volunteers of accommodation in view of the condition in which many evacuees had arrived; perhaps the most serious message came from the WVS organisers in Llanrwst who, speaking of the local contingent of evacuees advised that *'Unless steps are taken to remove these people I am afraid we shall have rioting here.'*[44]

Amongst all the complaints is a refreshing report from the Medical Officer of Health for Ruthin Borough who'd found that the general condition of children evacuated into her area was good and that there was less infestation there than elsewhere.[45] This, however, was rather a rare statement and the newspapers, needless to say, especially as they were so short of other war news, were not slow to exploit this controversy on the Home Front. The outcry accompanying this first evacuation also provided ideal fodder for Welsh Nationalists, and not merely for their case against the evacuation scheme. The October 1939 issue of the *Welsh Nationalist* absolutely slated the Government:

Welsh people will never forget the English evacuees. Some of the diseases they brought with them are well known - diphtheria, whooping cough, measles, TB, chicken pox. Congenital syphilis is not so well known in Wales, neither are bugs and body lice. One wonders whether the English government will compensate the farmers of Llyn for the destruction of bedding and furniture. One cannot but pity the evacuees but we are left in frank amazement at the inhuman smugness of a Government which allows such a condition of affairs to exist in its country, while preparing a war of many years in order to teach the German people about the inestimable benefits of English civilisation.

This, of course, was something of an exaggeration - it was nonsense to assert, for instance, that bugs and body lice were not to be found in Wales: pre-war logbooks for Welsh schools certainly refer to cases of impetigo and to 'unclean heads',[46] and the wife of one of the teachers evacuated to Portmadoc can still picture the backs of some of the young evacuees - covered with flea bites from their billets.[47] But the Nationalists had a point, and other newspapers, if a little less vehement, also carried shocking stories. Several reported the debate held in the House of Commons on 14 September on the condition of the evacuees. Major Goronwy Owen, Independent Liberal MP for Caernarvon, spoke of the situation in North Wales. He described not only the lack of cleanliness and clothing of the evacuees but also criticised the bad management that, for example, deposited mothers and children from the highly industrialised, bustling city of Liverpool to the beautfiul but remote and rather primitive village of Aberdaron. *'There are no public houses there'*, he said *'except two ... more in the nature of small hotels than anything else. There is no place of entertainment. They sent mothers and children from the Edge Hill District of Liverpool to that area. On 4 September, 424 mothers and children were sent there. What has happened? In the whole area there are not more than 50 left'*[48]

This, indeed, was what was happening in many places. Greeted with horror, themselves horrified by what they found, many of the evacuees within a very short time of arriving, began to drift back to the towns. The problems of health and of clothing could not be ignored by the local authorities; what these were exactly and how these and other problems were dealt with will be looked at later. The most immediate solution to evacuation difficulties, however, was provided by the evacuees themselves who, in large numbers, simply went home.

NOTES

1 *Birkenhead News* 30 August 1939
2 Ibid.
3 see Sheila Marriner, *The Economic and Social Development of Merseyside*, p.126
4 The title of one of Helen Forrester's novels, many of which paint a vivid picture of life in Liverpool in the 1930s.
5 Marriner, p.147
6 cited in Pat Ayers *Women at War*, p.3
7 Ibid. p.4
8 Quoted in the *Liverpool Daily Post*, 21 September 1939
9 Ibid.
10 cited in *Our Evacuee*, a commemorative booklet produced by Oswestry Heritage Centre 1995
11 *Birkenhead News* 2 Sept 1939
12 Ibid., 6 Sept 1939
13 See *Our Evacuee*, p.12
14 *Birkenhead News* 2 September 1939
15 Liverpool Daily Post, 8 September 1939
16 Satistics from the Great Western Railway Company show that they alone moved 35,606 evacuees from the region See *Great Western Railways at War*, Tim Bryan (Patrick Stevens, 1995) p.13
17 Titmuss, p.173
18 Mass Observation diarist 1057, 1 September 1939
19 *Liverpool Daily Post* 4 September 1939
20 Quoted in Ben Wicks, *No Time to Wave Goodbye*, p.72
21 Beryl Wade, *Storm Over the Mersey*, p.90
22 Quoted in Ben Wicks, *No Time to Wave Goodbye*, p.73
23 Liverpool Daily Post, 7 April 1939 (Montgomeryshire should also have been listed and Wallasey was allocated reception areas in the Wirral as well as North Wales)
24 Frank Smith to J.N. Sissons, 6 Feb 1985, cited Sissons, p.116
25 Quoted in *Cambrian News* 'Homefront Heroes Supplement', 1989
26 Flint Borough, File 13 (FC/4/2/50)
27 See Ruthin RO (Z1348); Caerns RO (DI/718); *North Wales Chronicle* 8 September 1939
28 *Wrexham Advertiser and Star*, 8 September 1939
29 Author's interview with A.M. Jones, former Billeting Officer for Holyhead UDC, 13 Oct 1975
30 *Our Evacuee*, p.28
31 Ibid., p.21
32 cited in the *Liverpool Daily Post* 'Wales at War Supplement', 25 April 1989
33 *Our Evacuee*, p.44
34 *Our Evacuee*, p.9
35 This was shown in the Channel 4 documentary 'Green and Pleasant Land' (1999)
36 Extract from *Welsh Rarebits*, the (unpublished) memoirs of a Liverpool teacher evacuated to Caernarvonshire 1939-43.
37 Reported in the *Wrexham Advertiser and Star* 27 October 1939
38 PRO file HO/186/128/643/3 (Ministry of Health meeting held on 10 March 1939, chaired by Sir George Chrystal)
39 Liverpool Education Committee Minutes - Report of the Medical Officer to the Education Authority for Year End 31 December 1939, p.10
40 See report on Education Committee meeting, *Liverpool Evening Express*, 26 September 1939

[41] Letter from Llewelyn-Jones, 6 Sept 1939, Flints CC file FC/4/2/50

[42] Mass Observation diarist 1057, 3 Sept 1939, also cited in Joan Boyce, p.13

[43] Reported in the *Sunday Pictorial* 24 September 1939

[44] Denbs CC file 8/9, Letter from N. Jones & J.M. Parry Jones, 4 Sept 1939 (Z1348 Ruthin)

[45] Report presented at Council meeting 10 Oct 1939, Ruthin Borough Council 'Agendae, Minutes & Reports', no.60

[46] See, for eg Llanfairfechan Mixed National School Log Book (1932-44), report of visit of school nurse, 25 Nov.1938 (Caerns. ES/1)

[47] Conversation with Ethel Kerry, widow of S.F. Kerry, master at Rock Ferry High School (1928-1967)

[48] Reported in the North Wales Chronicle 15 September 1939

3 - The Phoney War: About Turn

The return home movement began within hours of the Evacuation itself but gradually gathered momentum so that by Easter 1940, if not before, some local authorities had none left at all of their original evacuees. In Flintshire, for example, 60 per cent had returned by 8 January 1940 and by March only 2,417 of the original 9,994 received still remained; in Caernarvonshire the number of evacuated children in the county had fallen from 5,669 in September to a little less than 2,000 the following March. In many areas, despite great efforts by reception and evacuating authorities alike, the coming of Christmas in 1939 undermined the resolution of a large number who had until then managed to resist the urge to go home. Nevertheless, when the first national evacuation count was taken on 8 January 1940 it revealed that in Merseyside and its respective reception zones, evacuation was at least still a live issue - it was only here and in London that the scheme had survived at all.[1]

Two questions spring to mind - why did so many return so quickly and why was the scheme slightly more successful in Merseyside than elsewhere?

The reasons why many went home within such a short time are much the same as in other parts of the country - as will be seen, simple homesickness was a major factor along with a host of personal reasons and other causes which could be put under such headings as 'cultural clashes', 'social mismatching' and 'financial concerns'. A 'snowball' effect tended to operate - the return of one evacuee started others clamouring to be allowed home; then as more and more children returned, the pressure was on the Merseyside authorities to re-open the schools, which, when they did so, in turn encouraged even more parents to bring their children back.

The second question is less easily answered but there are several plausible explanations, possibly it was some combination of them all. Perhaps Merseyside evacuating authorities were more successful than others in persuading people of the need to go away and to stay away; maybe the Welsh host areas were more successful in making the evacuees feel welcome and in overcoming the problems thrown up by the scheme; or could it be that some of the evacuees themselves were more keen to leave and less keen to go home than those from other areas?

The last point seems a little cynical but as the condition of some of the Merseyside children showed all too clearly, for many 'home' was not 'sweet home' at all and there is no doubt that some evacuees, however much they may

56

have missed their families, did not regret leaving their homelife behind. It may well have been the case that some parents were also relieved to have a temporary respite from trying to bring up overlarge families in squalid conditions, and were happy to let their children stay away while the opportunity was there. This might also explain why more had registered for evacuation in the first place in Bootle and Liverpool than in other parts of Britain.[2] Equally it could be argued that Merseysiders do have a very strong sense of family and that both the decision to evacuate and the decision to leave the children away stemmed from concern for their safety, especially in the light of what had been forecast as the likely fate of Liverpool in the event of war.

Whilst the statistics may have been marginally better than elsewhere, the fact remains that thousands of Merseyside evacuees did quickly abandon their country retreats. Of course, one important reason why there was such a massive move back home, here as in other parts of the country, was that nothing whatever was happening in the so-called target areas. No doubt if there had been air raids the scheme would have been hailed a great success and even protests about the condition of some of the evacuees would have been muted. Indeed, with some justification Liverpool pointed out that those who were criticising them for allowing evacuees to leave in a poor state failed to appreciate the character and object of the evacuation scheme which, after all, *'was to enable the largest possible number of individuals in the "priority classes" ... to escape from the cities in the shortest possible time'.*[3] In the event nothing occurred in the first few months of the war which might have left evacuees feeling they'd had a lucky escape, and householders feeling their sacrifices were all in a worthy cause.

'I need a drink!'

Some of the quickest 'about turns' were made by the mothers who had been evacuated with their pre-school children and found they simply couldn't cope with the culture shock involved in moving from town to country. Whilst it might be obvious that Welsh villagers lived a fairly 'insular' existence, the fact is that these town people were in their own way rather 'insular' themselves. Many in this largely pre-car age rarely ventured beyond the narrow confines of their own little community; even after the war, Madeline Kerr in her study of a Liverpool slum discovered that 50 of the 61 families who comprised *The People of Ship Street* (a fictional name) had lived in the neighbourhood all their lives. Strictly in terms of mileage many evacuees were not very far from home, in other respects they were a million miles away!

As we've seen, Major Goronwy Owen made great play of these 'cultural' problems in the House of Commons debate on 14 September. His criticism would perhaps have been more reasonable had the authorities been organising a works outing rather than a wartime measure of civil defence; nevertheless, there is no escaping the fact that some adult evacuees were finding it very difficult - those returning would say impossible - to adapt to such a vastly different way of life. One of the teachers evacuated to the Caernarvon area explained that:

> ...the first deserters were the few 'expectant' mums and others with very young children. I know that they found village life dull and depressing; they also found no friendly bar-parlour where they could meet and exchange gossip over a glass of ale. Their manners, habits and conversation might possibly have been unappreciated by the women in whose house they were sharing. Yes! it was no surprise to me when they started to pack.[4]

The *North Wales Chronicle* similarly reported on 8 September 1939:

> In one district in the uplands where about 100 women and children evacuees were received, a correspondent observes that the experiment has not been a success: the mothers have been the problem. The children were very good for the most part, but the mothers 'were impossible'. It was unfortunate that all that had been sent to this particular locality, which is mainly Non-Conformist were Roman Catholics and their complaint generally is that 'there is no church here, nor an ale-house open on Sundays'.

Here were two problems peculiar to North Wales. The difficulty over religious differences will be looked at more fully later, but the connected matter of 'Sunday openings' also caused a lot of trouble. A memorandum by the Deputy Regional Commissioner for Wales on some of the early reception problems acknowledged these 'cultural' difficulties. It stated that:

> ... a number of evacuees from Liverpool and Birkenhead would appear to be of a very undesirable type and it is anticipated that their habits and customs will be resented by Welsh householders, especially in rural areas. For example some of these women are in the habit of frequenting public houses and several cases of drunkenness have already been reported. Today the County Clerk, Denbighshire, has been notified that a number of Irish women from Birkenhead, billeted in Eglwysbach, applied to be

billeted in an institution adjoining a public house, or in Llanrwst where there are public houses available, and stated that otherwise they would return home. Permission has been refused and it is hoped they will carry out their threat! [5]

Nesta Rushton, a schoolgirl living in Gerlan when the evacuees arrived, remembers it well:

A few of the mothers who came with their children found it difficult to adapt. I remember one Sunday morning after a new group had arrived the day before, going to a local farm for milk. There seemed to be a head out of every window. Three women and their children were billeted there. They were swearing and cursing about the place being too quiet and the so-and-so pubs being even closed on a Sunday. The farmer's wife was nearly out of her mind. A couple of days later they returned to Liverpool - civilisation and bombs!

The last point Nesta makes is important. The tendency to drift home was a feature of every phase of evacuation throughout the war, even during the height of the Blitz in Liverpool, and this somewhat undermines the claim that the absence of air raids had spelt the doom of the first evacuation scheme. The factor of a 'culture clash', when town found that country had few cinemas and even fewer fish and chip shops, and Liverpool found North Wales had no Sunday opening, was not only to influence the first mass movement home but would prove strong enough to drive some evacuees back to the towns even when the danger there was acute.

Quite apart from clashing cultures there were also practical difficulties facing the young mothers. Householders were given money for their lodgings only, the mothers were expected to buy and cook their own food: sharing someone else's kitchen is never easy at the best of times, but the country kitchens, often with no water on tap and only a range to cook on, could be quite a challenge. Ethel Kerry, evacuated with her three-month-old baby recalls:

Where we were billeted the kitchen wasn't up to much - there were mice droppings in all the cupboards. You felt you had to wash the pans out every time before you could use them. There was a stream running down the side of the house - an open sewer really. The people were very nice but the conditions were pretty grim - it was terrible trying to wash nappies in cold water.

59

In some areas, accommodation for mothers was provided in empty houses, but this didn't always prove a better option. The *Birkenhead Advertiser* on 16 September, praising the warm reception given by Llanidloes people, did mention in passing that there were a few problems in the area due to the fact that some of the Birkenhead mothers had been billeted 'in a row of dilapidated cottages' - though apparently they were trying to make the best of the situation!

There were very few places available for mothers with young families to eat out in the rural areas, yet shopping could be awkward. Country markets were not at all the same as the street markets back home, and a shopping expedition was often just that, an expedition across fields and down lanes, sometimes a walk of several miles to the nearest store. Nor, apparently, were local shopkeepers always quite as scrupulously fair with the 'visitors' as they might have been:

> *Our headteacher could speak Welsh and one day we saw him deep in conversation with the local postman who, as it turned out, was tipping us the wink. It seemed that the Bank Manager had been somewhat indiscreet - we [evacuated teachers and their wives] had to transfer our bank accounts across and the Bank Manager had been letting local shopkeepers know the details - with the result that we were all being horribly overcharged. So after that we just bought as little as possible locally.[6]*

As the above suggests, another problem for the evacuated mothers was the language difference - while this didn't of course prevent communication altogether, the fact that in some areas all the other adults spoke Welsh amongst themselves must have given the English evacuees an added sense of strangeness and isolation. Then there was the simple matter of homesickness - a longing to be reunited with husbands, friends and other family members - which drove many back home in no time at all.

'Take me home!'

Of course the children also suffered dreadful homesickness especially in the first few days. How bearable this was depended much on the response of the foster parents. Les Glover admits: *'I was very upset the first evening - terribly homesick - so the farmer took me hunting for rabbits to take my mind off things.'* Betty Aindow was only five when she was evacuated. She cried and cried and would not be pacified despite the best efforts of her hosts:

> *They had a big bureau in the room with a beautiful glass bowl on top into*

60

which they'd put the chocolate we'd brought with us. 'There there, now',
they said, going across to the bowl, 'have a bit of this chocolate.' 'I don't
want chocolate,' I cried, 'I want my mum.'

Eric Jackson also confesses to having been very homesick - *'I just couldn't stop*
crying at first - in the end the old lady kindly gave me some money for a home
visit.' Eric set off by bus, making several changes *en route*, only to discover
when he got home that his mother was away, visiting his younger sister who'd
been evacuated to another part of Wales! Luckily 'gran' was there to fuss over
him, after which he went back and settled down quite happily.

But for some children the homesickness was unbearable and the parents simply
hadn't the heart to refuse to allow them to come home, especially as it seemed
quite safe to do so. Pat Crick remembers walking back from school one day, a
few weeks after being evacuated, and seeing two figures in the distance who
looked rather familiar. *'As we got closer and saw it was our parents'*, she said,
'I burst into tears and started running towards them crying "Take me home, take
me home".' Later, when this really wasn't an option for parents, with
Merseyside under heavy bombardment, it must have been heartbreaking to have
to turn a deaf ear to such pleas, as Marjorie Lamb acknowledges:

On the rare occasions that my parents visited, which was usually on a
Sunday, my Dad used to bring us sweets and other goodies. I found out
later that he used to barter meat for the little treats he used to bring us ...
When it was time for them to go my brother would run behind the coach
shouting 'Don't go, please don't go.' He would do this until the coach was
out of sight. Can you imagine the trauma my mum and dad went through?

There were all sorts of reasons why the children felt so wretched. For many it
was the first time they'd ever been away from their mums and dads. It wasn't
just that they missed their family and friends (and a lot came from large, very
close-knit families) but that everything was so very different. A few of the
children were simply overwhelmed by the whole thing. One teacher, visiting all
his pupils within the first few days came across such a case. Speaking to the
despairing foster parents he learnt that the two brothers were upstairs and
wouldn't move out of the bedroom. They hadn't even been in their bed but just
sat huddled in a corner:

No sooner had I called upstairs to them than down they came with their
luggage, still unpacked, and entreated me to take them away. To me they

61

> *tearfully related their strange fear of rats racing round their bedroom,*
> *howling cats in the chimney, savage dogs that stole their 'emergency*
> *rations' and worst of all the people in the house 'that won't talk proper'.*[7]

Some of the children of course absolutely loved the rural way of life, the primitive conditions, helping on the farm, the country food, all the new sights and sounds - others positively loathed it. One Montgomeryshire hostess remembers *'the two evacuees did not stay long as they were not happy; the food provided for them was different. I remember they did not like butter.'*[8] One young evacuee refused to eat a french bean cooked in its 'long state' convinced it was some terrible kind of snake or other equally scary country animal![9] Roy Parry also confessed:

> *I did dislike a lot of the vegetables we used to get to start with, like*
> *cabbage and such like, because we did not get this type back home in*
> *Wallasey. I can remember being asked to wash the lettuce for tea and*
> *going outside and scrubbing it with a brush.*[10]

Pat Crick had been what she terms 'hand-reared' and hated life on the farm where she was billeted - having to share a bed with a stranger, help with the mucking-out and butter-making, bathe in a tin bath, listen to strange noises at night, walk miles to school, and put up with the antics of the local lads who were 'very rough'. She found it all *'totally foreign - completely and utterly'*. Catching nits and having her lovely ringlets cut off was the last straw. It was often little indignities like this that heightened the yearning for home. Pat Byrne although very young at the time, clearly remembers:

> *We were used to having a bathroom, so - although I was only five - I hated*
> *the indignity of being stripped and washed down standing on a kitchen*
> *drainer. I went home quite quickly.*

Enuresis, or 'bed-wetting' as it was commonly called, was a problem for many evacuees; for some of the older ones it made it simply too embarrassing to stay away. One lady recalls:

> *I was about 11 at the time but unfortunately bed-wetting became a*
> *problem. I felt so ashamed. I was sleeping in a bed with another evacuee.*
> *Mrs T got fed up and hinted that I'd have to leave if it continued. This was*
> *one of the reasons why my mother came and took me home, round about*
> *the end of November.*

It wasn't only the children who missed their parents but often the mums and dads who couldn't bear to be apart from their young families or from one another. Olive Murray remembers: *'My mother and father missed us a lot and decided to bring us home after a few weeks.'* Similarly Joan Brumfitt: *'We weren't away very long. Mother had also been evacuated, on 2 September, with a three-week old baby but Dad didn't like being alone so we all went home!'* 'Dad' was also the deciding factor in Mrs Williams's return: *'Dad had been away at sea when we were evacuated. He was furious when he found out and brought us straight home!'* ... and for Dorothy Wharton: *'We'd only been away about 10 weeks when Dad and my uncle came to get us. We arrived back at Woodside Station and I didn't want to get out because Hitler was out there. Dad gave me a big penny - that did the trick!'* But for Ernest Carvell it was 'mum' who was the problem: *'I only stayed away a month because my father joined the Forces and mum was lonely. I got booed by the others for going home!'*

The headmaster of the Liverpool Collegiate School, evacuated to Bangor, also blamed 'the mothers' for the return home of some of his pupils:

> *Some mothers have caused the withdrawal of their boys from the School back to Liverpool, with all that this entails in the matter of education, safety and health, simply because they (the mothers) are unhappy without the boys. (Home-sickness is natural, but the manly overcoming of this feeling has been indicated to them as their 'bit' in National Service - a small 'bit' in return for the immense benefits conferred on them.) I must ask such parents to think of others as well as themselves ...*[11]

Visiting

Even if parents didn't go and fetch their children straightaway, many did quite naturally at least want to go and see them in their new homes, but visits from the family often proved unsettling and sometimes these were actually the cause of speedy returns. Bryan Blades, a teacher evacuated with Aspen Grove School, Liverpool certainly felt this to be the case:

> *I am quite sure the children would have remained contentedly in the reception areas if their parents had not unsettled them by their repeated visits. This was, in my opinion, the main cause of the Great Trickle homewards.*

Rhona Parcell had been away for a few weeks and had begun to feel a bit closer to her new family, though still suffering bouts of homesickness:

> One Saturday morning I got a phone call to say that my brother had been
> called up for the RAF and that he was cycling from Liverpool to come and
> see me to say 'goodbye' ... He arrived hot, disheveled and saddle-sore and
> by the time he had washed and eaten a meal with us it was time for him to
> set off again. Naturally, this visit resulted in accentuating my
> homesickness, so the following day I wrote to my mother to let me come
> home. Margery [a fellow evacuee] had already left some time earlier and
> my mother was also missing me so she reluctantly agreed ...

Within a few days of the first evacuation an appeal was sent out from Hawarden,
Buckley and Connah's Quay, all quite accessible from Liverpool and the Wirral,
asking parents not to go and see their children until they'd had time to settle in.
Often the children's homesickness was at its most intense in these early days and
with no bombs falling it was very hard for parents to resist tearful pleas to be
allowed home. So, for example, in one district it was reported that:

> Some trouble has arisen as a result of parents who, having visited their
> children, decide to take them back to Liverpool. Some, indeed, are
> reported as having done so without even saying 'Thank you' to the people
> who have looked after the children since their arrival.[12]

A welfare worker in Chirk spoke of the difficulties that arose when parents,
some becoming quite aggressive, suddenly decided to take their children home
with them.[13] In one instance in Nant Conway, a father, supposedly taking his
evacuated daughter for a walk during his visit, hired a taxi and took her all the
way back to Merseyside.[14] In another case a six-year-old, billeted in Holywell,
received a visit from his father, a seaman home on leave. The father took an
instant dislike to the people at the boy's billet, took his son out, again
supposedly for a walk, and caught the train home, leaving behind all the boy's
possessions.[15] No doubt some of the parents felt too embarrassed to face the
householders, perhaps even felt guilty about removing the children so quickly
without good reason. But understandably the foster parents resented such
action, especially when they'd gone to the trouble of re-clothing the children.

On the other hand sometimes parents were simply furious at what they found
when they visited and either demanded a new billet or, quite often at this time,
simply took their children home in disgust. Matt M. explained the
circumstances of his return:

... Winnie and I were sent to an old Welsh witch in a dilapidated cottage ... we seemed to have fish-paste sandwiches for breakfast, dinner, and tea... [We] began to show the effects of our fish-past diet and what I suppose were signs of malnutrition began to become apparent. So much so that when our mother visited us, along with our Aunty Lily, the old 'Welsh witch' was sorted out in good style and we were promptly whisked home.[16]

Beryl Traynor remembers having nits and being sent to the barber by her foster mother:

I came back and was told that it hadn't been cut short enough - so I had to go back to the barbers and it was cut very short. I was so ashamed. Mum came to visit - it took her hours on the coach - and she wasn't at all pleased about my hair. In the end she took me home.

Still, at least Beryl's foster mother had tried to tackle the nit problem, sometimes parents were horrified to find their children's heads, which had been perfectly clean when they left home, were now 'alive' with headlice. Thinking their offspring were being neglected they took them back home without a second thought, as Bob Boyd explains:

One day our mother came to visit us on one of Harding's coaches, found that we had been neglected and took us back .. My wife was also evacuated to a village in North Wales, a few miles from Corwen. She was also brought home early as her head was infested with lice!

If some parents were annoyed by what they saw in the billets, some householders were equally annoyed when parents' visits unsettled the children. Mrs Redmund had worked hard to make her young evacuee happy and remembers, rather crossly, that *'his mother used to come and visit him and was always upsetting him'.* Other parents were more thoughtful. Mrs S.Davies relates how the Bank Manager (now Billeting Officer) had come knocking at their door, holding the hand of a little Moslem boy evacuated to the Wrexham area with his cousin, a fair-haired little white girl who'd been quickly offered a home. But no one would take the boy:

My mother was upstairs doing the bedrooms so I called her down. The little boy was crying - he wanted his cousin. I talked mum into saying we'd have him - not that she needed much persuading - and then we tried to comfort the little lad but he was still crying for his cousin. I said 'We'll

65

have to take his cousin as well' and mum sent me running after the Bank Manager who promised to see what he could do. A while later he came back with the girl. The little lad stopped crying straight away, sat down, opened his bag and took out an envelope which he handed to mum, saying 'Here you are, aunty' - just like that! She read the letter with tears in her eyes. It was a heartbreaking note from the little boy's mother saying she hoped Mohamed wouldn't be treated badly because he was black and that if it was all right she wouldn't come to visit him for a week in order to give him time to settle in. Well, within a week everyone loved him! When she came to visit, his mother was surprised that he was playing outside (she couldn't let him do this at home). He came rushing in, gave her a hug and a kiss, asked what she'd brought for him, said 'Thanks mum' - and rushed off to play again. His mother couldn't get over it!

In certain areas, householders felt that visiting parents were taking undue advantage of their hospitality, expecting to be provided with meals and accommodation for the duration of their stay. A.M. Gibson, headmaster of Liverpool Collegiate School, in his 'Evacuation Bulletin No.1' (October 1939) severely criticised certain parents:

One word I must add, and it must be a frank one. Some parents ... have acted in a most unreasonable and selfish fashion - in a way that may easily bring the name of Liverpool and the School into disrepute. Parents have come to visit their sons, planted themselves on already harassed householders for lunch and even badgered them into giving them beds for the night. They have gone away leaving handsome pocket money for their boys, and have not offered one penny towards the financial loss being sustained by householders.

In some areas this sort of problem caused such an outcry that local authorities or WVS groups eventually took it upon themselves to organise mass parental visits, providing meals and sometimes setting aside a hall for the parents to meet with their children.[17] Of course firm friendships were sometimes struck between parents and foster parents; others found the relationship a difficult one. If you were a parent - and being completely honest - would you be more concerned if your child was a bit fretful or was deliriously happy in a new home?!

Family visits occasionally created mayhem for other reasons. The evacuees, particularly those who stayed on for a long time, naturally looked forward to these visits - and to the presents that parents brought with them, but sometimes there was trouble over such presents once parents had left. In the worst instances children weren't allowed to keep their gifts at all. Often they were at the very least expected to share them around:

We got quite friendly with the farmer's daughter but our parents brought us little treats when they came to visit us and these were a source of resentment. One time my father gave me two and sixpence and said to share it with the other two evacuees. When he'd gone the farmer's wife insisted I share it four ways - to include her daughter. [Pat Crick]

After a visit from his brother and a parting gift of half-a-crown ('*an enormous sum*') Charles Crebbin took great delight in meeting up with his friends, evacuees and village children (though *not* the son of the house where he was billeted who was terribly spoilt by his parents, in great contrast to the way they treated Charles), and proceeding '*to spend most of my vast fortune on treating us all to such goodies as were available in the village - sticky buns, tizer, etc.*' For Charles, and perhaps for other children too, parental visits were a mixed blessing. They'd been told at school not to upset their parents by complaining at all. But another evacuee billeted with Charles had burst into tears during a visit from his mum, told her how unhappy he was and begged (successfully) to be taken home. The foster mother was furious:

I remember her taking me to one side and telling me that if I were to cry or misbehave in any way when my parents came to see me (a visit was planned), she would stop any further visits. So when my parents did come to see me and asked if I liked living in the countryside, I gave them the answer everyone wanted to hear - and cried into my pillow the night they left ... nearly every night I would pray for the courage to ask my parents to take me home... Yet each time they visited, my courage failed me: I thought they would never believe how unhappy I was, they would leave me in Meliden, then [the hosts] would discover my attempted escape and would take it out on me after my parents' departure.

Despite the fact that parental visits were sometimes troublesome and had contributed to the early flow home of evacuees, the government clearly felt that on balance a limited amount of visiting should be encouraged. Eventually reduced-cost travel facilities were introduced and special excursion coaches were laid on. Elsie Carvell, evacuated to the Towyn area, remembers '*Special buses used to bring the fathers on visits - dad loved it, especially watching the seals.*' Once the war was in full swing, these trips no doubt provided a much-needed break for the parents too. But for some, even when the cost was reduced, the sheer distances involved did make visiting difficult. Les Glover, evacuated from Bromborough on the Wirral to Sarnbach, near Abersoch, admits that it was a long journey for his parents to make: '*They had to get the milk train and stay overnight at a bed and breakfast place.*'

Perhaps because of the distance, perhaps for other reasons - travel did become increasingly restricted and many parents became very involved in the war effort, some of course, even injured or killed - certain children never saw their families for months, if not years. Frank Jagger remembers one boy, evacuated from Birkenhead to Bala, whose parents never wrote to him or visited him and never claimed him back! Similarly one evacuated teacher, when asked if visiting parents often took their children home from the Caernarvon area, replied that *'Very few parents ever visited their children - in fact the children were often ignored until they were 14 when they could become wage earners.'*[18]

Sad as this may seem, it could explain why the numbers returning home in the autumn of 1939 were lower here than elsewhere in the country. Without doubt, life was extremely hard for some Merseyside families and some of the children recognised that being evacuated may have been the best thing ever to have happened to them. Albert Houghton certainly feels this was true in his case. He'd been living in a poor part of Liverpool, in pretty rough conditions. Come Friday night, every week, his mother would warn him to hide before his father came in from the pub, ready to hand out a beating to anyone who got in his way. When he was evacuated with his friends from Aspen Grove school, Albert couldn't believe his luck. His new home in the little village of Carmel may have been primitive but he loved it, he didn't mind that there was no electricity or that the privy was at the bottom of the garden; he didn't even mind carrying big buckets of water or collecting dried dung to burn on the fire; he was in his element playing with the wild horses, roaming the countryside, collecting blackberries, helping with the harvests, learning how to tickle trout and even how to speak Welsh. The war had been over many years before Albert went back to Liverpool!

Upstairs Downstairs

Albert may not have objected to his billet but there were many who did, and equally many in the billets who objected to the evacuees they had billeted on them - both for reasons which can best be described as 'social mismatching'. As we have seen, the distribution process, despite foster parents in many areas being allowed to 'choose', was often rather haphazard and in practice could hardly have been anything else. While Billeting Officers could avoid bringing certain homes or people into the scheme on the reception side, they could rarely have advance knowledge of the character or 'class' of the evacuees seeking accommodation. Of course this was a time of national emergency, both sides were expected to make allowances, and many did (the whole issue of billeting will be looked at more closely later). Sometimes, though, the incompatibilty could not be overcome and was another reason why certain evacuees returned home in the early days of the scheme.

The heading given to one newspaper article - 'Bohemian Ideals versus the Puritan Ethic' - nicely illustrates one such situation, where prim chapel-going middle-class Welsh ladies found themselves having to share their homes with drunken, loose-moralled, Liverpudlian 'fishwives'. Stories of the antics of slum children billeted on middle-class or even aristocratic households are so common as to have become part of evacuation legend - children not knowing how to use cutlery, having no table manners, relieving themselves on the Axminster in a corner of a room and carving their initials on the grand piano! Yet this was only ever half the story, and Olwen Owen, a former evacuee, was quite justified when she adamantly declared herself *'rather weary of the "reception area" impression of lower class, lousy bed-wetting children invading "middle class" spotless homes of great cultural advantage!'*

Olwen was not the only evacuee to have come from a nice home and be billeted on a working class household in what was little better than a rural slum! Rhona Parcell, evacuated with fellow pupils from Calder High School, Liverpool, recalls:

> *After talking to others we realised we were lucky as some of our peers had been billeted in miner's homes which were small cottages where space was at a premium. There were no bathroms - tin baths were put in front of the fire and filled with hot water - naturally most of the girls took a dim view of this. The loos were usually 'privvies' at the bottom of the yard and quite a few of the girls begged to be returned home as they would rather risk being blitzed in Liverpool than suffer the indignities of living in these conditions.*

Rhona and a friend had actually struck very lucky and had been taken to a large, detached Victorian house, standing in its own grounds. Yet they had been allocated a bare-boarded room in the attic with a wash-hand basin and jug, and Rhona sensed that, although the scheme had only just started, *'various off-putting stories about evacuees had preceded us, leaving our hostess full of misgivings'*. After a week, Rhona screwed up her courage and when asked by her host how she liked living there told him frankly that she and her friend came from comfortable homes and were not used to roughing it:

> *Nothing more was said until the following morning when Mrs H. told us to move our belongings down a floor to a proper bedroom .. and we were*

69

also told that we could use the family bathroom. It was sheer bliss! From then on I felt more like a member of the family and was treated as such.

Marie B., evacuated with her sister Nancy, found a similar prejudice in their billet:

The family thought they were going to make young ladies out of us, and so they tried to teach us table manners. They were shocked to find that we already behaved well and that we knew our etiquette. I think they assumed that because we came from Liverpool we would be badly behaved and rough! [19]

Clearly there were some preconceived notions in the reception areas about the kind of 'gutter-snipe' children they were going to have to put up with, so this does rather beg the question: 'if they were expecting the worst why was there such an outcry when some of those who arrived fitted the bill?'!

Certainly class differences did cause mutual discomfort in some instances and led to rapid departures, as with Mrs Williams who felt *'It was quite obvious the people there didn't want us. They were Chapel people. He was a briefcase-and-bowler-hat type, with a permanent smell under his nose!'* Although Alex Anderson was a later evacuee he encountered much the same sort of attitude:

What they [the foster parents] thought of an uninstructed 9-year-old boy from Darkest Liverpool was made plain ... When I first arrived at the house, clutching my pillow-slip of 'spare clothing' I was taken to the front door. I was never allowed to use that entrance again. The back-door tradesman's entrance was good enough for me thereafter.

Yet there were many cases when potential 'mismatches' were overcome either by sheer commonsense or by pure and simple kindness. John Houston, along with another evacuee, unexpectedly found himself living with 'Miss Brooks', the daughter of a wealthy Manchester businessman, in her beautiful house overlooking the Menai Strait:

Miss Brooks was a wonderful person. Although she came from a very different social background from our humble beginnings we were never considered in any way inferior and were always treated as honoured guests ... Where, in many another similar household, the evacuees would have been relegated to the kitchen, we were waited on and fed in the dining room where she took her own meals. I expect our social graces left much to be desired but she never showed it ...

He Who Gives a Child a Home ...

Hundreds and thousands of householders all over Britain opened their hearts as well as their homes to evacuees in September 1939 and it would perhaps be unfair to claim that hospitality in North Wales was any warmer than that elsewhere. Indeed, again as in other areas, there were certainly instances (examined later) when evacuees were not at all well received. Yet so many testify to the welcome they were given that perhaps it is reasonable to claim that those who didn't quickly return to Merseyside chose to stay on in the hillsides because they felt genuinely welcome there. Again, the story is best told by those involved:

I remember learning this when I was very young: 'He who gives a child a home makes a place for himself in Heaven.' We shared our home with many people during the war but our fondest memories are of the evacuees. We lived in a village called Rhosesmor. We had our name down for 2 evacuees .. we couldn't have wished for nicer children. They were both from Liverpool. Fred was 10 and Norman 9. They were tired so I gave them their supper and took them up to bed. They were soon in their pyjamas and tucked up. I said a little prayer and gave them both a goodnight kiss. I left a light on and told them I would put it out when I went to bed. They slept all night ... [Doris Blackwell][20]

'Aunty' Rose and 'Uncle' Don were kindness itself and soon made us comfortable with a meal, a bath and a warm bed.[Edna Griffiths]

I was treated and loved as one of the family, and couldn't have asked for more. [D W Honey]

We were so well looked after and treated as two of the family all the time. Even when our relatives came to visit us Mrs Price would make them lovely meals ... [Vera Quinn][21]

We went to a lovely couple who had no children of their own and took us to their hearts. We were very, very happy ... [Mrs L Schofield]

I'm sure the villagers must have felt invaded by kids from outer space but they made us feel quite at home even though it was a very Welsh village. [Joyce Light]

71

I was evacuated to Barmouth and was one of the lucky evacuees who got billeted with one of the kindest, most loving families in the world.
[Tommy Murphy]

'The welcome accorded has been wonderful and the past weekend has been an experience we shall never forget. From the times of antiquity Wales has been noted for traces of gold, but this week has proved that everyone we have met in Aberystwyth has indeed a heart of gold ...'
[Liverpool teachers' tribute, printed in *Cambrian News*, September 1939]

'Let Them Remain'

Where there were contemporary glowing tributes and happy stories to relate, the evacuating authorities were naturally quick to seize on them in the early days of the scheme, anxious to reassure parents that the children were safe and happy. Birkenhead Councillor J. King, returning from a holiday in Wales in the first week of September, deliberately passed through Aberystwyth, Machynlleth and other areas which had just received Merseyside evacuees so that he could report back on how they were settling in. Shortly afterwards Alderman Deverell, the Mayor of Birkenhead, went on a tour of Montgomeryshire, Merionethshire, Caernarvonshire and Flintshire and found the evacuees perfectly contented and *'obviously settling in well in their new surroundings'*.[22] Local newspapers printed letters from teachers reporting on how well the children had settled down, from parents who had visited their children and wanted to reassure others, as well as happy letters from the children themselves. Ten-year-old Kenneth Richardson of Cole Street School, evacuated to Harlech wrote:

Dear Dad,

Its okay but for one thing we had to wait a couple of hours in a bloomin picture house and our Pat lost my bob, we were wakened the 'smornin by the mooin of cows and snortin of pigs and crying of cocks I hope everything is okay. When we stopped at the station in Wales the Welsh kids cum around with water and refreshments and oboy did we have some fun with them.

P.S. we do not have electric we have lamps. This farmer makes his own Home Killed Welsh Cow. It is hanging on a ceiling now.[23]

Roving reporters were despatched to the reception areas from where they sent back articles under such headings as REFUGEES IN WONDERLAND,[24] describing the warm welcome the children had received and how much they were enjoying discovering the countryside - 'a demi-paradise of green fields and mountains'.

Unfortunately, as early as 6 September, one local paper found itself having to scotch some 'ridiculous rumours':

While the evacuation of the schoolchildren was carried out without a hitch, considerable distress has been occasioned by persons who have persisted in spreading the most ridiculous rumours almost before the children had reached their destination. One such rumour was that a large number arrived in Oswestry and found no sleeping accommodation had been provided. This completely unfounded statement was in circulation at 1pm yet the trains for Oswestry did not leave until 11.20 and 3pm! [25]

Sadly, in the same edition came news of perhaps the first tragedy of the evacuation scheme. Nine-year-old Gordon Richards had been one of 62 children evacuated from Gautby Road Junior school to Caergwrle. Gordon had been playing with another two boys when he had stopped off to investigate a sewerage works in Hope near Hawarden. Tragically he had fallen into one of the sewerage tanks and had drowned. News like this would naturally have brought out the protective instincts of every parent reading the paper and no doubt influenced some to bring their children straight home. LET THEM REMAIN urged one editorial, speaking of the 'folly' and 'selfishness' of the parents and others whose homeward trek 'had not given the evacuation scheme a proper chance'. [26] Liverpool Emergency Committee also issued a stern statement condemning parents who had brought back their children for 'trivial reasons'. Yet there were more rumours to be countered the following week. A letter was printed in the *Liverpool Daily Post*, 11 September, from E.B. Pye of Clint Road School, Liverpool:

We are deeply concerned to hear that false rumours are being spread in Liverpool about the reception of children in this area [Gwyrfai]. Nothing could surpass the kindliness and hospitality of the people here. The children are being well cared for and are blissfully happy. Two children refused to go home when their parents, upset by these false rumours, came here determined to take them back to Liverpool with them.

A few days later, a *Birkenhead News* reporter offered further reassurance:
A second tour of evacuation areas convinces me beyond doubt that rumours of ill-treatment and bad organisation are entirely ungrounded. Those who, strenghthened by such rumours, have brought back their

children to the danger zone of Birkenhead have allowed sentiment to overcome reason.[27]

The head teacher of Woodlands School, evacuated to Bala had apparently told this reporter that the whole scheme was 'working perfectly' and that they had met with 'wonderful hospitality'. Only three children had been taken back - one of whom had written home and told her mother she was sleeping in a field! Could it be that some of the rumours had been deliberately started by homesick children?!

Local efforts to bolster the scheme were backed up by various government actions. On 14 September, just two weeks after the first evacuees had set out, the President of the Board of Trade broadcast a nationwide message, appealing to parents not to bring their children home. The Ministry of Health issued a circular urging *'tact, tolerance and understanding as well as administrative enterprise and ingenuity'* to help sort out the settling-in process for evacuees. Parents were warned not to be fooled by the current absence of air raids. There was also another fact to consider. If the children were removed from their billets now, there would be no guarantee that a place of safety would be available to them at a future date. As the 'Birkenhead News representative' explained in the 4 October copy of his paper:

> *Some of the parents have taken their children home - despite the Government's repeated warnings. They are very foolish and that is putting it rather bluntly - but, as a highly-placed North Wales evacuation official told me: 'Very soon billets will not be available, for thousands of "private evacuees" are pouring into North Wales at this very moment. They are paying their own way and one cannot refuse them. If mothers, at a time of real stress, clamour for the children to be re-registered, it may be impossible to deal with them.'*
> *This is exactly what the government warning indicated. Wealthy Mr Stockbroker of London is sending Mrs Stockbroker and the children to North Wales.*
> *The moral for Birkenhead parents - your child's safety comes first.*

However, on the very same day that the *News* carried this serious warning, the government made its announcement that parents were to be asked to contribute to the upkeep of their evacuated children. Newspapers throughout the evacuation area carried such headings as PARENTS TO PAY FOR EVACUEES and explained that parents were to be responsible for providing their children with clothes, boots, etc and that those who could afford it would be asked to pay part of the billeting allowance. The government had always intended trying to recover some of the cost of evacuation in this way, but the timing of its announcement could hardly have been worse. Some parents hadn't sent their children in the first place because the financial side of things seemed unclear; now the very mention of a 'means test' no doubt sent many other mums and dads scurrying off to North Wales to reclaim their youngsters. One WVS organiser certainly saw this as a blow to the scheme. Speaking of evacuees in Caernarvon, she said ' ...*I expect more than ever will be taken home now the parents have to pay. The whole position is difficult.* [28]

One week later (after the Health Minister had been asked in the House if he realised that large numbers of evacuees were being withdrawn due to his anouncement), local newspapers on Merseyside were again trying to stem the homeward flow, this time by publishing government reassurances that no one would have to pay who couldn't afford to do so. Birkenhead Education Committee passed a resolution to support Salford's Director of Education in asking the government to postpone collecting billeting charges from parents in order to prevent the complete breakdown of the scheme.[29] The Liverpool authorities did their best to allay parents' fears and quickly circulated some 25,000 parents with a personal letter from the Minister explaining the arrangements. Within a week, assessments had been made and parents notified of what contributions were due. Perhaps surprisingly, Liverpool's Civil Defence Emergency Committee reported one month later that: *'In spite of the levying of contributions from parents there has been a remarkable slowing up of the return of evacuated children from reception areas.'*[30] Yet certainly some damage had already been done and the evacuation scheme was soon to be further undermined when education authorities in the 'danger' areas found themselves forced to reopen their schools.

Early in October 1939, about 1400 parents of pupils attending Calder High and Quarry Bank schools, both evacuated from Liverpool to Wrexham Rural District, met in Liverpool. They resolved that, whilst appreciating the authority's action in organising evacuation, sufficient consideration had not been given to the human problems involved and they now called upon the Liverpool Education Authorities to re-open the two schools, which, they felt, could easily be provided with air raid shelters. The headteachers were anxious to stress that there was no question of the children being dissatisfied or unhappy in their billets, and indeed tremendous gratitude was felt to the people of Wrexham. The fact that a double-shift system was being used did not mean that the

CITY OF LIVERPOOL.

THE TOWN HALL
LIVERPOOL. . .

October, 1939.

GOVERNMENT EVACUATION SCHEME.

Repayment of Billeting Charges.

Dear Sir or Madam,

      I enclose a letter addressed by the Minister of Health to the parents of children who have been removed with their schools to places of greater safety under the Government Evacuation Scheme. You will see from this letter that the Government are asking parents to pay what they can afford towards the cost of the maintenance of these children, and the Government have directed this Council to act as their agents for the collection of the money due from parents in the County Borough of Liverpool.*

      Please fill in and return to the DIRECTOR OF EDUCATION, 14, SIR THOMAS STREET, LIVERPOOL, 1, within the next 3 days the form enclosed with this letter. An addressed envelope (which need not be stamped) is enclosed for this purpose. If you can pay the full cost (9/- a week) (or at least 6/- a week in respect of each child, you need not fill in Parts 2 and 3 of the form.

      If, however, you cannot afford to pay 6/- a week for each child, please fill in the whole form and you will be informed whether your offer can be accepted or, if not, of the amount which you will be required to pay.

Yours faithfully,

W. H. Baines

Town Clerk & A.R.P. Controller.

*Parents who are in receipt of Unemployment Assistance or Public Assistance will not be expected to make any contribution.

Some parents brought their children home when they realised they had to contribute to billeting costs! (Letter courtesy Peter Walker) education timetable had been halved. Nevertheless, apparently some parents believed that the situation was retarding the academic progress of their children and it was for this reason that they were now approaching the authorities.[31]

The matter was not pursued immediately but over the next few weeks the ever-increasing number of children returning to Merseyside, in addition to the sizeable number who had not gone away in the first place, put the education authorities in a dilemma. Because of the expected dangers and the implementation of the evacuation scheme, schools in evacuation areas had been closed, but as one non-evacuee commented as early as 16 September: '*...I wish someone would decide to send us back to school because my class and the others are surely as worthy of education as those evacuated.*' [32] In November 1939 a petition was submitted to Liverpool Education Committee from 'the parents of Liverpool scholars' who were similarly concerned by the lack of schooling. At the same time, the local Chamber of Commerce, in a letter to the committee, highlighted the annoyance being caused to shopkeepers by the large number of unsupervised children who were roaming the streets.[33]

The LEA realised that it had no option but to re-open the schools, though only after they had been provided with air raid shelters. In the meantime an appeal was put out asking local householders to agree to volunteer some rooms for use as temporary teaching centres. By this time, so many of the children had left the reception areas that some of the teachers who had been evacuated with them were no longer needed there. Helen Woodward explains:

> *I was among those sent back to Liverpool, with instructions to report in to the Education Offices. Next day I was there, among a surprisingly large gathering of teachers. We were informed there would be no access to any of our schools for any of us, or our children, until sufficient air-raid shelter accommodation had been installed. Meanwhile, would we be agreeable to assisting the City Engineers' Department in tackling the huge task of supplying shelters to civilians? So - off we went with lists and clipboards, and spent the next two weeks or so traversing hitherto unknown streets and roads, knocking on doors, and asking, 'Please do you want a free air-raid shelter?' and checking garden or yard areas suitable for installation. We were started off in pairs around the perimeter of the City, but when we had worked down to the less salubrious parts we were told to work in threes. The reputedly tough Scotland Road area gave us no trouble at all. There was a strange sort of camaraderie about it all. I never kept count of all the houses we visited, or of how many cups of tea we were offered!*

> *With this task completed we were able to get back to teaching the children. There was no school access yet available, but we arranged the teaching of small groups in various homes, where there was a room large enough. Eventually, sufficient shelters had been installed at Dovedale Road school to enable our children from the Morrison to be taught there on a half-time plan - alternately, mornings one week, afternoons the next.*

The difficulty was that once the Merseyside schools began to re-open, even more parents were inclined to bring their children home, so much so that Liverpool's Director of Education was obliged to issue a circular to all reception authorities explaining that: *'Owing to the advanced state of the construction of air raid shelters at many of the Liverpool schools, an impression is gaining ground that it is the intention of the Committee to withdraw the evacuated schoolchildren from the Reception Areas as soon as arrangements are completed for the re-opening of the Liverpool school attended by them.'* This, said Mott, was a completely false impression and he asked that Reception Officers *'authoritively deny any suggestion which comes to your notice that evacuated schoolchildren will shortly be officially re-called to Liverpool'.*[34]

But the rot was setting in. Christmas 1939 was particularly difficult. A letter signed by the Lord Mayor of Liverpool was sent to the parents of every child evacuated from the city, saying how inadvisable it was for them to consider bringing their children home at this time.[35] Many of the reception areas, sometimes funded by the evacuating authorities, went to great lengths to put on parties and other entertainments for the evacuees, to reduce the pull of home at this special family time. Liverpool allocated £2000 to provide Christmas gifts for evacuees and Birkenhead made a similar grant of 1/- per evacuated child.[36] Pupils of Cole Street Council school, evacuated to Harlech, were given a party, to which visiting parents were also invited. Each child received a present and the children put on a concert afterwards for their hosts and families. Temple Road Central evacuees were also treated to a party, in Towyn; in Caernarvon evacues were taken to local cinemas on Boxing Day, and had a party at the Drill Hall next day.

Many householders also made an extra effort to give their evacuees a special Christmas. Dorothy Kell, billeted with Miss Carter in her large house, 'Penmount', in Barmouth, writes:

> *Another lovely memory ... Miss Carter's mother lived in a very big house called 'Talafor' in Llanaber and at Christmas we closed Penmount and*

*went there - big log fire, Xmas carols and Xmas tree and stockings. On
Boxing Day we walked down from the house and were on the beach. Our
feet would be cold so we threw stones to get warm and it worked. By the
time we got back we were lovely and warm and ready for lunch.*

Hugh Jones has similar happy memories:

*I well recall Christmas 1939: in the parish hall Santa gave us all presents,
evacuee and Coedpoeth children equally. With those presents came an
orange. I was not to see another orange till after the war. The memory of
that orange has never left me.*

Pauline also has cause to remember her first Christmas as an evacuee - if only
because it was to be the last magical Christmas of her childhood:

*The first Christmas there was great, we had our stockings filled and mum
sent us dolls and toys which we opened on Christmas morning. It was the
last Christmas Father Christmas came to visit me as Mrs A didn't bother
with Christmas stockings after that - so at that tender age [6] I was told by
my brothers and sisters that there was no Father Christmas.*[37]

Some schools decided to give their pupils permission to go home, just for the
Christmas holidays, but this often proved to be the thin end of the wedge, as S.F.
Kerry, one of the evacuated schoolmasters, remembers:

*By Christmas there had still been no bombing. In consequence it was
considered safe to give the whole school Christmas leave. During the
vacation the situation was reviewed and the authorities decided to
discontinue the bulk evacuation and re-establish the school at Rock Ferry
in January but to continue facilities at Portmadoc for those whose parents
wished them to stay evacuated.* [38]

Much the same conclusions were drawn by the staff of St Francis Xavier's
College:

*...when parents were offered the chance of having their sons home for the
Christmas vacation, only about a score of boys were left in the reception
area for the three weeks' holiday. When parents were asked to choose
between bringing their boys home to Liverpool for full-time education and
leaving them in Wales for full schooling there, few, if any, chose the latter
course, so that when the Easter Vacation commenced on March 20th,
there followed what amounted to a complete return to Liverpool.*[39]

79

It was hard being away from home at Christmas but reception areas did their best to make it a happy time. Pictured here are some of the 300 children - locals and evacuees from Birkenhead - enjoying a party in Llanidloes. Looking on are Father Christmas, Mr. F.S. Higgs (the Mayor) and Mr. H. Guerra (one of the two beret-sporting Frenchmen who acted as local billeting officers). (By permission of the National Library of Wales)

The final nail in the coffin of the first evacuation scheme was perhaps hammered home by the weather, which after Christmas suddenly took on an 'arctic' feel. January saw the beginning of one of the worst winters on record. The Thames froze over for the first time since 1888. Closer to home a train on the Cheshire Lines railway, travelling from Liverpool to Manchester, was 'lost' in snow for three days and had to be dug out by soldiers. The Isle of Man ferry took three *days* to complete what was usually a four-hour crossing.[40] Many evacuees, often quite scantily clad but now of course living in much more exposed areas, some quite high up, and in houses with only very basic heating facilities and no hot water, still remember how bitterly cold it was. One of the things Ken Aird associates most with his period as an evacuee was the 'very cold, bleak weather'. 'B.R.' also recalled his first winter away:

80

The second term was progressing normally until one morning all awoke to find the world within their range of vision icebound and everywhere telegraph and telephone poles torn down. Worse was to follow for that night there was a heavy fall of snow and morning dawned to show the roads blocked by deep snow. There followed a period of arctic weather. Some of the temperatures recorded seem incredible - twenty eight degrees below freezing point was recorded one night. School was out of the question, so for ten days we had winter sports ...[41]

While most of the children managed to find some consolation - enjoying toboganning and the inevitable snowball fights - the severe winter gave an added headache to many of the teachers. One of them recorded that the early months of 1940 were:

A trying time particularly as the winter turned very severe, with settled snow. The heating system broke down in the school and we had to huddle around paraffin stoves. Nor was the situation helped by our being immobilised by heavy snowfalls for days at a time.[42]

Although there were still a lot of Merseyside children billeted in North Wales at this time, there is no escaping the fact that the whole evacuation scheme did seem to be running out of steam in this 'Phoney War' period. Even the Government had to concede this and early in 1940 set about the task of preparing a new plan, hoping at least to learn from the first evacuation, avoid some of the problems which had occurred and build on the improvised solutions which had been adopted. Many of the difficulties encountered did crop up again and some proved intractable. But by and large, the scheme came to develop a certain flexibility. Through a combination of more focused central guidance and more inspired local initiative the whole process of evacuation and reception became far better organised as time went by.

What then were the problems encountered and how exactly were they dealt with?

NOTES

[1] The count showed that some 900,000 out of a total of 1,473,000 over the country as a whole had returned to target areas (Titmuss, op.cit. p.173). Liverpool's Civil Defence Emergency Committee records show that at the end of December 1939, 58.3% of the city's evacuated schoolchildren were still away - marginally better than the nationwide figure of 55%. More importantly this meant that 38% of the schoolchildren from Liverpool's evacuation area were still away, compared with 14% in Birmingham, 11% in Glasgow and 34% in London.

[2] About 60%, compared for example with only 15% in Sheffield and a national average of 48% - see Titmuss, p.103ff.

[3] Report of the House of Commons debate, *Wrexham Advertiser and Star*, 22 Sept 1939

[4] Bryan G. Blades, *Welsh Rarebits*, p.365

[5] Denbs CC file 36 (Z1352)

[6] Author's interview with Mrs Ethel Kerry

[7] Bryan G. Blades, *Welsh Rarebits*, p.347

[8] Montgomeryshire Memories 1900-1960 (Powys Federation of Women's Institutes), p.89

[9] Detail from *Oswestry and Welsh Border Counties Advertiser*, cited in *Our Evacuee*, p.3

[10] *Our Evacuee*, p.48

[11] I am most grateful to Peter Walker for supplying me with copies of correspondence, bulletins etc sent to his parents from Liverpool Collegiate whilst he was evacuated with the School.

[12] *Cefn Chronicle*, 16 Sept 1939

[13] Ceiriog RDC Minutes 1939-42, report 21 Nov 1939 (Ruthin RO)

[14] Nant Conway RDC Letterbook 1941-42, letter to CF Mott 21 Jan 1941 (Caernarfon RO)

[15] cited in Sissons, *Planning ARP in Liverpool*, p.119

[16] cited in Boyce *Pillowslips and Gas Masks*, p.19

[17] Schemes like this were arranged for example in Menai Bridge, Twrcelyn, Caernarvon, Wrexham and Towyn.

[18] Extract from a questionnaire completed in October 1975 by Mrs M Jones, formerly Miss Kirkup, evacuated teacher in Caernarvon.

[19] Extract from Joan Boyce, *Pillowslips and Gas Masks*, p.14

[20] Extract from *Liverpool Daily Post* supplement 'Wales at War', 25 April 1989

[21] *Our Evacuee*, p.21

[22] *Birkenhead News*, 4 October 1939, also *Birkenhead Advertiser*, 23 September 1939

[23] Printed in the *Birkenhead News*, 16 September 1939

[24] *Birkenhead News*, 9 September 1939

[25] *Birkenhead Advertiser*, 6 September 1939

[26] *Birkenhead News*, 13 September 1939

[27] Birkenhead News, 16 September 1939

[28] Letter from Mrs Davies (WVS), 9 Oct 1939, Caern. Borough Evac Papers, Box 5 (DI/718)

[29] Birkenhead Education Committee Minutes, 25 October 1939

[30] City of Liverpool Proceedings of the Council, report of the Civil Defence Emergency Committee, 19 Oct-27 Nov 1939, (352/COU)

[31] The meetings were reported in the *Wrexham Advertiser and Star*, 6 & 13 October 1939

[32] Mass Observation diarist, quoted in Joan Boyce, *Pillowslip and Gas Masks*, p.22

[33] Liverpool Education Committee, November 1939, (352/EDU)

[34] Letter from Mott, 12 March 1940; Amlwch UDC Evac File 1939-41

[35] See Liverpool Civil Defence Emergency Committee 28 Nov-27 Dec1939

[36] See Titmuss, p.144, and Birkenhead Civil Defence Minutes, 30 Nov 1939 (B/025/1)

[37] Extract from *Cambrian News* 'Homefront Heroes' Supplement, 1989

[38] *With Oars and Sails*: An Illustrated History of Rock Ferry High School 1925-96, p.70

[39] St Francis Xavier's College Magazine, 1940, p.51

[40] Details from Ken Blasbery, Children of the Blitz, p.3

[41] Ibid. p.53

[42] *With Oars and Sails,* p.70

4 - *Tact, Tolerance, Enterprise and Ingenuity*

Many of the difficulties which were likely to arise following a full-scale evacuation had often been recognised in the months leading up to the start of the scheme but had rarely been rigorously addressed. With evacuation a reality they could no longer be ignored. The Ministry of Health issued a circular calling for 'tact, tolerance, enterprise and ingenuity' in sorting things out. The most pressing problem, or at least that given the most publicity, concerned the condition of the evacuees. This was a two-fold matter involving both health and clothing.

Wet Beds and Itchy Heads

During the first few weeks of September the Merseyside authorities received a barrage of complaints about the state of the evacuees, particularly the children - Wrexham Education Committee for example passed a severe censure on the municipal authorities for allowing children to be sent in a 'filthy' condition. Alderman Hampson, an ex-Mayor of Wrexham maintained that *'Picaninnies in darkest Africa were far healthier and happier'*![1] Inevitably questions were asked in Liverpool - the Labour Councillor Bessie Braddock, not known for mincing her words, demanded a full explanation from the Public Assistance Committee, whose chairman responded, much as C. F. Mott had done earlier, by claiming that the urgency of the operation had made it impossible to undertake pre-evacuation checks.[2] Others went on the offensive - Luke Hogan, leader of Liverpool's Labour Party issued a criticism of what he called 'drawing-room representatives' in the reception area who had no idea of the difficulties Liverpool had to contend with in the face of dire poverty.[3] Similarly, the *Sunday Pictorial*, 24 September 1939, carried a stinging rebuke of Alderman Hampson, declaring:

> *Wrexham's duty is to get on with the job of making the kids clean and happy - and showing a little charity. This nation showed plenty of charity to Wrexham, I remember, when they had their big pit disaster at Gresford. We are faced with a disaster that makes Gresford seem like a street accident.*

The priest at St Mary's Priory in the Tithebarn Street area also asked, though in a much gentler way, that Liverpool's evacuees be shown compassion. Equally aware that terrible living conditions were at the root of many of the problems,

84

he explained in a moving letter published in the *Chester Courant*, 13 September 1939, that many of the evacuees were

> *... people who normally receive more kicks than kindness from life and who do not have many of the opportunities of learning how to appreciate and requite kindness. Moreover our people were suddenly transported in circumstances representing grave urgency and they are naturally anxious ... Nevertheless, we who live on Dockside among them have a real affection for them, and a patience which is bred of an understanding of their privations. We believe that when you come to know them better, you will find, as we have found, some of the noblest qualities of human nature under an often unprepossessing exterior ... Once these people take you to their hearts they do not let go.*[4]

Once the immediate outcry had subsided, a less impassioned study of the situation often revealed that the health of the evacuees did not present a grave problem at all.[5] Many reports testify to rapid, if not miraculous, improvements in the condition of the children. A paper produced for the University of Wales Guild of Graduates[6] even suggested 'evacuees' should be renamed 'Dumplings' partly because they'd been 'dumped' in Wales but also because they were now enjoying the fat of the land (a comment which might have brought a wry smile to the faces of some, starving in their billets - but more on this later). The early improvements were usually put down to good country air and the solicitude of local householders, but do imply that the original reports may have been somewhat exaggerated! So, for example, Penmaenmawr's Medical Officer reported in November 1939 that the general health of the district was remarkably good; a recent measles epidemic had been almost exclusively confined to local children. Ruthin's MO expressed similar amazement at the very low incidence of infectious disease in 1939, especially in view of the addition to the population of some 600 evacuees. Officials in Holyhead and Ceiriog also reported good health amongst the evacuees.[7]

If the situation was not quite so dire as originally portrayed, there was still no room for complacency. The serious epidemic of diphtheria which broke out in the Nant Conway area in November 1939 proved the earliest fears of medical authorities were not totally unfounded. On the whole, the North Wales authorities did recognise the need both to protect their own children and to push for immunisation of evacuees so as to lessen any dangerous disparity. As with so many issues, this was at first made complicated by financial constraints (and by the need to obtain parental consent) but Liverpool finally agreed, in March

85

1941, to pay 3/6d per immunised evacuee. The importance of this was again underlined in November 1941 when diphtheria broke out amongst evacuees in Ruthin. Occasionally districts reported cases of scarlet fever which couldn't be accounted for by local conditions. The Health Ministry also decreed that with evacuation in process measles and whooping cough should be added to the list of notifiable diseases. By and large, however, reception areas were less troubled by these illnesses than by infectious skin diseases, such as scabies and impetigo; by an ailment known as enuresis (bed-wetting); and by infestations of 'pediculi' - otherwise known as head lice!

The problem of seemingly incontinent children often posed the greatest immediate worry for billeting officials in September 1939. Their offices were almost immediately inundated with outraged householders demanding compensation for ruined bedclothes caused by what they believed to be either dirty or lazy children whose parents had never properly toilet-trained them. Listening to descriptions of some of the billets it's perhaps not surprising that many of the children wet their beds! Although some were used to an outside 'privy', the facilities they now encountered were rather different. In many cases, a night-time visit to the toilet would involve getting out of bed in a strange house in the pitch black, making your way downstairs, out of the back door and right down to the bottom of the garden to use a primitive, often foul-smelling latrine. John Houston well remembers:

> The only toilet was in a wooden shed behind some empty stables. Inside was just a bench with a hole in the middle, suspended over a deep pit which, judging by the smell hadn't been emptied for years.

Ken McGunigle also retains a vivid picture of the 'plumbing' at his billet:

> The toilet was at the very bottom of the garden against the wall. It had a long wooden seat fixed into the wall, but there was no bucket. There was a piece of slate which sloped so that it went through the wall on to a dump on the other side which was collected by council workmen every so often and the slate was changed.

These were hardly places to linger at in daytime, let alone in the dead of night. As Maureen Weller puts it, it meant a difficult decision, even for the older children:

> Toilet arrangements consisted of a primitive privy in a draughty wooden

hut at the end of the garden. This constituted an agony of dilemma in the middle of the night. We had been provided with a chamber pot ... but embarrassment was the ultimate deterrent, equalled only by the scariness of the solo journey down the garden path in the dark.

Not all the hosts had the foresight to provide chamber pots, however, so some of the children 'improvised'. In Bethesda, one indignant householder reported that their evacuees had 'made use' in the night of the lower drawer of a chest of drawers![8] Similarly, Nesta Rushton recalls:

In those days we only had an outside toilet ... Well, one Sunday morning I went into [our evacuees'] bedroom for my best Sunday hat for chapel and was delighted to find that I couldn't go as the poor mites had used two of my hats for the toilet during the night!!

These circumstances alone would have been sufficient to explain the outbreak of bedwetting that heralded the arrival of the evacuees - but of course the real cause was the trauma of evacuation itself. Enuresis was actually a symptom of neurosis rather than bad training or laziness or fear of the dark. As a stress-related problem it was one which even affected the troops, causing problems, for example, to some of the soldiers evacuated from Dunkirk in 1940.[9] It was a condition commonly experienced in peacetime by children in public schools, homes, approved schools, holiday camps, and even by adults at training centres[10] - it was simply a reaction to loss of security and often passed when this was re-established in the new surroundings. As a neurotic ailment it was, not surprisingly, associated with every evacuation and despite attempts to explain its cause it continued to be a source of irritation. In November 1939, a welfare worker in Chirk reported:

Enuresis has been the chief complaint. Beds and sheets have been ruined. In every case this was due to laziness on the part of the child but I am glad to say that with a little advice both to householders and evacuees this complaint has entirely disappeared.[11]

Again in 1941, Penmaenmawr's Evacuation Officer made the following comment to C.F. Mott, which not only shows it was still a problem but also that it was still misunderstood:

During the past few weeks with the last evacuation from Liverpool, housewives with children billeted upon them have never had a more

87

arduous time in endeavouring to make the children better citizens owing to their habits. More money than ever has been spent on laundry charges owing to bed-wetting and bed-messing which is so surprising in children over 10 and 12 years of age, but we endeavour to appease the householders and ask them to give the children a further trial.

Within a few days of the first evacuation the government acknowledged the enuresis problem by authorising the payment of compensation to householders for damaged bedding - either a monetary payment or payment in kind from any existing bedding stocks held by the council. Records show that few districts escaped this problem, for appeals for compensation were received by Billeting Officers throughout North Wales. Of course, with this financial incentive the system was open to abuse and for this reason the extent of the problem may have been exaggerated. After 1941, when claims began to soar, an official Government enquiry was opened, but the North Wales authorities seem to have been vigilant before this. Reporting, for instance, in June 1940 the *North Wales Chronicle* noted that one claim from Portdinorwic for damaged bedding had amounted to £5 but the local council had allowed only £1/10/-.

Prevention was perhaps a better option and in the wake of the September 1939 experience the Welsh Board of Health was asked to send supplies of waterproof material, such as rubber sheets, which were issued to householders to reduce the damage from any 'accidents'. Frank Jagger writes, a little indignantly: *'I remember the rubber draw sheet on my bed. Mrs Davies asked me if I'd slept well. I said no I hadn't because of the stink of rubber!'* The Ministry of Health had, in fact, ordered Mackintosh overlays for young bedwetters as early as May 1939 but few had been delivered by the outbreak of the war and no provision had been made for older children despite reports showing a fairly high percentage of enuretics in schoolchildren.[12]

Towards the end of 1939, Liverpool University began to conduct a social survey into evacuation, including the problem of enuresis.[13] They used as their 'guinea pigs' children from the Alsop High School, evacuated to Holyhead. A list of known bed-wetters was compiled and helpers attached to the school (often masters' wives) interviewed the families concerned. The University then processed the information and published its findings. A.M. Jones, Holyhead's Billeting Officer, was highly sceptical of the whole thing, believing the survey team had been *'led up the garden path by complainants wanting to get rid of the children'*.[14] But many householders must have experienced the difficulty without making a fuss, simply treating their small charges with sympathy until the problem was overcome. Gwen Jones remembers when their evacuee arrived:

There were some initial problems, such as bed wetting, of which we were warned, but it had evidentally been caused by her unhappy experience in her first billet. She settled in with us very quickly and my parents treated her in exactly the same way as their own child. She and my young sister became very attached to each other and the bed wetting soon disappeared.

Yet undoubtedly there were others who took a much harder line, refusing not only to understand the cause of the ailment but also to give the child 'a further trial', especially in 1939 when this appeared as yet one more burden on country people out of all proportion to the war effort then being made by the nation as a whole. As a result, numerous councils found it necessary to establish hostels to take in children turned out of their billets by reason of their 'foul habits'. The Liverpool University survey suggested that even in these hostels there was widespread misunderstanding about enuresis, for a visit to one such institute *'gave the feeling that we still live in the Middle Ages. In this clinic the children were treated like little criminals, and threat and punishment were the means of teaching them clean habits. The result can easily be imagined: no progress was made at all.'*[15]

This particular clinic was not in North Wales and, in fact, though little evidence remains as to methods adopted, one report which does discuss the issue suggests that some of the Welsh establishments used a more enlightened approach. Ruthin Borough Medical Officer reported:

Several children whom foster parents have found wetting the bed have been sent to Whitegates [Hostel]. Most of the cases quickly recover without much treatment. In some cases there appears to be a tendency to expect too much of small children and the unsuitability of the billets are to blame...[16]

In other cases it seems to have been less the unsuitability of the billets than of the householders themselves, some of whom showed the evacuees very little compassion: a few were downright cruel. The harrowing experience of one Liverpool evacuee quite beggars belief. She describes in her own words how her 'hostess' reacted to wet sheets:

She came up the stairs and said 'Have you wet the bed?' I said 'No, I haven't.' She said 'You have, and for that and being naughty and crying for

your mother, I'll put the dog in your bed and you'll go in the dog's place.'
She brought up the little dog and took his collar off, put it round my neck
and put the dog in the bed. She put the chain round my neck, then she got
the lead and dragged me down the stairs on my bottom ... It was cold and
windy and she took me out into the back. I remember a black hole, which
was the dog kennel, and being pushed in it and chained. I was left there
all night, screaming and crying. She done that every time I wet the bed. I
hated it. I hated it when I went to bed and I would be saying in my prayers
'Oh God, don't let me wet the bed.' [17]

Despite all the advice being given out - writers like Anna Freud (daughter of
Siegmund) tried to explain the need for patience and understanding,[18] a message
reinforced in a radio broadcast by psychiatrist Donald Winnicot[19] - there were
those who persisted in feeling the short, sharp shock treatment would give the
quickest cure. Occasionally this did work, as in the case of Peter Sherlock and
his brother. Peter remembers *'the first night - we wet the bed. Mrs N rubbed*
the wet sheet in both our faces. We never did it again!' But this kind of approach
- humiliation or threat - rarely met with success and usually made the problem
worse. Charles Crebbin remembers that after visits from his family, when he'd
had to bottle in his terrible homesickness, *'tearful nights and embarrassing bed-*
wetting often ensued'. This also happened when, in his hearing, thoughtless
adults spoke of the terrible battering Liverpool was receiving. Charles felt
certain his parents were dead. *'The next morning,'* he recalls *'my bed linen*
once more wet, I was faced yet again with the indignity of being scorned by Mr
K as a "dirty little baby" and the punishment of taking my sheets and pyjamas to
the bathroom and washing them by hand, to show me just how much extra work
my incontinence was causing.'

Alex Anderson's bedwetting was also directly attributable to the coldness of his
foster parents who denied him any attention or affection, let alone any toys. No
doubt in an attempt to get at least some of these he one day took a few lead
soldiers belonging to another boy.

> *... I was branded a 'nasty little thief' and again spent a few more days of*
> *pariah status. This understandable reaction from the [foster parents] did*
> *nothing to ease my sense of insecurity and I repaid them by wetting the*
> *bed. This fairly regularly, especially during the early days.*

Jean McCarthy remembers her bedwetting, and the unsuccessful attempts at a
cure, with an added tinge of sadness:

I wet the bed seven nights a week. It was awful for that lady to have to put up with this dreadful habit. She used to have a maid, who would come up to bed us down and the maid would say, 'Whoever wets the bed tonight gets no storybook to read tomorrow.' I do not remember if my sister Doreen did ever wet the bed but to get that storybook next day I lied, and said it wasn't me - so no one got the book, and never did ... But oh my lovely dear sister, I miss her even now [The girls went home and Doreen was killed in an air raid] I would never blame her again for wetting the bed if I could have those times again.

Another set of sisters were also involved in a bed-wetting incident, though of a slightly different sort. Mrs Williams explains:

My older sister went to stay with some Fish and Chip shop people - they were more our sort and nicer than my billet - but she wet the bed and they took the sheets down to school to show everyone what she'd done. It was so humiliating. Of course the other children taunted her. I was the 'baby' sister but I was a bit of a tomboy and I battered some of the kids who were teasing her. They were rather straight-laced at my billet and they wouldn't let me stay when they found out what had taken place!

Others remember that sometimes mattresses were put out in gardens to dry - which was as good as broadcasting to the whole neighbourhood that there was a bed-wetter in the house. Children, being children, as Mrs Williams pointed out, weren't likely to miss such a golden opportunity for a bit of teasing. Some of the youngsters, of course, at a time when many had to share a bed, like Jean and Doreen, encountered the problem at rather closer quarters - hence a popular ditty of the time, along the lines:

Shine a light, shine a light, just for a minute
So-and-so's wet the bed - and I'm lying in it!

The provision of hostels and sick bays was the solution widely adopted in reception areas to deal with evacuee health problems (and a variety of other problems - see later). There was some confusion in the pre-evacuation planning as to where responsibility lay in providing accommodation for infected evacuees and as the government was slow to authorise expenditure, few local authorities were well prepared at the outset. The situation in 1939, however, called for swift action and within a week of the start of evacuation several councils had taken over empty houses to act as treatment centres or for isolation purposes.

Some of the first hostels set up were intended to help with bed-wetters, others were established in direct response to the discovery of skin diseases. School Medical Reports before the war had shown that scabies was on the increase and that impetigo was also common amongst elementary schoolchildren in the big towns[20], yet these, though not completely unknown in rural areas, were far less prevalent there. In practical terms this meant that North Wales householders were unfamiliar with the complaints and their local authorities had little in the way of established facilities to deal with them. As Portmadoc's Medical Officer confessed, *'The importation of scabies into the county found the districts unprepared in the matter of suitable accommodation and treatment and the provision of such treatment is proving to be a very slow process.'*[21]

As the first evacuation took place at the end of the school holidays, all the ailments usually controlled by the School Medical Services were likely to have been rampant. Even when children were sent away 'clean' and in good health, the travelling conditions, as we've seen, promoted the spread of infection. The tiny scabies mite burrows under the surface of the skin and isn't easily detected, so infected children could not have been readily segregated. Yet the mite thrives in the kind of hot atmosphere of a railway carriage, and with the children packed closely together it would only take a few scabies sufferers to have infected a large number of others. Impetigo is also extremely infectious and easily spread, and lice too, particularly head lice, were likely to have found many a new host during the course of the journey to Wales.

The conditions under which all these ailments were prone to spread became even more pronounced once Merseyside was thrown into chaos by the Blitz and people spent night after night in crowded air raid shelters. In Liverpool the number of children being treated for scabies, for example, soared from 693 in 1938 to 11,329 in 1943.[22] In some reception areas scabies was even referred to as 'shelter rash'. It was this sort of condition which led to evacuees in parts of Wales being dubbed 'ychafis'. Pronounced 'uchavees' so sounding quite like the English word 'evacuees', 'ychafi' actually translates to mean 'something nasty' and scabies certainly was a nasty thing to have. But it wasn't always the evacuees who were responsible for importing it. Gwen Jones remembers that *'the scabies epidemic was very unpleasant but it was never attributed to the evacuees. It was only when a large number of troops were billeted in the town [Llanidloes] that the trouble started and very soon we were all going around covered with sulphur ointment.'* In Caernarvonshire, however, the blame was placed fairly and squarely on the evacuees. When discussing the issue of who should finance treatment of locals who contracted the infection, Caernarvon Council informed the Welsh Board of Health in no uncertain terms that scabies was the direct result of evacuation: there had been no trace of it in the borough before 1939, furthermore it had been eliminated by August 1942 but broke out again when the evacuees returned from their school holidays.[23]

Whoever may have been responsible, the fact remains that during 1941 scabies did reach epidemic proportions in North Wales. Hostels and clinic records show a huge increase in the numbers admitted and treated; a census of absenteeism from schools in the Caernarvon area revealed that 597 children were away from school due to scabies and impetigo *'which seemed to be spreading at an alarming rate throughout the borough'*.[24] Authorities in Pwllheli, Criccieth and Portmadoc also expressed grave concern at the situation, the latter no doubt spurred into action when the Chairman of the Council discovered that two of the evacuees staying with him had caught the infection! In Criccieth the Evacuation Officer herself contracted scabies and had to enter a Sick Bay for treatment.[25] Many local people did become infected and feelings ran high, so much so that the Chairman of Menai Bridge Council, for example, felt it necessary to give a sharp warning against rumour-mongering. Whilst there had been a lot of scabies cases on Anglesey, he felt that undue alarm was being created over something which was not terribly serious.[26] Flintshire also experienced a large number of cases and here, too, one district Medical Officer found he had to 'scotch rumours about scabies'.[27]

There is no doubt that the scabies 'epidemic' at this time, when local authorities in North Wales were already under great strain from the sheer numbers of people pouring into their area, added to the overall tension. Medical Officers fell out with their district councils and councils fell out with the Welsh Board of Health. Each felt the other was not doing enough to alleviate the situation. Finally, on 14 November 1941, the Ministry issued a 'Scabies Order' intended to increase the powers of the local authorities to combat the spread of the disease. The problem was not just a shortage of centres to treat cases of infection but the fact that the treatment there wasn't always very effective. One supervising officer in Holywell reported:

> *The treatment of scabies is very unsatisfactory in that many children, sometimes within a few days of discharge, break out again and have to be sent back to the Sick Bay for further treatment. Some children have been sent back several times.*

Sometimes re-infection followed a visit home so eventually it was ruled that evacuees must be re-examined before being allowed back into the reception area but nothing was done to monitor the 'private' evacuees who were arriving in their thousands.

No doubt the children themselves had no desire to return to the hostels for further treatment as neither the treatment centres nor the cure itself were particularly pleasant. Jean Hennity remembers having to go to a scabies hostel and being stood on a big draining-board; then she had *'a disgusting-smelling ointment'* applied all over her *'with something like a large shaving brush'*. The McGunigle brothers also experienced the 'shaving brush' treatment. Ken writes:

> *One time Fred and I got scabies in our hair and between our fingers and toes, so they sent us to Waen Fawr Cottage Hospital. They used to stand us on a table with a newspaper under our feet and paint us by shaving brush with some white stuff. It used to burn like hell. I think we were there for about a week. It was awful.*

Margaret Jones never suffered the treatment herself but well remembers her cousin's ordeal:

> *A lot of the children got what they called 'shelter rash'. My cousin Edith had it. She was sent to the old Workhouse Hospital in Caersws and put in a ward among people who were tied to their beds! I remember going to visit her. Looking back, it was really Dickensian.*

It's perhaps not surprising that, as one evacuated scoolteacher recalls, children came to dread the thought of having to have their scabies treated:

> *Cases of scabies were sent to a special hostel, which soon became known as the 'Scabby-hole' and tears were often shed by prospective inmates. Innumerable rumours floated around relating to the inhuman treatment of patients in the 'Scabby-hole' so I visited the hostel and found everyone there perfectly happy - the only general complaint relating to the unappetizing food. I expected the rumours to cease after I had reported back to the evacuees but they continued to flourish. The same old tales were resurrected about the Matron flying out on her broomstick every night and black cats with tales like pokers stalking around the dormitory, about the evening bath in rancid fat, sleeping in canvas nightshirts ... and many more fantastic stories!* [28]

In May 1941, Caernarvonshire's MO suggested that to alleviate the strain on hostel accommodation, foster parents could perhaps be encouraged to treat

94

infected children at home. This encouragement took the form of an extra 5/- per week sickness billeting allowance and no doubt this, or a genuine desire to save their evacuee from the trauma of the hostel, led to many householders tackling the problem themselves. Sadly, sometimes the self-help treatment, or 'preventative' approach was over-zealous to the point of cruelty. One account tells how two girls on arrival at their billet were told to strip off all their clothing. When they refused their clothes were torn off and they were forced, naked, in front of the men of the house, into the kitchen where they were pushed into a tin bath containing Dettol. Then their hair was cut off, the excuse being that 'children from Liverpool brought scabies, lice and sores to country areas'. At school the following day they met other evacuees who were also bald.[29]

In the early days of evacuation many children did have to have their hair cut (though hopefully not too many in the way described above), or undergo treatment for head lice. As with the skin complaints, although by no means unheard of in the rural areas, nits and lice were less prevalent than in the towns and not all householders were familiar with the problem. So, one Billeting Officer, faced with a complaint from angry parents that their daughters had developed 'a verminous condition' in their billet, explained that Mrs R, the billetor

> ... had a beautiful clean house and is in fact very houseproud. She is not used to children but has kept their clothes clean. I imagine the idea that the girls' heads might be infected simply did not occur to her ... She is an elderly lady quite unaccustomed to the care of children and has failed to appreciate the personal attention that their maintenance requires.

This was perhaps particularly a problem in North Wales where the population was an ageing one and some of those called upon to provide billets simply couldn't cope with their young charges. But there were others too, younger couples, who for various reasons knew nothing about the rearing of children but now found themselves with a ready-made family. Recognising this, householders were offered assistance in the form of leaflets and in some areas members of the WVS gave lectures on various aspects of childcare. One of the WVS leaflets issued was specifically concerned with *The Cleansing and Care of Children's Heads*, adopting the motto 'Be Thorough', and in February 1940 Liverpool Public Health Authority drew up a circular giving *Advice to Householders on the Care of Children's Hair*. This explained about the head louse and suggested how it might be avoided by brushing with a fine bone small-toothed comb and regular washing, followed by use of a fine metal comb. The *North Wales Chronicle* also included some helpful hints in an article published in April 1940.

The government continued to stress the need to combat lousiness and not merely because it was someting 'nasty'. There had been concern at the beginning of the war that in the event of a typhus outbreak, body lice would rapidly transmit the disease throughout the population, and various medical research units were set up to assess the situation and the dangers.[30] The head of one such unit, Dr Kenneth Mellanby, reported that *'considerable numbers of children who were infested at the time when evacuation took place in 1939, have become and remained clean in the more open and healthy conditions that they have lived in since then'*. He added that even in large towns the rate of infestation had been successfully reduced following an intensive attack on the problem between the evacuation of 1939 and that of 1940. In line with this, in May 1941, Penmaenmawr's Billeting Officer was reporting that, personally, he had *'not had a single complaint regarding lice infestation either from the public, the medical practitioners or the school authorities'*.[31] No doubt other areas weren't quite so fortunate but perhaps familiarity with such problems was now beginning to make them less controversial.

There was also by this time a better medical support system in place to help with all aspects of evacuees' health. In the event of an evacuee becoming ill, a householder could call in a district nurse or doctor whose account would be dealt with by the Local Medical War Committee. Part of the difficulty in North Wales was that, at the start of the evacuation scheme at least, medical facilities and staff were quite sparse. Wrexham had asked Liverpool in September 1939 to send medical practitioners to help examine the newly arrived evacuees, and had been quite annoyed when none had come. The problem, as Liverpool explained, was that their staff were needed to man the hospitals and other centres which were expecting to receive heavy casualties with the onset of bombing.[32] When the raids failed to happen straight away, some medical personnel were despatched from Merseyside to help the reception areas.

On 9 September 1939, Anglesey's Maternity and Child Welfare Committee was notified by Liverpool's MO that a 'flying squad' of health visitors had been formed and would be available for work with evacuees. However the committee felt they needed at least two extra Health Visitors permanently stationed in Anglesey to deal with the evacuees; if the evacuating authorities couldn't make the appointments, they would do so, charging the cost to Merseyside.[33] Most of the North Wales authorities took similar action; Flintshire's MO for example reported on 27 September 1939 that he had appointed 8 additional health visitors and school nurses.[34] Evacuees in the Aberystwyth area were able to take advantage of a service provided by newly imported health workers of a rather different kind. The *Liverpool Daily Post* on 21 February 1940 pictured a group of Merseyside children receiving treatment for 'posture defects' by medical gymnasts of the Chelsea Polytechnic!

In May 1941, Caernarvonshire's MO submitted a Memorandum on General Health Services which gives some idea of the extra work that evacuation entailed. During the previous year, 1940 (when evacuation was by no means at its height), 13,900 local schoolchildren had been examined, but also 8,094 evacuees. Evacuees had been treated at several special clinics as well as at 8 hostels set up in the county. Additionally, in the early months of 1941, 1,690 children had been examined at various detraining stations. Arrangements had been made for all evacuated persons to receive local facilities; as the total population of the county had by that time increased by about 50,000 this *'entailed an enormous amount of additional work for medical, nursing and clerical staff'* and also caused *'many urgent and intricate problems of Infectious Disease and General Hospital Accommodation'*. At the time of writing, approval had just been received for the appointment of a full-time Medical Officer in Caernarvonshire to deal specifically with evacuees.[35] This was just as well for many more were about to pour into the area in the wake of the May blitz. A whole-time school dentist had also been transferred there from Liverpool[36] - many evacuees still remember his treatment!

Of course, while they were away from home evacuated children suffered with, and sadly sometimes died from, the same sort of ailments which may have afflicted them at any time. One of the Aspen Grove pupils, Eric Lowe, for example, died from appendicitis. Clifford Wrightson's brother Elston died from a childhood illness during the time he was evacuated to Montgomeryshire, and Mabel Grice, an evacuee from St Benedicts, attending Cwm-y-Glo School, also fell victim to appendicitis in February 1944.[37] Others had to have a stay in hospital - an ordeal for a child in normal circumstances, but how much worse it must have been with no mum or dad around to give reassurance, and precious little sympathy on offer elsewhere. Alex Anderson was whisked off by ambulance from his billet in Criccieth for treatment of an abscess on his jaw. Like many who underwent an operation in those days, Alex most vividly remembers the horror of the ether anaesthetic. He goes on to explain:

I still do not know the extent of the operation except from that day to this I have a piece of bone missing from my lower jaw. My stay in Bangor hospital appeared to me longish. However long it may have been, not once did anyone come to visit me ... but the nurses were all lovely and I don't recall being too unhappy. On the day of my discharge Dr. & Mrs D. [foster parents] came for me in their car. The journey back to Criccieth via Caernarvon is imprinted on my memory. When we reached the town square, in front of the castle, I was left sitting in the car with instructions not to open any windows, whilst my guardians went into a nearby cafe for a meal. On all my visits to Caernarvon, I still see myself as a little boy alone in that parked car, in strange surroundings.

Alex's foster parents may have seen adequately to all his physical requirements, but could they really have been so oblivious to his need for a bit of love? Marjorie Lamb got much the same treatment when, out of the blue one morning, in the evacuee hostel in Harlech where she'd been billeted, she was forbidden to have breakfast. Along with a few other unsuspecting souls, she was then whisked off, put into a nightshirt smelling strongly of disinfectant, lifted on to a table surrounded by strange people in long white smocks and hats, and informed that her tonsils were to be taken out. Despite putting up a strong defence against 'a horrid black thing being forced on to my face', the anaesthetic was finally applied and the tonsils duly removed.

I woke up lying on a mattress top to tail with other victims. My throat was very sore. After a sleep we were given ice cream and carried back up the hill. When we arrived back at the Hostel we were immediately put to bed. The Doctor used to come in every day and swab our throats. I must have been his worst nightmare - I fought like a tiger every time he came near me as I was never going to trust anyone again!

A few evacuee deaths occurred as a result of tragic accidents. Some of these might have happened anywhere at any time, such as that involving Billy Carroll (evacuated from Cole Street School, Birkenhead to Harlech) who was killed on a railway line. Marjorie Lamb and Walter Hurst both remember the incident - some of the boys had been playing hide-and-seek by the track; Billy had lain between the lines to hide, and had been run over by a train. 'It was a strange sad time', Marjorie says, 'the children talked about it for weeks.' Another little boy, Glyn Hughes, just seven years old and evacuated from Laird Street Infants to Penyffordd, died after he had been knocked down by a transport wagon, in December 1939.[38] But there were also accidents which happened as a result of the children being unused to the hazards of the country or the seaside. In Portdinorwic during the first week of evacuation, the authorities published a notice ordering a curfew for evacuees:

HOUSEHOLDERS IN CHARGE OF THE CHILDREN WHO HAVE BEEN EVACUATED ARE REQUESTED TO SEE THAT ALL CHILDREN ARE INDOORS BY 8PM EACH EVENING UNTIL FURTHER NOTICE. THIS PRECAUTION IS TAKEN TO PREVENT ACCIDENTS [39]

Yet accidents could happen in daylight hours also, such as the awful case of the boy who drowned in a sewerage tank only days after arriving in the Hawarden area. On 12 September 1939 the *Liverpool Daily Post* reported on serious injuries suffered by a thirteen-year-old girl, evacuated with St Oswald's, Old Swan, when she'd fallen fifty foot down a precipice whilst out rambling at Tower Hill, a beauty spot near Abergele. Almost a year later Abergele was the scene of a second tragedy when an evacuee, staying in nearby Towyn, ignored his foster parent's instructions that the sea was too rough, and sadly drowned. Another little Merseyside boy died after his leg had been caught in a threshing machine. One can hardly begin to imagine the anguish suffered by the parents of these children, who had thought they were sending them to a place of safety, or of the host families into whose care the children had been placed.

Birkenhead pupils from Cole Street School, Claughton evacuated to Harlech. Included are Miss Evans (teacher), Carl Larkin, Ron Carroll, Beryl Walker, Ken Gilbody, Walter Hurst, Billy Hennessey, Edna Hosker, Joyce Ashton and Daisy Nourse. The boy in the cap is Billy Caroll, sadly killed on the railway lines. (Photo courtesy Walter Hurst)

There were doubtless many other incidents involving the 'townies' which might have proved more serious but for the vigilance of their hosts. John Cox remembers:

> *We had two evacuees from Liverpool. They loved it on the farm ... We used to run the wheelbarrows of muck up a plank and tip the contents out at the top. I remember early on, young Jimmy ran up the plank and jumped off - right into the midden. He didn't realise what it was. They didn't know anything about farm life of course. We managed to pull him out and soon got him cleaned up.*

M.T. Whelan, another Liverpool evacuee, also encountered a hazard not usually to be met with on the West Derby Road!

> *I walked to school each day and one afternoon as I strolled home I heard loud shouts behind me. Glancing round I beheld the local bull charging at me and the farmer's men shouting 'run'. I scrambled over the nearest fence and fell into a deep snowdrift from which I was yanked without ceremony and sent on my way when the danger had passed.*[40]

R.E. Jones was farming in Tanycoed, north of Bala during the war. He well remembers the billeting officer arriving with two evacuated mothers and their two three-year-old children:

> *They were very happy here ... I had a concrete water trough in the yard for the cows. Soon the two children were taking a great interest in that water, as children often will. I was worried lest the children would climb up and fall into the trough. I had the idea of putting an eel in the trough to frighten them off. I caught a handsome eel about half a yard long in a ditch in the meadow, and put it in the trough. As soon as the children saw the white teeth they didn't go near the trough again, ever! The eel lived happily in the trough a long time after the evacuees went back to their homes at the end of the war.*[41]

George Parry didn't have any such guardian angel to save him from the cow's drinking water at his billet - quite the reverse, in fact!

> *There was a big pond outside the house, the cows used to drink out of it - it was quite deep. It froze over in the winter and we were given the job of trying to break up the ice. Their son was a little terror, always up to*

pranks, you had to be on your guard all the time. Well I set to, clearing a
semi-circle in front of me - I didn't notice that he was busy clearing
another semi-circle behind me. Of course I went down when the circle
cracked and had to be quickly dragged out, soaked and shivering.

Rita Holmes remembers that her brother, Nathan Griffiths, almost drowned once, too. They had been playing at the quayside in Barmouth and Nathan was walking along a pipe when he slipped and fell into the sea. Rita screamed as she watched her brother go under but a local fisherman out in his boat hauled Nathan from the water and managed to revive him. Rita now wonders if they ever properly thanked that fisherman for saving her brother's life.

Listening to accounts of how they'd played in slate quarries and near disused mine-shafts, swung on ropes across ravines, skated (literally) on thin ice, tried to 'break in' wild Welsh ponies and learn to swim in old sheep-dipping tanks, it's a wonder that Merseyside evacuees didn't occupy far more hospital beds in North Wales!

The health issue surrounding evacuation was not a one-sided affair. Although much of the early attention focused on the condition of the evacuees when they arrived in the reception areas, not all the billeting situations they encountered were particularly desirable from a health point of view, especially in 1941 when the sheer numbers arriving produced dangerous overcrowding in many areas. Criticism was directed at some North Wales authorities for allowing evacuees into homes where tuberculosis was known to be present. There is no evidence to suggest that any evacuee contracted TB after being billeted in a tuberculous household, but nor does anything suggest that the incidence of TB in a region was considered when evacuation plans were framed. Yet North Wales was known to have a poor record in this regard and even some parents were anxious about the problem, as one evacuee explains:

My mother was a bit prejudiced against the Welsh, well not prejudiced
exactly but very worried anyway - because of TB. She'd taught in a
children's hospital and was very frightened about this. When she heard all
the children [me, my brother and the little boy from the billet] had slept in
one bed she was horrified.

As with so much else, the issue seems only to have been appreciated in the wake of the first evacuation. Thus, Caernarvon Council resolved on 24 October 1939 that in any future evacuation steps should be taken to safeguard against billeting in homes where there were known TB cases; similarly, in May 1940, Nant Conway RDC agreed to remove from their list of billets any house where TB had been reported 'in order to avoid evacuees being *again* billeted in Tuberculous households' (my emphasis).[42] Obviously some mistakes had been made and some evacuees exposed to danger but the need for care had been highlighted and now seems to have been exercised. In Dolgellau in March 1942, a case where evacuees had allegedly been billeted in a house with TB present was reported to a meeting of the After-Care Committee. It was quickly investigated and proved to be untrue. The County MO at the time stressed that the committee's policy was clearly to discourage lodgers or evacuees in houses with a notified TB case. Yet, some apparently did slip through the net. A.W. Otter recalls:

> *We ended up in Aberdovey, in a wonderful billet - but they were all dying from TB! Eventually they wrote to my father to come and collect us because there was just too much sickness in the house.*

Happily the Otter children never suffered any ill-effects! In one instance, the region's problems with TB actually proved beneficial when one evacuee, suffering badly with tuberculosis when he arrived in Caernarvon, improved greatly after treatment at a local sanatorium.

In June 1941, a report in the *North Wales Chronicle* reminded the Welsh Board of Health of the 'Black Report' which it had issued only a few years earlier on health conditions in North Wales, and asked how, in the light of this, it could possibly have allowed the area to have become so overcrowded. Yet while facilities were undeniably strained and perhaps initially inferior to those in evacuating areas, many evacuees eventually received far better medical care than they'd been used to and returned home healthier than when they'd left. The medical scrutinies to which the children were subjected after the outcry in 1939, along with developments in welfare work which accompanied the blossoming of the evacuation scheme (see later) all tended to place a greater premium on the health of the child. Psychiatric social workers were appointed and special hostels established. Infections and disabilities, both physical and mental, were uncovered which otherwise might have been disastrously neglected.

For all this, is was sometimes simply just 'plenty of fresh air' and 'good country food' which most benefited the town children. Those billeted on farms in particular enjoyed dairy products, fresh meat, homegrown vegetables and homemade bread. Laura Jones admits:

We were very fortunate to be living in the country, in a market town [Llanrwst]. There was always plenty to eat and plenty of variety. Nan's sister who lived in Australia, also sent us food parcels, every item carefully wrapped in calico, and stitched securely. They were a joy to receive.[43]

But not everyone liked the 'freshness' of farm food. Doreen French remembers watching a cow being milked and the farmer directing the udder so that the farm cat could have a drink, then he offered her a glass of this nice, very fresh milk but to her horror it was still warm - she never touched milk again for weeks after that! Jim Barrow also remembers finding it hard to come to terms with watching a pig running round the yard one day then hanging up in the kitchen the next - salted and ready for eating:

I'd never much liked the fat on meat but [as an evacuee] remember having to sit at the table in the farm kitchen until I'd eaten it - and then being sick afterwards. I've never been a big meat-eater since then!

Jim has far fonder memories of the buttermilk which he used to help prepare - though his liking for this did get him into trouble on one occasion! Like so many other evacuees Jim had to attend church three times on Sundays but it was a long walk from his billet outside Llangurig. After a while, to save him one journey at least, it was arranged that he would stay for lunch at the Vicar's house and as a gesture of thanks Jim's foster parents sent over a bottle of buttermilk each Sunday, for the vicar's family. When summer came, however, Jim got so hot on the way into the village that he'd take a drink of the milk - filling the bottle up from a nearby stream so no one would notice. Needless to say, after a little while the vicar did notice, the culprit confessed all - and duly got a clout for his pains!

Sometimes the change of diet, particularly the increased consumption of greens, wreaked havoc with the children's digestive systems. As Ken McGunigle somewhat sheepishly recounts, *'We ate a lot of veg and during Sunday Evening Service one day I couldn't hold myself and 'let one go'. Everybody heard it. I got told off and sent to bed early!'*

Tommy Murphy, who was evacuated in 1940, will never forget the sight that greeted him on arrival at his new home:

I was billeted with Mr & Mrs Williams, they had the local butcher's shop and a farm. When I got there there was a wonderful spread laid out for tea

- I'd never seen anything like it - beautiful cakes and all sorts. Things had been quite hard at home, with rationing and everything, so it looked like a banquet!

Eric Jackson remembers that his sister Dorothy was equally delighted with her billet in Machynlleth - a cake shop *'which as she had a sweet tooth suited her down to the ground!'* Others remember blackberry-picking excursions and the wonderful jam and pies that followed. For some, however, blackberries, cobnuts and other edible items gleaned from the wayside became vital supplements to a less than adequate diet. Hetty Mowat was ten years old when evacuees arrived in her village outside Wrexham. Her father was a teacher at a local school but there's was a large family and she remembers that those times *'were not very pleasant as we never seemed to get enough to eat and clothes were mostly hand-me-downs'*. Rural areas had been just as hard hit by the depression as the towns and by no means all those who lived in the country were self-sufficient. When we hear of evacuees rooting up turnips and eating them raw to stave off hunger we must realise that with their ignorance of the countryside they would never have known to do this unless they'd seen this was what the local children did!

Certainly most householders in North Wales did the best they could and, with the help of the billeting allowance and a little ingenuity, kept their evacuees, if not in the lap of luxury, then at least adequately clothed and fed. Mrs Bert Morris of Middleton Terrace, Chirk, looked after nine Liverpool evacuees during the course of the war. Her daughter recalls:

Food, of course, was rationed but Mum was a wonderful cook and could make a meal out of anything. She would put the cream off the milk into a Kilner jar and when full we had to take it in turns to shake it until it set - to put with the butter and make it go further.

Sadly, however, a few householders seemed intent on turning evacuation into some sort of business venture, which involved taking in as many children as they could and spending as little on them as possible. In some cases, children were literally starving.[44] Several seemed to have fallen foul of one particular billet in Carmel. By and large, this Caernarvonshire village willingly opened its doors to the Liverpool evacuees and many loved it there. But there was one household which treated the children very poorly. The Aird brothers suffered in this billet as did Jean and Harold Lyle. None of them remembers ever having a square meal, only soup and bread, or bread (cut wafer-thin) and bramble jelly. They were so hungry they had to resort to eating raw carrots and turnips stolen from the fields, and even 'groundnuts'- the roots of a wild plant. The meals, for what they were worth, had to be eaten outside, whatever the weather, in the washhouse. Jean and Harold's mother sent the children a food parcel but they never saw it. Don, the eldest of the Aird boys, tried to write home to tell his parents what was happening but the letter was opened by the foster father and Don was beaten. The boys' grandmother came to visit one day with a basketful of homemade cakes. It was put to one side 'for later' but Gran would have none of that and for once the children had a treat. Finally the schoolteacher realised something was amiss and arranged for all the children to be re-housed.

Elsewhere, other evacuees were receiving similar treatment. At one billet, Ron Organ was only given water on his cornflakes when the rest of the household had milk; Barbara Smith got dry bread and beetroot for lunch, day in, day out; for Mrs D. Shaw it was treacle sandwiches and water for breakfast, dinner and tea. We've already seen that a similarly unvaried diet - of fishpaste sandwiches in their case - caused the rapid return of two other evacuees. Honor McGrath was evacuated with a party from St Vincent's, Liverpool. She comments:

> *My sister, a friend and I were housed with rather well-to-do solicitors in Anglesey. Their property was extensive, including a farm. However, the mistress of this manor was mean. The food was poor and our Government parcel of supplement food and chocolate was never given to is. We discovered this from school friends and the house-maid. We did see our bananas given to her dogs who ate at the table. At one point a teacher came to stay and seeing our plight had us re-billeted on a farm where then we were very well fed.*

In Mary Maher's billet too the meals were very spartan:

> *She was very mean with the food and we were always starving. In fact most of the children were in the same boat so we used to buy a homemade small loaf from a baker's shop for thru pence and we'd sit on the hillside and tear the loaf apart and eat it dry, but it helped to fill us ...*

Some of the evacuated children at Penmaenmawr were so underfed that the nuns at a local convent took pity on them and gave them extra food.[45] While many evacuees did thrive during their time in North Wales, clearly not all the children were becoming little 'dumplings'!

105

From Plimsolls to Clogs

Within the general division of the country into evacuation, neutral and reception areas, there was a further 'zoning' which meant the evacuation scheme operated mainly in the most congested sections of evacuation areas, the very sections which contained an abnormally high proportion of poor families. The government had belatedly recognised the problem but eleventh hour attempts by Merseyside Public Assistance Committees to try and alleviate the situation had not done enough to prevent Liverpool soon after the first evacuation being dubbed 'The Plimsoll City'. Reports from many North Wales authorities spoke of the 'deplorable unclad condition' of the evacuees, of their clothing being dirty and verminous or, where clean, totally inadequate especially to the needs of country life. An official circular entitled 'Points for Householders' had listed the items which the children were expected to have with them, and whilst admitting that *some parents would no doubt be unable to supply their children with all these articles* assured host families that they weren't expected to supply extra clothes or equipment.[46]

No doubt some householders interpreted this literally and felt no obligation to buy new clothes; some, as we've seen, expressed disgust at the situation. On the other hand, a great many householders responded sympathetically and did their best to make up any shortfalls. Eileen Crea remembers being chosen by Mrs Hughes and taken to what seemed to her a 'very posh' house. After being given a meal, Eileen and her sister were shown to their bedroom:

> I think she was trying to make us feel very welcome for the lady put us in her front bedroom. Then she left us alone to get undressed in privacy. I took my knickers off - these were very large. They must have been my mothers as they certainly weren't mine! My bottom wasn't that big! and they were soaking wet with the traumatic effects of the day. In my shame I pushed them behind the bedpost so no one would see them. When I got up the next morning they had gone. I was halfway under the bed, when I heard the voice of Mrs Hughes asking: 'Are you all right. Did you sleep well?' But, in my nervousness all I could think about was my vanished knickers. Then she said: 'I have run a bath for you both.' We had a lovely warm bathe and whilst preparing to get dressed I saw, laid out for us, lovely new knickers of the right size.[47]

Where foster parents had children of their own many felt that a double standard of dress in the household was simply not acceptable. What happened in Gwen

106

Jones's home was mirrored in homes across the country:

> *My parents treated [our evacuee] in exactly the same way as their own child ... She was given the same pocket money as my sister and if new shoes or clothes were needed they both had the same.*

Providing evacuees with adequate clothing was quite a problem in some areas - but many Welsh householders got out their needles and thread. Pictured here are nine Birkenhead evacuees who lived with Miss Levesley and Joyce Harne at their house, 'Greenhaven' in Fairbourne. For 4 years the two ladies sewed and knitted garments for all nine girls. Pictured are Jean Gibson, Betly Gladstone, Marie, Sadie and Millie Gaunt, Jean McAlery, Pat Roberts and Jean Corder (Holy Trinity School). (Photo courtesy Mrs Sadie Dawson)

Less affluent households, or those with a large number of 'visitors', set about making items of clothing for their evacuees. Sadie Dawson remembers the incredible industry of the two kind ladies that she stayed with, along with eight other evacuees, in their house 'Greenhaven' in Fairbourne (near Barmouth). She feels *'some recognition should have been given to Miss Joyce [Harne] and Miss Levesley. For all those years [all nine evacuees stayed for 4 years] they made most of our clothes and Miss Levesley knitted all our woollies.'* Newspaper and welfare committee reports testify to the efforts of many local people in this sphere. One evacuated teacher who remembers what took place offers the following tribute:

> *The billeting money would barely cover the cost of a child's board and lodging. It has never been generally known what personal sacrifices were made by the humble cottagers. They willingly accepted responsibility for evacuees, provided them with food and a bed then saved every spare penny to buy them something new to wear for Chapel on Sunday. In Wales I soon learnt that one must go to Chapel suitably attired. This was one reason, maybe the main reason, why the villagers wanted their evacuees to look respectable on one day at least during the week.* [48]

Another reason why new clothes, and shoes especially, were necessary was country life itself. It was generally 'harder': roads were rough and the children had to walk long distances - to and from school, on the many rambles that filled up school hours when classrooms were unavailable, to chapel, to the shops, or just playing outside, roaming around up hill and down dale. The weather was also more extreme, so that wellingtons and mackintoshes were high on the list of priorities, and of course as winter approached the situation became more urgent.

Individual initiative was supplemented by the effort of local voluntary organisations. Branches of the WVS everywhere began to organise 'make and mend' groups, arranged door-to-door collections of old garments or donations to special funds set up to purchase clothes, and struggled to find suitable premises to act as storage and distribution depots. In Flintshire, for example, although some Rhos-on-Sea ratepayers had sent a deputation to their MP about the evacuees, other residents got together to form the 'Rhos Voluntary Helpers for Evacuees' a group determined to try and help the many destitute children who had arrived in the area. *The Flintshire Observer*, 21 September 1939, had the following to report about their work:

> *Their depot is a scene of constant activity. All kinds of goods are being received and further parcels would be welcomed. Many children have been completely fitted up with new clothes and householders who had not enough furniture to cope with those placed in their care have been given crockery, furniture, beds and bedding. There is also a sewing room where a party of ladies, at times numbering well over thirty, are busily engaged in making clothes for the youngsters.*

Within a few days of evacuation, the *North Wales Chronicle* (8 September 1939) was publishing an appeal by the Mayor of Bangor, in which he explained that he was *'expressing the views of the majority of the people of Bangor when I say that a large percentage of the evacuees are very badly clothed and require other assistance such as nourishment and recreation'*. The Lord Mayor of Liverpool started the Bangor Fund rolling with a contribution of 50 guineas. In Portdinorwic, the WVS opened a Clothing Fund; in Bethesda the Ladies Committee arranged a house-to-house appeal; in Llandegfan a Welfare Committee inaugurated a variety of vital services; similarly in Colwyn Bay the 'Voluntary Social Service Welfare Council' was formed. These were typical of responses throughout North Wales and certainly much hardship must have been alleviated by this spontaneous and charitable reaction. On 8 September the Ministry of Health had also broadcast an appeal which produced several thousand second-hand garments, the sum of £1000 from the National Union of Teachers, gifts of clothing from America and a lakh of rupees (£7,500) from the Maharajah of Gondal![49]

Nevertheless, it quickly became apparent that private initiative could not, by itself, provide a complete solution. On 7 November, the Ministry of Health issued local authorities with a circular concerning the provision of clothing and footwear. This emphasised parental responsibilty but did outline other sources and, again with the understanding that nothing be said in public, arranged for Directors of Education to receive a sum of about £15,000 to help meet severe cases of hardship. As historian Richard Titmuss points out, this all marked the beginning of a new social service *'which arose from the shock experienced by the country in September 1939 in discovering the condition of the clothing of a large number of evacuees'*.[50]

Even before this government intervention the respective local authorities had already been in correspondence about the issue as Welsh Billeting Officers had been inundated with complaints and queries within hours of evacuation, and had naturally referred these to Liverpool and Birkenhead. Liverpool's Public Assistance Officer, whilst emphasising that at that time he had no authority to incur any expenditure, issued a circular letter to reception areas on 15 September, asking for detailed returns of clothing requirements. As with other aspects of the scheme, there was some confusion over where responsibility lay, but within two weeks Liverpool had despatched another letter to North Wales outlining an agreement reached between the Unemployment Assistance Board and the Public Assistance authorities over the provision of essential clothing and footwear for Liverpool evacuees.[51]

109

In the meantime, appeals had been broadcast across Merseyside, some parents had come forward with the clothing which children had left behind and charitable parcels began to pour in. Gifts were received from children at Hunt's Cross Council School and also from a group of St Helen's schoolchildren who in addition to sending clothes and toys, supplied woollen blankets *'ingeniously devised and manufactured from discarded articles of woollen clothing, which should prove invaluable in the really cold weather of the Welsh uplands'.*[52] By the end of October Clothing Requisition Forms were being distributed and certainly by late November North Wales had begun to receive items from the evacuation areas. A large clothing depot was set up at Emmanuel School, Liverpool and over 10,000 parcels of clothing and footwear had been despatched from this depot to reception areas by the end of December 1939.[53]

Individual teachers were also taking the initiative. An Evacuation Log Book kept by M.M. Granger, headmistress of Prince Rupert Steers Street school shows that clothing worries featured prominently in the early weeks of her school's stay in Caernarvon. She records that Liverpool teachers had met on 13 September to select a committee to work with local Council representatives in connection with the clothing of evacuees. In another area of Caernarvon two evacuated teachers, realising that many of the children possessed only the clothes they were wearing *'and judging from the quality of the material even these would be threadbare in a month's time'*, put their heads together and devised a makeshift scheme of their own. They decided to send an SOS to friends at home who might be able to spare some cast-offs.

> *We did so immediately and in less than a fortnight we had sufficient to stock a small shop. Two months went by before the Public Assistance Committee began to supply clothing and footwear, thus, our second hand clothes shop was well patronized.*[54]

The mere existence of a clothing scheme of course didn't immediately solve all the problems; it was an exasperating and difficult time for everyone involved with evacuation. The Birkenhead WVS seemed to be feeling the strain when they wrote on 6 November 1939:

> *We cannot send in response to individual requests for clothing. The supply is extremely limited now as we have bled the whole town in an endeavour to get these clothes which, as we all know, are the responsibility of the parents and not of charitable effort. So it is impossible to send, say boots to one district and vests to another, as we may have neither to send. We*

will endeavour to send parcels to each of our seven reception areas in turn, but please do not look for any great supplies as I must reiterate the fact that the stream of voluntary gifts is practically exhausted. It is of course quite definite *that gifts from [our] WVS are for Birkenhead children only.*[55]

The pool of goodwill in the reception areas was also in danger of running dry. A row broke out in the Colwyn Bay district in February 1940 when the chairman of the Juvenile Welfare Committee of the local Council of Social Service spoke of his committee's concern over clothing supplies and in particular over criticism that they hadn't done enough for the evacuees. Though they'd been assured by the Liverpool authorities that there was no need to do anything other than draw their attention to needy cases, the committee had actively intervened to help in some instances. There followed a certain amount of recrimination between members when it was claimed that Rhos had done more, and in the course of a heated discussion one of the members raised a point which was being increasingly voiced in this 'phoney war' period. He asked if the evacuees' parents were not responsible for their own children's needs as he felt there was *'plenty of poverty in Colwyn Bay without our being saddled with the responsibilty of providing for Liverpool children.'*[56]

This was the time when the first evacuation scheme was reaching an all-time low. In the same month, February 1940, one Caernarvonshire WVS leader also spoke of the clothing difficulties and added, *'… little comes in now. "Evacuees" is a bad slogan and we can get no support for them voluntarily. Most people's attention is now given to the Forces, naturally.'*[57] What was particularly galling was not only that so many evacuees were returning home but that they were taking with them the clothes that their foster parents had often just struggled to acquire on their behalf. One Rhos lady recalls the impression in her town was that the parents were deliberately sending their children away in their oldest clothes, waiting until they'd been supplied with new ones, then coming to collect them. Indeed, Liverpool University concluded from their investigation into evacuation difficulties that: *'Some people simply could not understand that people could be as poor as some of the evacuees. They thought it was ill-will and desire on the part of the parents to exploit the hosts by sending the children in poor clothes.'* However, their study showed that of the Liverpool mothers with one or two children evacuated, 32 per cent had genuine difficulty in supplying clothes, while as many as 52 per cent had difficulty if they had more than two children away from home.[58] Perhaps there was slightly more justification to complaints in later years when many 'city folk' had begun to earn good money

111

doing war work but the 'poor villagers' were still expected to clothe the children.

For the duration of the evacuation scheme the authorities did their best to ensure that parental responsibilities were neither undermined nor neglected. Certainly in 1944 there is evidence of a hard line being taken when one mother was actually reported to the NSPCC for not forwarding clothing coupons.[59] Unfortunately there doesn't always seem to have been such a stern approach adopted towards negligent 'foster parents'. Whilst there were very many caring householders who took pride in the appearance of their evacuees, there was also, as with so many aspects of the evacuation scheme, another side to the story. So, Ron Organ comments:

> We weren't really looked after properly - when our socks got holey, for instance. They were so uncomfortable, in the end I tried to sew them myself, but when I'd finished I couldn't get my feet in them. I asked one of the other lads how he'd fixed his. He took off his shoe and showed me - he'd got no foot in his sock at all. In desperation he'd cut it off and attached the remainder around his ankle with an elastic band to make it still look as though he was wearing socks!

The provision of footwear was probably the thorniest of the clothing problems. Towards the end of 1939, no doubt helped by the return home of many of the evacuees, the most pressing clothing needs had been met, but there was still a shortage of boots and shoes and some horrific bureaucratic muddles over existing stocks and over repair procedures. The Evacuating Officer in Penmaenmawr had great difficulty in getting anyone to sanction the issue of footwear, and even as late as 1941 one frustrated WVS worker in Caernarvon complained that *'Mr Molyneux knows that I hold a small stock of about 50 pairs of P.A.C. boys boots. These were only to be given out under instructions from him and for months he has preferred to leave this little stock untouched.'* [60] Any such stocks were used either to replace completely worn out footwear or to provide temporary cover whilst an evacuee's own shoes were being repaired. The problem of supplying and repairing boots and shoes was made more difficult as time passed, by the ever-growing shortage of leather. Many evacuees remember having their old boots converted into clogs, which a lot of the local children still wore, especially in the more rural areas. The blacksmith would attach an iron sole to the exisiting boot-top and the result was perfect - especially for making sparks fly walking along the road! Clogs did have their disadvantages in the winter, though. Then the snow would collect and compact under the iron. The Aspen Grove 'boys', evacuated to Carmel, remember the problem well:

You'd walk along on your clogs, getting higher and higher, then as bits of the snow fell off, you'd walk lop-sided and sometimes you'd actually fall over!

Evacuees from Woodchurch Rd School (Birkenhead) in Penrhyndeudraeth.
Ron Edmondson is pictured in the wellies - but not all evacuees had footwear suitable for country living!

(Photo courtesy Ron Edmondson who asks 'Anyone recognise the others?')

Again, amongst all the talk of the 'state' of evacuees, we must remember not to lose sight of the fact that many local Welsh children were hardly in a better state themselves. Those in some parts of North Wales vociferous in criticising the poorly-clad and poorly-shod arrivals from Merseyside would no doubt have been shocked to read the following entry in the logbook of one of their own schools, Bethesda British School (Caernarvonshire), dated 22 January 1940:

Attendance still low. The outlook in this area is very gloomy. Out of about 2000 men normally employed at the Quarry only about 800 have recommenced work today after a stoppage of 5 weeks. Many children are

113

absent due to lack of footwear. The local Bootless Fund is far from adequate to deal with the situation. Also we find that many children are unable to buy their usual quota of milk.

It must have seemed very strange to the teacher making this entry that there was such an outcry over the poor footwear of the evacuees when her own local children were in exactly the same plight! Eventually, in fact, it was decided that WVS supplies - of clothes as well as shoes - should be available for needy local children as well as evacuees.

The difficulties experienced over clothing and footwear in 1939 inspired a more positive approach when new evacuation plans were formulated in 1940. Liverpool sent out questionnaires to teaching staff and Welsh officials to establish the pros and cons of existing arrangements. Billeting officers were given assurances that evacuation parties would in future have spare clothing with them, but problems persisted.[61] The onset of the 'panic evacuation' with many of those arriving in North Wales forced to flee bombed homes with only the clothes they stood in created an added demand. More clothing depots came into existence: one of the largest in North Wales was that run by the Caernarvon WVS which administered the official Liverpool scheme for the whole of Anglesey and Caernarvonshire. In one two-month period alone, the depot received over £1,500 worth of clothing from Merseyside as well as a huge quantity of material, from the Ministry of Health and the American Red Cross, to be made up into items for evacuees. So much had been received that early in 1940 the depot ran out of space. Happily, more rooms were provided free of charge by the Dorothea Slate Quarry Company.[62] Eventually depots were also established in other parts of Caernarvonshire, in Conway and Pwllheli for example,[63] with a similar level of activity elsewhere in North Wales.[64]

Despite continued difficulties and occasional rifts between parents and foster parents, by and large the clothing problem was tackled vigorously and with much genuine goodwill in the reception areas. The scheme that evolved has been aptly described as *'a characteristic British mixture of Exchequer money and charitable gifts administered by local authorities and run by voluntary workers'.*[65] The sterling work of individual householders of course cannot ever be fully catalogued, nor perhaps the contribution of teachers. Whereas the WVS underdertook most of the work of making, collecting and distributing evacuee clothing (indeed in Connah's Quay the local branch was first set up specifically to provide this service)[66] the tedious work of assessing the precise needs of the children - the articles and sizes - and the delicate work of mediating between

114

parent and host usually fell to teaching staff. Their importance in this area was shown by the chaos which beset Holywell's clothing administration when several Liverpool teachers were suddenly called home.[67] The Consumer Rationing Order of June 1941 brought an added complication: clothing coupons. Some idea of what this now entailed can be gleaned from a letter sent to teachers by Liverpool Public Assistance Committee, 5 July 1941:

> ... *Requisitions may now be submitted only when you are sure the householder has sufficient coupons available and a note to this effect should accompany each application ... It should also be borne in mind that the needs of the children must now be considered in relation to the number of coupons available so as to ensure that the coupons are used to the best advantage over the whole year. It will be noted that a maximum of 26 coupons are available to each child, a further 40 becoming available with the issue of clothing cards in say 2-3 months time. Of these 40 coupons 20 will be usable this year, the remainder being valid only after December 31st 1941.*

On top of all this the teachers also had to contend with Board of Trade instructions on the issue of supplemetary clothing coupons for certain categories of children, depending upon a combination of their date of birth, height and weight - for example, those born on or after 1 September 1927, measuring 5ft 3ins or more in height and weighing 7st 12lbs or more, and so on. It's a wonder they found time for teaching at all!

Schooling in Wartime

In pre-evacuation planning there had not been a lot of attention paid to the difficulties which would arise when it became necessary to provide education for the thousands of extra children expected to arrive in reception areas. Several officials in North Wales had pointed out that existing school accommodation was already over-taxed but no alternative suggestions seemed to have been put forward as to how or where the educational needs of evacuees might be met. In 1939, reception was seen overridingly in terms of billeting - often there were no education officers present at detraining stations, with the result that schools were split up or children were sent to villages where there was no school accomodation at all. As the Director of Education for Anglesey commented:

> ... *the educational needs of the evacuated children had certainly not been the first concern of either the Evacuating or Billeting Authority nor indeed the Government Department concerned. For, not only were large schools*

evacuated into Rural Districts and the pupils scattered over a wide area,
but also the billeting arrangements had been more concerned with family
units than with school units.[68]

It was not long before the press was also highlighting glaring differences between treatment of evacuated elementary school children and those attending secondary or grammar schools.[69]

In the reception areas, schoolteachers had been informed at the beginning of September that they were not to open as usual at the end of the summer break due to the state of emergency. The schools themselves were often in use at this time as distribution centres and needed to be thoroughly cleaned before they could re-open. Indeed, in the wake of the publicity surrounding the condition of some evacuees there was general concern for the health of local children. The Denbighshire School Staff Committee, for example, decided not to re-open their elementary schools until the County MO had arranged to have all the evacuees medically examined. Similarly in Flintshire, Buckley's Clerk wrote in strong terms to his Director of Education on hearing of his intention to allow evacuees to share the local schools, urging him to consider the health hazards involved.[70] Precautions attached to allowing evacuees the use of local facilities were sometimes carried to ridiculous, if not downright insulting, lengths. Jean Moeller, evacuated with what she describes as 'probably one of the best schools in Liverpool at the time', Holly Lodge, remembers her first few days as an evacuee in North Wales:

> *We drove to Howell's school, a very superior boarding school, whose*
> *premises we were to share for lessons. They weren't back yet so we were*
> *allowed to use their swimming pool until the day before they came - when*
> *it was sterilised!*

When the education authorities addressed the problem of evacuees they found there were three possible solutions. The evacuated children could be fused completely with the home children in existing schools; they could be accommodated in schools on a 'Double Shift' system, locals on one shift, evacuees on another; or they could be kept completely separate if suitable premises could be found.

Anglesey authorities discarded the first possibilty almost at once *'for the evacuees spoke a different language and had formed different habits from native children'.*[71] Elsewhere, as noted, the notion of sharing premises seemed to spell a danger to health. The Double Shift system presented problems too, implying half-time and interrupted schooling. It also meant it would be difficult for visiting teachers to preserve the identity of their schools. But it was the Double Shift system that came to be adopted in most areas, though it wasn't always a popular solution. Local people complained that their children were being deprived of valuable schooling[72] and both local and evacuated teachers found the system particularly unsuitable for the young ones, hence the following logbook entries from three different schools:

The long hours are not suited to little children especially when they work almost four hours in the afternoon. After 3.30 it is difficult to hold the attention of the child.

Afternoon shift - the strain of the long afternoon seems to be having an effect on the children. By the end of the p.m. they are very tired and restless.

Working the afternoon shift this week. The children arrive in school tired out after playing all morning and in no frame of mind for schoolwork.[73]

Some authorities had initially suggested that evacuated schools should be allocated the afternoon sessions every day so that the premises could be disinfected before the local children attended the following morning. Fortunately, once it was realised that the evacuees were not such pariahs as initially imagined, most authorties agreed to alternate sessions. Anything else, as the above suggests, would have given the newcomers rather a raw deal.

The system seemed to work better where the Secondary Schools were concerned. St Francis Xavier's College, for example, found that sharing premises with Rhyl County School worked very well and that, far from leading separate existences the two schools were able to embark on some friendly rivalry on the sportsfield and even in the annual eisteddfod.[74] Arrangements also proved satisfactory in Bangor where the local secondary schools operated a double shift with pupils from the Liverpool Collegiate and Liverpool Institute. Reporting in October 1940 on how his school had adapted, the headmaster of Friars (Bangor) commented that

Paradoxically enough, the past year has been remarkable for our academic successes ... How much the Liverpool Collegiate School appreciated what had been done for them was evidenced by their gift to us of a cheque for 10 guineas for purchase of an athletics trophy.[75]

117

Many evacuees were taught in church and chapel vestries, such as this at Llwyngwril (nr Barmouth) where Ellen Baylis (nee Roberts) taught a class from Merseyside. (Photo courtesy Ellen Baylis)

The wife of one former evacuated teacher remembers that the Grammar School at Portmadoc was not at all pleased at first about having to embark on a double shift system to accommodate her husband's school - Rock Ferry High - but the arrangements actually worked quite well in the end. With slight adjustments to the usual routine it was made possible to provide education for 450 pupils in a school with accommodation for 250.[76] Former Rock Ferry pupils retain vivid memories of the 'slight adjustments' *they* had to make, especially when using the playing fields! As N. Westmore explains, *'Rugby in Portmadoc was certainly different. Cows grazed on the school pitches all week and on Saturdays cowpats abounded, it was difficult to avoid them!'* [77]

In 1939, with 360 pupils on its roll and new extensions just completed, Llandudno County School had thought its accommodation troubles were a thing of the past but within a few months over 200 new pupils had been admitted following the evacuation of the Inland Revenue Department to Llandudno. As an HMI report later comments (with deliberate irony?) *'the patience, ingenuity and tact of the headmaster were taxed to the utmost'*, but these turned out to be some of the happiest and most successful years in the history of the school.[78]

A Ministry of Health Circular (1871) of 12 September 1939 had directed that:

> *It may well only be possible to run schools in shifts, but other forms of activity, possibly under country conditions, which will provide occupation for the children outside the homes in which they are billeted should be developed as quickly as possible ... the general objective should be to ensure that the householder is relieved of responsibility between breakfast time and tea time, if possible by some form of organised care.*

Teaching staff, therefore had to organise games, excursions, nature rambles and other outdoor activities. Archie Manser, evacuated from New Brighton, on the Wirral, remembers:

> *School wasn't too bad. We even had a gardening lesson on Wednesdays. Amongst other things I learnt to bud a rose. We kept bees, taking the honey and making and feeding them sugar candy. We had a special allowance of sugar for this purpose.*

Enid Harrison also remembers encouraging her Liverpool evacuee pupils to grow fruit and vegetables in the school garden to supplement the school dinners. In the autumn term she took classes out for an afternoon of rosehip picking - these to provide rosehip syrup, an important part of children's diet because of its vitamin C content, making up for the lack of oranges during the war.[79] Hips were paid for at the rate of 2d a pound and 4 tons of these were collected in Caernarvonshire alone in 1943! Other children were given the task of collecting ferns, foxgloves and nettles which were then sent to Bangor University where they were used in the manufacture of dyes and medication. Horse chestnuts, or conkers, were also required, for the manufacture of a glucose preparation, with the residual pulp being used as experimental animal feedstuff.[80] Evacuees in Betws-y-Coed gathered bundles of sphagnum moss which grew in abundance in the nearby woods and, when dried, was used as a cotton-wool supplement for dressing wounds.[81]

A spokesman for Caernarvonshire County Herb Committee commented in 1942 on how very difficult it was ' *to make people realise that herb collecting is part of a vital National effort and is not merely a local "stunt"'*. He went on to explain that medicinal plants formerly obtained from Europe and America were no longer available due to enemy occupation and shortage of shipping space, and advocated more publicity be given to this vital 'Collect to Cure' effort. Appeals were to be made in particular to schools and youth organisations: *'Collect hips and horse chestnuts and you will help the war effort and at the same time earn money to contribute to worthy objects in which you are specially interested, to your club or society, to war savings or to your personal needs.'* The combined attraction of helping to win the war *and* earning some ready cash clearly did the trick - on 20 May 1944 the Committee issued a letter of thanks to various schools in the district, including particular mention of a number of evacuated schools at Penmaenmawr, Aber, Betws, and at Seion Vestry, Criccieth.[82]

The conkers no doubt provided hours of fun before, strings removed, they were all (apart from 'the champion' no doubt) consigned to the collecting sacks. There were also other nuts to be had - and eaten! Alex Anderson recalls his outdoor education and school foraging trips:

> *I remember the outside of the school building better than the inside ... because we often had our lessons transferred outdoors. We seemed to enjoy quite frequent rambles and journeys to the beach... A further favourite trip was to a nut wood, where we were allowed to gather up all the cobnuts we could carry.*

Eddie McKernan also remembers nut-collecting in Beaumaris:

> *We had to take our laundry to be washed every week and coming home we'd fill the cotton laundry bags with hazel nuts. We'd also fill our gas-mask cases with glorious chestnuts from Gas Work Woods and Baron Hill. There was a walnut tree in Baron Hill field. I can still remember breaking open the shell - it would stain your fingers and make it look as if you'd been smoking. We were a bit worried at first in case that got us into trouble - but you'd have to have been smoking all your life to get stains like that!*

Jean Moeller describes how their out-of-school hours were filled in Denbigh:

> *... we were glad to take advantage of a scheme to do our prep at school in the evenings - we were escorted to and fro by a mistress (in the blackout). A 3rd-year girl ran guides on Saturday mornings and on Saturday afternoons the staff organised rambles up the Clwyd hills or folk dancing, and this was also much appreciated.*

One evacuated teacher relates some of the 'extra-curricular' activities that he organised:

> *In the afternoons we had one lesson - Art, Drama or History - then went*

out to the fields, the hedgerows, the streams, the tarns and the mountains where the children learnt in a week far more Nature Study and Geography than a year's instruction inside a classroom. They learnt by asking questions. I taught them to use their eyes. Often I was unable to give a correct answer so it became a race between teacher and class as to which would discover the answer first.[83]

Country life was indeed often just as much a new experience for the teacher as for the pupil and, eventually, in Caernarvonshire for example, courses were arranged to help evacuated teachers make the most of their new 'facilities'. There was a one day Nature Study Course for evacuee teachers and another on the Historical Background of Caernarvon.[84]

Nature rambles became very much a part of evacuee school life. Here children from Alpha Drive Central School, Rock Ferry, staying in Caersws (Montgom.) eagerly examine what the countryside has to offer. (By permission of the National Library of Wales)

Of course, some parents, failing to appreciate the educational potential, complained about their children being permitted to roam around the countryside. An even greater outcry arose on one occasion when Liverpool teacher Bryan Blades arranged a treasure hunt for his pupils billeted around

121

Caernarvon. The children had been told to destroy all clues but one was somehow overlooked; when this was found by a local a few days later it produced a 'Fifth Columnist' scare in an area which had already convinced itself that German agents were operating in its midst![85] The message had read: GO FORWARD 500 YARDS TO A GATEPOST NEAR COTTAGE. LOOK FOR OXO TIN AND FOLLOW INSTRUCTIONS INSIDE.

The Double Shift system was gradually phased out either as a result of the fall in the number of evacuees or of a deliberate effort by LEAs to provide suitable premises for use solely by evacuee groups. By 8 March 1940, the *North Wales Chronicle* could reveal that of the 50 schools in Caernarvonshire which had been operating a double shift since the 1939 evacuation, only 10 were still doing so. Similarly in Denbighshire, the Director of Education was able to report as early as 30 October 1939 that the number of elementary schools on a double-shift system had been reduced from over 60 to 16, a reduction brought about partly by modifying the organisation of accommodation within schools and partly by hiring other premises. Rhona Parcell remembers that certain 'modifications' were made to the local school near to where she and fellow pupils from Calder High School were billeted:

> *Eventually our schooling was re-started at Wrexham Boys Grammar School and in order to separate us from the boys, thick white lines were painted across the corridors, over which none of us were allowed to step on pain of detention or the cane!*

Les Glover recalls that:

> *There was no classroom for us at first so the Liverpool teachers used to take us for rambles and so on, then the local school's woodwork room was cleared out and became our schoolroom. But we weren't popular with the Welsh kids because of this ...*

Elsewhere partitions were used to create extra classrooms as at Joan Brumfitt's new school where *'there was just one classroom so a curtain was put up to divide it into two - the English children were taught on one side, the Welsh on the other'*.

In Merionethshire the Education Committee quickly set up four sub-committees to look into education problems 'on the spot', with full powers to acquire and equip whatever buildings were necessary for schooling evacuated children.[86] A report presented on 2 October 1939 showed that 26 premises had already been brought into use, comprising old schools, chapel vestries, church rooms, Memorial halls, and so on. Anglesey's Education Committee, on the eve of evacuation, had arranged for its headteachers to make a survey of all local halls which might be suitable for use as schoolrooms. The survey was completed by 13 September and the Anglesey authorities decided to go ahead with any necessary works, such as sanitary provision, despite Liverpool dithering over sanctioning expenditure. Sanction was finally given but proved unnecessary as the Board of Education issued a rather belated Circular (1481) on 8 November to the effect that all extra costs of this nature would be met by the Exchequer.

Most of the halls acquired on Anglesey were the property of religious bodies of various denominations and were apparently preferred in a spirit of ready co-operation. Not so everywhere. In Pwllheli, for example, Chapel authorities were approached about using some vestry rooms: two refused, suggesting it would be far better to retain use of the existing schools! Elsewhere high rents were demanded by chapel authorities, and in Bethesda their outright refusal to allow the use of a room for school purposes led to the resignation of the local minister.[87] Numerous chapel vestries were eventually brought into use as schoolrooms across North Wales, as many evacuees recall. Ellen Baylis was in charge of a group of Birkenhead children billeted in the Merionethshire village of Llwyngwril:

> *At first we used an empty school in the neighbouring village of Rhoslefain. The village children of Rhoslefain were brought in to a school in Llwyngwril by car and the evacuees (Holy Trinity infants) were taken back to Rhoslefain to 'our' school in the same cars! We did this for a term then we were allowed to use the village Church Hall in Llwyngwril. This was much better for us - no more travelling and we were right in the village.*

Tony Lloyd also remembers his vestry schoolroom:

> *There was a small group of us in the village and at first there was nowhere for us to be educated. They tried putting us in with the Welsh children but this didn't work ... Then they got use of the Salem Chapel Vestry and that became our schoolroom. It seemed to take them a while to sort it out though. I don't know if there was some problem with the chapel authorities.*

In Caernarvon, which the *North Wales Chronicle* (29 March 1940) described as

123

'the Black Spot in the County with regard to part-time education', the difficulty experienced was not so much with the religious bodies as with the military authorities. The problem was that Caernarvon had for some time been in a depressed condition and the Council had sought to improve matters by applying to the War Office to have soldiers stationed there. In line with this, the National School had been officially requisitioned but this put the local authorities in a dilemma, caught between wanting the soldiers but also wanting full-time education for the children. As the prospect of getting the military seemed increasingly remote the Education Committee urged the council to appeal for release of the school but in March 1940 councillors narrowly voted against such action and the shortage of school space remained a problem.[88]

Sometimes it was the headteacher of an evacuated school who, by his or her own initiative acquired premises for their evacuees. Portmadoc Council received a letter early in September 1939 from Sister J. Francis, Head of the Rock Ferry Convent Secondary School, stating that she'd had difficulty in securing suitable accommodation for the children in her charge and asking whether the Council would help by allowing them room at the Town Hall. They agreed to this, at least as a temporary expedient.[89] Liverpool Blue Coat School sorted out their own accommodation in Beaumaris. At first Blue Coat children were billeted privately and shared the local schools. Eventually the Liverpool school rented 'Red Hill House' from Sir Richard Bulkeley, purchased 'Bryn' and another property 'Woodgarth' from the estate of F.F. Tattersall and settled into a very happy routine - not returning to Wavertree until the spring of 1946.[90] The Blue Coat pupils must have made quite an impression on the Anglesey town, especially on Sundays! John Houston was a pupil at the school during its time in Beaumaris:

There were at that time about 300 pupils, boys and girls, with an age range from 8 to 16. As well as our everyday uniforms we also had, especially for Sundays, the old traditional uniform, in which we paraded through the streets, led by our band of brass and drums, to attend the parish church each Sunday. The boys' Sunday uniform consisted of long serge trousers, a long-tailed cut-away coat and a waistcoat with silver buttons down the front. Around our necks, in place of a tie, we wore an old-fashioned white clerical neckband. ... The girls wore a long sleeved navy blue pleated dress, buttoned up to the neck and belted at the waist. On top of this was a big white starched collar arrangement, the points of which extended to the waist. Long black stockings completed the outfit and on their heads they wore straw poke bonnets which were tied with a broad ribbon under the chin.

124

Of course, as with other solutions to the education issue, the idea of providing evacuated schools with what was essentially make-shift accommodation did have its drawbacks. School halls, for instance were frequently set aside for use by the evacuees. Winifred Litten remembers that, on the Monday following evacuation:

> *We reported to Hawarden Grammar School. The six lots of evacuees (Holt Hill Convent, Maris Stella Convent, Oldershaw High School, Oldershaw Grammar, Wallasey High and Wallasey Grammar) were kept together. Our 'mixed' sixth form had as a 'classroom' part of the School Hall. Teachers were 'pooled' so whilst we had our own 'Mamselle' for French, we had Masters for History, English and Maths.*

A school hall might have worked all right for sixth-formers but it wasn't always ideal for younger ones, as one evacuated teacher testifies:

> *...the hall as a classroom was not conducive to concentrated study, being a public footpath to all classrooms, cloakrooms, toilets and playgrounds. Whenever a Welsh boy clattered through the hall in his clogs he would loiter idly on the way or stare impudently at the evacuees or gape in wonder at the strange teacher speaking in a foreign tongue.*[91]

Later, this same teacher was in charge of a group who were given use of a converted local chapel vestry which, if not ideal, was a slight improvement on the hall:

Left and over. Evacuees from Liverpool's Blue Coat School must have made quite an impression in Beaumaris as, led by the school band, they marched to church in their traditional uniform. (Photos courtesy Blue Coat Old Blues Association)

125

*Our vestry schoolroom was attached to the chapel. It was a fine large,
rectangular room with a wood-blocked floor, an open fire-place, electric
light, a low platform on one end and windows on the east wall only. We
had no cloakrooms or washbasins. One small W.C., somewhat like a
sentry box, had been erected near the entrance. This was used by the girls.
The boys used an open latrine at the rear of the building.*

One of the biggest problems was lack of heating. One evacuee group, having
enjoyed a few months of independence, had to move back into the local school,
forcing the reintroduction of a double-shift, as there was no means of heating
their rooms and winter - a particularly harsh winter in that first year of

evacuation - was fast approaching. On the whole, however, even somewhat inadequate premises were better than grossly overcrowded 'normal' classrooms. Merseyside and local school inspectors tried to keep a watchful eye on what was happening.

The teaching situation was also made difficult by lack of equipment. Liverpool Education Committee had explained in a Circular on 20 September 1939 that

Owing to uncertainty as to the actual number of schoolchildren who would report for evacuation in an emergency and to the possibility that trains might be diverted from their original destinations, it was not possible to arrange for furniture or stocks to be sent in advance to the reception districts. It may now prove practicable to send supplies to evacuated schools but the actual quantity transferred may have to be limited owing to shortage of road and rail transport.

Details of items required were to be submitted through local education officials; sometimes the host schools helped by lending text books, pencils and paper or chalk and slates in some cases. They weren't always too keen on sharing their facilities, however. Jean Moeller, looking back, feels the Welsh school *'were NOT very welcoming - we were not allowed to use their lab facilities so for zoology we had to sit in the library and draw some cockroaches. They were in a glass box - Barbara Thomas knows how they got out!'* Harold Beckett, evacuated with Birkenhead Institute, remembers that they had some problems with laboratory facilities too:

Ours was a science-orientated school, the Oswestry one favoured the Arts more, so our masters found the labs there rather inadequate. The chemistry master used to return home regularly to pick up supplies of chemicals and equipment.

For many teachers it was often a case of improvisation. One evacuated headmaster, trying to encourage a colleague in February 1941- by which time there was a general shortage of paper - explained how he was collecting backs of envelopes for his pupils to write on.[92] Another teacher, Enid Harrison, recalls that teaching materials were so scarce every part of a notebook was used - margins and covers included, and pencils down to the last stub.[93]

The mass return home within months of the first evacuation created new educational problems in both the reception and evacuation areas. Liverpool had

127

been forced to re-open some of the schools in priority areas and to recall some of their evacuated teachers; in many North Wales districts, teachers were often left with a mere handful of children until these were either absorbed into local schools or joined with other pockets of evacuees, possibly drawn from a number of Merseyside schools. Ethel Kerry remembers that eventually there was only one Rock Ferry boy left in Portmadoc, keen to stay put as he had formed a close relationship with a local girl! He couldn't be forced to return so she and her husband, the master responsible for the school's evacuees, were also obliged to stay on in Portmadoc until arrangements were eventually made for the boy to attend a Welsh school. Another teacher, J.C. Andrews of Friary RC School, Liverpool, outlined his predicament. By then (early November 1939) he explained, of one school evacuated to Denbighshire there were 370 children still in the reception area but 850 back in Liverpool, many of whom were running wild about the streets as practically the whole of the teaching staff was still in Wales. He proposed that if evacuee children in outlying districts could be concentrated in two centres some of the teachers could be freed to return and the education work in the reception area might also be improved. The Council's response shows what a tricky problem this was:

While recognising the difficulty with which this teacher is faced, I believe … his proposals will meet with resentment and opposition in this area … From a public health point of view, it would appear to be unwise to evacuate five parishes and overcrowd one. Owing to the diminution in the numbers of evacuees, those remaining scattered all over the district are all placed in suitable billets, but if they were all 'crammed' into one parish it is almost certain that a proportion of the billets would be unsuitable. From the point of view of ARP, concentration is not advisable … Owing to the uncertainty of the future with regard to aerial warfare the possibility of another exodus from Liverpool cannot be precluded. Many householders in this area have gone to considerable trouble to get their evacuees into something resembling a respectable condition and it would be abusing their hospitality to take these children away from them while the possibility remained that another evacuation, as hurried as the one in September, might involve them in a repetition of the trouble and unpleasantness they then experienced. On the other hand, should no further evacuation take place, you can well imagine the outcry if one parish was overcrowded with evacuees while the remaining 9 parishes in the district had none.[94]

As with other aspects of the first evacuation, the chaos experienced over education in some areas in 1939 didn't go unheeded when the subject of a new scheme was raised. Almost every local authority in North Wales now identified the need to co-ordinate educational and billeting facilities. Attention was focused far more on matters of schooling: quotas were discussed in terms of education facilities, LEA representatives were brought on to evacuation committees. In Flintshire, for example, a Conference of Education Officials was held at Mold on 30 April 1940 *'to ensure that the billeting arrangements and the education facilities in each area would harmonise'.*[95] Proposals were amended to take account of the fact that certain schools already had a nucleus of their pupils in a particular district or had developed good relationships in an area during the course of the first evacuation. There were, however, some added complications. While many official evacuees had returned home certainly by Easter 1940 many other 'private' evacuees had begun to pour into North Wales from Merseyside and from all over the country. In October 1940 the Welsh authorities were instructed:

> *As Liverpool Education committee are responsible financially for the education of all the children who proceed from the 'priority' area of the City to the reception area, it has been agreed with the Directors of Education for Anglesey, Caernarvon, Cardigan, Flintshire and Denbighshire that children now arriving in the reception area shall be absorbed, as far as accommodation and teaching resources permit, into the existing groups of Liverpool evacuees ... Teachers should therefore accept on to their registers, as many Liverpool children as possible, whether they are officially billeted or not.*

Many school logbooks show the extent to which their numbers were now inflated. Denbigh Central School for example recorded a gradual increase in the number of private evacuees admitted in the autumn term of 1940; by the end of October they were having to make use of the hall for classwork and were pleading for more staff. Numbers continued to rise and when in September 1941 the school was asked to accommodate a group of official evacuees, the Head was forced to admit that *'accommodation and staffing are totally inadequate'.*[96] Flintshire schools were experiencing a similar influx and the Medical Officer pointed out in November 1940 that schools and school clinics in Rhyl and Prestatyn were seriously overcrowded, making it difficult to maintain efficient supervision and treatment.[97] Alf Bryce was evacuated to Prestatyn - but had no complaints about his schooling arrangements!

> *School was situated on the beach in what was a holiday camp and our classroom was the restaurant. The ballroom became the school hall for prayers, etc. and this opened on to a swimming pool with a slide - it was heaven ...*

129

As the air raids became more and more intense, especially over Merseyside in 1941, schools in many parts of North Wales began to reach saturation point. In one area of Caernarvon, for instance, three evacuee groups were merged into one in April 1941 but more Liverpool children arrived in June, making a total of 66 pupils and one schoolroom; a double shift had to be employed within the evacuee group itself for a while.[98] Winifred Litten who'd been originally employed to look after a group of 28 Catholic children evacuated from Liverpool and Bootle, found herself at one time in charge of a class of 93! These evacuee groups no longer necessarily comprised a single Liverpool school unit and, especially in the villages, often contained children from many different areas and covering a wide age-range. The Bronyfoel Council School, for example in June 1941 had 42 children from a total of 9 different Liverpool schools as well as 1 child from Birkenhead, 2 from Barrow and 1 from Nottingham.[99]

Jessie Wynne was a schoolgirl in St Asaph in Flintshire during the war. There were two classrooms in her school *'but when the evacuees came one was divided into two, there was also a classroom set up in the cloakroom and one in the back of the church. We were full to overflowing!'* School-life was chaotic for Marjorie Lamb, too:

> *After a while school was organised; it was not very successful as for a long time children of different age groups were all taught in one big hall. It was very distracting as you could hear and see other lessons in progress.*

Looking back, Joyce Light appreciates just how difficult it must have been for the teachers:

> *We had our own teachers with us, one science teacher for the girls and a music teacher for the boys, both of whom had to teach all subjects to children from age eleven to fourteen in the same room. I'm not sure we learnt very much but the teachers did their best in a difficult situation.*

There is no doubt that evacuation brought teachers many challenging situations. Not only were they called upon to teach a variety of subjects and a wide range of age-groups in difficult surroundings but to assume entirely new responsibilities to do with the welfare of the children. It is hard to over-emphasise the importance of their role. For the children, he/she also often represented a vital link with home, a familiar and reassuring adult presence in a strange new world. Yet it was also a very strange world for some of the teachers

130

themselves. Many had no idea where they were heading when they boarded the trains in that first week of September, and when they arrived in the reception area it was often to discover that no arrangements had been made for their accommodation. Joyce Clarke was a Liverpool teacher evacuated to the Aberystwyth area with children from Anfield Road School. Like all the others they'd been provided with carrier bags of iron rations and the teachers had done their best to clean up after the children on the way. Thinking back to that first day of evacuation, Joyce relates:

> *At the end of the day, when the children had been housed, the teachers were still without shelter for the night. Finally, dishevelled after a long journey from Merseyside and many wearying hours, they were taken to a posh hotel on Aberystwyth promenade. They arrived just as the guests, ladies in evening gowns and gentlemen in dress suits, were drinking their after-dinner coffee. As they followed the porter through this lounge of elegantly dressed people - horror of horrors - the bottom fell out of one of the carrier bags. Not only did the iron rations spew out over the thick carpet but also half-eaten soggy sandwiches, a half-empty bottle of pop and a lot of apple cores. There was a ghastly silence from the guests as a porter stood snootily looking on as the mortified teachers picked up the rations from a carpet now covered in crumbs and sticky pop.[100]*

Of course the teachers were only human, some were very homesick and very lonely, others found it hard to adapt to country life. The left-wing politician Leah Manning, a former teacher herself and an active trade unionist, was given a roaming commission by the NUT during the war, to travel around the country's schools acting as a sort of troubleshooter. She explains:

> *On one occasion ... I found a telegram awaiting me to go to Anglesey at once and investigate a complaint of an urgent nature. It was an unpleasant journey, especially when I reached Anglesey. It took me hours to find the house and I could not understand a word anyone spoke. ... At last I found an old mansion where a young teacher had been sent with her class from one of the great cities of the north. I do not mention the city because I think it was a bad bit of planning to send a city girl to such a remote area. She had no one to talk to except the children, and no books. I stayed with her for a week-end enjoying the delicious country food cooked most beautifully by the Welsh-speaking housekeeper. The best I could promise was that I would try to fine another teacher or an educated person who wanted to be evacuated and would return as soon as possible loaded with paperbacks. Both promises I was eventually able to keep.[101]*

131

The fact of being evacuated into an area where Welsh was the first language must have given many teachers an added sense of loneliness. Bryan Blades admits that he was surprised, when making his first visit to the children's billets, to find that many of the foster parents, especially the older ones, had difficulty understanding English. The children, as we will see, often picked up Welsh very quickly, but the teachers didn't find it quite so easy. Jessie Paisley, wife of the famous Liverpool football manager, remembers that as a newly qualified teacher in charge of an evacuee class in Silian, she had been very slow at learning the language - *'I remember especially taking part in the village Christmas play and being given the part of Mary as she was the only one who didn't speak and the play was in Welsh.'*[102] Similarly, Miss Crosbie, Head of Liverpool's Salisbury Street Infants School (evacuated to Bangor), describing in the summer of 1940 how easily her pupils were learning Welsh, added ruefully:

> *The only one who can't learn the language is myself. I tell them that I cannot learn it because I have turned 30 years. When I say 'Leslie bach' (little Leslie) my own pupils correct me! They say 'You don't pronounce 'bach' properly, Miss.'*[103]

Once the air raids started in earnest it was particularly hard for teachers with families still in the danger zone. Helen Woodward revelled in her time as an evacuated teacher but admits:

> *From talk which I had later with other teachers who had served in evacuation duties, that not all were happy during the experience did emerge, caused mostly by billeting problems, unsettled children or continuing anxiety about being away from their homes and families in Liverpool. I was fortunate ... for me it was a stimulating experience.*

It sometimes fell to teaching staff to have to break sad news to a pupil. Frank Morris remembers:

> *We went to school in a Vestry. I remember that awful feeling when a teacher called one of the pupils out to the front in private - you knew that it was to tell him his parents or someone in the family had been killed in the Blitz.*

It wasn't only the teachers who were called upon to perform unaccustomed tasks; sometimes their wives had to (quite literally) roll up their sleeves as well. In Portmadoc, the ladies found themselves with the job of doing washing for the

Margaret Hughes age 9.

What I think of Carmel.

I came here on the 3rd of September 19 And we were taken home by our present land lady. The snow is very deep.

We can get a lovely view from Carmel. We can get some black-berries in the summertime The worse fault is falling in the streams. The people in Carmel are kind to us. There are a lot of lambs and mountain ponys. In the sumer time we go to help with the hay. Carmel is a pretty place. I n Carmel there are beautiful walks to go. We have some fun in the snow. We go to Wesh chapel twice on sundays. We have a vestry for a school. I n the in semmer time we go up the mountain to play little house. We go up the mountain for picnic. There are sports here. I go with some of my friends for wild flowers. There are a lot of cows here. Carmel chapel was built in D. M. C. 10. I n the summertime we can go to the seashore. In Liverpool we do not have band of hope or socity. We had have been on the radio. There are some farms here. There are only a few shops here. I have tried wes wesh butter milk for the first time in my life. We go to playscenter in winter time We are very glad to stay here in such a beautiful place to stay in.

Children's essays showed how different life was as an evacuee in North Wales - eating butter (not marg.), helping with the hay, going to chapel and 'Band of Hope' and even making a radio broadcast! (Margaret Hughes was evacuated with Aspen Grove School, Liverpool, to Caernarvonshire. Letter courtesy A.E. Houghton)

Rock Ferry boys in their husbands' care. Ethel Kerry can still picture the scene vividly - the masters' wives, no less, lined up in front of long trestle tables in the Church Hall scrubbing away: *'Talk about washing socks for England!'* she laughs. Incidentally, Lilian Jones, evacuated to Beaumaris as a pupil with Blue Coat School also lists among her memories: *'Darning and washing those dreadful boys socks'* - adding ruefully *'where was Women's Lib in those days?'* [104] Some girl evacuees had laundry problems of their own. As one recalls *'... in those days most people had home-made sanitary towels and we had to send a monthly bundle home to mum for laundering!'*

Some teachers, either on the outbreak of war or shortly after (perhaps following their experience as evacuees?!) left to join the armed forces. The resulting shortage of staff was overcome partly by increasing mobility - evacuated staff in particular as well as being occasionally called back for spells of duty on Merseyside were moved from place to place in North Wales as the size of units fluctuated with various waves of evacuation. Elderly teachers were brought out of retirement and more women were employed. The teacher shortage in North Wales was partly alleviated by making use of trainees from Bangor and Liverpool Training Colleges. It must have been rather a 'baptism of fire' for the students, with evacuation bringing challenges to tax the ingenuity of even the most experienced teachers.

What exactly were the duties of the evacuated teachers? Bryan Blades kept a diary throughout his years in charge of Liverpool evacuees and recorded details of the many tasks he was called upon to perform:

> A class to be kept constantly at work whether I was in the vestry or visiting another group. Lessons to be prepared and exercises to be marked.
> Playtime duty and the organisation of games and P.T.for the boys.
> Supervision at the Play Centre, held every Friday evening from 5.30 pm to 7 pm.
> Occasional Saturday excursions.
> Evening 'police' duties and investigating complaints about the behaviour of evacuees out of doors or inside billets.
> Sunday services; every child attended because there was nothing else to do.
> Frequent visits to the groups in neighbouring villages. The visits, nearly always on foot, meant walking either $3/_4$ mile uphill or $1^1/_2$ miles downhill. I was always paying bills for shoe repairs.

Journeys to the Education Office in Caernarvon; the Clinic; the W.V.S. Centre; and the Chief Billeting Officer. These visits were usually made on Saturday mornings.

Clothing and Boot repairs. This was a real headache until the W.V.S. came to our aid. We had to take the measurements of children requiring new clothes, exchange unsuitable articles or try to fit them on another child; and label boot repairs; check prices and send bills to the P.A.C.

Requisition lists for school stocks to supply the three village groups.

Collection of library books once a month from the Education Office in Caernarvon.

Removal of sick children to hospital. We had one case of scarlet fever. Bed wetters were sent to a hostel for a period. This hostel was known as the 'Plumbers' to distinguish it from the hostel where we sent cases of scabies.

Clerical work to be done in my spare time. The following are some of the forms which had to be filled in - part of my war effort: EV12 (weekly to evacuees' home authority, on admissions and departures); EV42 (weekly to Caernarvon); Milk records, Attendance records; School MO records (milk, pills and capsules, dental); WVS (clothes and shoe records), PAC (bills forwarded on clothes and shoe repairs), etc.[105]

Mr Blades was a remarkable man and many former evacuees still remember him today with great affection. But many other teachers were also very dedicated to the welfare and happiness, as well as the education, of their evacuated pupils. Most made it their first priority to set up some sort of system for checking on the children in their billets and sorting out any problems there. M.M.Granger, headmistress of Prince Rupert Steer St School kept a logbook during her stay in Caernarvon. One of the first things she organised, after of course arranging for the children to complete and send off the all-important postcards home, was for her teachers to be allocated groups of billets to visit. Ronald Lascelles, Head of Newsham Boys School, evacuated to Llandudno Junction, also remembers how he and his staff were directly involved in ironing out problems between pupil and householder - usually simply a matter of resolving cases of *'people who did not really want to be evacuated to homes of people who really did not want any evacuees'*.[106] Winifred Litten (an evacuee herself at the start of the war but later a qualified teacher in charge of a group of evacuees) relates how:

I had to order shoes, boots, jumpers etc from the WVS. I also had to visit billets especially if the children were unhappy. One little Bootle girl was very unhappy. The bombing of Merseyside had ceased so I thought she would be better off at home. I wrote to her mother and she went home - I received an irate letter from Bootle Education Committee but I wrote back and said Bootle seemed now to be safe and the child's happiness came first!

On another occasion Winifred took direct action on behalf of an older pupils whose parents had been killed. *'He was a sad child,'* she remembers, *'He had reached 14 and did not need any longer to go to school. It seems the first billet he'd had was awful. He was abused and made to sleep in a barn. He used to appear at school with huge flea bites all over him.'* He wanted to join the Navy so Winifred got in touch with the authorities and paid her own way back to Liverpool to plead his cause - eventually he did join the Naval School in Penrith.

Most of the teachers felt responsible for their evacuees during out-of-school hours, especially in the early days when it was not quite clear who did have powers 'in loco parentis'. The Headteacher of Alsop High School issued certain 'instructions' to Holyhead householders, though prefaced with many thanks for their hospitality, and worded with the utmost tact:

At this time you must be put to great inconvenience but I hope the boys will play their part and help you as much as possible. Boys must clean their own boots and shoes. It will not be amiss if they learn to make their own beds so that occasionally they can rely on their own efforts in this direction. I shall much appreciate it if the boys will give you a hand with washing up, running errands and gardening, etc. but in no case should a material reward be given for helping those who are so kindly helping them. It is my wish that the boys should be in bed by the following times: Under 11 years of age, 8 pm; 14-15, at 9 pm; 16 at 10 pm. Boys should rise at 7.30 am. No boys make smoke. Please encourage this rule ...[107]

The Blue Coat School also imposed certain restrictions on their pupils. Don and Eddie McKernan remember it was a case of 'No bikes! No skates! No boats! No pier!', also no one was to venture beyond a one-mile radius of Beaumaris - *'But rules are made for breaking! These restrictions only made life more exciting - everything was even more of an adventure. We weren't supposed to go to the cinema at first either - but of course everyone sneaked in!'*

Keeping tabs on what all the children were up to wasn't easy! Ken Blasbery also relates how:

Miss Bell, Head of the Morrison School, was in charge of the evacuation party. The girls were sent to school in Greenfield. Discipline was strict,

> *the evacuees were told by Miss Bell that if they went to the local cinema*
> *to see the Alfred Hitchcock thriller 'Dial M for Murder', they would be*
> *sent home. Needless to say they all went to see it but nobody was sent*
> *home!* [108]

Mary Formstone was amongst those evacuated from Birkenhead Girls Secondary School. Looking back, she now feels rather sorry for the teachers who went with them:

> *With the approach of winter a sort of curfew was imposed - the girls were*
> *supposed to be in by 6.30. Most of us succeeded in convincing our*
> *hostesses we would be safe in groups out of doors till about nine. I now*
> *sympathise with our teachers! We were sometimes caught - but how*
> *innocent were those joints, usually with the local boys. We went to*
> *darkened cinemas, to railway carriages or just strolled around the maze of*
> *passages behind the houses.* [109]

Perhaps the safest solution was simply to keep the children in sight as much as possible, and as we've seen many teachers did organise their own out-of-school activities sessions. With teaching staff having so very many extra responsibilities, inevitably the question arises: Did the children's education fall by the wayside? Some former evacuees will answer with a resounding 'yes!', others recognise that they acquired a much broader type of education. Certainly Lord Addison in February 1940 declared that: *'The first major casualty of the war has been the national system of education.'* [110] Yet, looking back on it all, several teachers maintain that the standard of schooling during evacuation was not inferior at all.

Apart perhaps from those children who were evacuated in 1939 and remained away for the duration of the war, there can be no denying that the majority did suffer a terrible disruption to their school life. Those who stayed in the towns experienced months with no schools open, followed by months where attendance was constantly interrupted by air raids, then further free time because school buildings had been destroyed. Many of those whose parents opted for evacuation found themselves on a merry (or not so merry)-go-round - sent away in 1939, back in 1940, off again in 1941 and (for those evacuated from down south) back home in 1943, then re-evacuated for one last time in response to the 'V' bombs in 1944!

Rita Holmes, who was aged nine when war broke out, didn't go with the first wave of evacuees but stayed at home in Birkenhead where the schools of course were closed. Later she was evacuated - first to Buckley for 18 months, where she did have a little schooling though the classes were very overcrowded, and

137

then, after a spell at home in the raids, on to Barmouth where she got no schooling at all, by which time she was 14 and old enough to leave school anyway. Rita summed up her war years as *'Plenty of memories but no education!'* Marjorie Lamb feels *'very aggrieved that I did not receive a proper education'*. Nellie Doyle recalled being evacuated with her three sisters from Liverpool to North Wales where all but one of them went to work in the mills. She was only thirteen at the time and her sisters were twelve, eleven and nine.[111] Stan Wallis, evacuated to Abersoch in 1941 writes:

> *The only time we went to school was on Monday mornings - we stood in line for a roll call, then went home again. While it may sound like every boy's dream it did me no favours later on as when I did return home the other kids were streets ahead in maths and English ... I feel I've played catch-up the rest of my life.*

Jack Richardson also felt that he hadn't had much education during the years he was an evacuee in Llangurig, having spent more time helping out on the farm than in the classroom. Yet when he returned to school in Alpha Drive in 1945 he found he was top of the class! Certainly education was disrupted in the early months of the war and again in 1941 when some schools in reception areas were grossly overcrowded. Yet there were many times during the war years when evacuees found themselves in small groups with a far better pupil/teacher ratio than in normal circumstances. Later, educationalists would actually come to advocate the sort of mixed-age, mixed-ability classes that evacuees were often taught in. So, one former evacuated teacher writes:

> *In later years I often refuted the statement that the standard of work - and the teaching - in the reception areas was shamefully poor. Such accusations were made by teachers who had never been evacuated, or by teachers who had served their three months and become homesick. I know how difficult it was trying to obtain results from a class with its roll of pupils rising and falling like a restless skylark. It is surprising to me that any recognisable progress was ever made at all. Yet I am convinced that our work in the vestry compared very favourably with that of any school at home. The fact that some of our children won City Scholarships in the years 1940, 1941 and 1942, proves it.[112]*

This opinion is borne out by a study made of developments in education in Caernarvonshire during the first half of this century which, speaking of the war years, concludes that:

On the whole ... it is true to say that where Liverpool Grammar or Secondary schools were moved 'in toto' to Caernarvonshire, with their staffs, as in the case of Rock Ferry High Schools to Portmadoc, and the Liverpool Collegiate and Liverpool Institute Schools to Bangor, arrangements worked well.[113]

The Vice Principal of the Liverpool Institute confirmed that their examination results had remained high throughout the duration of evacuation.[114] Nor was it all bad news from the Elementary Schools. Although the Head of Caernarvon British School had worried that the operation of a double-shift system may have handicapped those sitting their Scholarship in June 1941, a month later his pupils were enjoying a half-day holiday to celebrate exam successes. Of local children gaining the Scholarship, 11 of the first 17 on the list, as well as the top scholar of Caernarvonshire, had come from the British School.[115] There was, apparently, a slight drop in the standards of attainment of Liverpool children sitting the eleven-plus whilst evacuation was in progress,[116] but despite concern about having to employ double-shifts, many schools did manage to fit a full timetable into their half-time sessions and the supervised activities of the remainder of the day had a considerable educational value of their own.

Sometimes evacuated teachers had taken the opportunity to try out new approaches, often with good results, as Mimi Hatton explains:

We used the environment for teaching purposes as much as possible and went beachcombing, using driftwood to make handicrafts, and slate [to make paper weights and lamps]... Because I was interested in the educational ideas of Homer Lane and A.S. Neale, the evacuee children elected a Children's committee - one member for each age group - and the committee helped to organise events and to deal with delinquents, and to run the evening Play Centre ... The children took any examinations they would normally be due to take and I think the contact with the beauty of Snowdonia and the Welsh culture was an excellent educational experience for them. [117]

Helen Woodward, who in 1942 had taken over a class of 21 Liverpool evacuees in Cefn, in Denbighshire, also concludes that evacuation brought the children broad educational benefits:

Having no prior knowledge of the academic achievements of the children before evacuation, it was difficult to assess the level of their progress

139

during the time I worked with them. But progress they did. As one would expect in a group mixed in age and ability, some achieved more than others. How they fared after returning home I never knew ... I do think though, that the evacuee children I met did benefit from experiencing a new way of life and, in their social development, in coping with the unknown.

As Miss Hatton and Miss Woodward both explain, the children acquired learning not only from the blackboard but from their new environment - country skills, and from the very experience of evacuation itself - what today we might call 'life skills' (though some evacuees might ruefully suggest 'survival skills' more like!).It is now almost a cliche, but nevertheless true, to point out that some town children really did not know that milk came from cows, and apples grew on trees. Certainly not all evacuees were ignorant of 'country' things - horses were a common sight on city streets and one carter in Liverpool kept not just horses but goats, hens and pigs at his stables in Stitt Street;[118] dairy cows were kept at farms in the near-suburbs, even inside the evacuation area in the case of one farm - in Penny Lane; many a backyard housed rabbits or a few hens. Yet to many evacuees their new life was a great eye-opener. Joan Brumfitt admits that she'd never seen a cow before - *'I remember writing to tell my dad that I'd had milk "straight from the cow". He wrote back, joking, and asked if I'd been lying under it at the time!'* Ron Organ also explains:

If anyone ever had an apple at school he always got chased until only the core was left and then whoever caught him got to have the core. I won one once and it had a funny thing attached to it. One lad said it was a leaf. 'What?' I asked. 'It is, it's a leaf. Apples grow on trees you know,' he answered. I knew he was having me on. But on that first morning in Bodfari, when I opened my curtains the first thing I saw was an apple tree in the garden. So he hadn't been lying after all!

Archie Manser made a similar amazing discovery at his billet. *'The summer was very hot,'* he recalls *'I can remember the surprise of seeing Victoria plums growing on the trees behind the Cross Keys pub. I thought plums were only grown overseas.'* If Archie couldn't believe his eyes, Alf Bryce couldn't believe his ears:

With another lad I went to live in a house called 'The Nook' ... It was a lovely place and we were looked after by two ladies. The first morning I asked one of the ladies where she kept all her canaries. She told to me it was the wild birds I'd heard.

140

Charles C. Carter, Head of St Saviour's, Liverpool told a meeting of the Wrexham Rotary Club in December 1939 how one of his little evacuee boys on seeing pigs for the first time had said to his playmate, *'Hey, Fred, come and look at these 'ere wolves'*![119] Another evacuee, picking a dandelion on the side of the road in Anglesey, was scolded by her older sister, who told her to *'Leave them lovely flowers alone.'* Even six months after being evacuated some Merseyside children were still amazed at being able to cross a green field without a 'parkie' chasing them![120] Alex Anderson sums the matter up well when he says:

> *For a boy brought up in the back streets of Liverpool, where the sun rarely shone and it took a longish journey by tramcar just to see a tree, the North Wales countryside was like being on another planet.*

Evacuation opened up whole new vistas for some - Liverpool boy Roy Hill would never have thought to join the Lovat Scouts in 1941 but for a love of the mountains acquired as an evacuee in Bangor. There were new skills to be absorbed, too. Many helped with milking and butter-churning, with feeding the hens and collecting the eggs; there were potatoes to be picked, beets to be pulled and the harvest to gather in. S. Griffiths got a job plucking chickens, and Archie Manser helped out at the local blacksmith's, learning how to strike with a 7lb hammer and how to re-hoop a wheel. The land offered opportunities beyond just part-time work - a point not lost on the Liverpool juvenile employment authorities. *'Slowly, and almost solely as a natural development of the evacuation scheme,'* they acknowledged, *'boys are beginning to see that when they reach school-leaving age, work in a farm will help the country to fight its war as well as furnishing them with healthy, interesting employment.'* In the autumn of 1940 it was also reported that two Liverpool *girls* of school-leaving age had taken up agricultural work.[121] Whilst they may not have minded helping on the farms, many of the girls weren't too thrilled at having to acquire certain 'domestic' skill. Yet Margaret Ferguson was actually quite pleased to do so:

> *I had never been very domesticated in my own home. Mrs B. taught me a lot, every morning before school I dusted the hall, dining room and sitting room and on Saturday mornings we baked fruit pies and cakes for the forthcoming week.*

The children learnt from their foster parents as well as from their teachers, sometimes they acquired refinements such as good table manners or a passion for poetry, sometimes more dubious talents, such as how to snare a rabbit or tickle a trout! Many evacuees, even those with caring foster parents, developed

141

a little useful independence, a bit of confidence. For those unlucky enough to get a 'bad billet', any learning tended to come from the school of hard knocks: how to stand on your own two feet, keep cheerful in the face of adversity, protect younger siblings, shield your parents from worry, survive in a love-less environment. It may have been 'character-forming' but it wasn't always pleasant - and was certainly one aspect of 'learning' that should never have been part of the evacuation experience.

Even evacuated teachers found they could learn a thing or two, as Helen Woodward admits:

> Looking back on those days in Cefn, I realise what an enriching time it was for me. I learnt much and was given much in true care and friendship, and being able to explore the countryside around the Vale of Clwyd in leisure time was an added bonus.

Many others seem also to have enjoyed their time in Wales; some formed life-long friendships, some even married local people and made a permanent home there. Merseyside teachers on the whole enjoyed good relations with the communities in which they and their pupils were billeted. Nor is there anything to indicate the sort of attitude described by H.C. Dent when he wrote that 'Urban teachers, though obviously mental paupers in a land of plenty, affected an air of lofty superiority over their country colleagues.'[122] On the contrary, school records for the period suggest there was much genuine goodwill and co-operation between the two sets of staff. Naturally, local head teachers didn't relish the prospect of having to share their schools and frankly admitted to being relieved when the evacuees left, but this was an objection to the difficult situation their presence created rather than the personnel involved. Dr Elfed Thomas, who was the Director of Education for Caenarvonshire during the war, recorded in 1960 that:

> My strong impression is that after the first shock of the impact of evacuation, personal relations were on the highest possible level. I have the happiest memories of some of the people I worked with at the time and it may be taken as some small indication of the prevailing atmosphere of good will that when I myself married in August 1940, I received a very handsome wedding present from the Liverpool teachers evacuated to the Caernarvonshire area.[123]

Dr Thomas's opinion is supported by N. Bullock who was the wartime Inspector of Schools for Liverpool. He, too, records that:

142

So far as I can recall, co-operation among the teachers was good despite the strain put on the accommodation of some of the schools. The Caernarvonshire heads had a difficult task in trying to be fair to the local children and to the evacuees. I found the headteachers very co-operative and I was well received when I visited the schools ... The main problem of personal relationships arose within the Liverpool services as teachers from a variety of schools had to work under the general direction of certain head teachers from Liverpool, under whom they had never worked before.[124]

There was, however, one distinct area of friction which did develop in parts of North Wales, and that was between local people and teachers from some evacuated Roman Catholic schools. Difficulties arose in particular when these teachers, and Catholic priests, attempted to take action to safeguard the religious welfare of their pupils.

Chapel - and more chapel!

Ask anyone who was evacuated to North Wales what they remember most about their time and almost all will mention having to go to chapel, not once or twice, but very often three times every Sunday, and sometimes on a weekday too! Where the services were in Welsh these visits must must have been very tedious, as Ron Shaw explains:

Every Sunday, three times, a trip to church HAD to be undergone, with the language something of a problem to me - the result: boredom and a nip on the ear (nothing malicious) to awake my dormant Christian beliefs.

Indeed, perhaps some of the children *were* in need of a little religion - if the comment of one Welsh minister is to be believed! Interviewed in 1989 about evacuation, the minister recalled that he'd asked the children from Birkenhead, *'Tell me children, have you ever heard of Jesus Christ?'* Apparently the children looked at each other for a few moments before one of the older ones ventured: *'Sorry we've never heard of him. You must remember Birkenhead is a big town, so we don't know everyone!'*[125] Certainly Ron Edmondson's foster parents thought he was in need of 'salvation':

... my carer felt it necessary for me to have a modicum of religious instruction, but I think the only Sunday service was at the Welsh-speaking chapel. Although I had mastered a few Welsh swear words (which I vividly

143

remember) I was quite unable to follow the proceedings. I was therefore sent to the local branch of the Salvation Army ... I still have a copy of Hans Anderson's Fairy Tales presented to me by the Salvation Army 'For good conduct, diligence and regular attendance' having obtained 30 marks out of a possible 102. I recall being very embarrassed at the nature of the prize as another of our group got a copy of a Biggles adventure book. It's possible that he scored more than my measly 30 marks!

There was some 'bribery' involved in Peter Sherlock's regular attendance at Sunday School, which he enjoyed *'because you got a star for each attendance'*; others were rewarded for reciting Bible verses - especially if they managed to do so in Welsh. Stan Wallis remembers:

I attended church at least twice each Sunday ... Mrs Jones had her own pew, in which we sat. Each week all the children were expected to learn a Bible verse - in Welsh. If you couldn't remember it we always reverted to our favourite one - the shortest: God is Love.

The 'Sabbath' was strictly adhered to in many Welsh households, as Hugh Jones explains:

On Sundays we either went to church or we went to chapel, nothing else was debated. The good book was all that we could read on the Sabbath, certainly no Dandys or Beanos. A game of cards? Heaven forbid!

Some evacuees remember that only cold meals were eaten on Sundays and of course there was no Sunday opening of the pubs. In fact in certain areas 'Sabbatarianism' was carried to quite extreme lengths, as Moya Jones's family discovered:

...Mother and I went off together to a solid grey stone house in what is now called Snowdonia National Park. It came as a shock to realise we were not welcome in the village. I could not understand why people did not like us just because we were English. Of course mother did not help by opening up the parlour for tea every day when previously it had been sacred to family funerals; or gardening on a Sunday. They had meetings of the chapel committee about that! [126]

Little Doreen French couldn't understand why she was getting such stern looks from passersby one Sunday as she sat in the sun on the front step of her billet, embroidering a doyley as a gift for her mother. Even such a 'labour of love', it seemed, was not acceptable. It may have been all very strange to some of the evacuees, but many came to love even the regular trips to chapel and church, and, like Jim McHugh, Billy Moffitt, Ken McGunigle, and numerous others, became enthusiastic members of the choir. As John Manuel recognises, chapel was also a great 'integration system' - *'Certainly my own Chapel, the Wesleyan, had a number of evacuees as regular attenders and we happily mixed with them.'*

Some, of course, did rebel. Maureen Weller, having been first evacuated to the south coast and then re-evacuated to North Wales after Dunkirk, was getting a bit fed up with the whole thing. At the age of 14 she suddenly discovered a stubborn streak - over the issue of chapel!

> *There was a sensation of being irreversibly sucked in to the strange ways of unknown powers. All else I had suffered ... but chapel-going was where I took an intransigent stand - as also did [my foster parents]. They would do their part in the war effort by accepting two evacuees. They would put up with the inconvenienc and the problems. But they would NOT keep a heathen under their roof. So once again I was moved, ironically thanking the Lord for deliverance!* [127]

Despite the earlier story of Christ and the Birkenhead children, many evacuees were already practising Christians and attendance at church or Mass gave them great comfort - a sense of continuity with life at home, of something familiar at a time when so much else was very strange. Alex Anderson, evacuated with Sacred Heart School explains:

> *Happily, my presence at Mass worked for me here [in Criccieth] as it has worked for me in all the other Catholic Churches I have ever been in ... Nothing is strange. Nothing is unfamiliar. ... The same friend. The same feeling of being at home and in safe hands.*

But the experience of evacuation far from bolstering their faith introduced serious doubts for some, like Doris Coxon. She and her sister were not well treated at all, given only meagre meals, made to do all the chores, including cleaning the family gravestone, and forced to stay in the garden shed whenever visitors called. Doris writes:

> *It was the worst experience of my life. Not one person of any authority*

145

checked on us in all that time, they probably thought we were OK because the Rogers were stalwarts of the church. I was and am a Christian but nearly lost my faith then.

Another youngster, evacuated to near Welshpool, was anxious about 'this church and chapel problem' and wrote for guidance to his minister at home, Revd Eustace Hand of Tranmere, Birkenhead, who offered the following advice, what you might call a working compromise:

> *...Chapels were started to bring men into the Church. Now they take men away from the Church. You must be on your guard and not let them take you away. It won't do any harm to go with your pals in the evening so long as you treat it like one of the Meeting Houses that John Wesley founded, to help you to know God better and worship Him better when you go to Church. It will never do <u>instead</u> of Church. I think you realise that. The very fact that you want to stick to church in the morning shows it. Here of course I absolutely forbid our children to go to a Chapel, but where you live there are so many Chapel people and you are sure to make friends with Chapel people that I feel it would be unkind in your case. However, by now you know my feelings about it. Stick to your Church ... if you find that Chapel helps you to become a better child of God, and a better son of His Church, use it merely as a Meeting House and not as a substitute for Church ...*[128]

The danger of evacuees losing their faith or having it in some way corrupted became very much a concern of the Catholic hierarchy following the billeting of many Roman Catholic children on to non-Catholic householders. This concern in turn became the source of much friction. Welsh householders, the majority of whom were Protestant and Nonconformist, deeply resented the regular visits from teachers and priests, which they viewed as unwarranted interference in the running of their homes. The records of evacuation in North Wales contain numerous complaints on these grounds, especially in the counties of Denbighshire, Merioneth and Caernarvon. One example typifies the prevailing attitude. Referring to the use of compulsory billeting powers, the Evacuation Officer for Aled Rural District explained that:

> *The Billeting Officers generally, whilst disliking the task, are prepared to carry out these duties and to use compulsory powers, providing that Protestant children only are sent to the district. They all explain that householders will not, under any circumstances, receive Catholic children*

into their homes again, and the Billeting Officers have threatened to resign rather than use their compulsory powers, as their sympathies are all with the householders. They all emphasize that this attitude is not the result of religious bigotry, but because of the interference and religious intolerance of the Catholic priests and teachers who accompany the children.[129]

The Catholic Church was anxious about so many of its young members being deposited into the heart of Welsh Methodism, where facilities for Roman Catholic worship were very limited or non-existent. But householders objected to being chastised if their Catholic charges failed to attend Mass or, perhaps worse in Catholic eyes, were taken along with their foster parents to chapel services. A.M. Jones, Billeting Officer for Holyhead remembers one occasion when:

Revd John Puw Jones, a highly volatile Welsh Wesleyan Pastor stormed into my office or my home (trouble often came right to the doorstep!) demanding that something be done in the case of Mr & Mrs So-and-so who had some Roman Catholic children from Liverpool. The Priest had called at their house laying down the law with regard to the evacuees in no uncertain terms. Possibly they'd been taking the evacuees to chapel through lack of any alternative. Anyway they'd call in their Minister who then came to me to sort it out![130]

Having young Catholic children billeted on them did pose quite a dilemma to many Welsh families. On Sundays it meant having to choose between missing chapel altogether, going to chapel and leaving the children unattended, or taking the children with them. Most householders, not unreasonably, chose the latter but then had to face the wrath of the Catholic priests and teachers. One priest apparently felt it necessary to call upon the parents of some evacuees and insist they be brought home, alleging that any physical danger they might incur from air raids was trifling compared with the spiritual dangers they ran by remaining away![131]

Where there were Catholic places of worship nearby, householders often did make a determined effort to ensure that the children were regular attenders. If others failed to send the children to Mass it was usually due to concern over their welfare rather than any intentional undermining of their faith. Mrs Lily Powell, whose family took in two evacuees from the Birkenhead girls' Catholic school of St Werburghs, remembers:

147

They were very strict, going to Mass each Sunday they stayed with us. To go to Mass they had to walk from St Martins to Chirk, to the Catholic Church, later there was one on the Rhewl. The teachers would accompany them. They would not have a drink and it would be winter time and my mum used to worry for them. She would say just have a drink to warm your tummies. No way - they would not have anything pass their lips. They would walk to church which was three miles and walk back, and they would be starving - we were so worried for them.

Sometimes a special bus would be laid on to collect the children and take them to Mass. But, more often than not, attending a Catholic service in the scattered rural districts involved a very long walk, and poor footwear occasionally made this simply impossible. One Penmaenmawr householder expressed her concerns to the council, describing how the children in her care *'are being taken to the Roman Catholic Church after school in all weathers, walking both ways; one child is 7 and the other is 5 years old and it is after 5.30pm when they get in. The journey is far too long for these children and especially when they have to walk, and come home unaccompanied, wet or fine.'*[132] Nant Conway's Clerk made the point to Mott in April 1940 that *'during the last evacuation, children were made to walk as much as 8 miles to attend mass on Sunday mornings'*, adding that he considered it especially *'a hardship on the younger children to have to do this in all weathers'.*

In the districts where there were no established Catholic places of worship within remotely possible travelling distance, other premises were bought into use. In this respect, Anglesey set a very enlightened example by permitting its Catholic evacuees the use of chapel vestries and church halls for their worship - an action which, if not appreciated by all, was warmly welcomed by Father William Hodson of St Vincent's, Liverpool.[133] Elsewhere other halls or large rooms were set aside for the purpose. In Portmadoc, Catholic evacuees were granted use of the Town Hall for teaching on week days and for religious services on Sunday evenings; in Llanfairfechan they were given use of the Promenade Pavilion on Sundays and Fridays.

Sometimes, however, such arrangements were either impossible or unsatisfactory and, even if happily billeted, Catholic evacuees were moved at the request of a teacher or priest, simply in order to accommodate their religious beliefs. In November 1939, however, having handled a large number of re-billeting requests, Denbighshire's Clerk decided to dig his heals in on this issue. Writing to Evan Evans, Evacuation Officer for Wales, he declared:

I am tired of these attempts to move children simply because they belong to one particular faith and intend to take as firm a stand as I can against any further nonsense of this kind. I hope I can have your support.[134]

Even where there were Catholic churches available, accommodation was strained by the large increase in the number of worshippers. Winifred Litten explains what happened in one area:

The Catholic church in Hawarden was too small to accommodate over one hundred more parishioners and the 'outsiders' chapel at the Convent [of Poor Clares] could not cope either, so with special permission from the Bishop we went to mass in the 'Enclosure'. The Enclosure chapel floor was covered with coconut matting. When we had to kneel on it our knees were like 'nutmeg graters'. The benches were 'sideways on'.

December 8th was an important feast for us at Holt Hill - the Feast of the Immaculate Conception. We had always had a procession in the afternoon. We had our 1939 procession in the Convent Enclosure singing our traditional hymns ... It was very nostalgic because we thought of our homes and our school. Instead of our lovely chapel organ, one of the Poor Clares played a wheezy old harmonium.

The education of Catholic children, at least where the teaching of religion was concerned, also posed a problem for, as was pointed out at a meeting of Denbighshire's Education Committee in October 1939, it was, strictly speaking, illegal for denominational instruction to be given on Council school premises in school hours. An amendment was put forward that as evacuees were taught separately there was no justification for refusing to allow them to receive such lessons, but this was turned down in favour of a resolution that the Catholic teachers should *'make an effort to secure separate premises wherein such instruction could be given'*.

As far as North Wales was concerned, the religious clash stemmed from what must be one of the more glaring examples of lack of forethought in an evacuation scheme which sent large numbers of Roman Catholic children to an area of staunch Calvinistic Methodism without making arrangements for their religious needs. As a result, when the later evacuation scheme came under discussion, district councils were inundated with resolutions from their parishes and they themselves sent resolutions to the Welsh Board of Health, to the effect that if a further evacuation was to take place, no more Roman Catholic children should be sent into the area. The Clerk to one of the Denbighshire districts left his County authorities in no doubt as to the prevailing sentiment. He explained how his householders, regular chapel-goers, had had to take their young evacuees with them on Sundays but had then been visited by Priests and instructed - in terms which left no room for argument - that they must not do this. He added:

> *This, in the opinion of my council, interferes far too much in the life of the community and in view of the district being so scattered, it is impossible for the Catholic authorities to make proper arrangements for the religious welfare of their evacuees, and I am directed by the council to ask you to use your influence with the Evacuation Officer for Liverpool to arrange for further evacuees who may come to the district to be of any other religion than Roman Catholic.* [135]

Much the same request was put forward by numerous other parish and district councils.[136] The Catholic authorities were also up in arms over what had occurred in 1939. Cardinal Hensley, head of the Catholic Church in Britain, appointed a commission to look into the status of evacuated Catholic schools, and in March 1940 demanded a meeting with government officials. He wanted some assurance that Roman Catholics would only be billeted in areas amenable to Catholic principles.[137] Eventually a map was produced marking the precise location of Catholic schools and churches in all reception areas but the Minister responsible, Walter Elliot, was clearly less than amused by the whole affair. Testily, he asked his civil servants to let him know in future 'when you wish me to arrange for further distributions so that Methodists, Plymouth Brethren, Freethinkers and Quakers can each enjoy their particular brand of spiritual comfort'!

In an attempt to pacify all parties over this matter, C.F. Mott, in April 1940, declared that in future his authority would make an effort to ensure that Roman Catholic evacuees were sent to areas where the required facilities were available, although, he added, the very high percentage of Catholics among the Merseyside population obviously meant that there would have to be exceptions. However, when details of the quotas were issued by Liverpool, shortly afterwards, one Clerk at least challenged the notion that Liverpool had made any such effort. He pointed out that 200 Catholic children had been allotted to Llanrwst - with no RC facilities - whereas Abergele, which possessed a recently built and large Catholic church, was to receive 500 Nonconformist and Church of England children only![138] Nor were the Catholic authorities happy: in fact Father Doyle, priest for Liverpool's Holy Cross School, disliked the situation on Anglesey so much that he allegedly visited Menai Bridge in person and threatened to wreck the whole evacuation programme there.[139] As late as July 1941, Dr Downey, Archbishop of Liverpool was still expressing his concern at what he described as 'mismanagement and muddle' over evacuation of Roman Catholic children: '*A little careful forethought and planning on the part of the evacuating authorities*', he wrote in the *Catholic Record*, '*would result in Catholic children being sent to congenial surroundings where they could receive schooling from Catholic teachers and be ministered to by Catholic priests.*'[140]

It was not only the Catholic clergy who showed concern over the welfare of the children - the Revd T.W. Isherwood, for example, Vicar of Christ Church, Claughton (near Birkenhead) visited the Towyn area to check on evacuees from his parish and to thank the foster parents who were looking after them. Revd G. Wynne Griffiths of Tabernacle Church Bangor, 'funded by a friend interested in the welfare of evacuees', produced *A Wonderful Life: A Handbook for the use of English evacuees attending Welsh Sunday Schools*. Evacuees of yet another faith in Bangor also caused some concern. Rabbi Teretski visited the area when some difficulties arose due to the presence there of a number of Jewish children, several of whom were Orthodox and would not accept the same food as other members of the households in which they were billeted.[141] This was a relatively isolated incident for North Wales, however, where the main religious problem continued to centre on Catholic evacuees.

There was an interesting twist to the religious issue when in April 1941 Bethesda and District Evangelical Council lodged a protest against the sending of Roman Catholic evacuees into essentially Welsh and Protestant districts, and urged its local authority, Ogwen RDC, '*to use its influence to safeguard the best traditions of Wales and the religious susceptibilities of the nation*'. It seemed that the Catholic hierarchy was not alone in seeing the potential for 'spirtual contamination'. Clearly this Evangelical Council regarded the Catholic children as some kind of religious 'fifth columnists'! Perhaps alarm bells had rung when, a few weeks earlier, the Clerk to Ogwen council had sung the praises of the Catholic evacuees, particularly their strict church attendance, and had added, '*They are an example to Protestant children*'![142]

The Catholic Church authorities remained opposed to the mixing of Catholic and Protestant schoolchildren and were duly criticised by several non-Catholic organisations for what they regarded as religious intransigence in a time of national emergency. But, equally, some Welsh districts, even in the chaotic Spring of 1941, continued to protest when Catholic children arrived. There were discontented mutterings in Penrhyndeudraeth about householders being

151

not only forced to send their evacuees to Mass but pay their bus fares there as well. Catholic teachers from Our Lady's School, Birkenhead, which had been evacuated to the village, felt compelled to write a letter to the local press refuting the accusations levelled against them at a meeting of the parish council, and adding: *'This definitely hostile attitude of the Councils undermines our influence as it incites even the majority of householders who have been hitherto very friendly and helpful, to keep the children from church. Surely everyone is entitled to live their own lives and to follow their own religion; that is why this war is being fought.'*
143

As with so many of the problems which arose over evacuation, some of the best solutions were adopted at 'grassroots' level. Thus in Hawarden, there was something of an ecumenical breakthrough during a 'clothing' at the Convent. *'All the Sixth Form evacuees were invited, Catholic and Non-Catholic alike,'* Winifred Litten explains. *'Quite a lot of us went and were very moved by the whole thing.'* Elsewhere, complaints from the reception areas gave way to more positive attempts to make a place for the Catholic children in the local communities. In one Wrexham parish special clubs were set up for the Catholic evacuees when it was discovered that their religion prohibited them from joining existing clubs.[144] In time, meetings were held between representatives of the Liverpool Catholic Churches and those in charge of reception arrangements in North Wales so that amicable arrangements could be reached.[145] Gradually some of the sting was taken out of the controversy. In fact even the Catholic Church seems to have become a little blasé over the individual evacuee souls which had caused it so much concern in 1939. When, many years after his evacuation with Sacred Heart School, Alex Anderson wrote to ask the Catholic Church at Portmadoc for a certificate of his confirmation there in 1941, he was told that the priest at the time had entered the names of all the local children and then added the words *'and 129 others'* . So much for individual souls!

From the beginning of the evacuation scheme it had been mostly the Catholics who seemed to fear for their religion as a result of enforced encounters with Nonconformity but there was an interesting counter-blast from one Welsh Evangelical Council which, faced with an influx of Catholic evacuees, urged the need *to safeguard the best traditions of Wales and the religious susceptibilities of the nation.* In the planning stages of evacuation the 'best traditions of Wales', not just its religion but its whole culture, especially its language, had been very much the concern of the Welsh Nationalists. How right were they to have been worried? The final problem to be looked at in this section will be the matter of the Welsh language.

'We're in Germany!'

It seemed like hours before we arrived in North Wales and were taken into a Market Hall in Aberdovey. We (Betly and I) were sitting on our cases, listening to the Welsh voices around us; Betly, panic-stricken, whispered "We're in Germany!" (Sadie Dawson)

For some young evacuees, like poor Betly, the fact that the people waiting to meet them after their long journey were speaking in some peculiar language must have been an added source of confusion in an already bewildering day. To some, it was almost the last straw - Glenys Thomas remembers the evacuees arriving at Bontnewydd, on a bus from Caernarvon, and being 'chosen' by their various foster parents:

> *... and on the following morning the police were picking them up all along the road going home. They didn't understand Welsh - and a lot of the people didn't understand the Scouse they talked - but it worked out in the end!*

Others were mildly amused by the 'strange gabbling' that greeted them - though less amused as time went by and they discovered that the 'gabbling' could be used to exclude them from certain conversations! As John Houston recalls:

> *The family I was sent to stay with lived in a small terraced house. There was a father and mother, a boy of about my age, and an old grandmother who couldn't speak a word of English. Not that it bothered her very much, as the others talked to each other in Welsh all the time, and the only time they spoke in English was to me, which wasn't very often ... although I couldn't undersatnd what was being said, it was made very obvious that I was the subject of their conversation, and that I wasn't a very welcome guest.*

Tony Lloyd also remembers being *'sometimes conscious that we were being spoken about in Welsh - and none of us liked that much'.* No doubt many Welsh householders, especially in the early days of evacuation, were quite oblivious to the fact that their new charges felt in the dark. As Margaret Brent explained, she'd been evacuated on 1 September and was living in a 'Welsh' billet - the grown-ups spoke Welsh to each other and all the newspapers in the house were in Welsh - so it was over two weeks before she even discovered that the nation was at war! Of course there were very few adults in Wales who couldn't speak

English when necessary and did so when addressing their evacuees. The worry for Nationalists was that through having to speak English in the presence of English children in their homes, Welsh people would lose the habit of conversing in their native tongue. Welsh was also widely used as a medium of instruction in primary schools and it was feared that this, too, would have to give way to English if non-Welsh speakers had to be admitted into the classrooms.

The first alarm bells had begun to sound amongst Welsh Nationalists during the Munich crisis back in 1938 and as the evacuation plans were finalised and then actually put into operation, fears for the future of Wales continued to dog sections of the community. A member of the Caernarvon Town Council urged the need for a Consultative Committee to watch the national interests of Wales during wartime, and within three months of the first evacuation a National Conference for the Safeguarding of Welsh Culture was duly convened in Shrewsbury, intending to establish local committees 'for the supervision and protection of Welsh cultural interests'.[146] Though a staunch supporter of the stand taken by Britain, W.J. Grufydd was also worried that *'England could win the war and Wales could lose it!'* It was the presence of evacuees that concerned him most. *'In the village of Arfon'*, he wrote in *Y Llenor* (autumn 1939), *'there are almost as many English children as there are Welsh children.'*[147]

Yet while the Nationalist Party continued to rail against evacuation and insist that the Welsh language was doomed, others took a different view, more in line with that put forward in the *Caernarvon and Denbigh Herald* on 1 September 1939. The paper acknowledged that one of the duties facing Welsh people was 'to see that the essential Welsh life does not suffer by the influx [of evacuees]' but went on to suggest a more positive approach:

> *... one must rely on the good will of the people generally, hosts and visitors alike. Given common sense and consideration the difficulty should be capable of solution and the children from the English towns may be all the better for coming into contact with another type of life.*

Many Welsh people set about doing exactly what the Nationalists should arguably have advocated from the outset, namely trying to teach their English visitors something of the ways and language of their newly adopted country. As Angela McDonald testifies:

> *I learnt to speak Welsh ... The whole experience was unforgettable and*

*enabled me to become aware of Welsh language and culture. I was so
lucky that the family whose home I shared did everything to encourage me
and make me appreciate what they held so dear.*

Walter Hurst regrets that he never learnt Welsh whilst he was an evacuee, but
adds, *'my sister did and spoke and wrote it quite perfectly - she took her school
certificate in Welsh and got a merit'.* For those evacuees who were billeted with
Welsh-speaking families (on Anglesey, for example, 97 per cent of the
population spoke Welsh), learning some Welsh became almost a matter of
survival. As Tony Lloyd explained, the lady in his billet didn't speak very good
English *'so I had to learn some phrases. I was never fluent but picked up enough
to get by.'* Learning Welsh also helped Beryl Bellier-Moudray to become very
much a part of her new 'family', as she explains: *'I was taught Welsh and I, at
the very grown-up age of 7 was able to teach their small daughter English!'*

Often it was the desire to make new playmates which acted as a spur, as for Les
Glover, who, because he was billeted on a farm quite far out of town, couldn't
easily meet up with other evacuees, *'But I got quite friendly with the bailiff's son
- he was about the same age as me. He couldn't speak any English and all the
farmhands spoke Welsh so I picked it up - well enough to communicate OK.'*
Elsewhere there was a more formal approach to helping the children acquire a
new language, as Elsa Chatterton explains:

> *We went to the village school and were taught by our own teachers ... but
> once a week the local headmaster taught us Welsh. We learnt to count to
> ten, say the Lord's Prayer and sing 'Jesus loves me'. I'm sorry to say I can
> only remember the counting now. On the way home we were taught in
> our innocence some different Welsh by a local teenager. When Mrs
> Williams-Ellis discovered what we had learnt she told us not to walk home
> with Owen any more! Perhaps it is fortunate that I have forgotten that bit
> of Welsh too!*

The fact that Welsh was widely used in primary school classrooms did create
problems for those trying to sort out educational arrangements. Tony Lloyd
remembers:

> *There was a small group of us billeted away from the rest of our school
> and at first there was nowhere for us to be educated. They tried putting us
> in with the Welsh children but it didn't work out - there was a lot of
> fighting and the language was a problem. In the end we were given the use
> of a room in the Chapel and we had our lessons there.*

155

This was the usual procedure adopted - finding alternative accommodation for the schooling of the English children, but when numbers dwindled and evacuees were absorbed into Welsh primary schools it occasionally became necessary to conduct lessons in English, and this did cause minor resentment amongst local teachers and parents. In fact if there was a problem over the language issue it was usually the adults who were the cause. Whereas hearing Welsh may at first have been rather bewildering to the English children it wasn't long before they picked up at least 'colloquial' Welsh and reached some form of working understanding with local children. For some of the mothers arriving with their babies and toddlers, the language difference was less acceptable. One Evacuation Survey, produced in 1940, concluded that:

> ... under the most favourable circumstances it would have been an obstacle to social intercourse and mutual understanding. But ill-educated adults who find themselves surrounded by people speaking an unknown tongue are apt to be suspicious and resentful and such an attitude naturally provokes resentment on the other side. This, like so many other aspects of evacuation does not seem to have been considered in advance by anyone.[148]

The issue of the Welsh language was certainly one of the factors causing the rapid return of many adult evacuees in the early days of the scheme, but not all were so easily put off. Some made an effort to acquire at least a smattering of the language of their hosts. Ethel Kerry, evacuated with her schoolmaster husband, remembers that the young daughter of the family they were billeted with used to go around singing a well-known little Welsh song, 'Mi welais jac-y-do'. Ethel recalls: *'I asked her to teach me the song . She was absolutely thrilled that I managed to learn it - and I've never forgotten it to this day!'* As we've seen, some teachers found it harder than their pupils to pick up the language; others were more determined. When Helen Woodward joined an evacuee group in Denbighshire, the Liverpool children had a head-start on her, having been sharing a Welsh school for over a year:

> Morning assembly was always taken with all the children together in the 'Infant' room - and always in Welsh, so I had to catch up and learn the Lord's Prayer and the various hymns used. ... Mrs Williams [at the billet] helped so much in enlarging my knowledge of the neighbourhood and also helped with my first struggles with Welsh. It was her firm rule that we only spoke in Welsh at the tea-table - a good start ... Occasionally attending chapel services helped too, the local minister steered me through mutations and the differences between literary Welsh and colloquial speech. I found it interesting and learnt a lot of vocabulary ...

156

Some of the evacuated teachers were, of course, themselves of Welsh origin, some were fluent Welsh speakers and had perhaps even volunteered for evacuation duties for this reason. Even quite a number of evacuated children - especially 'private' evacuees - had relatives in North Wales and were also at least familiar with the language. Historically, there were strong ties between Wales and Merseyside - many Welsh people had 'emigrated' there: Wallasey in fact means 'the island of the Welsh'. Liverpool had a Welsh quarter around the 'Flower' streets off Stanley Road[149] and there were Welsh places of worship in Windsor Street (the Presbyterian Church of Wales) and Princes Road, which housed what one historian calls 'the cathedral of Welsh Calvinistic Methodism'![150] There had even been eisteddfodau held on Merseyside in the past - in Widnes, but also, since the 1920s, in Lewis's Department Store![151] Indeed, according to the *Wallasey News*, 18 March 1939, there had been a strong possibility that the 1941 Royal National Eisteddfod might be held in Wallasey Borough. So, for some at least, the Welsh language was perhaps not so strange - but for the majority it was, like so many other aspects of evacuation, a whole new experience.

Whilst the *Welsh Nationalist* continued its vitriolic attack, against seemingly complacent compatriots as well as *'the English evacuees whose skins Welsh people consider more worth saving than their own language'*,[152] there was growing evidence to discredit its gloomy forecasts. In March 1940, Flintshire's Director of Education reported that

> *...not only has the presence of evacuees not been a menace to the Welsh language and culture but in addition to giving the evacuees new knowledge which they appear to value, it has been an actual stimulus to the local children in their study of the language and its culture, since they (as well as their parents on their behalf) do not care to take up an inferior position in a matter which so initimately concerns their national status and their national pride.*[153]

Even in Caernarvonshire, heart of Welsh Nationalism, the Director of Education conceded that the danger to Welsh culture from evacuees had been grossly exaggerated if, indeed, it existed at all. Addressing the Llandudno Cymrodorion Society he reported that the evacuated children seemed anxious to learn Welsh and were rapidly absorbing Welsh culture. Within twelve months of the start of evacuation the local Education Committee had been told that *'some of the evacuees show an appreciable ability to converse in Welsh and it is regrettable that no scheme has been adopted for giving all of them simple*

157

lessons in the language and its literature during school hours'.[154] As one Liverpool Schools Inspector later recalled:

> *Linguistic problems arose in the bilingual areas when small numbers of school children had to be absorbed in to Caernarvon schools. On the other hand, many of the Liverpool children learnt Welsh very quickly. When a second batch of evacuees reached the Borough of Caernarvon, some of the first batch of evacuees had to be stopped from chasing the others round the town calling them uncomplimentary names in Welsh!*[155]

As early as February 1940 a BBC Broadcasting Van had been travelling around the Caernarvon area recording evacuees. This tour, it was reported in the *North Wales Chronicle 'has dispelled the Jeremiads of some ardent Welsh people who feared Welsh culture would suffer as a result of the advent of English children. The contrary has taken place. English children are learning Welsh ... attending Welsh places of worship and Bands of Hope.'*

Elsie Carvell remembers her very first trip to a Welsh place of worship. *'What are they saying?'* she asked her hosts eagerly, and was told, *'They're saying "God bless all the little English children."'* It was indeed often in church or chapel that the children picked up their first smatterings of Welsh - some under sufferance, like Mrs Williams who remembers *'I had to stand straight and try and recite something in Chapel - and I hated it!'* Others, like Joan Brumfitt, were spurred on by the promise of a shiny penny as reward for mastering 'Duw cariad yw' (God is Love). Soon English children were winning prizes for reading whole passages of the Bible in Welsh - feats that even won them the grudging admiration of local children, such as the small Welsh boy who agreed that English could be used in a game of marbles because his playmate had recited a Welsh verse in chapel![156] Before long, English evacuees were even competing successfully against native Welsh children at local eisteddfodau. Dorothy Formston remembers:

> *I was very happy there [Criccieth] and learnt to speak Welsh. There was an eisteddfod with about 80 children taking part and 'Anti Nel' taught me how to recite in Welsh using the right expression ... I won and was very proud!*

Similarly, Ellen Baylis, teacher in charge of a group of Birkenhead children in the little village of Llangwril, recalls with great satisfaction that *'Lilian, who was probably about 8 or 9 then, actually won first prize for sight reading a passage*

158

from the Welsh Bible at a local eisteddfod.' On 8 April 1941, the *Liverpool Daily Post* proudly reported further evacuee successes - this time at the eisteddfod held by the Nevin and District Sunday School Union:

> *An outstanding feature was the success of a party of evacuee children from Anfield, Liverpool, who are attending the Welsh Presbyterian School at Edern. They beat a Welsh party from Nevin in a party-recitation competition!*

In September 1941 several English children took part in the BBC's 'Welsh Children's Hour' and revealed *'a remarkable proficiency in the language'*. The children involved had been living in Merionethshire and Anglesey for periods varying from two years to only twelve months *'yet the majority of them spoke Welsh like natives. They sang, recited and conversed without the slightest embarrassment.'* [157]

Kenneth McGunigle and his brother spent most of the war in the little village of Carmel, outside Caernarvon:

> *Fred and I got good at the Welsh language. Just before we came home we were rehearsing Welsh poetry for the local eisteddfod. Singing with the church choir was good too. Even now when they play Welsh songs I like to join in, especially when Welsh choirs are on the telly.*

Despite all the evidence to the contrary, the Welsh Nationalist Party, while conceding that their stand was not popular even among Welsh people, continued to oppose the Evacuation Scheme and to claim it had 'concrete evidence' that the presence of English evacuees was 'harmful to the Welsh way of life'. Those who took a more positive view noted that Welsh children, particularly in remote rural areas had become less self-conscious and more confident in their use of English, though where an element of 'scouse' crept in this was not always appreciated! As Caernarvonshire's Organiser of Infants' Schoolwork and Language observed:

> *Unfortunately, some of our children are copying certain inaccuracies of speech which have been brought into reception areas and heads say that new grammatical mistakes are occuring in written work ... more opportunities must be given for oral speech training practice. This should go a long way to check a habit which might do harm to Welsh children anxious to be proficient in English - a disturbing factor in their lives since the advent of the evacuees.* [158]

Some still maintain that in certain areas the Welsh language did suffer from the necessity of speaking English when evacuees were present. Figures show that 909,261 people claimed to be Welsh-speakers in 1931 but only 714,686 in 1951.[159] But it is almost impossible to calculate the effect of evacuation alone on the language when there were so many additional influences at work during the war: many Welsh girls left to find war work in English factories and young Welsh men joined the Forces - both groups would have to have spoken English; then there was the presence in Wales of a host of other visitors besides evacuees - not least the GIs.

As for the English evacuee children, they'd often proved themselves willing and able to learn Welsh and to take part in the country's cultural activities. Those returning home with a heavy Welsh accent were teased by friends who hadn't been away, but those who could actually speak the strange foreign language often found themselves the centre of attention. As Mrs Hughes relates: *'After nearly two years we finally returned, speaking fluent Welsh, which was a source of great entertainment for the local children who had stayed behind.'* Many evacuees remained in Wales after the war, continued their use of the language, and acquired an intense loyalty for their new land. But for those who returned, little seems to have been done to help retain the interest in Wales that evacuation had aroused. Ironically, it was from Merseyside itself that, in December 1944, an appeal was made for the names and addresses of those who had learned Welsh during their time as evacuees so that efforts could be made to sustain their pursuit of the language. If only some of the most ardent nationalists had viewed their enforced 'entertainment' of so many visitors in a more positive light, as numerous Welsh householders had done, who knows what the outcome may have been?

NOTES

[1] *Sunday Pictorial* 24 Sept 1939, see Liverpool RO Newscuttings HF 301 13EVA
[2] *Liverpool Daily Post,* 21 Sept 1939
[3] see Sissons, *Planning ARP in Liverpool,* p.136
[4] quoted in Sissons, ibid
[5] Later, the Liverpool University Survey showed that 17% had arrived verminous; 11% both dirty and verminous (from a sample of 685 children in 3 different reception areas).
[6] Article by R.I. Aaron, Guild Annual, July 1940
[7] See Wrexham MO's report, *Wrexham Advertiser and Star,* 29 Sept 1939; report in *North Wales Chronicle,* 16 Feb 1940; Penmaenmawr UDC Health Committee Minutes 1932-41; Ceiriog RDC Minutes 1939-42, Welfare Worker's report 21 Nov 1939, Ruthin RDC Minute Book 1939-44, Ruthin Borough Council 'Agendae, Minutes & Reports' No.60
[8] Letter from Emyr Owen, cited by P E Owen [PhD Thesis, ref UCNW 15234]
[9] See *The Lancet,* 12 August 1944, article by Anderson, Jeffrey & Pai, cited in Martin Parsons, *I'll Take That One,* p.194
[10] As explained in, *Our Towns,* produced in1943 by the Women's Group on Public Welfare.
[11] Ceiriog RDC Minutes 1939-42, 21 November 1939
[12] London County Council, for example, had made studies of the problem in 1919 and 1934, see Titmuss, op cit. p123
[13] Published in 1940 as *Our Wartime Guests. Opportunity or Menace?*
[14] Author's interview with A M Jones, 13 October 1975
[15] *Our Wartime Guests,* p.20
[16] Ruthin BC 'Minutes, Agendae & Reports', No.61, 21 January 1941
[17] Quoted in *The Evacuation: the true story,* M. Parsons & P. Starnes, p.116
[18] Anna Freud & Dorothy Burlingham, *Children in Wartime* (1940) see Ruth Inglis, *The Children's War,* p.154
[19] See Bob Holman, *The Evacuation: A Very British Revolution,* p.88
[20] *The Health of the School Child* in 1938 showed routine medical inspections had uncovered the following steady increase in skin diseases: 9.4 per 100 examined in 1936, 9.7 in 1937, 10.5 in 1938.
[21] Portmadoc UDC Health Committee Minutes, report 27 October 1941
[22] Liverpool School Medical Service Reports 1938, 1943, cited P. Ayers, *Women at War* p.42
[23] Caernarvon BC Minutes, Special Evacuation Committee, 26 Oct 1942
[24] Caernarvon BC Minutes, Health Committee, 19 Nov 1941, D1/763
[25] Portmadoc UDC Minutes 1938-42, letter from Mrs McEwan 13 Oct 1942
[26] Menai Bridge UDC Minutes, 10 Feb 1942
[27] Buckley UDC Minutes 1940-45, Sanitary & Highways Committee, 15 June 1943
[28] Bryan Blades, op cit, p. 419
[29] Extract from Lillian Evans, *Yesterday's Children,* cited Parsons, *I'll Take That One,* p.14
[30] For the work of Dr Mellanby and other wartime medical research into scabies and lice - see Jill Wallis, *Valiant FOR Peace: A History of the Fellowship of Reconciliation,* pp.137-9
[31] Penmaenmawr file 'MoH Evacuation - Welsh Bd of Health', report May 1941
[32] Reported in the *Wrexham Advertiser and Star,* 29 Sept 1939
[33] Anglesey CC, Committee on Maternity and Child Welfare, 28 Sept 1939
[34] Flints.CC, Minutes of Meetings 1939-41, FC/1/41, p.1287
[35] Caerns. CC, Meeting of Establishment Committee, 27 May 1941
[36] Penmaenmawr UDC file 'Evacuation MoH circulars etc'
[37] Cwm-y-Glo School logbook, 3 Feb 1944; Birkenhead Civil Defence Committee (B/025/1) also

records the deaths of June Bennett (at Corwen, Jan.1942), Derek Lee (Portmadoc, March 1942), Joan Gallantry (Welshpool, June 1943) - causes unspecified. Parents of children who died whilst evacuated were usually awarded a grant of £6-£12 to cover funeral costs.

[38] See Birkenhead Education Committee Minutes, 20 Dec 1939

[39] Printed in the *North Wales Chronicle*, 8 September 1939

[40] Extract from *Liverpool Women at War*, p.156

[41] Extract from a letter at Dolgellau RO (Z/M/735/1)

[42] Caernarvon BC Minutes, Housing & Health Committee, 24 Oct 1939 D1/763; Nant Conway RDC Evac File, Letter from MO to Evan Williams, 17 May 1940

[43] Extract from 'Wales at War' supplement

[44] One evacuee child is alleged to have actually starved to death in Welshpool but I have not yet been able to find further details of this.

[45] See Joan Boyce, *Pillowslips and Gas Masks*, p.39

[46] A copy of this circular is contained in Penllyn RDC file '1939 Evacuation Arrangements'

[47] Extract from *Liverpool Women at War*, p.26

[48] Extract from *Welsh Rarebits*

[49] Titmuss, *Problems of Social Policy* p.118

[50] Ibid. p.120

[51] It had been agreed that the PA Committee would deal with their own cases and also those of the Unemployment Assistance and Unemployment Insurance Boards; cases of hardship not involving any of these three Boards fell to the Emergency Clothing Committee. All the authorities were to co-operate in investigating claims and teachers were to certify need.

[52] Liverpool City Council Proceedings, Report of PA Committee 28 Nov-27 Dec 1939

[53] Liverpool City Council PA Committee Report, as above

[54] *Welsh Rarebits*, p.347

[55] Letter from Dorothy Jacob, WVS Organiser, Birkenhead (Caern.Boro. Evac Papers, Box 5)

[56] Colwyn Bay Council of Social Service, Minutes 8 Feb 1940, DD/DM/121/1

[57] Mrs Davies to Mrs Lake, 15 Feb 1940, Caern. Boro, Evac Box 3

[58] *Our Wartime Guests*

[59] Ceiriog RDC Minute Book 1942-47, Welfare Report 16 January 1945

[60] Caernarvon Borough Evac Papers , Box 1

[61] Letter from R.T.Griffiths to billeting officers, 6 January 1941. Gwyrfai RDC File 'List of Evacuee Arrivals 1941', see also Ruthin BC 'Minutes, Agendae & Reports', No.61, Jan 1941

[62] see Caernarvon Borough Evacuation Papers, Box 3

[63] Caernarvon Borough, Evac Papers, Box 3; Conway Boro, Evac Cttee Minutes, 13 May 1942.

[64] In Wrexham for example, see *A Record of War Service - Wrexham RDC*, p.101

[65] Titmuss, op cit p.375

[66] Connah's Quay UDC, Minutes of Evacuation Committee, 8 Sept 1939 (Hawarden RO)

[67] See Holywell RDC Minute Book, no.36, Evac Committee, 10 June 1942

[68] *The Education of Evacuated Children*, E O Humphreys, 27 Nov 1939, (UCNW V4594)

[69] See for example, the *Birkenhead Advertiser* 21 October 1939

[70] See Wrexham Advertiser and Star, 15 Sept 1939; Flints CC Clerk's Dept, file Evac Minutes, letter Ll. Jones to J. Bevan Evans, 6 Sept 1939

[71] Report by E.O.Humphreys, as above

[72] See for example protests from Penmaenmawr, Llanfairfechan and Bethesda, reported in the *North Wales Chronicle*, 8 Jan 1940, 8 April 1941

[73] Hirael Infants, 22 Sept 1939; Bethesda (Carneddi Infants Council), 18 & 25 Sept 1939; Caernarvon British School, 19 Feb 1940 (all Caernarvonshire)

[74] See St Francis Xavier's College Magazine, 1940, p. 50
[75] Reported in *North Wales Chronicle*, 25 October 1940
[76] Personal notes of William Rowlands, headmaster Portmadoc School, cited P E Owen, p.280
[77] See *Oars and Sails,* 'Reminiscences of the 1940s'
[78] County Education Minutes, 24 Nov 1950, cited P E Owen
[79] *Our Evacuee*, p.45
[80] See Caernarvonshire County Herb Committee records 1942-46 (UCNW Gen.IX, 8733 & 8734)
[81] see Reg Chambers Jones, *Bless 'Em All*, p.12
[82] Herb Committee, as above (8734)
[83] *Welsh Rarebits*
[84] See log book of Prince Rupert Evacuee Group (in Bronyfoel, Caerns.) Nov 1941, Feb 1942
[85] Caernarvon people had been convinced that there were enemy agents within when they woke one morning in August 1940 to find their streets littered with copies of a speech by Hitler. Later it emerged that these had been distributed by the Luftwaffe but at the time it was felt they were too bulky to have been dropped from planes. See *Daily Post* 'Wales at War' supplement, 25 April 1989.
[86] See Merionetheshire Education Committee Minute Book 1939-40, A/1/6
[87] *Caernarvon and Denbigh Herald*, 3 Nov 1939 'Notes of the Week'.
[88] Caernarvon Borough Council Minutes, 5 March 1940
[89] Portmadoc UDC, Special Committee Minutes, 8 Sept 1939 (Caernarfon RO)
[90] See *Liverpool Blue Coat School Past and Present 1708-1995*, ed. P.Healey
[91] *Welsh Rarebits*
[92] 'Memo & Minute Book', headteacher Groeslan Churchroom (Caerns E.A.9)
[93] Quoted in *Our Evacuee*, p.45
[94] Letters from J.C. Andrews and R.T. Davies, Nov 1939, Denbs CC File 8/1
[95] Report on Conference of Education Officials, 30 Apr 1940 (Transferred to Hawarden RO)
[96] Denbigh (Love Lane) Central School Log Book 1938-46, ED/LB/24/8
[97] Flints Educ Cttee, School Medical Service Sub-Cttee, 13 Nov 1940, FC/1/41
[98] Log Book 'Gwyrfai "A" Groeslon' (Caerns) E.A.9
[99] Bronyfoel Council School records (Caerns) EA/9/5
[100] Extract from the *Daily Post* supplement, 'Wales at War', 25 Apr 1989, p.29
[101] Leah Manning, *A Life for Education*, p.150
[102] *Cambrian News* Supplement, 'Homefront Heroes', 1989
[103] *North Wales Chronicle*, 26 July 1940; For more on Miss Crosbie, see Sinclair, *Welsh Scouse.*
[104] See Liverpool Blue Coat Brotherly Society Annual Report Sept 1989 (Beaumaris Reunion)
[105] Appendix to *Welsh Rarebits*
[106] Letter from Lascelles, 27 Sept 1960 cited by P E Owen (Appendix 33)
[107] Printed in the *North Wales Chronicle*, 8 September 1939
[108] Ken Blasbery, *Children of the Blitz*, p.6
[109] Extract from *Daily Post* Supplement, 'Wales at War', 25 Apr 1989
[110] Cited in St. Loe Strachey, *Borrowed Children*, p.107
[111] Cited in Julie Craine, 'Evacuation from Liverpool'... unpublished BA thesis.
[112] Bryan Blades in *Welsh Rarebits*, p.450
[113] P E Owen, op. cit.
[114] Ibid, Letter from Vice Principal to P E Owen, 4 November 1960
[115] Caernarfon British School (Boys) Log Book 1941 (Caernarfon RO)
[116] Letter from HMI Inspector, N. Bullock to P E Owen, op cit
[117] Transcript of oral account by Miss Mimi O. Hatton of Plymouth and Porthmadog, talking about

the Porthmadog Evacuee School 1944-45. XM/T/380 (Caernarfon RO)

[118] see Sissons, *Planning ARP in Liverpool*, p.117

[119] Reported in the *Liverpool Daily Post*, 6 December 1939

[120] Reported in the *North Wales Chronicle*, 8 September 1939, 9 Feb 1940

[121] See *Liverpool Daily Post*, 25 October 1940

[122] H C Dent, *Education in Transition*, p.22

[123] Letter from Dr E Thomas, 13 Sept 1960, cited in P E Owen, op cit (UCNW 15234)

[124] Letter from N. Bullock, 11 October 1960, cited in P E Owen op cit

[125] I am grateful to Frank Jagger for relating this tale.

[126] Extract from 'Our War' supplement

[127] Quoted in *Goodnight Children,* p.242

[128] The letter, dated 15 July 1941, was left behind at the farm where the evacuee was billeted after he returned to Tranmere. It is now lodged at Dolgellau Record Office (Z/M/735/1)

[129] W. Brookes Parry to Wm Jones, 24 Jan 1941, Denbs.CC file 35/4 (Ruthin RO)

[130] Interview with the author, 13 October 1975

[131] Padley and Cole, *Evacuation Survey* pp.236-7

[132] Letter to Penmaenmawr UDC from householder, 17 Nov 1939, file 'Ministry of Health - Evac - Welsh Board of Health'

[133] Liverpool Daily Post, 16 Sept 1939, see also letter from N. Bullock, P.E.Owen, op cit

[134] Denbs. CC file 8/1, W Jones to Evan Evans, 13 Nov 1939

[135] John Roberts (Hiraethog RDC) to Wm Jones, 1 March 1940. Denbs CC file 35/4

[136] For example, Cerrig-y-Drudion parish; Llanrwst, Llanfairfechan, and Pwllheli UDCs; Aled, Edeyrnion, Deudraeth, Nant Conway, and Lleyn RDCs, to name but a few.

[137] See Carlton Jackson, *Who Will Take Our Children*, p.47

[138] Letter, Emrys Wynne (Llanrwst) to C F Mott, 26 Apr 1940, Denbs CC file 35/4

[139] Carlton Jackson, p.49

[140] Cited in the *Liverpool Daily Post*, 10 July 1941

[141] Caerns CC held an Emergency Meeting over this, see *Caerns & Denbs Herald*, 10 Nov '39

[142] See *North Wales Chronicle*, 7 Feb & 4 April 1941

[143] Reported in the *North Wales Chronicle*, 6 June 1941

[144] Wrexham RDC Minutes, Welfare Worker's Report, 12 May 1942 (Ruthin RO)

[145] See *A Record of War Service Wrexham RDC*, p.72

[146] Reported in the *North Wales Chronicle*, 12 January 1940

[147] cited in Davies, *A History of Wales*, p. 602

[148] Padley & Cole, *Evacuation Survey*, p. 239

[149] See Peter Aughton, *Liverpool: A People's History* (Carnegie Press, 1990), p.185

[150] D. Ben Rees, *Wales: The Cultural Heritage* (Hesketh, 1980), p.55

[151] *Wallasey News,* 15 April 1939, described the Lewis's Store eisteddfod as 'the 18th annual event'

[152] *Welsh Nationalist*, December 1939

[153] Flintshire Education Committee Minutes, 13 March 1940

[154] See Morgan Humphreys Mss, 28 Nov 1940

[155] N Bullock, cited in Owen op cit

[156] Padley & Cole, *Evacuation Survey*, p.239

[157] *North Wales Chronicle*, 19 September 1941

[158] Miss Thomas's report was quoted in the *North Wales Chronicle* 20 November 1939

[159] Davies, *A History of Wales*, p.644

5 - *Preparing a New Scheme*

By early 1940, the Government had reviewed its original Evacuation Scheme and in February issued all Local Authorities with a copy of its findings (Memo EV8). This contained comments on the 1939 experience as well as details of a new scheme (known as Plan IV) which was to concern itself solely with unaccompanied schoolchildren and was to come into force only if and when air raids began. Aspects of the new plan were designed to avoid earlier pitfalls: parents again had to register children but now had to also give a written undertaking that they would not bring them home whilst the scheme was still in progress. At the reception end, children were to be given a medical examination before being allocated accommodation and hostels would take those not immediately suitable for billeting on householders.

Memo EV8 also gave suggestions for *'the mobilisation of billeting resources and the stimulation of the community effort'*. Recognising the fact that the first evacuation had undermined much of the goodwill of host families, reception areas were advised to leaflet householders, inviting them *'to enter their names on a roll as being willing when called upon to share with their neighbours in the work of receiving and caring for children sent to the district under the Government Evacuation Scheme'*. Anyone who failed to respond was to receive a personal visit from a local official, but if sufficient voluntary accommodation was not forthcoming, compulsory powers were again to be available.

As with the first scheme, it was recommended that county conferences be held to allow representatives from the evacuating and receiving authorities to discuss arrangements; a series of these was held across North Wales in March 1940. By this time some Welsh officials had already had one meeting with their Merseyside counterparts - and the new scheme had come in for heavy criticism. Reception areas were worried about school accommodation and about complications likely to arise where some districts had been allocated to more than one evacuating authority. Overriding all, however, was the feeling that allocations had been made without regard to the facts; the Government had been far too high-handed and the first step should clearly have been for the Ministry to confer with the reception authorities themselves.[1]

These concerns were voiced in no uncertain terms at the county meetings. In Denbighshire the Clerk to the Council fully endorsed the protests already being made, exclaiming, in high dudgeon, that *'the Ministry and Liverpool are taking the County Council and the Local Authorities too much for granted and will one day find that it is the Reception authorities who count in regard to Evacuation, even more than the Evacuation authorities'* ! Flintshire officials meeting in Mold also pointed to the lack of consultation over quotas, adding that only the reception areas themselves were aware of all the changes that had occurred in their districts since the outbreak of the war.[2] In response, Dr D.J. Roberts, of the Welsh Board of Health, reminded delegates that the original census had revealed sufficient accommodation far in excess of that required not only for those evacuees still left but for the additional newly allocated quotas. He seems to have missed the point. Quite simply, the situation was now very different. In fact, of the eight authorities represented at the Flintshire conference, six claimed they would not be able to accommodate the numbers allocated to them under Plan IV due to the presence in their districts of large numbers of troops, war workers and other visitors.

Leaving aside the vexed numbers issue, the Conferences proceeded to discuss other aspects of the new scheme. The Medical Officer of the Welsh Board of Health was at pains to emphasise to all receiving areas that any future evacuation would include far greater medical safeguards - all the children would be examined before departure and again on arrival; those who were wholly unfit would be excluded from the scheme. The Liverpool authorities, no doubt stung by earlier criticism, had already put in place a system of medical checks on children who were about to be evacuated. With all the talk of evacuees returning home in the autumn of 1939, it isn't always appreciated that there were still parties being dispatched to reception areas at this time. Thus on 4 October, in a 'Review of ARP work', Liverpool City Council reported:

> *A supplementary registration of schoolchildren ordered by the Ministry of Health resulted in 1700 names being registered. Evacuation of these is now proceeding… Future evacuations will, of course, be dealt with under more favourable conditions [than in September], and parties of children, about 1500 in number, were last week carefully inspected and treated before they were sent away.*[3]

This was perhaps the most vital aspect of any new plan in view of the outcry that had accompanied the arrival of evacuees in 1939. Indeed, Denbighshire's Clerk announced that:

> *It must be clearly understood that any case of lack of cleanliness or disease found on inspection will not be accepted by a reception authority, and*

166

arrangements must be made by the evacuating authorities for the return to Liverpool of such children. The Reception Authorities will not accept children in the state many Liverpool children were in on the last occasion.[4]

Will you share a small burden with your neighbour?

This little girl is billeted with Mrs. Brown. She is one of 400,000 children now safely in the country. She came last September with a label nearly as big as herself, a fugitive from a danger zone.

There were difficulties at first. It took her quite a while to pick up the ways of country folk. But when she settled in, Mrs. Brown grew quite fond of her. Mrs. Brown will miss her when she goes.

But go she must. Mrs. Brown's circumstances have changed. Just as the circumstances of many other foster-parents are changing. They need someone to take over their small burdens.

These children must not go back to the cities. There may be raids at any moment. New billeting volunteers are badly needed. Will you enrol your name for this splendid national service? You may be asked to take a child now, or your name may be kept against the time when raids make a second evacuation necessary.

The Minister of Health, who has been entrusted by the Government with the conduct of evacuation, asks you urgently to join the Roll of those who are willing to receive children. Please apply to your local Council.

In the spring of 1940 newspapers in North Wales featured a series of government notices designed to persuade householders to join in a new evacuation scheme. (North Wales Chronicle, April 1940.

I WISH TO MARK, BY THIS PERSONAL MESSAGE, my appreciation of the service you have rendered to your Country in 1939.

In the early days of the War you opened your door to strangers who were in need of shelter, & offered to share your home with them.

I know that to this unselfish task you have sacrificed much of your own comfort, & that it could not have been achieved without the loyal co-operation of all in your household.

By your sympathy you have earned the gratitude of those to whom you have shown hospitality. & by your readiness to serve you have helped the State in a work of great value —

Elizabeth R

The government expressed its thanks to Mrs Bert Morris and to other householders in North Wales - and hoped that more would volunteer to give evacuees a home! (Courtesy Mrs I.B.Pierce)

Such a statement, of course, underlines the artificial, or 'phoney', conditions under which these plans were being formulated. It was a strange scheme which could be devised in response to a nightmare scenario of enemy bombardment, killing and destruction - and which yet proposed to send children back into this nightmare if they arrived in the countryside in an unclean state! Nevertheless, if the scheme was to be 'sold' to householders, and parents, they would need to be convinced that some of their unsavoury experiences of the first evacuation would not be repeated in the second. With this in mind, the government instigated a huge campaign designed both to convince parents in evacuation areas to send their children away, and householders in reception areas to take these children in.

On 15 February 1940 a nationwide appeal was broadcast by Walter Elliot, leaflets were distributed and the local press carried a series of large notices depicting children playing serenely in rural surroundings with menacing bombers just visible on the horizon - all aimed at persuading housewives to join the Roll of those willing to receive evacuees. Even the pulpit was used in some areas to urge members of the congregation to offer their help.[5] As a further 'sweetener', host families who had taken part in the 1939 scheme were presented with certificates bearing a personal message of thanks from the Queen.

Local WVS groups also met to discuss the new scheme, particularly to prepare for likely clothing requirements - the Caernarvonshire group, for example, recognised the need to stockpile clothing as it was now known that the county had been allocated 3,000 children from some of the poorer districts of Liverpool. The WVS ladies were no doubt greatly encouraged in their work by a visit from the founder of their organisation, the Marchioness of Reading. Addressing an audience at Bangor University in January 1940, the Marchioness also praised the contribution of North Wales householders: *'I have been round this district to see what you have done. I don't throw many bouquets'*, she added, *'but I think what you have done here is simply stupendous.'* She went on to say that when tributes were paid after the war she hoped the small householders in the reception areas with no maids would be remembered - it was the women in these areas, she said, who had first gone 'over the top' in this war![6] But could they be persuaded to go over the top again?

A Ministry of Information film, *Westward Ho!*, was issued in 1940; painting a rosy picture of all aspects of evacuation, it was blatantly designed to persuade city parents to sign up to the new scheme. In Merseyside parents were 'given a peep into the life of their children evacuated to North Wales' in a feature programme broadcast by the Home Service in February 1940. This, too, emphasised the beneficial aspects of evacuation. Recordings had been taken of the children, some now speaking in Welsh, in schoolrooms, homes and recreational centres. Miss J. Crosbie, Head of Liverpool's Salisbury Street Infants, who compered the programme said:

> *When we arrived in Wales last September many of the children were pale, tired and not very healthy. Today, most of them are bonny, healthy and content. This is the miracle that is going on all over North Wales. To the children it seems that place where dreams and fairy tales come true ...* [7]

Local newspapers, scotching rumours that a future evacuation would be compulsory, explained that *registered* children would this time be sent away in school parties in the event of air raids actually taking place. Anyone wondering what kind of a reception they might now expect, particularly those who'd 'upped and left' the first time round, was blandly reassured that *'if bombs began to fall the grievances that have arisen out of the original evacuation experiences would be quickly forgotten and householders would willingly take evacuees again'.* [8] This was not altogether contradicted by a report issued in early March which showed 38% of hosts had approved unconditionally of the first evacuation scheme, 30% had approved under certain conditions, and only 32% had actually thought the scheme a failure. [9]

Yet despite all this effort, the response to the plans, from both sides, was disappointing. In Caernarvon Borough, only 116 householders had responded to the appeal for billets by May 1940 - and of these, 23 said they already had evacuees, 48 refused outright, and just 45 volunteered their services. Similarly in Flint Borough, of 3,500 letters issued, only 60 replies had been received by the end of April, with a meagre 51 offers of accommodation; only 45 of the 2,500 letters issued in Denbigh Borough brought a reply. [10] A second series of conferences held throughout North Wales in May showed that this lack of enthusiasm was widespread.

The attempts of the evacuation authorities to sell the new scheme were also met with apathy. But parents were receiving conflicting messages: one week papers carried headlines about the re-opening of schools - FIFTY CITY SCHOOLS TO OPEN ON MONDAY blazened the *Liverpool Daily Post* (8 February 1940) - and the next week, about PLANS FOR RE-EVACUATION *(Daily Post*, 15 February 1940). The Minister of Education was clearly aware of the confusion: *'Does this determination to rebuild education in the evacuation areas mean that*

170

the Government no longer believes in evacuation?' he asked, *'I say most definitely it does not. It is a thousand pities that these children are not in reception areas, and it may well prove to be a tragedy. It may be that we will have some warning before a general assault by Germany. But equally it may be that we will not.'* The Minister underlined this approach in an address at the opening of an extension to a school in Wrexham. While reaffirming Government commitment to the education of children in the evacuation areas he again spoke of the necessity of evacuation:

> *To remove children from the nervous strain as well as the actual danger of bombing is not an act of cowardice. Everything points to the desirability of their removal ... As a nation we are going to need them in future, healthy in mind and body, to make good the loss and wastage of this struggle.*[11]

The fact that schools were being rapidly equipped with air raid shelters - not to mention the lack of bombing - clearly undermined attempts to convince parents. Although many hundreds of children were still away, for the most part happily enjoying life as evacuees, these rarely made the news. On the other hand, Liverpool papers did carry details of a court case in late February, where a Hove man was sentenced to six-months hard labour for ill-treating two London evacuees in his care. When the children's mother visited the billet she had found her five- and six-year-old suffering with scabies and impetigo, heads and bodies verminous and covered in bruises.[12] This was hardly a good advertisement for evacuation.

For whatever reason, the new scheme seemed to have little appeal in Merseyside. During the first week in March, the Post Office, acting on behalf of the Government, had distributed 160,000 registration forms to all households in Liverpool's priority areas; in April Liverpool's Director of Education was forced to notify reception areas that they were temporarily suspending detailed arrangements pending guidance from the Ministry - only 5,000 children had been registered, whereas the Government scheme had envisaged a number nearer 30,000! Even this was a slight exaggeration as actually at this time only 4,285 had registered, though by the end of May (no doubt in response to developments in Europe) this number had increased to 9,024.[13] The Birkenhead authorities had fared little better - 18,025 forms had been issued, of which 1,281 had been returned with a request to be registered for evacuation, 1,576 had come back with a definite 'No', and the remainder had produced no response at all.[14]

Despite these set-backs, further conferences were held in May - the government advised that preparations should still be based on the estimated quotas. It was felt that when bombing actually began, many who had not registered would in fact request evacuation. At each of these conferences the morning sessions concentrated on trying to match billeting and education facilities, afternoons were spent sorting out transport and accommodation (many districts still maintaining they could not billet the numbers allocated, certainly not without resort to compulsion). Unlike the first scheme, on this occasion no rations were to be distributed (no more brown carrier bags!) but mothers were expected to provide their children with food for the day and to send their ration books with them, rationing having been introduced in January 1940. The Flintshire authorities were concerned about food supplies and submitted a request to the Food Ministry that shops in reception areas be sufficiently stocked with essential foods to take account of the increased demand which would accompany evacuation.[15] Other detailed provisions concerning detraining, initial reception and distribution of evacuees had also to be arranged, much as in 1939. This usually meant simply re-activating the machinery employed the previous September, which in most areas was thought to have run quite well. There seems to have been no official recognition of the need to avoid the kind of cattle-market approach which had inadvertently caused so much distress to the first evacuees.

All these arrangements for a second evacuation were still being formulated against a 'phoney war' background which no doubt partly accounted for the public's apathetic response. However, within days of the second round of conferences, the war took a turn which rendered Evacuation Plan IV inadequate. The 'twilight war' came to an end as Germany began her long-postponed attack on the West, breaking through to the Low Countries on 10 May 1940. As the German Armies made lightning progress a new danger became apparent: the possibility of an all-out air attack was now augmented by fears of actual invasion. By mid-May, the British Chiefs of Staff, assuming French collapse inevitable, affirmed that there were three ways in which Germany could defeat Britain: unrestricted air attack aimed at breaking morale; starvation through attack on our shipping and ports; and occupation following invasion.[16]

As far as evacuation was concerned, this turn of events, hastened by news from Dunkirk, produced a new priority - the removal of several thousand children from the now-vulnerable coastal areas of Kent and East Anglia. Over a two-week period in May and June some 25,000 children were moved from the coastal zone. They were mainly housed in South Wales but some, like Maureen

Weller, did end up in the North and many other 'unofficial' evacuees flocked there under their own steam. Nor was it only civilians who were relocated to North Wales at this time. One Anglesey Billeting Officer remembers the arrival of some soldiers from the Middlesex Regiment who had travelled directly to Holyhead from Dunkirk. He recalled:

We offered to put up one group of men ourselves. They hadn't slept for 48 hours - their clothes were still full of sand from the Dunkirk beaches. It fell out all over the bedroom floor.[17]

With the news that the French front was disintegrating it was decided to operate a hurriedly re-cast version of Plan IV for London and Thameside, incidentally reversing the decision that a new evacuation should only take place in response to actual air attack. Each week during July and August a 'trickle' scheme (known as Plan V) took away parties of schoolchildren, whilst mothers with younger children were also encouraged to take themselves away from the danger area by use of a 'Special Scheme'. This was a form of assisted private evacuation, offering free travel vouchers and billeting certificates to London mothers who had found their own accommodation in reception areas. In time this scheme would be extended to other areas of the country and would give the evacuation scheme much more flexibility.

Not surprisingly, all these developments forced the government to inform local authorities that Plan IV had been scrapped and by early July they were hearing of yet another scheme - Plan VI, or to be precise, Plan VIA (for children already registered) and Plans VIB and VIC (for children whose parents belatedly wished their children to be evacuated). These plans were to operate consecutively rather than simultaneously, the object being *'to secure the maximum amount of elasticity in their working, to enable any particular section to operate separately, and to secure as equitable a distribution as possible between the receiving authorities'.*[18]

Although reception authorities were bemused by all the chopping and changing of plans, there were remarkably few complaints when officials were faced with a new, this time even more complicated, set of figures. For most, the overall statistics were not greatly different, though the continued lack of consultation was annoying. But there was a loud outcry from areas whose total allocation under the three new plans was considerably higher than under Plan IV. Deudraeth RDC for example responded to the new allocations with the comment that: *'It will be definitely clear that plans C and B will be absolutely*

173

out of the question after plan A is put into operation. I have not the slightest doubt that owing to the recent influx in the district, very little, if any, room will be available.' Although there were only 155 official evacuees in the Deudraeth area, at least 1,000 people had entered the district as private evacuees during the preceding few weeks. Similarly in Betws-y-Coed there were also approaching 1,000 unofficial evacuees, in addition to the 230 official ones still present. By November 1940, the population of Pwllheli had risen from a peacetime figure of 3,599 to close on 6,000.[19]

Correspondence from local authorities in all parts of North Wales at this time indicates the presence of large numbers of unofficial evacuees. To some extent, the government was a victim of the success of its own 'Special scheme'. As Holyhead's Billeting Officer reported:

> *During August and September there has been a constant stream of evacuees arriving in the town, principally from London and the East Coast. This movement is individual and is the subject of a special Government scheme which allows certain classes of persons to make private arrangements for accommodation in reception areas and also qualify the person for payment of billeting allowance.*[20]

The steady exodus from the south which had begun with the invasion scare, of course assumed new proportions with the onset of the Battle of Britain over London. As far as North Wales was concerned, there were now also bombing raids taking place much closer to home. In the early summer of 1940, Grand Admiral Raeder, Commander-in-Chief of the German Navy, implored Hitler to authorise a concentrated air attack on Liverpool:

> *He felt that destruction of this vital port would bring Britain to its knees and advised Hitler that after the destruction of Liverpool the British people would listen to a peace offer without Germany having to resort to an invasion of the British Isles.*[21]

Fortunately for Liverpool, Raeder's advice was not heeded at the time - almost a year was to pass before the heaviest of the raids, but Merseyside was subjected to some enemy bombing from as early as July 1940. On 29 July a bomb landed on the Wirral, dropping harmlessly in fields around an area ironically designated for receiving evacuees! Ten days later, 6 high explosive bombs fell on Birkenhead, and Merseyside recorded its first fatality when one of these bombs took the life of a maid working in Prenton. On 10 August, Wallasey was hit by

174

11 bombs, causing 4 deaths and 4 serious injuries. Over the next two and a half weeks 150 enemy aircraft attacked Liverpool, Birkenhead and Wallasey. Amongst the fatalities was a little girl, killed by a direct hit on an Anderson shelter in Liverpool's Dovecot Estate. Two nights later, another two children were killed.[22] In *Children of the Blitz*, Ken Blasbery records:

On Monday 2nd September whilst we were at school, the siren sounded ... we set off for home. We didn't hurry, but played marbles in Stonefield Road with four other boys. When we turned into Shellingford Road we heard the sound of an aeroplane flying low over the houses. Looking up we saw it was a German bomber, then we heard what we thought was the sound of hailstones. It was in fact the sound of machine gun bullets hitting the road around us! We soon ran to safety ...

It seemed not a moment too soon to implement the new evacuation plans, yet for some reason the Government delayed setting in motion the official movement of children from Merseyside and also extending 'Special Scheme' status to the area.[23] The Liverpool authorities were placed in a quandary by this prevarication, as C.F. Mott explained:

Since the intensification of air attack on Liverpool, the number of applications for the evacuation of individual children has increased considerably and it has been considered desirable to take up no further cases officially of individual children except in very special circumstances, in view of the fact that there are some 10,000 children who have been registered for evacuation earlier in the year who are still waiting for the Government instruction to put plan VIA into operation. [24]

The receiving authorities were also growing anxious. At a meeting of Aled Rural District Council on 2 October it was reported that 422 persons had moved into the district since June, 137 of them during the previous fortnight; the council was concerned as they were due to receive 400 Merseyside evacuees under the Government scheme. '*We could have taken 400 fairly comfortably two months ago*', commented Brookes-Parry, Clerk to the Council, '*and we might perhaps be able to take many of them today, but if evacuation does not take place for a month or two it looks to me as if we will not have room for a dozen, let alone 400!*'[25]

In the meantime raids on Merseyside continued to intensify. Although, no doubt for reasons of national security, the newspapers played down the effects of the bombing, the number of casualties and fatalities grew, and certainly included women and children. Birkenhead and Wallasey were particularly badly hit during the first week of November, prompting a visit from the King and Queen. The royal party spent some time in the area on 6 November, looking at the destruction and listening to tales of heroism and of miraculous escapes, offering their sympathy and support before going on to view the situation in Liverpool and Bootle the following day. Spirits in the region seemed remarkably high - a radio programme broadcasting 'How Merseyside Goes To It' when a raid was actually in progress, concluded with a call to London *'If you can keep it up, so can we!'* Yet the continued delay over implementing evacuation began to draw increasing criticism from the press.

The state of the local evacuation scheme was reviewed in the *Liverpool Daily Post* on 7 November 1940. This showed that of 60,000 Liverpool children who had been evacuated in September 1939, about 10,000 were still away; another 5,000 had left the city in September under the scheme allowing mothers with under-5s to take up places in reception areas, accompanied by their school-age children if desired.[26] A further 8,727 were registered 'to be sent away when the Government thought the appropriate time had come'. The report added:

All details for this evacuation have been worked out by the Liverpool education authorities but so far the Government has refused to allow the scheme to proceed. It is understood that the Liverpool authorities have urged that the plan should be put into operation, but so far without success. In the meantime some of the accommodation earmarked has been taken up by private evacuees from London and elsewhere.

Originally only those within the 'priority areas' had been eligible for evacuation but the onset of bombing was now causing concern amongst parents outside the designated zones and Liverpool City Council decided that emergency evacuation provision should be extended to certain cases, regardless of where exactly they lived - namely, to children of families rendered homeless by enemy action, to children with family members who had been killed or injured, and to other persons who had themselves been injured during air raids. As the Government would not agree to extend the scheme in this way, costs were to be borne by Liverpool Corporation, supplemented where possible by voluntary contributions.[27]

November brought further casualties and new tragedies, including a direct hit on the Blackstock tenements, both the flats themselves and the underground shelter. Sadly, in the case of one family caught in the blast, several of the children who died that night had been evacuated once but had returned home a few months earlier. The night of 28/29 November saw the worst disaster yet on Merseyside. At the time, the local press again reported 'Casualties Not Heavy!' but in fact a shelter in Durning Road had suffered a direct hit with horrific consequences.[28] There had been 290 people in the shelter. Eventually some 163 bodies were recovered, a further 96 had been seriously injured; many had been gassed, crushed or burnt to death when a furnace in the basement ruptured and a boiler exploded. Churchill would later describe this incident as *'one of the worst of the entire war'*.[29]

The planned evacuation of Merseyside children away from such terrible sights and dangers was finally put into progress in December 1940. A circular letter, issued by Birkenhead Education Committee explained that this particular scheme, however, was

> *...primarily intended for those registered schoolchildren resident in the evacuable part of the Borough whose parents have regularly submitted them for medical inspection and have signed the undertaking to leave them in the Reception Areas once they are evacuated. The Education Authorities have been asked by the Ministry of Health to make it clear to the Headteachers and parents that the scheme does not constitute a general evacuation scheme as, for example, that set out in Plan VIA of June last. It is an endeavour to assist parents who, unable to make private arrangements for their children, do not wish them to remain any longer in Birkenhead. Consequently, the arrangements under this scheme will not, at the express wish of the Ministry, be broadcast or given publicity outside the schools. Parents of unregistered children should not be refused facilities under this scheme provided they sign the official form of application, undertaking to leave their children in the Reception Areas.* [30]

The plan appears to have been the end-product of repeated pressure from the Merseyside authorities on an oddly reluctant Government. No doubt the parents didn't care whether it was Plan VIA, a Special Scheme or a plan by any other name, just so long as the children could be moved to a place of safety. But it was unfortunate that the go-ahead for the evacuation only came in late December; the fact that the arrangements were timed to operate just five days before Christmas doubtless explains why, despite the continued bombing, the numbers actually leaving were lower than expected and offers of accommodation were also reduced. One billeting officer went so far as to inform the Birkenhead authorities that *'to expect the householders to billet children so near to Christmas will not be at all satisfactory. You will no doubt agree that at this time of the year there are many relatives and friends etc who will have come for a short period and I am afraid we will have much difficulty in finding comfortable accommodation for all the evacuees.'*[31] Responding to criticism from various quarters, the Merseyside authorities retorted that the timing 'was selected by the Ministry of Health who said that the war does not wait for Christmas'. It was inconsiderate of Hitler to have started the war at the height of the summer holiday season - and now it seemed he was going to spoil everyone's Christmas, too!

Notwithstanding these reservations, the evacuation did occur on 20 December and although compulsory billeting notices had to be issued in some North Wales areas, the fact that only a small number of children were involved meant that few problems were encountered. In Bootle, for example, where plans had been made to remove 4,000 children to safety, only 300 actually left. Over the three days, 20, 22 and 23 December, 1,399 children were evacuated from Liverpool. The Reception areas did their best to compensate the children for having to be wrenched from their families at such a time, organising parties and cinema outings, and trying to ensure that all the evacuees, those who'd been there for some time as well as newcomers, received a gift from Santa. Liverpool Education Committee sponsored a big Christmas event in Aberystwyth with evacuees from the surrounding areas - pupils from Anfield (Holy Trinity and Anfield Road) and Everton (Brookfield School and St Saviour's) - being entertained in the Pier Ballroom. Even evacuees confined to Sick Bays didn't miss out on the fun - those at New Park Road Sick Bay, Holyhead, for example, were given a party and received a visit from the billeting officer, A. Maldwyn Jones - on this occasion heavily disguised with a white beard and a big red coat! In Montgomery it was the Mayor himself (A. Reg Jones) who donned a Father Christmas outfit in order to delight the town's evacuees. Nor were the mothers and pre-school children forgotten, as one local paper reported:

> *No fewer than 165 evacuated mothers and children under five years of age were entertained to tea at St Mary's Church Hall ... They had come to Bangor from all parts of the country but mostly from Liverpool and London. The tea party was made possible by the kindness of Bangor residents.*[32]

The movement of children in late December 1940 was in effect the first of the 'Trickle Evacuations' from Merseyside which set the pattern for the operation of the Government's scheme in 1941. Whether or not Plan VI was ever

178

instigated is unclear - certainly there was never a single large movement of children into North Wales over a few days as there had been in 1939 - but some of the elements of the plan were employed in a staggered version which moved groups of children from Merseyside to different parts of the Welsh countryside at monthly intervals throughout the spring of 1941. In May, however, came a serious intensification of bombing over Liverpool and the monthly trickle was replaced by a weekly flow. For the first time since the evacuation scheme had begun to operate, the numbers arriving in North Wales were now actually larger than those expected. Even areas which were not scheduled to receive organised parties found themselves required to accommodate 'panic evacuees' - people who were quite literally fleeing from the bombs. Anglesey's Billeting Officer in May 1941 addressed a letter to all the councils on the island appealing for their co-operation in finding accommodation for those in need. Llangefni's Public Assistance Officer seconded the plea, adding that *'The number of persons to be billeted is indefinite!'*[33]

NOTES

[1] See, e.g., Nant Conway RDC Evacuation file. Report on a Conference in Liverpool. 21Feb.1940.

[2] See Denbs.CC file 15 (Wm Jones's notes); and Flints. file 241/334

[3] City of Liverpool Proceedings of Council 1938-39, Review of ARP work, 4 Oct 1939

[4] Denbs, CC file 15

[5] See *North Wales Chronicle*, 26 July 1940

[6] Reported in the *North Wales Chronicle*, 19 January 1940

[7] Quoted in the *Liverpool Daily Post*, 12 February 1940. The children who took part in the recording came from Salisbury St School (evacuated to Bangor), Netherfield Rd (to Ty'n-y-Maes), Prince Rupert Junior, Whitefield Rd (to Llanllyfni) and Aspen Grove Junior (to Carmel).

[8] *Daily Post*, 15 February 1940

[9] Liverpool University Department of Social Science Evacuation Survey ('Opportunity or Menace?'), extracts of which appeared in the *Daily Post*, 4 March 1940.

[10] See Caernarvon BC , Evac Committee meeting 29 Apr, 1940 (file DI/763); Flint BC Supplementary Scheme (Box 1619), Denbigh BC, Evac Cttee 16 Apr 1940

[11] de la Warr, quoted in the *Daily Post*, 23 February 1940

[12] The case was widely reported, eg *Daily Post* 24 Feb 1940

[13] Liverpool Civil Defence Emergency Committee 26 Mar-22 Apr 1940, 23 Apr-27 May 1940

[14] See Birkenhead Education Committee, 3 Apr 1940

[15] Report of Conference, 30 Apr 1940 (Overton Supplementary Scheme, Transferred Records)

[16] T.H.O'Brien, *Civil Defence*, p.355

[17] Author's interview with A.M.Jones, former Billeting Officer for Holyhead,13 October 1979

[18] Circular 2071 (see Menai Bridge UDC, file Governement Evacuation Scheme 1939-40)

[19] Deudraeth RDC Evacuation Letter Book, 4 Oct 1940; Betws-y-Coed RDC Minute Book, 23 Nov 1939; Pwllheli BC Minute Book, 8 Nov 1940

[20] Holyhead UDC Minute Book, Report of Sanitary Inspector, 5 Nov 1940

[21] Rodney Whitworth, *Merseyside at War*, p.3

[22] For details of the bombing of Merseyside, see Rodney Whitworth, *Merseyside at War*; Richard Whittington-Egan, *The Great Liverpool Blitz*, *Bombers over Merseyside* (Liverpool Daily Post and Echo); *Walking through the Blitz*; Bryan Perrett, *Liverpool: City at War*.

[23] Even as late as Dec 1940, Holywell's Billeting Officer was under the impression that Merseyside was still, curiously, omitted from the special scheme (Holywell RDC File 'Correspondence - Billeting & Evacuation', letter to Welsh Bd of Health 19 Dec 1940) yet some mothers and children do appear to have been removed from Liverpool under this scheme in September 1940.

[24] File as above, letter 27 Sept 1940

[25] Reported in the *Liverpool Daily Post*, 3 October 1940

[26] Although, according to a report in Liverpool's Civil Defence Emergency Committee, 29 Jan 1941, the government only brought Liverpool into the scope of Circular 2170 ('Special Scheme') after the bombing on 20/21 December; in the month following, 2,500 mothers with 5,200 children were evacuated from Liverpool through this scheme.

[27] Liverpool Civil Defence Emergency Committee, 17 Oct 1940, cited in Julie Craine, op. cit.

[28] For a personal account see Bryan Perrett, *Liverpool: A City at War* , p.84

[29] Perrett, *Liverpool: A City at War*, p.84

[30] Extract from Circular Letter, Portmadoc UDC, file Evac Letters No.2. Despite this letter, some areas, like Towyn UDC, clearly regarded this December evacuation as the start of Plan VIA

[31] Deudraeth RDC Evac Letterbook, letter to Dempsey, 17 December 1940

[32] Various reports of Xmas entertainments for evacuees see *North Wales Chronicle*, January 1941

[33] Twrcelyn UDC Minute Book, letter on 'Panic Evacuation', 27 May 1941; Amlwch UDC Evac File 1939-41, letter from PA Committee, 9 May 1941

6- *Fleeing the Bombs*

Exodus

Although it was unfortunate that the evacuation at the end of 1940 was so close to Christmas, in other respects it was very timely, for over the course of three nights, from 20-22 December, a total of 500 bombers hit Merseyside. Norman Ellison describes how by the afternoon of 21 December, *'ALL Liverpool seemed to be on fire'*. Lena Roberts had only just left the entrance to Birkenhead Park Station when a huge explosion rocked the whole area *'and Park Station was no more'*.[1] Many evacuees who had come home from Wales to spend Christmas with their families, were speedily sent back; for other children it proved the final push that their parents had needed and they too were hastily signed up for the first available evacuation train.

Archie Manser was living in 36 Duke Street, New Brighton at the start of the war. He was ten years old and can still remember sitting in the kitchen listening to Mr Chamberlain explaining why 'a state of war' existed between Britain and Germany:

> We went through the 'phoney war' [at home]... As school children we had the bonus of several weeks off school whilst brick and concrete air raid shelters were built in the school yard. We had to call in once a week to get homework, which I can remember scrambling through to get out to play ... My Dad wanted to keep us at home so he converted the middle (dining) room into an air raid shelter which he had also made gas proof ... We were beginning to have one or two sporadic raids, single aircraft dropping the odd stick of bombs ... According to the records, I was in Wallasey for 30 air raids. The next significant thing was the series of raids at Xmas 1940. The excitement had gone and I was getting frightened, The 'Xmas Blitz' as it was called was pretty frightening. We were bombed out of our house in Duke Street, one bomb landing opposite and another next door... These raids culminated in my being evacuated in early January 1941.

Frank Jagger, like many other evacuees, had gone away in 1939, only to be brought back home just in time to experience the bombing!

> ...The Blitz started. Air-raid shelters sprang up in the streets and back yards. We had one in our yard in 58 Peel Street. I wore a 'siren suit' at night and would be snatched up and taken downstairs when the warning sounded. In

our air-raid shelter a canvas bunk on two tubes of conduit had been specially erected for me. My sister, brother, mum and a couple of neighbours sat on benches underneath me. I remember well the whistles followed by explosions. As far as I was concerned, as long as you put your fingers in your ears to deaden the bang everything would be all right ... Then one night as I settled in my bunk a faint drone was noticeable at first, then we had to speak louder ... The whistles started, lots of them this time, followed by a crescendo of explosions. I wasn't scared, I was shaking a bit ... I recall that I never saw an adult scream or panic during one of these raids. The women would just say our lads would get even one day...

One of my friends that night was in the communal shelter in Mersey Park and told me about the exciting happening. His mother had fractured a man's skull with her high-heeled shoe because during the raids he was panicking the children. She had to appear in court for this and was fined 10 shillings. She was alone with four children, her husband in the Cheshire Regiment was taken prisoner at Dunkirk by the Germans. She wasn't in the mood for Hysterical Men.

We emerged this time from our shelter to a changed scene ... we found barriers across our street. Lots of rubble was strewn across the road. The block where my mate's sweet shop stood had received a direct hit. He was at a friends and was alive but his mother was never found. Her iron bed was found on the Birkenhead to Chester railway line over 150 yards away. The raids got worse. Then the King and Queen came to Birkenhead. We all lined up along the New Chester Road ... The Rolls carrying the King and Queen stopped and the Queen got out and spoke to the mothers, telling them the children would soon be moved out of danger. We were immediately on our way again to Wales!

Tony Lloyd had returned from North Wales so that he could take the Liverpool scholarship exam but he, too, was soon packing his bags again, as he explains:

My brother and I were both happily billeted in Ruthin but it was a tricky time because I was about 10 - coming up to doing the scholarship - so we came back home, just in time for the start of the Blitz! I was home a few months, started the new school [Liverpool Collegiate] and then got evacuated again - this time to Bangor.

For some parents, especially those whose children had been desperately unhappy during the first evacuation, the decision to let them stay or make them leave again was terribly difficult. Sometimes they were allowed to stay - with

182

tragic results. Jean McCarthy and her sisters had returned home early in 1940 because the son of the household where they had been staying was moving back home and there was no longer a room available for them; in any case they had not been very happy:

We had to go home, <u>thankfully</u> - I was never so happy to see our parents and siblings again. But what a terribly sad ending. The May Blitz began - my mum grabbed my mentally handicapped oldest sister and shouted to get Doreen and myself up, out of bed, and follow. But my dad never did get the chance - the bombs dropped on our block of flats in Lower Tranmere, opposite the Tanyard and Glue works. The whole of the end block collapsed with all three of us in, two of us in bed and dad in the living room. Three days later my dad was got out safe, then my sister Doreen who was dead, and then myself. I was in Clatterbridge Hospital for six weeks and to this day have problems ... But oh! my lovely dear sister. I miss her even now.

Many Merseyside children joined the ranks of evacuees after a 'close shave' during the Blitz. Archie Manser headed off for North Wales after his home, 36 Duke Street, New Brighton, pictured here, was bombed 21/22 December 1940.

(Photo courtesy Archie Manser)

183

John Manuel similarly remembers that where he had been evacuated *'around the corner, living with a very elderly lady was a lad, Kenny, who didn't stay very long and who, we heard, later lost his life in an air raid'.* Margaret Jones recalls another tragic incident:

> *Six brothers were evacuated to Newtown - all settled well apart from the youngest who missed his mum very much. A friend of the billet family was due to travel to Liverpool and offered to drop the little lad off in Birkenhead to reassure him that his mother was still there. He arranged to pick the boy up to take him back to Newtown the next day. He duly called - only to find the boy and his mother had been killed in an air raid that night.*

For some, luckier ones, it was a near miss which finally persuaded parents that evacuation really was the better option. Jean Cruickshank was playing under the table at her Everton home when her mother nipped out to the market at St John's. When the bomb fell Jean felt the table lift and everthing fall off; her mother had literally just left the market when it received a direct hit. Jean was soon on her way to Wales! Les Glover explains how he came to be an evacuee:

> *I was at home for a lot of the Blitz - we seemed to spend most of our time under the table or under the stairs. One day there was a 'dogfight' just outside - a bullet from the German plane went right through the house, through my bedroom and on to smash the toilet. I think that was when it was decided I'd be better going away!*

It was after a close shave that Bill Turnstall left Liverpool in 1940, with his two brothers and sisters - '*I was twelve-and-a-half years old and a pupil at Holy Trinity School, Liverpool, when a German bomb dropped on the school. Hundreds of children were taken to Brickside Park Railway Station - we didn't know where we were heading for ...*' [2] And for Gordon Nash's family, the bombs were also getting too close for comfort:

> *When the Nazi bombing of Liverpool area took place, some bombs landed in Wallasey, and this changed the lives of many people, including my own family. Every night families would sleep in their garden Anderson air-raid shelters until one night a huge landmine (parachute bomb) landed on the school at the rear of our house and the widespread blast shattered all our windows, brought down ceilings, etc. My mother (father had died the year before) decided to evacuate the family to Oswestry and mother's relations.*

184

Ernest Carvell had been brought home from his billet in 1939 because his mother was lonely. He wasn't evacuated again, but remembers how grim it all was during the Blitz. He was only a lad yet *'helped pull the bodies out when a bomb fell on Clarence Road, near St Joseph's Church. There were 100 soldiers sheltering in a cellar there. It got a direct hit and they were nearly all killed.'* Although a report issued in December 1940 concluded that children were, psychologically, actually less affected than adults by bombing and shelter life,[3] there is no doubt that some found it all terrifying. Bryan Blades, teacher-in-charge of a group of Merseyside evacuees in Caernarvonshire recorded in his memoirs that:

Many of the evacuees now arriving were in an extremely nervous state ... one little girl had a horror of being enclosed within four walls and whenever her mother brought her to school in the vestry in the mornings their arrival was heralded by the child's frantic screaming. For days no amount of persuasion could cajole her into entry - she finally came in in the midst of a game of ring-a-roses which the other children deliberately carried on with within the vestry to take the child's mind off her 'enclosure' indoors.

Ken Blasbery similarly relates in his *Children of the Blitz* how one night his cousin Betty became separated from her parents on their way to the air raid shelter during a particularly heavy attack on Liverpool. All around there were bombs dropping and flares blazing out from gunshots and searchlights. Betty, by then quite hysterical, was found by a warden and safely reunited with her family *'but to this day is terrified of thunder and lightning and has to go into a cupboard or somewhere completely enclosed so that she cannot see the flashes'.*[4]

Whatever initial misgivings parents may have had about evacuation, seeing the fear in their children's faces was now incentive enough for many to sign up to the scheme. After careful thought, Alex Anderson's parents decided this was the best option for him, as he explains:

The almost nightly bombing of Liverpool in the early part of the war did not have a good effect on me. In fact, I was becoming quite badly disturbed and depressed by it. At that time, there was a general move towards the evacuation of the children into the countryside. After much debate and some delay, during which I sought to hurry things on a bit by wrapping up my toys, it was arranged that I should join the exodus.

185

Victoria Massey recalls how after one severe raid when she and her brother had been sobbing with fear, her parents had obviously decided things couldn't go on as they were. The children had lost weight, their faces were pale with big blue rings under their eyes - *'we became aware of some secret and massive campaign in operation. This, of course, was evacuation!'* [5]

Peter Sherlock was only five when the bombing began. He didn't understand very much about what was happening but he has vivid memories of it all:

> *We were less than a   mile from the Dock area, living off Gorsey Lane, Wallasey. The planes were overhead, and dropping bombs, we were on all fours, my dad leading, making our way to the back door, then out to the Anderson shelter which had been built in the back garden. Overhead I could see the barrage balloons in the sky. My dad left us - to help put the fires out caused by the bombs falling on the houses close by.*

A few days later, Peter and his twin brother found themselves boarding a yellow double decker outside their primary school (Poulton Infants), and being whisked off to catch a train at Woodside Station. They had joined the ranks of evacuees just in time to miss the May Blitz.

Marjorie Baker recalls how she and her sister had gone home after the first evacuation but her sister had been so frightened by the bombing that she'd begged to be re-evacuated:

> *We stayed near Oswestry till Christmas but because up to then there had been no air raids, we came home. Later, when the air raids began, Margaret was terrified, so my mother wrote and asked Mrs Watkins [their first billet] if she could take Margaret back [which she did]... By that time I had left school so I spent most nights in Air Raid shelters. It was very bad on 12 March 1941 with a lot of damage and deaths ... ten of us were crowded into my Aunty's shelter in Vincent Street, off Grange Road ... The Air Raid Warden came to tell us to move out because there was an unexploded bomb down our street so they shepherded us all down Grange Rd, stepping over the broken glass as all the shop windows had been blown out, to a Public shelter in Coburg Street. But some rowdy youths were making us feel uncomfortable, saying the next Bomb was for us, so we were moved again to the British Home Stores staff shelter ... After that we were able to go every night about 6.30pm to a shelter underneath the Roxy Cinema on Charing Cross ... you had to go every night even if there was no air raid, to keep your place.*

Beryl Traynor had also come home from her first billet during the 'phoney war' and when the bombing started she, too, was very frightened *especially as mother used to cry when it got close'*. As with many other families, when things got especially bad they would head for a public shelter but, like Marjorie, found the various options less than ideal:

> *... some went every night and got their own speck, so it was no good if you weren't a regular. Some people slept on the stations - there were bunk beds on all the platforms; also in a tunnel built into the rock face at Rock Ferry - I went there once with the family - but it was quite a long walk.*

Production of Anderson shelters had been halted in March 1940 due to a shortage of steel. These, in any case had only been available to the few who owned gardens. Later in the war an indoor shelter, the 'Morrison shelter' was widely distributed and gave protection to people in the relative comfort of their own homes. The 'Morrison', named after the Home Secretary of the day, Herbert Morrison, was in fact designed by a Wallasey man, John Fleetwood Baker. It comprised a sort of cage with a reinforced steel top which could not only withstand the force of a collapsing house but could also serve as a useful bed or table when it was 'all clear'!

In the meantime the authorities sought to build surface shelters to serve groups of residents. Unfortunately many were erected hastily and, due to an apparent misinterpretation of Ministry instructions, with inferior materials. When bombs dropped anywhere near they simply collapsed - inspiring little confidence in their ability to offer protection! Even those that were structurally sound were often insanitary and either poorly ventilated or too draughty. Given a choice, people preferred to opt for basement shelters - but as the Durning Road incident revealed, these sometimes proved terrible death-traps. While some communal shelters provided a comforting camaraderie, others, as the Baker family had found, held 'rowdy youths'. The Merseyside authorities did try to address this problem, setting up a Shelter Welfare Department not only to introduce public health measures but also to act as 'moral guardians'. Behaviour within the shelters was monitored and harsh penalties imposed on anyone causing a disturbance - but arguments and scuffles still broke out from time to time.

With shelter life leaving much to be desired, Beryl Traynor found herself evacuated not once but twice more, on one occasion going privately to stay with family in Belfast - which proved every bit as dangerous as Liverpool! Beryl's parents, like Ken Blasbery's, had toyed with the idea of sending the children abroad - Beryl to stay with relatives in Canada, Ken and his brother to an aunt who'd emigrated in 1927. [6] One Liverpool schoolgirl, Meryl Reed of Rodney Street had been on her way to stay with foster parents in America when the ship she was on was torpedoed and sank. Miraculously, Meryl was rescued and returned to Liverpool but the attack on the '*Volendam*' and the sinking of the '*City of Benares*' caused many parents, and eventually the Government too, to think better of sending the children overseas. [7]

For those families who wished to stay together in Merseyside but were not happy with using air raid shelters, 'trekking' proved a possible alternative. This involved moving out of the danger zones each evening, bedding down in the nearest safe area, and returning to the city at first light the following day. Eileen Byrne should have been evacuated with her school, St Joseph's Primary, but at the critical moment she had gone down with chicken pox so had to stay behind. Her parents ran a pub right in Liverpool city centre:

> *I was very frightened during the Blitz - one of our neighbours was killed, also some people in the tenements opposite (Gerard Crescent). I was a nervous wreck as a child - especially when the sirens went. My brother used to say, 'Don't let the bombs get me, mummy.' I became one of the 'trekkers'. We'd be picked up by a lorry at night and taken to Norris Green - it was countryside then. We slept in a Church Hall. Finally the pub got hit ... we went with mum to North Wales. I slept on a stage in Pensarn Hall with lots of others (and got scabies!) After a while we got a cottage in Abergele...*

Barbara Smith was with her parents in Bootle when the raids were at their height in 1941. Like many other Bootle inhabitants, the Smiths lost their house and they too became trekkers:

> *... We were bombed out of our house, all the windows were blown out, we were in total darkness, our feet were cut and bleeding having to walk through broken glass. We were directed to a local underground smelly shelter, and lived there for three days until they defused a landmine ... The following days we were herded into meat wagons which had no windows, and taken out to Dovecot and slept in a church hall until dawn the following day, then brought back to Bootle.*

Maghull was another popular trekking 'resort'. With a normal population of about 8,000, it had planned to receive perhaps as many as 1800 refugees - one night some 6,000 trekkers arrived, taking over every available church, school and hall, and even a local hospital.[8] Others (as many as 4,500 a night at one stage[9]) made their way to the safety of Huyton Woods:

> *At night, lorry after lorry goes down our road (the only one open at all) with men, women and children, with blankets and pillows, etc. They are taking them up into Huyton Woods to sleep - but they are laughing and cheering all the time ...* [10]

But not everyone in Merseyside was laughing. In fact, especially after the May Blitz, morale was at an all-time low. All sorts of wild rumours were circulating: Liverpool was under martial law; trainloads of nameless corpses were being sent for mass cremation; food riots were taking place; and protestors were marching around Merseyside waving white flags.[11] Liverpool was never actually under martial law though two cordons placed around the city for a while did limit access - but only to help speed up the clearing-up operation. There was also some truth in the talk of 'nameless corpses' - on 13 May 1941 a mass funeral was held at Anfield Cemetery at which 550 (some claim 1000) victims of the May raids were buried in a common grave. There may not have been riots but there was a lot of anger directed at the authorities - perhaps understandable when word on the street had it that some 20,000 had been killed!

The fact of the matter was that in the first week of May 1941 Merseyside had been subjected to seven consecutive nights' bombing with over 800 bombers taking part - one of the most concentrated attacks in the country. It was no wonder that rumours abounded - but Norman Ellison insists that morale on Merseyside, although severely strained, never was broken - *'Liverpool was groggy'* , he claimed, *'but very far from being down and out.'*[12] Bryan Perrett in his book, *Liverpool: A City at War* supports this view. Statistics show that between August 1940 and May 1941 almost 4,000 people were killed on Merseyside (nearly half of these in the May Blitz alone) with a further 7,000 or more seriously injured. Out of a total of 282,000 Merseyside homes, 184,300 were damaged and 10,840 destroyed. Bootle suffered the most, with about 80 per cent of its housing stock affected in some degree; over 25,000 dwellings in Birkenhead were damaged.[13] The people were naturally heartbroken at the loss of their families, their homes and their beloved landmarks. Mrs A. Jones remembers:

> *A friend of mine who was living in quite a poor part of Liverpool told me how once their whole street had had to leave because of an unexploded bomb - she was only a child but she remembers them arriving at William*

*Brown Street and seeing their lovely museum burning, it was a
heartbreaking experience. Then they were hustled on to coaches and
ended up in North Wales - whole families of them.*

With so many needing re-housing and so much damage to the housing stock, the
only real solution was for people to be helped to get out of the region and into
the areas which had been designated for reception of evacuees. The exodus was
not now merely of child evacuees but of entire families - often extended families
at that:

*The area we lived in was badly damaged and an unexploded bomb had
landed outside our aunt's chip-shop in Vescock Street. This was the
deciding factor for the whole extended family to organise themselves and
get away to a safer area. The local coal merchant offered his services and
took thirty-two of our relatives down to Lime Street on the back of one of
his lorries. The station was crowded with people, all trying to evacuate.
There were so many of us that the Station Master had to add an extra
coach on to the North Wales train just for us!*[14]

It also included evacuees from areas that had not originally been recognised as
dangerous, as Joyce Light explains:

*The powers that be were of the opinion that New Ferry was going to be
safe ... Consequently in 1939 no plans were made to evacuate any children
living there. However, after the next 18 months and the May Blitz in
1941, when we who lived near the river watched Liverpool burn, a swift
decision was made to evacuate all children whose parents wanted them out
of the danger, to North Wales.*

There was one final group seeking refuge in North Wales - not exactly evacuees
or 'trekkers' but what came to be known as passengers of the 'Funk Express', a
derogatory term used to describe city workers who fled from Liverpool every
evening to avoid fire-watching duties. Although thousands of men did enrol for
this vital but highly dangerous service, at one time volunteers were in such short
supply that the Government decided to allow women to register. In fact
Britain's first 'Jill Crow' was a Liverpool girl - Miss Dorothy Trumbell, a 21-
year-old laundry worker who'd actually taken up fire-spotting during the
earliest raids of the war but was only in November 1940 allowed to offficially
attend a four-day spotters' course - at Everton Terrace Spotters' School.[15]
Members of Liverpool's Emergency Committee were mildly horrified at this -

prefering to try and track down all the male 'shirkers' (in December 1940 it became compulsory for all men aged 16- 60 to perform up to 48 hours fire-watching duties per month). Alderman Ernest Shennan, leader of Liverpool City Council explained:

> *Since the air raids began, hundreds of men who earn their living in Liverpool have made their homes in the 'safe' areas of North Wales, Cheshire and the upper and coastal parts of Lancashire. Every evening we see them streaming to the stations to pack the 'funk' trains and get out of the city before dark. The practice has become a by-word in Liverpool, but the Emergency Committee is going to stop it.* [16]

No Vacancies

As Llangefni's Billeting Officer had commented in early May 1941, the number of persons seeking billets in North Wales did now appear 'indefinite'. In addition to the official 'trickle' evacuations from Merseyside, from the summer of 1940 people had been pouring into the area from all parts, either as 'private evacuees' or under the 'Special Scheme'. The numbers arriving, from Merseyside and elsewhere, grew as the bombing began - and then intensified.

Shortly after Dunkirk, the Ministry of Food had moved to Colwyn Bay, taking over 2 schools, 35 hotels and other buildings along the coast to house the 5,000 clerks now administering Britain's rationing system. 'Foaming in-the-Mouth' and 'Somewhere-in-Britain', the secret locations of two popular radio shows - *ITMA* and *Hippodrome* - were actually Bangor and Llandudno. *Hippodrome*'s 'canned laughter' was provided by an audience of tax officers (proving they do have a sense of humour!) evacuated to Llandudno, and a not-so-subtle clue was given to *ITMA*s new Welsh home by one of its characters being called Sam Fferffeckan![17] Pam McNaught, who'd been evacuated to Bangor as her father was a master at the Liverpool Collegiate school, remembers the various BBC people around the town - one of the lodgers they took in (to help pay the rent) was a comedian - *'and one day "Mrs Mop" (Dorothy Summers) came to tea!'* In July 1940 some 300 staff from the London office of the Liverpool Victoria Friendly Society took up residence in Bangor, which also provided refuge to staff and students from London University and to a group of Dutch and Belgian diamond-cutters.[18]

A whole variety of war workers were being drafted into the area, some with unusual tasks to perform - such as the men helping to make the Manod Slate mines suitable for housing the country's art treasures from the National Gallery, and others on a highly secret mission on the River Conway, building and testing the Mulberry Harbours which would be so crucial to the D-Day landings.[19] With Liverpool Docks coming increasingly under attack, ammunition ships were transferred from there for unloading to Holyhead and housing had to be found nearby for the dockers. Sea-plane manufacturers Saunders Roe were also relocated to Anglesey, setting up their works in Beaumaris, whilst another aircraft company - the North East Coast Aircraft Company - moved from Newcastle to Llanberis. The wooden three-rigged training ship ' *HMS Conway*', vulnerable on the Mersey, found a new mooring in the Menai Strait - many evacuees recall the cadets coming ashore to stock up on provisions.[20] There were refugees arriving from Poland and the Channel Islands[21] and of course there were army, navy, RAF and sea-rescue personnel in need of billets. Soon overseas troops arrived, too, then the POWs.

Not surprisingly, accommodation in North Wales was now at a premium and at the height of the May Blitz there was serious overcrowding in some parts. Alf Bryce remembers at one time he was billeted in a house in Meliden Road, Prestatyn - '*a Liverpool lady with some children of her own and some vacees - it was six in a bed and a rush to get to the middle berth!*' Similarly A.W. Otter recalls:

> *We were evacuated after the May Blitz and went to 3 different places in Wales. We were away for about eighteen months, a mixture of horrific times and marvellous times. We were literally starving at one of the places - the woman even stole our sweet coupons. One billet was so overcrowded that one of my sisters had to sleep in the bath and another shared a bed with the foster parents!*

As Laura Jones explains, some houses appeared to have 'elastic walls':

> *When the air raids intensified over Birkenhead and Liverpool my parents decided I should go to my nan in Llanrwst ... We lived in Station Road, above a shop and in 1941 nan's youngest daughter was widowed and came from Birmingham with her four-year-old daughter to join us. Nan was shopping in Llanrwst one day and met a cousin she'd not seen for a long time. She and her baby had come from Birkenhead to escape the bombing and were staying in a cottage up the mountainside, but they moved in with us shortly after this meeting - our nan's house had elastic walls!* [22]

If it was a choice between housing child evacuees or taking in some adult war-workers, it was often the children who missed out, as a former headmaster of the Blue Coat School explains:

On the whole the Billeting Scheme was very successful and some boys made lasting friendships with their hosts. Nevertheless .... with the advent of Saunders-Roe to Friars Bay and the urgent need to accommodate the employees, billeting difficulties increased and there was not the same willingness on the part of the townspeople to billet boys. [23]

As early as September 1940 a special meeting of Bangor City Council was held to discuss the 'chaotic' situation which was developing with many people from bombed areas simply roaming about the town in search of somewhere to stay. Local papers were asked to appeal for those with rooms available to come forward so that some sort of central bureau could be set up. A similar approach was adopted in other areas, like Holyhead and Portmadoc. On 10 May 1941, after the heavy raids on Merseyside, the *Rhyl Leader* carried an urgent appeal:

ACCOMMODATION IS **URGENTLY REQUIRED** FOR PERSONS RENDERED HOMELESS BY ENEMY ACTION. PERSONS WITH AVAILABLE ACCOMMODATION ARE ASKED TO FORWARD PARTICULARS TO THE BILLETING OFFICER, HEALTH DEPARTMENT OR THE UNDERSIGNED **IMMEDIATELY.** VOLUNTEERS WITH CARS ARE ALSO REQUIRED FOR TRANSPORT OF HOMELESS PERSONS

A.E. EDWARDS,
Clerk to the Council

Eventually in September 1941 the Government ordered all reception areas to make a Survey of Accommodation because of *'constantly increasing demand for accommodation for people of various classes'*. By and large billeting officers had simply coped as well as they could:

The train travelled very slowly and stopped at every station when we arrived in North Wales ... officials would be waiting ... They shouted out the number of evacuees they could accept - 'No more than 20 ...', 'No more than 10 ...'. Sometimes they couldn't take any at all so they would signal to the driver of the train to carry on to the next station ...[24]

As had been anticipated, once the bombing started, many Welsh householders did respond generously. Edith Duncalf of Wallasey spoke of the kindness she and others had received:

> ...after I had been in Rhyl a few days, my husband arrived with about half a dozen friends who had, the previous evening been 'bombed out'. They were 'dirty' with soot and grime - there was no water with which to wash - and tired out. I wondered how we would manage, but thanks to two Rhyl ladies who offered blankets and sleeping accommodation and whatever else was required, we managed very well.[25]

It was often a case simply of 'rallying round' as the authorities now had little if any advance notice of arrivals (though invariably bombers heading for Merseyside did first pass over North Wales). Even when councils were informed beforehand to expect a contingent of evacuees, the figures were rarely accurate. Local newspapers for the period carried numerous accounts of unexpected arrivals, such as that described in the *North Wales Chronicle*, 16 May 1941:

> Members of the Llandudno WVS had a sudden demand on their services late on Thursday night last week when a party of about 40 evacuees arrived unexpectedly at Llandudno Station. They had fled precipitously from a blitzed city and were homeless. The authorities closed up one of the schools, where the evacuees were housed for a couple of days. The WVS workers made a hurried collection of blankets and provided food, though as one helper remarked, the evacuees seemed too dazed to eat. Most of them slept on the boards of the school floor. Efforts were made to find accommodation for them - no easy task - and on Sunday they were removed to more suitable premises. It should be pointed out that Llandudno is not a 'reception area' and the evacuees arrived unofficially.

Where a party was expected, some councils clearly tried their best to be welcoming by at least laying on a hot meal for the new arrivals. The *North Wales Chronicle* for 7 February 1941 carried a message of thanks 'to Major Platt and Dr Starkey' for supplying rabbits, free of charge, for one such meal. Other evacuees had to make do as best they could. Matt and Winnie recorded what happened when they, along with the thirty other members of their family, finally arrived unannounced, very late one evening, at Abergele station:

> There were no officials at Abergele to attend to us. The local vicar opened up the parish hall. He allowed us to stay until we were fixed up by the billeting officer the following day. It turned out to be one of the funniest

nights we had ever experienced. Local people generously came to our assistance with blankets and items of food. The men organised one section of the hall as a sleeping area, the women organised a meal. The numbers to be catered for were many and this posed a problem for the cooks. One of our aunts came up with a bright idea. She acquired two white enamel buckets from God knows where! With help from the other women she proceeded to prepare an enormous amount of stew (scouse). This was enjoyed by all, including the friendly vicar. Before going to bed we all joined together for a raucous singsong! [26]

If ever there was a time for people to Go Forward Together as Churchill required, this was surely it. Unfortunately, it seems, there were just a few who were out of step! Even in 1939 when evacuation had been getting a very bad press, most billeting officers had prided themselves on *not* resorting to use of compulsory powers, feeling that enforced billeting would create an atmosphere of discontent, particularly undesirable where the children were concerned. Aberystwyth's Billeting Officer, however, had laid his cards on the table from the outset. He was expecting 3000 evacuees and had allocated a place for each one. To forestall any possible problems he inserted a notice in the *Cambrian News* on 1 September 1939:

Every effort has been made to meet objections to billeting but we are sorry we have not been able to meet the wishes of all objectors. We would therefore call your serious attention to the following:

> *1. Should a billeting officer call at your home with evacuees for billeting you are to receive them whether you consider that you should or not. Section 56 of the Act authorises the imposition on summary conviction of fines ... or imprisonment .. for failure to comply ...*
> *2. Any case of hardship and any objection to billeting would be considered during the few days following evacuation and a tribunal has been set up for that purpose.*
> *We would therefore urge all householders to have their accommodation in a reasonable state of preparation so as to save time for the billeting officers when they deliver their charges.*
>

Signed OSBORNE J. EVANS
Chief Billeting Officer, Aberystwyth

On the other hand, WVS members in Bala and Dolgellau, and billeting officers in Deudraeth had refused point blank to use compulsory powers in 1939, and several other councils had passed resolutions specifically directing their officers to avoid compulsion as far as possible.

By 1941, however, such was the demand for accommodation that it was no longer possible to ignore householders who refused to co-operate. In Denbighshire, for example, most of the local councils had been informed by June 1941 that voluntary billets had been exhausted and compulsion was having to be introduced. The Deudraeth authorities in Merionethshire were able to report in February 1941 that all evacuees had been billeted without compulsion but only after threats had been issued about the possibility of strong measures being taken. Many councils favoured this approach - sending out letters to explain the extent of their powers, hoping this alone would 'persuade' householders to comply. Others felt the time had come for more drastic action, as the following account of the Portmadoc Council meeting indicates:

> *The Chairman said that 81 children and 5 teachers were received in the last evacuation, of which they were given 48 hours notice. He was sorry to say that they experienced more trouble than usual in fixing them up and police assistance had to be called in some cases ... The Council decided to approach the police with a view to instituting proceedings under the billeting regulations against certain persons for failing to comply with the billeting notices served upon them ...*[27]

The compulsory notices informed householders of the number of persons they were required to take in and explained that failure to comply could result, on conviction, in a fine of up to £50, a term of imprisonment up to 3 months, or both. Tribunals were available to which appeals or complaints could be addressed - though until an appeal date was set the billet had to be provided. So that the situation in his area was quite clear, the Billeting Officer for Portdinorwic inserted the following notice in the *North Wales Chronicle*, 17 January 1941:

> *... when a billeting order is served upon a householder it must be complied with but the householder can appeal to a tribunal against the ruling of the local Billeting Officer. Pending the hearing of the appeal the householder must take in the evacuee. Further, it is to be noted that compulsory powers have been served on those who did not get evacuees in 1939. This is in accordance with the suggestions of the local committee.*

Billeting Tribunals had been set up at the outset of the war. Although rarely used to begin with they had sometimes helped to smooth things out. One tribunal for instance had been called upon in October 1939 to arbitrate in a so-called 'clash between Puritan and Bohemian ideals'. As a result three Llangollen foster parents were relieved of their six evacuees, having applied on the grounds that the children weren't happy, that 8/6d was not enough to keep them on, especially with parents visiting, that the children suffered some physical difficulties and that there was an incompatability of temperament. On the other hand a tribunal had met in Ogwen in November 1939 to hear householders appealing *against* removal of their evacuees - though they lost their appeal as there were 'strong educational reasons' behind the transfers.[28]

<u>GWYRFAI RURAL DISTRICT COUNCIL</u>

Cwellyn,
CAERNARVON.
............................1941

To...............................
....
....

<u>Defence Regulations, 1939.</u>
<u>Government Evacuation Scheme.</u>

I hereby require you to provide in the above mentioned premises accommodation for .... child(ren) as from .... 1941, and to provide them with board and lodging and to care for them to the best of your ability until relieved of the responsibility.

Failure to comply with the above request will render you liable on summary conviction to a Fine not exceeding <u>Fifty Pounds</u> or to imprisonment for a term not exceeding <u>Three Months</u> or to both such Fine and such imprisonment.

CHIEF BILLETING OFFICER

P.S. A Tribunal has been constituted to deal with complaints against billeting notices. If you feel aggrieved by the service upon you of the billeting notice which will be served upon you when the child(ren) arrive you may lodge a complaint which should be forwarded to me <u>in writing</u> at the above address. You will then be afforded an opportunity to appear before a Tribunal. You must, however, take custody of the child(ren) until your case has been heard and decided upon by the said Tribunal.

Local councils had compulsory powers of billeting and householders could be fined or imprisoned for failing to comply. Billeting Tribunals were set up to hear appeals.

In many areas, however, tribunals only really became active when compulsory powers were used more widely Although most households were sympathetic to the needs of the evacuees there were certainly some who either never had been or had had such a bad experience in 1939 that they were prepared to challenge any billeting notice. In Llanfairfechan, for instance, 104 billeting notices were sent out in April 1941, in response to which no fewer than 80 appeals were received. Excuses, here and elsewhere, tended to fall into one of three categories - lack of space; lack of time; or ill-health (usually endorsed by a medical certificate). A.M. Jones, Billeting Officer for Holyhead, remembers the tribunals as dreadful affairs - *'sitting in judgement on those wanting to get rid of children billeted on them'*. But in the end, with the accommodation situation getting quite desperate, his sympathy had begun to wane:

> *We were presented with medical certificates elaborating all sorts of female diseases that no one had ever heard of. Some of the women really would make themselves neurotic over the issue but on the whole the tribunal wasn't terribly sympathetic and many applicants were turned down.* [29]

Shortage of space was usually put down to the presence of war workers, private evacuees, or relatives; lack of time to war work or a particular occupation. Especially in the spring and summer months farmers tended to claim they'd no time to look after evacuees. In one case in 1941, however, where a farmer (also actually Vice Chairman of Caernarvon County Council) was being prosecuted for refusing to take in two young boys, the prosecuting attorney made it quite clear that farmers were not exempt from billeting regulations. The farmer lost his case as did a VAD officer in Bangor who'd refused to take in a child on the grounds that she might be called upon at short notice to go as commandant to a military hospital. [30]

Tribunals tended to turn down this sort of appeal, arguing that almost everyone was involved in war work of some kind. Local newspapers for 1941 contain regular reports of cases, with fines ranging from a few shillings up to £6. Occasionally, local authorities lost on a technicality and the Ministry went to some length to ensure that councils knew the proper procedure to be followed when serving billeting notices. From May 1941, officers had power of entry to ascertain the exact accommodation in any house. Tribunals examined cases individually but occasionally did lay down a general ruling - one in Bala decided that bachelors or widowers relying on domestic help should be relieved from taking evacuees unless it became absolutely necessary. [31] Had the young man in Michelle Magorian's moving story been evacuated to this part of North Wales, he may never have found himself saying 'Goodnight Mister Tom'!

Local authorities were also empowered to prosecute in cases of fraud concerning billeting allowances, where, for example, foster parents continued to draw money for evacuees who had returned home. Often quite large amounts were involved, as in two cases in Caernarvon Borough concerning sums of £19/15/0 and £23/2/0.[32] A slightly different case of fraud was uncovered in Denbighshire where the authorities, suspicious over one particular billeting allowance claim, found that the so-called 'evacuee' had in fact been adopted by the foster parents in 1937! Sometimes it was the evacuees rather than their hosts who were attempting to defraud the system. Known as 'twicers', these were evacuees suspected of taking themselves off to reception areas now and again just for a holiday, or of sending their children away at intervals to allow the mother to earn good money for a while doing war work. The government eventually countered the possibilty of such 'multiple evacuation' by requiring that having once returned home an evacuee must show just cause before re-evacuation.[33]

Some cases where allowances were drawn illegally were genuinely due to ignorance or confusion; sometimes it was even the fault of the billeting officials. A careful system of checks was in place (payment books were returned every eight weeks for scrutiny) - the need to monitor payments being an added incentive to local authorities to provide for regular visits to billets. Nevertheless, it was always difficult to determine whether any wrongdoing was deliberate and there was, perhaps understandably, a certain reluctance amongst local councillors to prosecute members of their own community over evacuation matters.[34]

There is no doubt that the whole period of evacuation was a very stressful time for all concerned - certainly a number of billeting officers in North Wales did resign because they felt unable to cope with the enormous amount of work involved and the strain of having to bear the brunt of complaints from local people and from evacuees; various others - evacuating officers and headteachers - also fell victim to stress at this time. However, if too much paperwork was proving a headache to Welsh reception officials, it was a sudden lack of paperwork in Liverpool which created huge problems for those in charge at the evacuating end! At the start of the scheme, Liverpool City Council had stored all its records relating to evacuated children at premises in St Thomas Street. When the area was slightly damaged by bombs in March 1941, the Education Department decided to move all the paperwork to Drury Buildings, Walter

Street - an unfortunate decision as it happened, since these buildings were completely destroyed in the May Blitz! One of the officials in charge later explained:

> *To compile the records of all the children again was a herculean task. In the midst of that reconstruction work, a second evacuation was going on of 30,000 children and we had to cope with parents as well. We borrowed records from other departments, from other towns, the various schools, and brought everybody in to help that we possibly could. Schoolteachers whose schools were out of action worked with us, while Liverpool University Social Science students assisted by carrying out interviewing of parents. It was a time I will never forget. We had people coming to see us covered with bandages ... However, we were able to contact the parents of all the children, and set up new lists.* [35]

Of course it was vital to keep records of where the children were being housed, but billeting officers were increasingly asking, 'Just where are we to put them all?' On 13 June 1941, the *North Wales Chronicle* published a Resolution passed at a meeting in Abergele, which read:

> *Abergele Urban Council consider evacuated persons have arrived in reception areas at a rate incompatible with the available accommodation. Despite the congestion it is our duty to pursue the task, vigorously and relentlessly, of finding suitable accommodation for the victims of ruthless bombing, but the problem of billeting bristles with difficulties. Having exhausted all other means ... the Council feel wooden chalets should be erected by the Government for families rendered homeless. Such a scheme would help councils and would be a source of comfort to the afflicted ...*

As early as February 1939, the Government had in fact agreed to build a limited number of camps for evacuees and through the Camps Act in May 1939 gave a contract for 50 camps, each housing some 300 people, to the National Camps Corporation Ltd and the Scottish Special Housing Association. Although none had been completed by the start of the evacuation scheme, over half were under construction by the following summer[36] and one was opened for the use of Merseyside evacuees in April 1940. This was the Colomendy School Camp, located near Loggerheads in North Wales and managed by Mr Greenwood of the National Camps Corporation with headteachers, Mr T. Pennycuck and Miss J.L. Macdowall.The camp was a series of schoolrooms, dormitories, assembly and dining halls made from Canadian cedar and acacia wood. Set in 150 acres of wooded ground, it was soon being described in the local press as 'Liverpool's New Lung'.[37] By mid-March 1941 'Colomendy' housed 544 children (boys and girls); the children followed a full school curriculum but also benefited from having 'a whole mountainside on which to play'. There were organised rambles, the children helped look after pigs and poultry and tend an orchard and a 3-acre field of potatoes. They also enjoyed games, concerts and cine shows. There were ample rations - in fact a report issued on the first anniversary of the camp recorded that since arriving the children had each gained an average of one and a half pounds per month, with an average development of one and a quarter inches in height. There were apparently hardly any cases of illness at the camp - a feature which was soon attracting the interest of the Education Board.[38]

Merseyside evacuees were also expected to benefit from another camp, being constructed on Deeside, on the Clayhill estate at Neston. But the buildings - not wooden chalets here but an estate of one-storey hostels - were not completed until 1942. As the bombing had significantly decreased by this time, the estate was not used to house Liverpool evacuees but did give refuge to a number of families who arrived in 1944, fleeing the 'V' bomb attacks in the south. It even received an 'official' visit on 8 August 1944 from Florence Horsburgh, Parliamentary Secretary to the Minister of Health, and Sir Francis Hindle, Deputy Regional Commissioner.[39]

Abergele's resolution about housing evacuees in chalets produced a mixed response - many felt the idea impractical because of shortage of material and labour. Indeed, the Ministry itself rejected the suggestion on these grounds. But several North Wales authorities were already making use of existing wooden chalets to house evacuees and many, no doubt to the delight of the children, found themselves living in holiday camps, such as the Lyons Camp, the Bolsover Camp in Rhyl (owned by Bolsover Colliery Company) and the Alavowlia Camp in Denbigh. The Bolsover camp had been requisitioned by the army at the start of the war but in May 1941 Rhyl Council got authority to take it over as a Receiving Centre; by 18 June it was occupied by some 150 Merseyside women and children who had fled from the bombs.

Most billeting officers did try to spread the burden of taking evacuees evenly over their community and to keep both evacuees and hosts happy. As the wife of one officer recalls:

Mr Pritchard knew the village people and because it was such a small community he had a pretty good idea what the home atmosphere was like

201

in each house, also whether there were any children there - so there was some selection of billets. The locals used to turn up in batches asking him to give them 'nice people'. His criterion for judging if a person was 'nice' was whether or not she had on a fur coat! On one instance he sent such a fur-coated 'lady' to one of the big farms (where they'd asked for someone nice) but she left very rapidly because, nice or not, she couldn't stand the cocks crowing! [40]

Inevitably there were some complaints and accusations, the most common one being that evacuees were forced on to working-class homes whilst upper-class ones remained exempt. An anonymous but angry correspondent to the *Rhyl Journal*, 26 July 1941 had this to say:

Sir - The billeting of evacuees in Rhyl is being carried out in a manner causing bitterness which will long be remembered. After two poor years, lessees of apartments houses are, in the middle of the season, forced to take evacuees even to the exclusion of war-weary relatives from bombed areas, sorely in need of a holiday. Objections are overcome, if necessary, with the help of the Police, who courteously but firmly explain the powers of the Authority. Meanwhile, in the next road, private residents occupy large houses with well-furnished rooms standing empty. These people are not even approached ... This position is apparently well known to all except those who carry out the billeting. Why?

This was not a complaint peculiar to North Wales. Titmuss, in his official history of the wartime evacuation, concluded that some of the wealthier members of society had managed to evade responsibility in this sphere[41] and a more recent study by Travis Crosby supports this view.[42] Anyone who has read Evelyn Waugh's *Put Out More Flags* will immediately picture the unscrupulous Basil Seal, successfully extracting large sums from local dignitaries in return for relieving them of the dreaded Connolly family of evacuees! Many aspects of the whole evacuation business were certainly potentially open to exploitation. At times, for example, there were accusations that exorbitant rents were being charged - Bangor City Council were informed in July 1941 that tenants of some Corporation houses were illegally sub-letting the properties to evacuees. These 'racketeers' as the Housing Committee chairman described them were leaving the council houses in the possession of strangers, charging them enormous rents and not even staying in the area themselves! Elsewhere council house tenants had taken in so many evacuees that there was serious overcrowding - five houses in one Bangor district, usually occupied by a total of 27 local residents were discovered to have 72 occupants!

There was always a possibility that money would change hands either to secure a 'nice' billet or to ensure 'nice' evacuees, or none at all. Some such activity may well have taken place although, as has been seen, billeting officers were selected from people of the highest integrity - ministers of religion, headteachers, senior council officials and bank managers. Underhand dealings by their very nature are not likely to have been documented but one case of attempted bribery that was recorded amongst official papers in North Wales was flatly refused by the officer concerned.[43] If the poorer sectors of a community did take large numbers of evacuees, this was certainly in some instances because they chose to do so, sometimes for altruistic reasons, sometimes for profit. Equally, whilst some wealthy families may have sought to avoid billeting, there are many instances when the doors of 'upper-class' houses were willingly opened to evacuees, from the very beginning of the scheme.

Just days into the first evacuation of September 1939, Janet Davis, a Welsh woman living in New York, cabled the British Foreign Office, offering her home The Cliffs in Merionethshire, to evacuated children. The authorities quickly accepted and made much of the offer, hoping others in a similar position would follow suit.[44] Many did. Sir Francis Joseph, a Liverpool man, told the *Liverpool Daily Post* on 8 September 1939 how proud he was that his home, The Hall, Alsager, was sheltering children from his native city. A few days earlier, the paper had carried news that another gentleman in North Wales - who wished to remain anonymous - had given over his residence to house 60 evacuated children. Mrs Pritchard, whose husband Robert Alun Pritchard, Head of Clynnog School (Caerns) was also the local billeting officer, remembers that there were no accommodation problems in Clynnog *'because Canon Elsie and his two sisters opened up their big house which then functioned as a communal billet'.*[45]

Numerous evacuees also testify to having found themselves in sumptuous surroundings. Arthur Martin remembers arriving on Anglesey, being bundled into an old green Austin Seven, driven out of the town and into the grounds of 'Plas Megan', home of Sir Williams Bulkely. After a warm greeting and a meal of fish and chips, Arthur was shown to his bedroom:

> *... the largest I had ever seen with a huge bed, magnificent furniture and beautiful ornaments and pictures. On waking up in the morning I pulled back the curtains of one of the three large windows in the room to see a view which was truly remarkable. Over the top of the wood stood the whole of Beaumaris, with the Menai Strait and Snowdonia beyond. On the*

lawn in front of the house, rabbits were eating, a dog was watching them quite unconcerned and a gamekeeper was walking across the lawn with a gun and two pheasants under his arm - it was like paradise! [46]

Similarly, Mrs Roper recounts:

... After a while I moved to live with Mr & Mrs Phillips at 'Plas Wilmot'. I was one of five evacuees staying there. It was a lovely home with a beautiful big garden. Mrs P. was very kind to us all and went to a lot of trouble. The big lounge downstairs had been furnished as our room. We had 5 beds there, a piano, tables and chairs. We had happy times in there. A french window opened out on to a big lawn with a huge tree in the middle; on warm summer days we used to sit under the tree and have our tea ... I discovered that Wilfred Owen, the war poet, was born at Plas Wilmot and then his family had moved to Birkenhead to live, it seemed a coincidence that he had moved to Birkenhead from Plas Wilmot and I had moved from Birkenhead to live there! [47]

During the course of his time as an evacuee John Houston took up residence in a number of large properties - some more desirable than others! The first was dark and gloomy - *'two old cottages and some stables made into one big house with a lot of rambling rooms and passages with steep narrow staircases and low ceilings with dark old beams'*. It was a spooky place - John wasn't sorry to leave. Later came a spell in another imposing residence - a house used by the local Masonic lodge, but John and his 'tearaway companion' were *'summarily expelled when we were caught peeping through the keyhole of the door in the room in which the Masons were in session'!* Finally, John 'fell on his feet' when he got to live in a beautiful house overlooking the Menai Strait and was, at last, shown great kindness by the owner.

Freda Beetson found her billet not only very grand but very 'convenient'!

Millicent and I were taken by a Captain and Mrs Williams to their fine home. It had a big drive and lovely gardens, but the thing that really amazed us was the double-seated toilet outside!

Elsa Chatterton clearly remembers the house that she and nine of her friends arrived at:

It was huge and very old and we were to stay together there with two of our teachers. Mr and Mrs Clough Williams-Ellis owned the house, Plas

Brondanw, and we were their guests. Clough Williams-Ellis was the architect of Portmeirion amongst other things and Amobel [his wife] was a collector and editor of children's folk tales ...

Some of the girls evacuated from Birkenhead Secondary School found themselves billeted in a twelfth-century mansion in Ffestiniog. The girls slept in a wing of the house and took their meals in a large room opening on to a courtyard, with wonderful views of a terraced garden, famed for its rhododendrons. The lodge keeper still wore Welsh national costume![48] Other requisitioned properties became in effect small 'boarding' schools. Elizabeth Belger explains:

We all went to a large farmhouse, Cafnan, near Cemaes Bay, Anglesey. There was a matron in charge, with helpers. The whole party of ten children (girls) were in this large house (there were boys to start with in 1939 but they were blamed for the death of a sheep and sent back to Liverpool). A room in the house was turned into a classroom. A dentist would come with all his equipment and gas to the house ... We were treated very well. [49]

Dorothy Formston's sisters *'...were taken to 'Parciau Mawr' [Criccieth] which had a long drive, a huge house and lots of surrounding grounds, kitchen garden and areas of grass and trees. The owners were Captain and Mrs Leslie...'* Criccieth also boasted another large house - though this was was perhaps not quite so amenable to inquisitive evacuees, as Beryl Traynor who was evacuated to Criccieth, recalls:

Lloyd George was still alive then - he had a house in Criccieth (I think some evacuees stayed in the Lodge). Well once we knocked at the big house to ask for a drink of water though we knew someone famous lived there so we hoped we'd get lemonade. A maid answered the door - she was all dressed in black and white. She made us stand on the doorstep till she got us a drink - of water!

Joan Boyce, author of *Pillowslips and Gas Masks*, writes:

In Liverpool we lived in a small terrace in the dockland area of Stanley Road. Our house had three bedrooms, a kitchen, a back kitchen, parlour and basic amenities. In Penmaenmawr we lived in a minor 'stately home' which had many large bedrooms, several bathrooms, huge 'parlours' and extensive gardens bordered by tall trees.

Joan was actually living in the one-time home of the Owen Owen family whose department store was a well-known landmark in Liverpool. It had been converted into the convent of the Seafield sisters and became a temporary home for many Merseyside evacuees during the war, as did the nearby Franciscan monastery. It's hard to decide who would have been most affected by these new living arrangements - the city children trying to fit into the strict routine of convent life or the nuns and monks, their serene existence rudely shattered by the arrival of dockland evacuees! Religious houses in other parts of North Wales also opened their doors: Poor Clare Convent in Hawarden, St Beuno's in St Asaph, and the Jesuit House, Barmouth.

Billeting was not permitted in furnished houses where the owner was not in occupation; if required for accommodating evacuees, such property had to be requisitioned - and as accommodation became increasingly scarce more and more Requisition Notices were issued in North Wales. Large houses acquired in this way tended to be used as homes for aged and infirm evacuees or for children with special needs, such as 'Hafod Eithin' in Harlech and 'Morfa Lodge', Portmadoc - both used as a wartime home for children from Claughton Road Special School, Birkenhead. Other large properties accommodated nursery units for the under-fives (like Bryn Afon Nursey set up in Wrexham in October 1941 to house young children of expectant mothers evacuated from Merseyside). Some served as hostels for the expectant mothers themselves, as centres for children not readily 'billetable' due to medical or temperamental difficulties, or, particularly in 1941, as Emergency Receiving Centres. Titmuss writes that in 1943 there were 103 institutions in Wales catering for about 2,800 evacuees needing different kinds of care.[50] The figure for 1941 would certainly have been much larger.

Sometimes centres were set up as a result of private initiatives - such as that reported in the *Liverpool Daily Post*, 7 November 1940. What were described as 'three North Wales mansions' had been converted to accommodate 100 evacuated babies. The scheme had been made possible thanks to two local artists - Carolyn Townsend and Joan Howson - who had a studio at Morfa Bychan. Miss Howson, daughter of Archdeacon Howson of Liverpool was certainly well qualified to run such a centre, having cared for Austrian refugee children during World War I and helped evacuate French children from the front line.

Smaller vacant properties in reception areas were often used for housing one or two families as complete units. In 'communal billets' like these councils occasionally found it necessary to issue a set of rules to ensure harmony

206

prevailed! But a solution of this sort tended to work to the satisfaction of both evacuee and local authority. When for example one extended family of Merseysiders arrived in Abergele (thirty of them!), they were given the option of renting a large boarding house which had been requisitioned for evacuation purposes. The arrangement worked so well that the family ended up staying there, all together, for over a year.[51]

In 1941 many authorities had to resort to housing children, at least for a short time, in large properties run as hostels. Merseyside parent I.T. Jones (from New Ferry, belatedly included in the evacuation scheme) felt that his two children were being treated well in their hostel (Craig-y-Don) at Borthygest when they were evacuated there. He wrote to Pormadoc Council to express his appreciation and to pay tribute to the hostel's efficiency. *'It is a relief and pleasure to parents'*, he added, *'to know that their children are being so well looked after.'*[52] Mrs Williams, otherwise known as 'Aunt Sally', also worked hard to look after evacuees in the hostel she ran at Oak Alyn Hall:

> *I looked after 300 children when the city [Liverpool] was being bombed in 1941. I then lived in a lodge. The hall was empty and I, with some friends, got it open and ready for children the very next day . I was shocked when the ambulance arrived with 15 children - all not suitable for private billets - boys and girls, black and white, aged 4 to 14. I took them all into our church hall and we managed to feed them. During the evening, beds and bits of furniture arrived - the rest we borrowed. As no one came to look after them I was asked to stay until help came - that's how we started. A week later, 15 more arrived, all medical cases. I was then appointed matron. It was meant to be a short stay hostel. When they were well, clean and clothed they went to private billets ... We had lovely grounds for them to play in and trees to climb. Some were not without the spirit of adventure which caused me a lot of anxiety, but to town boys it was great fun ...*[53]

But hostel life wasn't such fun for all children. Mrs Marie Moore had been evacuated in 1939 and like many others had returned only to be re-evacuated when her home was destroyed in the May Blitz. She ended up in Llanfairfechan, in a big house with about thirty other evacuees, a place, she said *'where kids with a stigma label were stuck'*. Scabies, impetigo and dermatitis were rife and food was in very short supply.[54] Frank Jagger spent his first stint as an evacuee at a youth hostel [55] - Rhos-y-Gwaliau in Bala. He wasn't unhappy there, but the regime was quite harsh. It was strongly rumoured that the hostel was haunted:

That scared us so I can recall going to the lavatory always with a mate ...
When you pulled the chain that disappeared through the ceiling you ran
like crazy back to the dorm. The older boys at night would creep about
with flashlights under their chins frightening us until they were caught and
punished in front of us with the slipper across their bottom ... Each of us
had a cotton sheet sleeping bag and blankets. The older boys had to repair
these when they got torn, which was frequently. To go to school we had
to cross a foaming river on an old rotten wooden bridge. That scared me
because in parts you had to sidle along the handrail to get past the holes.

Others who spent time in evacuee hostels were positively unhappy. Walter
Hurst was evacuated from Birkenhead to Harlech. The people in his first billet
had been very kind but they ran a shop and having two boys to look after proved
too much; the lady at his second billet also had to give up her evacuees due to
illness:

I landed up at the YHA with 19 other boys and 20 girls. It was very
spartan with good plain food, bunk beds with very thin mattresses and one
fireplace to serve the whole place - no central heating! It was run like a
school - no one showed us any real affection ... The one thing that I
remember most was the longing to feel someone's arms around me, to
give me a big hug and love - the deprivation at times was awful. There was
one man at the hostel - Jimmy Stafford - he would beat unmercifully any
child who wet the bed.

Marjorie Lamb also has bad memories of this hostel. During her stay there both
she and her brother were bullied by one of the older evacuees and she too
remembers Stafford's cruelty. Little affection was shown to Marjorie either -
no attempt to explain things to her before she was sent off unceremoniously to
have her tonsils removed, or later to be temporarily billeted elsewhere.
Marjorie spent much of her time there feeling frightened, unloved and rejected:

I remember two boys running away from the hostel, they were going to
walk home. I remember one of the helpers saying "They have been caught"
as if she was referring to criminals. They were not criminals, just unhappy
evacuees wanting to go home.

It was not altogether unusual for evacuees to try and run home - from hostels or
billets. Joan Boyce writes of two boys running away from Penmaenmawr - they
were picked up by the police at Edge Hill and returned to North Wales; James

Sinclair tells how the procedure for evacuees trying to get back to Liverpool from Bangor became known as 'the Aber run';[56] John Doyle, Barbara Smith and Mrs D. Shaw all made abortive escape attempts. Hilda Wilkes ran away - but only to another billet where her friend was staying. Bill Wilkinson also recounts how fellow-evacuee George Bowen 'did a bunk' from Beaumaris, with two other lads:

> *They'd got as far as Menai Bridge - haversacks on their backs, a couple of sarnies for the journey, an apple, a few cough sweets. They were just approaching the Bridge when a bus pulled up - the Head and another master jumped out and collared the three of them!*

Billy Moffitt tried to run home from the hostel he was living at in Ruthin. As the oldest boy there he was always given lots of jobs to do and felt constantly picked on. He used to get regularly 'clipped around the ears' - and more - from one particular staff member. In the end, he hitch-hiked to Birkenhead, was duly returned to North Wales by an uncle, but, not to be defeated in his bid for freedom, was back in Birkenhead again even before his uncle was! The urge to run away like this may have been caused simply by homesickness - but it could also have been a sign that something was seriously wrong. The children were after all extremely vulnerable - so just how, and how well, were they safeguarded?

NOTES

[1] See Waller and Vaughan-Rees, *Blitz* - several eye-witness accounts of the bombing of Merseyside, including these by Ellison & Roberts are included in the chapter 'The Provinces'.

[2] Quoted in *Cambrian News*, 'Homefront Heroes', supplement August 1989

[3] See Jackson, *Who Will Take Our Children*, p.61

[4] Blasbery, *Children of the Blitz*, p.42

[5] *One Child's War* (which tells of Victoria Massey's time as an evacuee in Abersoch) p.33

[6] See Ken Blasbury, *Children of the Blitz*, p.30

[7] The story of overseas evacuation is told in Johnson, *Exodus of Children*, also chapters in Jackson, *Who Will Take Our Children*, and Crosby, *Impact of Civilian Evacuation*. See also Elspeth Huxley, *Atlantic Ordeal: The Story of Mary Cornish* (1941). Many of the CORB children, of course, set sail from Liverpool having first met up with their escorts at Fazakerley School and at Fazakerley Cottage Homes.

[8] See Angus Calder, *The People's War*, p.246

[9] Liverpool Civil Defence Emergency Committee Report, 15 May 1941. The local resources of Huyton-with-Roby UDC were so taxed that the Medical Officer urged eveything possible be done to discourage this, even threatening that 'trekkers' would be sent straight back.

[10] Extract from *Bombers Over Merseyside*, p. 16

[11] See Calder, p.246, citing a Mass Observation entry for 17 May 1941

[12] cited in Waller & Vaughan-Rees, *Blitz*, p.159

[13] For various casualty and damage statistics, see Whitworth, *Merseyside at War*, pp. 81, 87-8; also Whittington-Egan, *The Great Liverpool Blitz*, p.62, and *Bombers Over Merseyside*, p.13

[14] This account by 'Winnie and Matt' is quoted in J. Boyce, *Pillowslips and Gasmasks*, p.39

[15] Reported in the *Liverpool Daily Post*, 13 November 1940

[16] Details of the Funk Express, but also of the heroic efforts of Merseyside fire-fighters, professionals and volunteers, appear in 'Our War', *Liverpool Echo* supplement,1989.

[17] 'Wales at War' (A Souvenir Special from the Daily Post) 25 April 1989, contains some interesting facts about these and other wartime 'visitors' to Wales. The official in charge of the billeting and welfare of the Inland Revenue officials during their stay in Llandudno was none other than the future Prime Minister, Jim Callaghan.

[18] For a fascinating account of various aspects of the war in North West Wales, see Reg Chambers Jones, *Bless 'Em All* (Bridge Books, 1995)

[19] The National Gallery collection had been moved at the beginning of the war to be stored in the National Library, Aberystwyth, in Penrhyn Castle, and at Bangor University but the paintings were moved again after a bomb was dropped on the area and it was recognised as being on the route of bombers heading for Merseyside; prototypes of the Mulberry harbours were designed by Iorys Hughes of Bangor. See 'Wales at War' and Chambers Jones, *Bless 'Em All.*

[20] See J. Sinclair, *Welsh Scouse*, p.199

[21] Guernsey evacuees were also sent to the Wirral, staying in Heswall, Irby and Neston

[22] Quoted in *Wales at War*, p.31

[23] See *Liverpool Blue Coat School Past and Present*, ed. P.Healey, p.24.

[24] Charlie's account, reproduced in *Pillowslips and Gas Masks*, p.39

[25] Letter to the *Rhyl Journal*, 24 January 1941

[26] Quoted in *Pillowslips and Gasmasks*, p. 39

[27] Reported in the *North Wales Chronicle*, 11 July 1941

[28] *Liverpool Daily Post*, 13 October 1939; Ogwen RDC Committee Minutes 1930-47 - Meeting

of Tribunal, 27 November 1939

[29] Interview with the author, 13 October 1975

[30] Both cases reported in the *North Wales Chronicle*, 15 August, 30 May 1941 respectively

[31] Bala UDC Minutes, 3 June 1940

[32] Caernarvon Borough Evacuation Box 2

[33] See Crosby, *Impact of Civilian Evacuation*, p.55

[34] See Wallis, *North Wales 1939-45*, pp.221f. for a bizarre chain of events in Bala in 1942 when the council refused to make a prosecution over a billeting matter.

[35] *Liverpool Daily Post*, 16 June 1948 (Liverpool RO, Newscuttings Book, HF 301 13 EVA)

[36] See M.Parsons, *I'll Take That One*, pp.202-3

[37] *Liverpool Daily Post*, 7 March 1941

[38] See *ibid.*, also *Liverpool Echo*, 25 April 1941. Some officials subsequently claimed that the constant exercise regimes which were a feature of most Camp Schools actually retarded growth! - see Parsons, *Evacuation - the true story*, p.83

[39] See *Liverpool Daily Post*, 8 August 1944; some details of the camp are also included in *Neston at War* (Burton and Neston History Society, 1999).

[40] Author's interview with Mrs M. Ptitchard, 29 October 1975

[41] Titmuss, p.372

[42] See Travis L. Crosby, *The Impact of Civilian Evacuation in the Second World War*, p.49

[43] Caernarvon Borough papers (Evac Box 2) show that one woman, searching for a house for herself and a child, had enclosed a postal order for the billeting officer in anticipation of his 'kindness'; this had been immediately returned.

[44] See Carlton Jackson, p.66

[45] Interview with the author, 29 October 1975

[46] Quoted in Liverpool Blue Coat Brotherly Society, Annual Report, September 1989 (Beaumaris Evacuation Re-union), p.31

[47] '*Our Evacuee*', p. 40

[48] Reported in the *Birkenhead News*, 16 September 1939

[49] Another hostel in Cemaes Bay served as a convalescent home for the armed forces and for traumatised children, see Jean Carter's account in *Goodnight Children Everywhere*

[50] Titmuss, *Problems of Social Policy*, p.383

[51] See *Pillowslips and Gasmasks*, p.39

[52] Report of Portmadoc Council meeting, *North Wales Chronicle*, 11 July 1941

[53] Quoted in *Wales at War*, p.31

[54] Quoted in 'Our War', *Liverpool Echo* supplement, 5 Sept 1989

[55] Many local Youth Hostels housed evacuees, eg Bala, Bangor, Barmouth, Oswestry, Abergele, Harlech, Chester, Roman Bridge, Idwal, Llanrwst Nantgwynant and Llanberis.

[56] Boyce, *Pillowslips and Gasmasks*, p.39; Sinclair, *Welsh Scouse*, p.166

7- Minding the Children

In February 1940 Liverpool headmistress, Miss J. Crosbie, compered a Home Service programme called 'Minding the Children', broadcast from Bangor. As we have seen, in introducing the programme she commented:

> *When we arrived in Wales last September, many of the children were pale, tired and not very healthy. Today, most of them are bonny, healthy and content. This is the miracle that is going on all over North Wales. To the children it seems that place where dreams and fairy tales come true ...*[1]

This was undoubtedly what the majority of evacuated children did feel; yet for some, evacuation was not a dream at all - it was one long, seemingly never-ending nightmare. Recent 'retellings' of the story of evacuation have highlighted cases - some truly shocking cases - where evacuees were treated terribly. Certainly some Merseyside children too, far from being welcomed, became victims of abuse during their time in Wales. Without doubt, they were *all* extremely vulnerable; indeed several evacuees have made the point that there could easily have been many more such cases. The sad truth is that child abuse - mental, physical and sexual - took place *before* the war[2] and *after* the war. Reported cases of cruelty increased dramatically during the first waves of children returning back to their parents in 1944 and 1945![3] Children continue to be ill-treated despite a far greater recognition of the problem and the availability of enormous resources to try and counter it. The Waterhouse Inquiry which reported in February 2000 revealed 'truly appalling' abuse in some children's homes in the 1970s and 1980s. Nor is such abuse confined to children 'in care'; even in 1999, 100,000 children (a quarter of whom were under-11s) were recorded as having run away, mainly due to violence at home. However unacceptable, it is perhaps not surprising then to find that abuse did take place *during* the war.

Whilst it is vital to record cases where evacuees were treated cruelly and to acknowledge that this should never have been allowed to happen - that the government did fail these children - it is also important to acknowledge that perhaps many more might have suffered but for the vigilance of those involved in running the evacuation scheme. We've see how, from the onset, teachers and billeting officers, working in conjunction with the children's parents, foster parents, medical staff, churchmen and volunteers had undertaken all sorts of welfare activity and regularly visited children in their billets. Evacuated teachers could have no real knowledge of the householders taking in the children but

212

billeting officials had a better idea of the character of would-be foster parents, and the local community itself often acted as a vigilant 'watchdog': On 27 May 1940, for example, June Warren was admitted to a school in Bangor as an evacuee. On 2 July the school logbook records that June had left for home 'on the request of the Inspector of Cruelty to Children'as it 'had been reported' that the foster mother was in the habit of leaving the little girl alone in the house for hours on end.[4] Unsatisfactory or even only potentially unsatisfactory situations in the reception areas were constantly being uncovered and acted upon. Children found to be undernourished or neglected were removed from the offending billet; prosecutions were brought in more serious cases.

Yet it is always difficult to monitor what goes on 'behind closed doors' - even more so when society is suffering the dislocations of war. Occasionally, unless the problem was blatant, children's complaints were not taken seriously, sometimes simply because it was the word of a child against that of an adult, sometimes because the adults deliberately concealed the true state of affairs in front of outsiders. Letters home were quite often 'censored' or, if not exactly censored, then at least read by the foster parents, which amounted to much the same thing - though perhaps the practise was sometimes well intended, as Olive Murray believes: *'I remember Mr & Mrs Davies reading the letters we sent home - making sure we were happy, I suppose.'* Whatever the reason for reading the letters, it did make it rather difficult for evacuees to 'tell all'. Doreen French had written home to her mother in 1941. Fifty years later, sorting through her mother's things just after her death, she was very surprised and moved to discover the letter - which her mother had never mentioned in all those years - carefully stored in the purse she used every day. The letter comprises two pages: the first, with general bits of news, Doreen had duly handed to her foster mother (supposedly to check the spelling), the second had been secretly added before the envelope was sealed and posted. It reads:

> *Could I come home please. If you decide, please don't let Mr & Mrs C. know. I do not like it all. You can just say you are coming to see me and then you can arrange it with Mrs. C when you get here. I can pack and come home with you.*
> *Your loving daughter, Doreen.*

Even today Doreen is amazed at how wonderfully restrained this was - and yet how desperate is the homesickness which leaps out of the page! Fortunately Doreen's mother recognized her daughter's desperation and took action, but some parents were effectively advised to ignore any such letters. The headmaster of Liverpool Collegiate, for instance, issued a bulletin warning parents that if any boys wrote home with a complaint instead of going through the proper channels *'it probably means they are "trying it on"'*. Charles Crebbin, young as he was, had also been imbued with the belief that he must adopt a 'stiff upper lip'. If anything, he was even more desperate than Doreen to get away from his billet, yet, driven by fear of his foster parents and concerned not to add to his family's worries he somehow managed to write home as if he hadn't a care in the world. As he explains:

> *My mother kept all the letters I wrote home from Meliden and none of these letters show any desire to return to Liverpool despite the fact that nearly every night I would pray for the courage to ask my parents to take me back, blitz or no blitz.*

Letters home didn't always paint a true picture. This one from Charles Crebbin gives no idea of how desperately unhappy he was in his billet

(Courtesy Charles Crebbin).

214

Perhaps the most common cases of ill-treatment of evacuees concerned those children who were grossly underfed, but some were beaten, others felt they were over-worked or subjected to 'psychological' cruelty, a few were even sexually abused.[5]

Mrs D. Shaw was given 'a horrible time' in the pub where she was billeted - living off treacle sandwiches and water, put to bed at 4.30pm, and having to undertake all sorts of unpleasant chores, including cleaning out spitoons:

> *...my brother came to visit one Sunday and we actually had a roast dinner. We couldn't say anything to him of course whilst Mrs Evans was about. However, when we saw him off to the bus stop we immediately told him what life was really like. He refused to believe it (I expect like most older brothers would do then) and went home without saying a word. Time and time again I reported to my teacher at school what life was really like at the Rock Tavern but nothing seemed to be done. I also spoke to several other people in the village but when that happened I would be confronted by Mrs Evans about the awful lies we were telling ... Eventually we came across a young woman in the village who listened to our tales of woe and allowed me to write home from her house... About a week later I went into school to be informed that that they had finally found us a new billet.*

Despite a system of regular checks, Billeting Officers weren't always successful in detecting problems, either because they were misled, as in Betty's case below, or because, as with Doris, the householder was thought to be above suspicion:

> *I was very unhappy. I had to sleep on a bed chair on the landing. I wasn't allowed to play and my brother who was only eight used to sit outside crying for me. I found out later that the billeting officer had been shown a bedroom which was supposed to be for me but it was the lodger's room.* (Betty Catlow)[6]

> *If the Rogers had visitors, which was quite often, I had to stay in the garden shed ... It was my birthday while I was there; they never even wished me happy birthday. I cried every night ... Not one person of any authority checked on us in all that time - they probably thought we were OK because the Rogers were stalwarts of the church.* (Doris Coxon)

Evacuation officials certainly did advise householders if they felt a situation

215

needed rectifying - though even then the solutions adopted weren't always quite what they'd had in mind! J. Iorwerth Davies recalls:

> ...Not every evacuee was so well looked after and checks were made of the homes at regular intervals to ensure that the evacuees were 'in safe hands'. One of the supervisors [in Llanrhaeadr] was Mr. Pat O'Brien, Headmaster of the local Infants school. It was said that on one occasion he reprimanded one family for having boys and girls sleeping in the same bedroom and suggested they should be separated. When he later visited the house he found that the owners had separated the boys and the girls by fitting wire netting across the bedroom![7]

Not only could 'abuse' take various forms - physical, sexual or, perhaps the hardest of all to detect, mental; it could also be perpetrated by a variety of people with whom evacuees were thrown into contact - not just foster parents but teachers, billeting officers, doctors and even other children. Quite a number of evacuees were bullied either at school or by other members of the household on which they were billeted. Barbara Smith remembers:

> Mr Hughes had a granddaughter Margaret who was a menace to say the least, she must have been jealous of our stay there. She was always taunting me about being an evacuee ... One day she went too far and I decided I'd had enough. I got on my bike telling her I was heading for the railway station to find my way home, and she knew I meant it ... Needless to say I was taken back and to Margaret's satisfaction given a good telling off.

Jean Hennity recalls:

> Mrs Jones had a horrible son - he was terrible to me, and we would often be attacked by older gangs of Welsh boys. They'd call us 'trash from England'. I worried about this later on in life - the memories of the bullying preyed on my mind.

May Hornby was also plagued by a member of her host's family:

> ... we always felt hungry. The woman used to promise me a digestive if I ran an errand - this involved walking miles to her mother's house. I had to pass a big pond covered in green slime - she used to call it Jinny Green Teeth. I was terrified of it and when I arrived there was a young lad there who tormented me - locked me up in the chicken coop and things like that. I was petrified.

216

Hilda Wilkes ran away to a friend's billet because the boys in hers were so rough with her. To avoid the local bullies Ron Organ always had to take a back route from his billet to school and hide in a hedge until the bell went. It was one thing to be bullied in the playground - quite another to be bullied in the classroom. Yet this is precisely what happened to Ron, who on top of hostility from local children, found himself at the mercy of a Welsh headmaster with clearly no liking for evacuees!

> *The headmaster, in front of the whole school announced the presence of us evacuees. 'These Liverpool kids think they can rule us,' he said, 'but I intend to nip their antics in the bud - you Welsh children report anything they get up to, do you understand?' Not long after, a Welsh boy accused me of weeing on him in the toilets. It was a complete lie but of course the head wouldn't listen. He said he was going to cane me in front of the whole school next day. That was a terrible sentence to have hanging over my head all night … He caned me over and over until I pulled my hand away but then he started hitting me anywhere he could - giving me a terrible beating. In the end the Infant teacher jumped on to the stage to put a stop to it - he could see things had gone too far …*

This was a particularly unpleasant incident but there does seem to have been a tendency to 'blame the evacuees' if fights broke out - which they often did between the 'newcomers' and the locals - or if any property or equipment got damaged. Jim Barrow recalls:

> *On the very first day I got into a fight in the schoolyard with a big Welsh farm lad - he was bullying one of our girls - Lillian Edwards I think. Anyway we had a stand-up fight. The Welsh head gave me the cane in front of the whole school - just me, not the local lad! I got on fine with the Welsh boys after that, though.*

Don and Eddie McKernan also remember that the children had a 'war' of their own in progress in Beaumaris - Welsh boys versus evacuees - and this was true in many areas. Yet while there were odd skirmishes of this type, these were only a version of the sort of gang rivalry which took place between local children. Indeed, sometimes evacuees were absorbed into different existing gangs and became ranged against each other! Of course some evacuees were downright badly behaved - Ralph Broster recalls how one lad carved his name into his host's grand piano! A few did get into serious trouble. As early as 13 September 1939, barely a week after the children had been evacuated, the *Liverpool Daily Post* was reporting that a nine-year-old boy had been sent back to Liverpool after stealing £1 and two flashlamps from a shop in Colwyn Bay! Juvenile delinquency as a whole increased during the war but Merseyside evacuees were no more guilty in this respect than other youngsters. In fact in an article headed 'Juvenile Crime - Alarming Increase in Caernarvonshire', the *North Wales Chronicle*, 21 February 1942 quoted Dr H. Lloyd Williams as actually remarking that *'they could* not *fasten the blame on the evacuees'*. Of the 51 children proceeded against for indictable offences in the past quarter, only 10 had been evacuated into the county.

Any evacuees caught stealing, or breaking the law in any other way, were subject to standard policing procedures but the issue of disciplining or punishing evacuees for simple misbehaviour in the home was more difficult. A 1939 Ministry of Health memo (EV4) had stated in respect to unaccompanied schoolchildren that *'the householder will be in loco parentis and should have no great difficulty in controlling the children and preserving reasonable discipline. The children will be accompanied by their teachers, who will know them and will be able to assist in their control.'* Some foster parents did solve the problem of 'disciplining' their evacuees by reporting any antics to their teachers, leaving them to sort out a punishment. But one group of foster parents wanted the matter clarifying and asked Liverpool Education Committee if they were be allowed to smack any evacuees who were naughty - but no firm ruling was ever given. The whole question of guardianship was only really thoroughly debated in respect of overseas evacuees[8] and in the absence of any instructions to the contrary, certainly some foster parents did mete out corporal punishment. Where children were accustomed to this (and it was fairly common practice in those days), it seems to have been accepted, especially if the host's own children got the same treatment. Harold Lyle remembers one particularly strict foster mother who gave her evacuees the strap but as her own son got it too it was somehow acceptable. What was not acceptable, however, was the kind of punishment being administered in a neighbouring house where Don Aird was beaten for trying to tell his parents that he and his brothers were literally starving, or the kind of severe beatings which seem to have been given out in some of the hostels.

Don Aird is reluctant to dwell too much on the downside of his evacuation experiences. Like many others he had good times and bad times whilst he was away from home but has overall a huge sense of gratitude to the people who offered him a refuge from the bombing. But he did meet with cruel treatment in one house. The same 'foster father' who attacked Don for alerting his parents to the poor conditions in the billet took him out hunting rabbits one day - with an ageing dog in tow. At one point Don was asked if he would just hold the dog for a minute. The little lad duly obliged, only to look on in utter horror as the man stepped back, raised his gun, pointed it at the dog and shot it dead. Regrettably, it seems that some children were quite simply billeted with sadists. The worst case must be that mentioned earlier of the little Liverpool girl forced to spend night after night in a dog kennel. But there are others.

Rita Holmes, for example, unhappy in her Barmouth billet and bullied by local children, tried to run away; caught and returned to her billet she was punished by having copious amounts of iodine poured into her scabies sores, with excruciating stinging. John Doyle was evacuated from Birkenhead to Gobowen when he was just seven years old. He and two of his sisters were billeted with a Mr & Mrs Jones. It was not a good billet; the children were neglected and always hungry. To make up for the poor meals John got into the habit of taking three apples each day from a bathful stored by the back door, one for himself and one for his sisters:

> *Mrs Jones found out and I got a good thrashing with a large cane she kept by her chair. I was convinced she didn't like little boys as I always seemed to be getting caned for something. During the few weeks I was there I ran away several times, I followed the railway tracks, thinking I'd end up at Woodside Station, but I was brought back every time - to another caning … My older sister visited unexpectedly one day in the middle of one of these canings. My sister took the cane from her, there was a lot of shouting and my sister packed up our things. Mother was horrified when we got home. She took us to the Town Hall to show the Authorities the state we were in - covered in lice and underfed.*

Mrs Hughes felt that she, too, was punished unnecessarily:

> *…Another haunting memory was the day I was shut in the cold, dark pantry. I cannot remember if I had been trying to answer the telephone - however, the village Post Mistress had informed Mrs H. that someone had been 'messing' with the phone and this was my punishment.*

Marjorie Lamb was also locked in her room, for nothing worse then the sin of being a frightened, confused little girl. She'd already concluded that her mother didn't want her, having never had any explanation of 'evacuation', and had just about got used to life in a hostel when, again with no explanation, she was taken out and put into a private billet. It seemed as if even the hostel didn't want her:

*I broke my heart crying - and was immediately sent to my new room
which was a dismal attic ... I was lonely, sad and confused. I think that
awful woman only wanted a servant. I had to do housework for her, if it
was not done to her liking I was punished ...*

Marjorie was not alone in feeling that she was, if not exactly abused, then at least
taken advantage of when it came to having to do work for foster parents. It's
difficult to decide at what point overworking the children actually amounted to
ill-treatment. As a recent TV documentary revealed, children in rural areas
were regarded as a vital part of the economy and did indeed have to work
extremely hard on the farm, in the house and in the fields.[9] Some Merseyside
evacuees looking back at their time in North Wales do feel they were exploited
- that the choice of a 'suitable' evacuee in the first place was with an eye to
securing a good farmhand or domestic worker and that they then did have to do
far more than was reasonable. Often it was those billeted on or near farms who
found out what hard work really meant:

*... we had to help muck out and feed the calves ... you'd think it would be
fun, but not when the calf, trying to get the last drop out, tossed the
bucket up and cut your chin. And making butter was such hard work too -
hand churning, on and on, thinking it would never thicken and then
patting and paddling the salt in - really hard work. We had to clear away
the dishes as well and wash up and sweep the floors.* (Pat Crick)

However, although many do remember having had to work hard, especially at
harvest time, most thoroughly enjoyed it. Ken McGunigle and his brother
certainly had their fair share of chores to do, but they didn't find the farm work
such a hardship:

*They used to delegate jobs for us. My job was chopping wood for the fire.
Fred's job was going round farms and houses to collect money for the
catalogue she ran. It used to take him ages - in all sorts of weather.
Another job on a Thursday - Mrs Jones made a lot of dough for bread,
about 8-10 loaves. She'd put it in a big basket and wrap up the dough in a
cloth. Fred and I had to carry it up to the Bakery in the centre of the
village. It was heavy. I used to have to have a rest because it was up hill as
well. Mr Jones had relatives who had a farm - every summer we' go
down and help with the harvest. It was great fun.*

Having had a terrible time in his first billet, John Doyle was very pleasantly surprised by the kindness shown him during his second spell of evacuation. This time he was sent to Montgomery and was allowed to help on a local farm:

> *...I loved the animals, especially the horses. I often went to a local market with the farmer to buy horses and rode them back to the farm bareback. I learnt a lot about animals during my stay in Montgomery. The farmer would also give me eggs, butter and bacon which I would take back proudly to Mrs Woods. After some time I was allowed to feed the other animals and collect the eggs in the evening ... I enjoyed the opportunity to work on the farm with the animals which at the time was a big achievement for a townie lad like myself who'd never seen some of the animals that were on the farm.*

As the war progressed and more and more land was brought into production it wasn't only the evacuees who were expected to lend a hand, especially at harvest time. Local children, shop girls, even office workers were brought in to help and special camps were set up to give this army of farm labourers somewhere to eat and sleep. For the 1941 harvest, 300 camps housed 12,000 young people - including boys from the Liverpool Institute who were paid 8d an hour when they went to work at the Schoolboy Harvest Camp at Plas Newydd, on Anglesey.[10]

Far from being exploited other evacuees too were paid for their labour. Archie Manser worked on a farm and at the local blacksmiths and used his earnings to buy sweets, chips and later (he confesses) cigarettes. Roy Parry put the money he earned - from pulling beets and potatoes - towards buying clothes. Some of the Fazakerley children, evacuated to the little village of Llanasa, received the princely sum of 1/- a week for helping out on the farm of Sir Percy Bates. At other times they went around with Lady Bates collecting scrap metal - in her car (a great treat for most). Of course many of the children - evacuees and others - were encouraged to take part in 'war work' - helping to fill sandbags, dig for victory, knit comforts for the troops, gather herbs and nettles, fruit and rosehips, conkers and acorns (to feed the pigs), scrap metal and bags of bones. Moya Jones remembers *'Saturdays spent in the exciting if draughty world of Caernarvon Barracks, helping to pack parcels for prisoners of war. As a great concession I was allowed to wrap the tablet of soap and place it in its accepted spot in the carefully designed jigsaw of tinned meats and rice puddings.*[11]

Some work was less than savoury though - we've already heard how two girls had to clean out spitoons (luckily they thought they were ashtrays!). Doris

221

Coxon and her sister had to clean their hosts' family gravestone each weekend. Yet, of course, children being children, some of the worst-sounding jobs were those enjoyed the most! Barbara Smith admits:

> One job we were given and didn't mind doing was to take the two cats and pick the fleas off them, one at a time, and throw them in the fire. I bet you are shuddering, me too now, but we thought it was great fun then!

Honor McGrath recalls *'being despatched to the local abbatoir to get black puddings. I had to wait and saw the pig slaughtered, then wait for the end product!'* Many of those evacuated to Carmel remember following the thresher machine to kill the mice. One school logbook records in July 1940 that 65 boys volunteered to assist farmers exterminate a current pest of caterpillars![12]

Although much of the 'work' asked of Merseyside evacuees was on the whole enjoyable, nevertheless, there were some, like Marjorie Lamb, who felt they were simply being used as 'skivvies'. As we've seen, Ken McGunigle and his brother worked hard but didn't feel they were being unduly exploited. Their sister's situation, however, was a different matter:

> Two of my sisters were in a good home but Charlotte (Totty) was in a terrible house. We used to go and see her but the woman wouldn't let us in. Totty was always cleaning and washing-up and had a terrible time. Fred and I used to feel sorry for her.

Others, like 'Jimmy Sinclair' (whose hosts even provided him with an unwieldy cart for all his fetching and carrying) and Charles Crebbin felt like glorified 'errand boys'. *'Although Graham [the son of the household] and I were the same age'*, Charles recalls *'... I became the person to be sent on 'messages'.* It wasn't unusual for him to have to walk two miles carrying heavy bags of groceries - though his foster mother once told Charles's father that she only sent him 'round the corner'! Jim Barrow found himself in a tug-of-war situation in his billet, fought over by his foster father who wanted him to help out on the farm (which he enjoyed) and his foster mother who wanted him to dust and polish around the house (which he hated!).

Ron Organ felt that his situation was abused; he was constantly being made to run errands - backwards and forwards to the shops, as if his foster parents took sadistic pleasure from having him at their beck and call. What he also found distressing was the fact that they never introduced him to anyone by his name but only ever as 'our evacuee'. Indeed some of the ill-treatment suffered by evacuees was not so much physical as mental. In a wartime broadcast, the eminent psychiatrist, Donald Winnicroft had emphasised how the distress naturally felt by many evacuees could be greatly eased by understanding foster parents providing them with security and affection. But not all foster parents complied! Charles Crebbin, the 'errand boy' mentioned above, evacuated from Anfield in 1939, spent the next two years in Meliden:

> *Those two years were probably the unhappiest two years of my life. I was not physically ill-treated in any way but was subjected to psychological bullying and insensitive treatment ... Mr K. was a cold, sarcastic type who had no scruples about taunting a six/seven/eight year old child evacuee in front of his own similarly aged son and persuading his own child to join in those taunts ... Mrs K.'s 'misbehaviour' was I think in allowing Mr K.'s actions to be allowed to continue.*

There was, of course, no law against 'insensitive treatment' nor any way in which the hosts could be forced to give a little love or affection to their young charges. Many of course did so unreservedly; one survey undertaken in 1941 concluded that only 8.2% of evacuees had an unhappy relationship with their foster parents.[13] Some evacuees actually escaped abusive situations at home; others found their foster parents showered them with far more love than they'd ever had from their real parents. But for those who ended up in households who had either been forced to take them or did so only for financial gain, the evacuee years were very bleak. Ron Organ comments - *'we just wanted someone to put their arms around us'*; Walter Hurst also remembers *'the longing to feel someone's arms around me to give me a big hug and love'*. Jean McCarthy, who hated every moment of separation from her family, recalls:

> *The lady who took us in would only allow us to call her 'Madam', we could never ever talk unless spoken to, she was very cold in as far as affection went, we never got any hugs or stories at bedtime.*

Pauline, evacuated to Aberystwyth at the tender age of five, was also starved of affection. *'One couldn't get away from the feeling of not really belonging,'* she explains, *'the sense of not getting any affection, not being wanted or loved.*[14] Alex Anderson felt equally *'denied of love or even simple affection'* during his time in Criccieth. He adds:

> *I cannot say that the Dobies were deliberately unkind to me, because they*

223

weren't; there approach to me was just starkly functional. Probably
summed up in the formula:
Little boy = unstable element (therefore) handle firmly.

In some households it was more the inequality or sheer unfairness of treatment which was hard to swallow - when for instance Alex Anderson was left sitting in the car whilst his guardians went into a cafe for a meal, when Ron Organ got water on his cornflakes when the rest of the household had milk or where, in one billet, George Parry remembers the evacuees had to eat in the kitchen whilst the family took their meals (rather better meals too) in the dining room. And Charles Crebbin, again drawing the short straw:

> *Naturally, evacuees like Charlie and myself were very much 'second fiddles'*
> *to the treasured [son] Graham. Sometimes this was hurtful; for example, I*
> *remember the time when Mrs K. said she had to take Graham to see the*
> *doctor straight after school and that us evacuees could have a picnic meal in*
> *the back garden and we should play quietly until they returned. That night*
> *Graham let the cat out of the bag by describing the meal the family had*
> *enjoyed in Prestatyn and the plot of the film they had seen at the cinema!*

Barbara Smith remembers her father leaving them pocket money *'but when I asked for tuppence from it to go to the chip shop, Mr Hughes refused'*. Others remember parcels arriving for them from home but mysteriously disappearing, much as happened to Mrs. Shaw:

> *Any monies sent by our mother, along with comics and sweets was*
> *immediately confiscated - 'This money is needed for shoe repairs, sewing*
> *threads, etc' we were told. Incidentally this cash was apart from the*
> *money our parents had to contribute for our keep. Mr & Mrs Evans had*
> *one married daughter with twin sons ... We always knew where the*
> *comics and sweets went but could not say anything. When the daughter*
> *visited we would be sent to bed whilst they all sat down to a good meal.*

For a small number of evacuees the problem was not mental or physical abuse, but sexual. Understandably, those affected do not find this an easy matter to discuss; sometimes the problem was not even fully appreciated at the time, as in the case of one Liverpool evacuee who in adult life suffered emotional problems but only realised when she underwent analysis that she'd actually been sexually abused as a child - by her billeting officer. Not all such cases remained hidden, however, even at the time. In July 1940, 38-year-old Dr Arthur Merfyn

Rhydderch who had a practice in Llandudno and Prestatyn was found guilty of indecently assaulting eight under 16-year-old boy evacuees from Liverpool. He was sentenced to 15 months imprisonment. In all cases the doctor had initially been called in to examine the children for routine complaints such as styes or German measles but had then asked them to attend his surgery for examination of 'lumps in their groins'. One of the foster mothers became suspicious when her two little evacuee boys said the doctor had given them both some money but told them 'not to tell'.[15] The authorities were swift to respond. Indeed the need to safeguard the welfare of evacuees had been recognised from the outset of the scheme but it came to attract even more attention as numbers grew again following the start of the air raids.

We've seen how in 1939 various *ad hoc* measures had been devised as a means of 'minding the children'. In addition to the work of teachers and billeting officers typical of the sort of thing speedily arranged were: the Welfare Centre for Evacuees set up at the Palladium Cafe, Prestatyn, within days of the start of the evacuation scheme; the communal meal service, under way almost immediately in parts of Anglesey; a Children's Aid Committee in Bethesda, comprising teachers, members of the Nursing Association, the WVS, and WI - quickly formed to deal with a whole variety of evacuee welfare issues; 'welfare committees' appointed by many local authorities; and of course 'clothing action' groups which had sprung up all over North Wales. A Government Committee which reported in January 1941, recognised the extent to which such improvised solutions had helped the situation at the time, and sought now to build on these achievements, acknowledging that *'the provision of adequate welfare facilities is the essence of good reception arrangements'*.[16]

The report prepared under the auspices of Geoffrey Shakespeare, MP,[17] gave particular attention to two aspects of evacuation: How can the burden in the Reception areas be eased? and What provisions can be made to induce evacuees to remain? Amongst the 'essential elements' of a successful evacuation it listed: adequate reception arrangements; good medical treatment; assistance allowances; publicity and propaganda; and welfare arrangements - specifically urging an increase in the number of welfare committees and the appointment of Welfare Officers in all areas to co-ordinate and stimulate welfare activities.

The findings of the Shakespeare Report were incorporated into a circular which was despatched to all reception areas in March 1941. In North Wales this coincided with the arrival of a heavy influx of evacuees which, along with a request from the Welsh Board of Health for detailed accounts of welfare arrangements, no doubt encouraged many authorities to act. Several areas had already gone some way towards rationalising their approach by appointing welfare committees[18] and, in rare cases, even already had district welfare workers submitting monthly reports of their work, visiting billets and schools.[19] The problem in NorthWales, as in many reception areas, was not so much one of extending peacetime welfare provisions but rather of devising what had never, or barely, existed before. But wartime conditions meant there were a number obstacles impeding the development of 'social services' - namely, shortage of trained personnel; scarcity of accommodation; and lack of money.

First, in this pre-Welfare State period, there was simply no large pool of professional social workers available. Although a few had accompanied the evacuees at the outset of the scheme in 1939, once the air raids began most trained welfare workers, who serviced the relatively sophisticated provisions of the city, were needed back home for Civil Defence duties. Some however had already made a mark. In Caernarvonshire, a member of staff of the London Child Guidance Committee had been voluntarily engaged as a Psychiatric Social Worker with evacuees at the outbreak of the war. 'Child guidance' ideas and techniques had been imported into Britain from the USA in the 1920s and involved the use of psychiatric social workers, as well as psychiatrists and educational psychologists. A central Mental Health Emergency Committee had been set up in 1939 to establish a register of qualified workers and circulate local authorities about the likely value of child guidance work in the event of evacuation.[20] Indeed, Caernarvonshire's Mental Health Committee were so impressed by the work done by the psychiatric social worker, and so convinced of the need to continue it, that they decided to appoint such a person at their own expense for three months from 1 January 1940, strongly urging the Welsh Board of Health to extend the appointment.[21]

On the second matter - accommodation - as we've seen, throughout North Wales this, especially the type of large empty house needed to set up a hostel, club, nursery or maternity centre, was increasingly hard to come by, competed for by government departments and businesses, voluntary organisations, the armed forces, and the local authorities themselves.

As for the third issue - finance - the local authorities, extremely wary of undertaking large-scale expenditure at the best of times (particularly in the wake of the 1930s), were certainly not inclined to burden themselves with hefty costs to meet the needs of non-local residents. Typical of the response to proposed welfare schemes was that displayed by Caernarvonshire County Council in June

226

1940 - the Medical Officer was authorised to make arrangements, as required by the Welsh Board of Health, for the possible arrival of 100 expectant mothers *'so long as the expense involved should not be the ultimate responsibility of this county'.* [22] If new forms of welfare provision were to be provided for evacuees in the reception areas it was vital that the government promote a more liberal financial policy - which it now did. As Titmuss put it, local authorities were in effect told *'to forget the economies of the past and not be "niggardly" with Government money in establishing welfare services'.* [23]

Whilst the Welsh authorities remained watchful of demands on local ratepayers, it was therefore not so much the financial issue as the shortage of trained personnel and suitable accommodation which tended to hinder establishment of welfare arrangements. Nevertheless, shortly after publication of the Shakespeare Report, welfare committees were active in almost every district to which Merseyside evacuees had been sent. [24] The Welsh Board of Health was also keen to establish some level of county and regional co-ordination; in December 1941, for example, Miss Margaret Rowlands was appointed as Social Welfare Organiser for Anglesey, having *'the capacity for developing new services necessitated by evacuation',* [25] and in February the following year a Regional Welfare Officer was appointed to act for the whole of North Wales (including Montgomeryshire). Beneath the Regional and County Welfare Officers, many areas appointed 'District' Welfare Officers. The advertisement placed by Holywell RDC illustrates the type of person required:

> *Applicants are invited for the appointment of a temporary Woman Welfare Officer ... salary to be paid will be £200 pa plus travelling expenses. Candidates should have good training and experience of social work, organising ability and knowledge of social legislation. The officer appointed will be required to organise and stimulate social and welfare activities among evacuated mothers and children.* [26]

Menna Lloyd Williams was Caernarvonshire's Welfare Officer. Her reports, covering general issues, communal billets, hostels and individual casework show both the variety and pioneering nature of the work. She recognised how important it was to involve the whole community in looking after the evacuees and for that reason recommended welfare committees should comprise representatives from local voluntary groups and religious organisations as wel' as council officials and evacuated teachers. [27]

Those responsible for the welfare of the children also had to take what might be termed 'preventative' action directed at addressing the second problem outlined in the Shakespeare Report - the tendency for evacuees, regardless of the bombs, to want to return home. At the time of the first evacuation, much was made of the 'cultural' difficulties involved when town met country: the problem of a lack of entertainment or recreational facilities in rural areas. But the issue had been tackled quite speedily in some districts. As early as 26 September 1939 the County Games Organiser in Caernarvon suggested local councils provide pitches for evacuated children and others to play on; even before many of the first evacuees had arrived, the Mayor of Bangor had pointed out the need to develop 'the religious and social sides' of the City's 'adopted children'; the *Flintshire Observer* reported on 28 September 1939 that many movements were on foot at Abergele to make evacuees feel at home - a committee was hard at work arranging communal recreation for children aged 7 to 16. Elsewhere there were attempts to provide centres for evacuated mothers to meet - and 'make and mend'!

Most of these early efforts had been thwarted by the large-scale return home of evacuees to the as-yet unbombed streets of Merseyside, but when evacuation began again in earnest towards the end of 1940, many of the schemes were revived and more were devised. Some were quite successful, such as the social centre for evacuated mothers and children set up in Denbigh Borough's Conservative Club, a similar centre in Rhostyllen Parish Hall (near Wrexham), and 'a happy meeting place' for evacuated mothers and their young children, run by Caernarvon WVS on local Liberal Club premises. In Portmadoc the Labour Party allowed evacuees to use the club games room. Elsewhere attempts to provide centres were sometimes thwarted by lack of suitable premises until an Local Education Authority (LEA) memo, issued in January 1941, encouraged LEAs to allow use of school premises out of hours as centres of recreation for mothers with young children as well as for the schoolchildren themselves. This not only alleviated the problem of finding premises but also of supervision - the onus for which in these circumstances tended of course to fall on the teachers. As we've seen already, many rose to the challenge - Bryan Blades for instance held a Play Centre every Friday evening for evacuees in the Groeslon and Carmel area in Caernarvonshire. Concerts, put on here and elsewhere by evacuees, were often attended by the foster parents and helped build bridges between the 'newcomers' and the 'locals' - Liverpool Institute's Drama Society entertained their hosts at Penrhyn Hall in February 1940 with four performances of Sheridan's *The Rivals*; Salisbury Street Infants put on a show in July 1941 to thank their Bangor 'Aunties'. [28]

Unfortunately not all teachers were quite as enthusiastic as Mr Blades or Miss

228

Crosbie. J. H Leakey was master-in-charge of Dulwich Preparatory School, evacuated to Betws-y-Coed. His was not the only school in this village - there was also a contingent there of some Liverpool-Irish Roman Catholic children. These children, he recalls, who were frowned upon from the outset by the local strongly Nonconformist population, were quickly becoming ever more unpopular because of various antics born of boredom. Leakey explains:

> *I approached their teachers who, after taking lessons returned to their digs without attempting to do anything for the children and, at the same time, grumbled about how bored they were. I offered them use of our playing fields, plus all our equipment ... The only stipulation I made was that they should supply the supervision. I pointed out we were all working 12 hours a day and couldn't provide any ourselves. Not one single teacher offered to take advantage of this and the children were unable to make use of my offer.* [29]

This highlights the vulnerability of the government evacuation scheme - despite the work of many conscientious paid officials it still relied very much on voluntary co-operation and goodwill. Where these were lacking or unsuitable, problems did arise.

While social centres offered a period of respite to harrassed foster parents they also sometimes offered a lifeline to unhappily billeted evacuees. John Houston, remembering one of his less happy evacuation periods, writes of *'two bright spots in this period'* - one was the discovery of a large friendly pig who loved having his back scratched and responded with 'a few companionable grunts' but, more importantly, listened attentively as John poured out all his troubles! The second was *'a small social club in the village school for us evacuees, which we could go to for a few hours in the evening. Here we could meet and talk to our friends in our own language and I was able to meet up with my brother. They had even found a few books and games for us so we were able to while away a few happy hours ...'*. Pauline wasn't terribly happy either in her billet in Aberystwyth and so she and her sister *'joined every 'movement' possible - Band of Hope, we signed the pledge vowing never to drink [they were aged five and eight at the time!] watched Magic Lantern whenever possible - anything to get us out of the house and away from Mrs A. ...'* [30]

Of course there were numerous existing organisations for young people in reception areas, like the Band of Hope mentioned here, which many evacuees did join. Some, like the Scouts and Guides, were already familiar meeting

229

places. By January 1941 it was reported with regard to Anglesey for example, that *'All the evacuees now belong either to the 1st Anglesey Guides or to the Brownie Pack and are working hard for the salvage scheme and knitting comforts for the troops.'* [31] Peter Walker, evacuated with Liverpool Collegiate school to Bangor recalls:

> *Out of school, the 1st Bangor Scouts filled much of our time. We had quickly found this unique crowd in a loft in Berllan Bach, somewhere behind the town clock, where Old Woodhead, lovingly nicknamed Penpren [Welsh for 'wood-head'], reigned supreme. ... He seemed to be adored by his troop as much for his discipline as for his unorthodox methods, not to mention his extensive knowledge of plants and the mountains ... He and his lieutenants took us to the mountains whenever conditions permitted .... [we] spent many happy hours on Snowdon in shorts and gym pumps, when he would lead the troop up the slopes of Lliwedd to lunch on bilberries.*

Other organisations were peculiar to Wales but now found they were attracting new, English recruits - the Welsh League of Youth organised sports activities and camps and produced a regular magazine. By 1943 its membership had leapt to 50,000. [32] The Urdd Gobaith Cymru also flourished during the war, partly because the Welsh Board of Education insisted that every teenage child should join a youth club or cadet force. [33] Many evacuees joined local youth clubs, such as the thriving club in Caernarvonshire known as the 'Aelwyd' group. Others became involved in local cadet corps which were being extensively developed at this time, although these were not quite so popular in parts of North Wales which retained the old anti-militarist tradition. When a conference was convened in Caernarvon to 'develop the county spirit in the Air Training Corps', the Higher Education Committee expressed *'the hope and conviction that it will be possible to foster county activities without unduly introducing a militarist spirit into our secondary schools'.* [34] Nevertheless, squadrons were established in the county. Young Farmers' Clubs also thrived in the more rural areas. Evacuation had, in general, raised awareness of the need to safeguard the moral and physical welfare of young people. More Youth Committees were appointed and Welsh children benefited as much as evacuees from these developments.

One of the most successful Army Cadet Companies was that founded at Beaumaris for the evacuees of the Blue Coat School. The Company was affiliated to the 2nd Battalion of the Royal Welsh Fusiliers and soon gained an excellent reputation, with the boys achieving high pass rates in First Aid, Signalling and ARP (Gas Test) exams. The Blue Coat cadets took an important part in the Wings for Victory and War Weapons Weeks and on one occasion performed the changing of the Guard at Caernarvon Castle in the presence of the Grenadier Guards stationed in the town. The School Band were all members of the Corps and sometimes marched at the head of parades of the Royal Welsh Fusiliers; they took part in the last march-past of the 2nd Battalion before it was disbanded in 1945. The cadets enjoyed summer camps at Rhosneigr and Holyhead. Occasionally, they were responsible for maintaining communications in an area of about 8-miles radius from Beaumaris Gaol (HQ of the local Home Guard) especially during the mock invasions of Anglesey which were part of regular army training at that time. This seems to have involved the cadets in hair-raising, break-neck journeys on dubious army-issue bicycles but no doubt the boys revelled in such 'real action'.

Not that evacuees entirely missed out on the sort of 'excitement' enjoyed by those who'd stayed behind in the bombed cities. Many witnessed 'dog-fights', such as that which saw a Junkers 88 being shot down in the Clywedog Valley after an encounter with two Spitfires on 7 September 1940. Other evacuees were all too aware that the bombers they heard droning overhead were intent on trying to destroy their own Merseyside homes. Some even had close encounters themselves! Bill ('Will') Wilkinson recalls what happened one day just after he'd arrived back at his billet for lunch. His 'honorary' gran ('Nain' in Wesh) was frying black pudding and asked him just to hold the handle of the pan for a minute while she set the table:

> *As soon as I grasped the pan handle there was a sudden, almighty deafening explosion, then silence. A second or two later all the willow pattern plates on the old Welsh dresser toppled forward in unison and fell to the floor with a crash. Then more silence and my ears were ringing. Nain looked at me. 'Whatever was that, Will?' and as she surveyed the debris at her feet she began to cry. I thought to myself, 'What have I done now?' I ran to the open doorway of the kitchen and looked up into a clear blue summer sky and saw a plane flying at maybe 5,000 feet, heading off towards Snowdonia ... 'It's a bloody Jerry!' I shouted. 'He's dropped a bomb on us.* [35]

In fact, as Will found out later it was not a bomb but a plane crash-landing on the house next door, and it wasn't a German plane but one of our own Spitfires - fully armed as well. The occupier of the house, her evacuee, Will and Nain all had a lucky escape, being pulled to safety just as the ammunition in the wing of the plane began to go off as the whole thing burst into flames. Luckily the pilot had bailed out in time. Though Will was wrong on this occasion, bombs were dropped in north and mid-Wales, some simply 'offloading' on their way back from Merseyside, some aimed at Welsh targets, such as factories and RAF bases. The first such incidents actually took place even before anywhere on Merseyside came under attack![36]

Evacuees didn't miss out on all the 'excitement' of the War. In Beaumaris a plane crash-landed on this house, 17 New Street, just as Bill Wilkinson (a Blue Coat School Pupil) was about to have lunch in his billet next door. (Photo courtesy Reg Chambers Jones)

Despite being set up with the best of intentions not all the 'organised' ventures for evacuees thrived. In Portmadoc a proposal to establish a centre for indoor games and entertainment for evacuated children was eventually dismissed as *'impracticable and unnecessary in a small town like Portmadoc, seeing that the evacuated children joined with the local children in enjoying the amenities and social life of the place generally'*.[37] Indeed, many of the areas to which the children were evacuated had excellent amenities - some were holiday resorts - and the original much-publicised cries about the so-and-so countryside having no pubs or cinemas was, of course, like so much else at that time, much exaggerated. In Barmouth, Rita Holmes was actually billeted with the manager of the local cinema and never had to queue to see a film! But Laura Jones even enjoyed the queuing:

> *Llanrwst boasted a cinema called The Luxor. There was a nice entrance foyer and there were stalls and a circle. Outside there was a canopy so if it rained you could keep reasonably dry. The 'still' pictures of the current film and future attractions were to be seen outside the cinema and in the foyer, this passed the time while we waited to go in.*[38]

Ron Shaw remembers:

> *... I also attended the local picture house - Eric was told to take me. He was about 13 and I think he had his eye on a local lass so I cramped his style. Still, I went - the picture was called 'Rage in Heaven'. I didn't understand a thing about it but it was an occasion for a picture to be shown in Bethesda.*

Lilian Jones, a former Blue Coat pupil, includes among her memories of being an evacuee in Beaumaris:

> *... the Saturday afternoon matinee serial of 'The Scorpion' - not to be missed - and the one-liner from the cinema usherette after she sprayed the area where we were sitting, with sickly sweet perfume: 'Blue Coats - first four rows only.' (Is that why some of us today still walk as though we are studying clouds?!)*[39]

Cefn Mawr may only have been a little place but, as Edward Mandaluff recalls, even there there was a 'picture house': *'it had one of everything - one school, one newsagent, one fruit shop, only one pub and - my favourite - the Palace Picture House'.* Alex Cross has similarly fond memories of *'the Derby Cinema on Castle Street'*, which he used to frequent on Saturdays when he was an evacuee in Caergwrle. Others remember magical pantomine trips.

For many evacuees, though, it was the countryside itself that provided the best possible entertainment. Clifford Wrightson recalls that a local farmer's son still laughs today remembering how one of their newly-arrived evacuees, when asked where he was going, replied *'Out to play in the street'.* Of course there wasn't 'a street' as such for miles around! But what there was around, for many, was one enormous play-ground which was a source of sheer delight for those who loved their time as evacuees and a huge compensation for those who were otherwise unhappy in their new life - as Marjorie Lamb put it: *'All my memories [of evacuation] seem to be unhappy ones - but I do remember the lovely countryside and the beautiful beach.'* Alex Anderson also drew solace from his surrounds - exploring the castle at Criccieth, playing on the beach, watching fishermen repairing their nets, roaming the nearby hills. At a time when Ron Organ was suffering bullying at school, neglect from his parents and a lack of love in his billet, he too could take tremendous pleasure from the 'rural experience':

> *I once saw an old man lying flat on the floor. I thought he was dead. I went up to him and gave him a poke - he nearly jumped out of his skin, and so did I! It turned out he was ferreting for rabbits - he'd been lying down and listening - I stayed and watched what he was doing and at the end he gave me a rabbit. It was worth about two bob - I thought to myself 'This is the life!'*

Pupils from Liverpool's Blue Coat School learning to swim in 'chilly' water in Beaumaris Baths! Included are Maurice Cureton, Stan ('Ratto') Mason, Don and Eddie McKernan, Freddy Davies, Frank Trowler, 'Marsh' Harrison, Tommy ('The Swat') Joynson, Don Tweedale, Walter Street, Paddy Ryan, Geoff Wise, Cyril Morris, John Topping, Pollit, Bill Wilkinson, Alan McLaren, Tommy ('Bomber') Arnold, Tommy McHugh and Frank Teague. (Photo & details courtesy Blue Coat Old Blues Association and Bill Wilkinson)

As Ron's account suggests, the countryside provided not just entertainment but also nourishment for some of the children who could supplement sometimes meagre meals in their billets with gleanings from fields, hedgerows and orchards. Many of the children were only too pleased to think they might be able to help out their hosts. Some were a little misguided - like the boy who came struggling home to his billet in Mold, laden down with potatoes, explaining that he'd found them growing wild in a field and could have got a lot more if only he'd had a bigger bag![40] Others, like W.D. Jones and his pals, evacuated near Llanddona on Anglesey, thought they could be helpful *and* enterprising! Following a night disturbed by an unusual amount of explosions, the boys had walked to White Bay to see if they could spot anything unusual - perhaps an ammunition ship ablaze in Liverpool Bay. They noticed the beach itself looked a bit strange, rather whiter than usual. Then they realised why - it was absolutely covered with fish *'literally thousands of fish of all varieties, flapping around the edge of the water as the tide went out, leaving them high and dry'*. The explosions in the night had been mines jettisoned from damaged German bombers and as they'd detonated above the surface of the sea, they'd concussed and beached all the fish in the area. W.D. Jones explains:

> *During this period of the war food was getting scarce, particularly fish as most fishermen had been called up, so you can understand our enthusiasm when we saw this potential food supply. The problem was how to get it back to Beaumaris? Off came our raincoats which we turned inside out to make a waterproof carrier bag, then we bundled in as much choice fresh fish as we could carry, and off we went ... As each mile went by our bundles seemed to double in weight but the prospects of sudden and unexpected wealth sustained our perseverence and we finally arrived back in town undetected. After giving my hostess all the fish she wanted the rest was disposed of to various people in return for small amounts of cash which relieved my dependency on postal orders from home for a while.*

The venture seemed to have been highly successful, at least until the next time the boys needed their raincoats - which unfortunately happened to coincide with a special Sunday Service, involving the whole school. The intrepid 'fishermen' became very self-conscious as the hot, packed church began to smell like a fish-market - they couldn't wait to escape. For once the senior master present had a good reason to suspect that something 'fishy' had been going on! [41]

With the enormous influx of evacuees into North Wales in the summer of 1941 there was some genuine fear that food supplies would prove inadequate. At a meeting of Caernarvon County Council in June 1941, for example, it was pointed out that the quota of foodstuffs allowed the county was still on the 1938-39 basis yet the population had increased by some 70,000.[42] There was also a growing clamour that billeting allowances were insufficient. The government had already raised the levels of payment once to try and encourage householders to take in evacuees and to compensate for steep price rises in 1940 (food prices had risen by 14% in the first few months of the war). Portmadoc UDC had been one of the first councils to raise this matter with the Ministry, as early as October 1939, and had been readily supported by all North Wales authorities. Many evacuated teachers had also felt that the allowances were insufficient. Even at the time of the first evacuation, the Head of Liverpool Collegiate school, for example, had written to parents of evacuees in the following terms (28 September 1939):

> It is unnnecessary for me to say to parents that 8/6d per week does not cover the normal cost of housing and feeding our boys here ... The growing boy of 11 to 19 ...will consume more food than most adults, particularly from the age of 14 or 15 ... I therefore must appeal to all parents to agree to subscribe the difference between 8/6d and the real cost [which he calculated to range from 2/- for younger boys to 8/- for boys over 14].

The billeting rates were eventually increased in May 1940 from the original flat rate to a sliding scale of payments according to age - children aged 10-14 were entitled to 10/6d; 14-16, 12/6d; over 16, 15/-. Many still felt the allowances were inadequate and this was repeatedly cited by officials in North Wales as a cause for lack of co-operation from householders. Pat Crick recalls that *'when my parents came to visit, the farmer's wife told them the 10/6d wasn't enough - they'd have to give her more. Mother said she wouldn't give any more money but she would bring a food parcel next time she came.'* Even Mrs Redmund, whose family had taken great pleasure from providing a home in Corwen for several evacuees from Birkenhead comments that the allowance *'wasn't enough to keep them - and we had to buy clothes so as not to be ashamed of taking them out'.* In the end a further increase was introduced in July 1941, this time at the instigation of Ebbw Vale UDC, with one final rise in 1944 (urged by Camarthen).The government had appreciated that the billeting allowance wasn't keeping pace with rising costs but was anxious to avoid the inflationary effect of increasing the amount of money in circulation at a time when supplies were diminishing.[43] Eventually, however, the need to try and encourage offers of accommodation won the day: the 'stick' of compulsory notices may have been available but clearly the 'carrot' of a reasonable billeting allowances was the better approach. Several North Wales authorities certainly felt that the increased rates would produce a better response; on hearing news of one such rise, Buckley UDC even re-published their notices inviting volunteers of accommodation.[44]

Further measures were also introduced to try and ensure that evacuees, and others, were adequately fed. Mrs Gwladys Jones from Pwllheli remembers:

Foster parents received an allowance each week to feed each child. In due course the allowance proved too frugal for hungry growing lads and it was decided to feed them en masse for a midday meal and tea, at a cost of 6d for dinner and 4d for tea, Monday to Friday, with Saturday and Sunday to be provided by the foster parents. Bread was sliced by the bacon machine of the grocer and potatoes scrubbed and peeled by the local fish and chip vendor. For a couple of months all went well but we were very short of cooking equipment. So helpers lent cooking trays and pans and we strained cabbage through wire waste paper baskets that had been scrubbed in the kitchen sinks! [45]

In many parts of the country, canteens were set up and manned by WVS volunteers. Pam McNaught remembers her mother helping out at the canteen in Bangor - but it wasn't any delicious smell of cooking that came to mind when Pam recalled that particular feeding centre: *'The Royal Welsh Fusiliers were stationed in Bangor and used the canteen - but their goat [the RWF mascot] used to go with them: it smelt the whole place out!'* It was the WVS that organised the canteen in Llandegfan. This was originally intended for the Liverpool evacuees and provided a midday meal for 3d per child. At first only a few attended but by the end of the month it was serving all 40 evacuees billeted locally, and some Anglesey children too. Indeed as rationing began to affect everyone the government agreed to raise the rate of grant-in-aid to local councils to enable an increase in provision of school meals and free milk for all children.[46]

Many authorities took up the idea not only of a school meals service but also of a more general Communal Feeding scheme - often better known as 'British Restaurants'. The main stumbling block, as ever, was often shortage of suitable accommodation. Holyhead UDC had decided in June 1941 that five rooms of the Railway Institute would be ideal for such a centre but the Institute objected and it was not until September 1942 that all work on the Restaurant was finally completed. Caernarvon Borough had even greater difficulties with the chosen site for their British Restaurant and spent over two years discussing the matter. Perhaps only those who dined in British Restaurants could understand why no greater sense of urgency was displayed! Former council official Lesley Twist remembers:

> *We had a British Restaurant in Bangor. You could get a meal there for a shilling. It was awful. We didn't really know what we were eating! But we had to try and popularise it so we held a NALGO evening there. We 'endured' it rather than enjoyed it!*

Nevertheless, Bangor Restaurant which housed a maximum of 100 persons was reported in September 1940 to be serving on average 250 meals per day. In Wrexham a British Restaurant at Rhosddu School, officially opened by the Mayor on 21 August 1941, was soon advertising MEALS AT MODERATE PRICES.[47] A 'Communal Dining Centre' was also set up at Rhyl Town Hall, *'for the purpose of providing a hot mid-day meal at moderate prices for evacuees'.*

The provision of meals, then, was just one of many expedients adopted by the reception areas both to ease the burden on local homes and to help the incoming evacuees. Many of those arriving from the bombed areas were in a dreadful condition - often dirty and verminous - but there was no longer a howl of protest from householders. It was appreciated that many of the children, and adults, had spent night after night in shelters which left a lot to be desired; Liverpool's water supply was constantly being interrupted as mains pipes were shattered; soap was hard to come by; a change of clothes was impossible to secure from a house which had been reduced to rubble; scabies was rife. But what had been viewed as unacceptable in the phoney-war days of 1939 was now dealt with on the whole far more calmly, partly because the evacuees were by this time quite obviously victims of Nazi aggression, and partly because there was a new pool of experience to draw upon - householders now knew all about nits and scabies and wet beds, and there were officials and hostels to help bear the burden.

The point has been made in a study of evacuation in Cambridge[48] that had there been more skilled services available when things went wrong the great ebb home of the first evacuation might not have occurred. This is plausible, but at least in the Merseyside/North Wales experience of evacuation, seems unlikely. Admittedly much was learned from the first evacuation, and welfare services did expand and mature as the war progressed. But some services had been available in 1939 - billeting officers and teachers had quickly adopted a routine of billet-visiting; social centres were established; and far more 'helpers' accompanied the first evacuees than subsequent arrivals. On the other hand, when, later, certain services were provided (like nurseries and women's clubs), demand amongst evacuees was not always sufficient to warrant their continuation. Undoubtedly the establishment of some hostels or institutions and the growing presence of paid social workers did help both householders and evacuees. These developments are important both to the history of the Evacuation Scheme and to the history of the Welfare State. Yet it is crucial not to lose sight of the fact that in most of North Wales, reception of evacuees was by no means 'institutionalised'. It remained largely a 'homely' affair - the householders cared for the evacuees; where either needed help this was provided by the teacher, or a local lady (even if she was now a 'WVS'), or the local Clerk, Surveyor or Bank Manager (who happened to have the new title of Billeting Officer) and it was often 'the village' itself which acted as the keenest watchdog of evacuees' welfare.

One retiring billeting officer (in Deudraeth RDC) felt confident enough to declare in September 1941 that the Evacuation scheme *'has become a well organised affair in this very rural district'*.[49] It was true that reception had become largely a matter of routine to many North Wales counties by the end of 1941. Merseyside had survived all that the Luftwaffe could throw at her in the spring and early summer of that year, and North Wales had survived the huge influx of people that had followed in the wake of the raids. The pinnacle of the scheme, in terms of sheer numbers arriving, had been reached in May/June 1941; although trickle evacuation continued to occur at monthly intervals during the rest of the year, a slow voluntary trickle home was also now in progress. There were occasional official arrivals of small groups from Merseyside in 1942 and 1943 but by this time many more were returning home and the whole machinery of evacuation was being allowed to slowly wind down or, rather, to be put into cold storage. The government wished to retain the framework of the administration in case of future emergency. This in fact came in 1944. With the horrifying 'V' bomb attacks on the south of England, the reception services of the counties of north and mid-Wales were once again in demand.

NOTES

[1] Quoted in *Liverpool Daily Post*, 1 February 1940

[2] It was only in 1933 with the passing of the 'Children and Young Persons Act' that children were given some protection from parental abuse. This Act decreed than anyone over the age of 16 who 'wilfully assaults, ill-treats, neglects, abandons or exposes [a child] ... in a manner likely to cause unnecessary suffering' was deemed guilty of misdemeanour. See Inglis, p.164

[3] See Carlton Jackson, p 132

[4] Glasinfryn Logbook 1931-43, entries 27 May & 2 July 1940

[5] Penny Starns in *Evacuation: The True Story* (BBC radio broadcast) maintained that 10%-15% of evacuees were sexually abused. This particular enquiry into the Merseyside/ North Wales experience has not uncovered anything like that amount of abuse. This does not necessarily mean it did not exist. Often those who were ill-treated find it difficult if not impossible to talk of what happened.

[6] *Our Evacuee*, p.17

[7] Ibid. p.53

[8] See Jackson, *Who Will Take Our Children*, pp.91-3

[9] Channel 4 documentary 'Green and Pleasant Land', November 1999

[10] UCNW (PNP5723), cited Chambers Jones, *Bless 'Em All*, p.47

[11] Extract from 'Our War'supplement, 3 September 1989.

[12] Bangor Modern School Logbook 1935-49, entry 2 July 1940

[13] Susan Isaacs (ed), *The Cambridge Evacuation Survey* (1941)

[14] Cited in 'Home Front Heroes', *Cambrian News* supplement, 1989

[15] See Flintshire Quarter Sessions papers, 1940 (Hawarden RO)

[16] From the *Report on Conditions in Reception Areas*, being the Report of the Shakespeare Committee, January 1941 (Penmaenmawr UDC file 'Welsh Board of Health Circulars')

[17] Shakespeare was then Parliamentary Under-Secretary of State and chairman of the Children's Overseas Reception Board; he had earlier served as Parliamentary Secretary to the Ministry of Health and Board of Education.

[18] See e.g. report on Llandegfan Welfare Committee, *North Wales Chronicle*

[19] Ceiriog RDC Minutes, 21 November 1929 *et seq.*

[20] See Holman, *The Evacuation: A Very British Revolution*, p.120

[21] See Caerns Education Committee Minutes (Bk 28), School Attendance& MI, 9 Apr 1940.

[22] Caerns CC Minutes of Maternity & Child Welfare Committee, 25 June 1940

[23] Titmus, p.372

[24] For example, in Bethesda, Llanfairfechan, Nant Conway, Portmadoc, Lleyn, Penmaenmawr, Betws-y-Coed, Conway, Caernarvon, Towyn, Deudraeth, Twrcelyn, Valley, Menai Bridge, Beaumaris and Denbigh Borough

[25] Extract from the advert for the post, *North Wales Chronicle*, 1 August 1941

[26] Holywell RDC Minute Book no.36, Evacuation Committee, 26 Feb 1943

[27] Caerns CC Minutes, Report of County Welfare Officer 1941

[28] Miss Crosbie wrote a special poem, reproduced in *North Wales Chronicle*, 18 July 1941

[29] See J H Leakey, *School Errant - The Story of the Wartime Adventures of the Dulwich College Preparatory School.*

[30] Extract from 'Home Front Heroes' (Cambrian News supplement) 1989

[31] See *North Wales Chronicle*, 3 January 1941

[32] It had been founded by Ifan ab Owen in 1922 - see John Davies, *A History of Wales*, p.602

[33] Ibid.

[34] Caerns. Higher Education & Curriculum Minutes, 2 October 1941, cited P E Owen, op cit

[35] See Liverpool Blue Coat Brotherly Society, Annual Report 1989, p.24

[36] For an account of some of the enemy activity in North Wales, see Ivor Wynne Jones, *Air War over Denbighshire and Flintshire, 1939-45*

[37] Penmaenmawr UDC Welsh Bd of Health file, 23 June 1941; Portmadoc UDC Evac Cttee 20 July 1942

[38] Extract from 'Wales at War' supplement

[39] Quoted in Liverpool Blue Coat Brotherly Society Annual Report Sept 1989

[40] See the *Flintshire Observer*, 21 September 1939

[41] See Liverpool Blue Coat Brotherly Society, Annual Report, Sept. 1989, p.29

[42] Reported in the *North Wales Chronicle*, 13 June 1941

[43] See Titmuss, p.398. By 1941, for example, a 2lb loaf cost 4d, milk was $4^{1}/_{2}$d a pint, cheese 1/1d per lb and a pound of butter was1/7d)

[44] See Buckley UDC Evacuation Comittee Minutes, 16 May 1940; *North Wales Chronicle*, 17 May 1940

[45] Extract from 'Wales at War', supplement

[46] By March 1943, Flintshire for example had at least 50 school meal centres, see Flints Education Committee Minutes, 31 March 1943

[47] see *Wrexham Leader*, 15 August 1941

[48] Isaacs, S. (ed.), The Cambridge Evacuation Survey, (Methuen & Co., 1941)

[49] Deudraeth RDC Minutes, Report of Billeting Officer 8 Sept 1941

8- *More Comings and Goings*

By the end of 1943 the Ministry of Health had already begun to study the problem of returning evacuees to their homes and a final report on the ending of the Evacuation Scheme was presented in December. It wasn't until September 1944, however, that the North Wales authorities received their first notification that return home arrangements were to be put in motion regarding evacuees *whose homes lay in areas other than London*. Indeed, many of the London area evacuees had only just arrived in Wales, fleeing as they were from Hitler's 'V' bombs. Telegrams about this new influx were received by most Welsh reception authorities in July 1944 and caused a hasty reassembling of the reception machinery - which happily hadn't actually been disbanded even though many evacuees had already left for home. It was in some ways fortunate that the authorities were called upon to make arrangements for the 'V' bomb evacuees for having been 'reactivated' they were then better prepared shortly afterwards to tackle the far from simple repatriation arrangements for all evacuees still in their care.

The 'V' bomb attacks had begun in the middle of June. First came the V1s (the 'buzzbombs' or 'doodlebugs') which caused extensive damage and horrific injuries, spraying shrapnel up to $1/4$ mile from their point of impact. In September they were joined by another new weapon - the V2. At first the government had tried to play down the effect of the 'V' bombs but with growing casualties along 'Bomb Alley' an official evacuation was ordered in early July and school parties joined the large numbers of private evacuees trying to escape this latest terror.

Throughout July and August a steady stream of evacuees made their way up to North Wales from London and surrounding districts - almost 3,000 arrived in Flintshire alone. The success of arrangements made to receive them all seems to have surprised even the billeting officers themselves! Portmadoc's Clerk, reporting on this latest reception of evacuees, commented that whilst 'considerable effort' had been involved, the whole process had worked *'efficiently and with surprising smoothness and expediency'*.[1] Much the same sort of arrangements were made in 1944 as for earlier evacuations though on this occasion Rest Centres were brought into use across North Wales from the outset, allowing local authorities not only to feed the evacuees on arrival but also to accommodate them, in some cases for up to six days, until satisfactory billets could be found. Popular resorts like Rhyl and Colwyn Bay, at the height of the summer season yet again, struggled to find space for even more visitors but in most areas householders seem to have come forward willingly despite the claim in *The Welsh Nationalist,* August 1944 that '*We divulge no secret when we say that there is in Wales intense opposition to the present evacuation scheme.*' Holywell RDC reported the 'very ready assistance' of householders, evacuees in Mold were given 'a ready welcome', in the rural district of Lleyn they were met 'with great kindness' and in the Wrexham area there were so many volunteers of accommodation that the authorities found they had a surplus of billets in several parishes.[2]

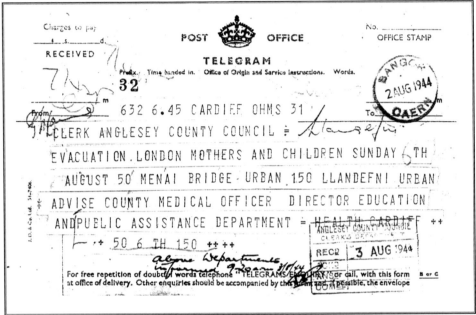

There were more comings and goings in North Wales in 1944 as many Merseyside evacuees went home to make room for evacuees arriving from the South, fleeing the dreaded 'V' Bombs. (Telegram courtesy Anglesey County Record Office)

As far as provision of schooling was concerned the problem with this latest evacuation was not so much one of finding accommodation as of securing sufficient teaching staff to meet the increased needs. Many of the teachers who'd been evacuated earlier had by this time been recalled to their home schools to deal with the children who had already returned; evacuees who remained had been grouped together or assimilated into local schools. With the onset of this new influx of pupils in 1944, the evacuating authorities in the south were asked to provide extra teachers, but local Directors of Education were also authorised to make representations to the Ministry of Health '*with a view to arrangements being made where possible for the Liverpool and Birkenhead evacuees at present in the county to return home again*'.[3]

The importance of the 'repatriation' arrangements were highlighted in a WVS Evacuation Bulletin which announced:

> *Those in Reception Areas who are preparing evacuees for their return home must have the satisfactory feeling of making a good end to a good job, and this last step is by no means the least important, since the future happiness of the children depends on their successful re-uniting with their parents in normal family life.*

The Evacuation Scheme had turned full circle. Now evacuation authorities found themselves in charge of detailed reception arrangements whilst reception authorities were responsible for organising the orderly despatch of children, families, expectant mothers, the aged, blind and infirm, to their designated destinations. The main onus fell this time on the evacuating authorities; and with London still under threat it was the provincial towns that now had to take the lead in establishing a suitable procedure for receiving home vast numbers of people often scattered throughout the UK. As far as Merseyside was concerned, the situation was further complicated by the fact that as well as welcoming back their own children, they were also receiving evacuees from down south, seeking refuge in what until recently had been a target area itself! The *Liverpool Daily Post* noted on 22 July 1944 that Merseyside was to receive some 3,000 evacuees, about half of whom would be staying on the Wirral (including 400 detailed for Wallasey)[4] with the remainder bound for various parts of Liverpool. Dave Molyneux recounts an all-too-familiar story, even if the boot was now on the other foot!

> *When I was living in Liverpool, during 1944 when the V-1 flying bombs and the V-2 rockets were directed on London, my grandmother (my mother lived with her) took in two evacuee sisters who came from Harrow. I was four years old and remember them both very well ... Sheila, the youngest, was a bit of a devil. When they arrived, through no fault of their own, they both had hair lice, and my mother had to bring in the health officer. Sheila had very long hair which had to be cut short, and I remember her screaming mad because she had to have it cut. However, the lice soon cleared up and never returned. Both sisters were sent to our local school, Lawrence Road, in Wavertree, a C of E School. They were Catholics but had to attend this school as there was no room in the local Catholic school. They spent a few months with us until the V-1 and V-2 threat subsided.*

It was actually Ministry of Health Circular 129/44, issued on 23 September 1944, which ordered the termination of the Evacuation Scheme. Evacuation areas were instructed to send lists of evacuated children to all reception areas who were then to check that the children were still present. The Liverpool Education Offices began a process of interviewing all parents whose children were still away, in order to discover if they were in a position to receive them back, and if not, why not. Schedules were then forwarded to reception authorities giving the names of those to come home, the names of those to stay a while longer and the names of those for whom no firm decision had yet been made. The Birkenhead authorities were conscious of another problem. On 18 October the Education Committee agreed to forward to the Ministry of Education a resolution:

That this committee urges the Ministry to give sympathetic consideration to evacuees now in attendance at Secondary Schools in Reception areas. Many such pupils have been away for five years and the background of their education has been entirely rural. Returning to urban conditions in the middle of their Secondary School course would be a handicap to which they should not be subjected, and especially does this apply to those pupils who are due to take their School Certificate or Higher School Certificate examination within the next two years.[5]

Having had little response to this resolution, Birkenhead's education officials turned to Graham White MP for assistance and, eventually, in early December, won at least a partial victory when the Ministry agreed that evacuees who were due to sit exams the following summer would be allowed to remain in reception areas.

Meanwhile, the reception authorities were themselves sending out 'Notices to Evacuated Persons', explaining the return home procedure and the circumstances under which certain evacuees were to be allowed to stay, and requesting completion of a tripartite form. All evacuees were to fill in Part A - giving name, age (if under 14), billet address and home address. Where evacuees were to return home within 4 weeks, Part B enabled them to apply for a travel voucher; those unable to return were requested to explain why in Part C. Liverpool outlined a number of reasons which were acceptable causes for non-return: bomb-damaged homes where children couldn't yet be received; children being due to sit the School Certificate exam; and children having left school and found approved employment in the reception area - these could remain if parents agreed (subject also to the approval of the Ministry of Labour and National Service). If, for other private reasons, parents had arranged for their children to stay in their billets, householders were to be forewarned that billeting allowances would cease, and Liverpool Education Committee made it clear that in such cases, if misunderstandings did occur they could not undertake to pressurise parents into paying.[6]

Despite the mass of paperwork involved, the first organised return of Liverpool children from North Wales took place on 28/29 November 1944. It was decided that certain measures should be adopted in an attempt to avoid complaints - both sides clearly drawing on past experience! Doctors were to be available at Dispersal Centres in Liverpool for the medical examination of returning evacuees; billeting officers were asked to arrange for lists to be sent with the children, detailing all articles sent home with them, so as to avoid any recriminations; it was also declared that anyone who left the reception area without first handing in their billeting forms would be liable for prosecution. Householders billeting unaccompanied children were given details of travel arrangements - fares could be refunded if a householder had to take a child by public transport to a departure terminal. Children would be medically examined before departure; coloured labels were to be attached to the child's outer garments (there was no escaping those labels it would seem!); particulars of excess luggage were to be given to the Billeting Officer but the children themselves had to carry certain necessities all of which had to be labelled. Householders were to ensure that the children took with them their identity cards, ration books and clothing books, and had a parcel of food sufficient to last their journey.[7]

In fact, by late 1944, so many had returned home independently that the numbers to be despatched were usually not large. In Wrexham RD for example, the organised party which left for Liverpool on 28 November numbered only 55 (with an additional 8 escorts). Of those who were leaving, 24 had been in Wrexham since the very first evacuation in September 1939 and, not surprisingly, the scene was an emotional one.[8] The Wrexham children were joined by a much larger contingent from the Aberystwyth area, making a total of some 300 in all, including helpers (one for every eight children), with J.D.Bonner, Head of Holy Trinity School Anfield, in overall charge. All the children from the outlying rural areas had been brought to Aberystwyth the previous day and had stayed overnight in a large hostel. When it came time for the special train to leave, the evacuees were given an official send-off by a party of local dignitaries including Aberystwyth's Mayor, Town Clerk, Medical Officer and numerous Billeting Officers. Four evacuees who'd been staying in

Llanfairclydogan, a tiny village on the Teifi, had apparently been looking out for Dr Ernest Jones (MO) at the station. Just before boarding the train they rushed over and proudly presented him with a small parcel wrapped in newspaper. It contained four trout which one of the boys had caught the previous day!

Next day the *Daily Post* described the scene as the evacuees arrived back in Liverpool. It may not have been such a dramatic event as the departure in 1939 but it was poignant nonetheless:

> *A party of school children stood on a platform of Lime Street Station yesterday, singing in sweet unison. Passers-by stopped in their steps to listen. They were attracted in the first place by the sweetness of the singing but then stopped also out of curiosity. For the words of the song sounded like a foreign language. Where the children little French, Dutch or Belgian refugees?*
>
> *They were Liverpool children all right greeting their native city with a rendering of 'Calon Lân'. They were the first contingent of the children who were evacuated from the city to North Wales at the outbreak of the war and who are now being returned to their homes. Many of them have been living in areas where English is scarcely ever spoken and they can now speak Welsh as well as their mother tongue. A few of them have forgotten practically all the English they have ever learned!*

The following day a further 540 Liverpool evacuees as well as 120 or so Birkenhead children arrived home from North Wales, Cheshire and Hereford. The special train which brought the children from Caernarvonshire had started its journey in Portmadoc, picking up children at intermediate stations *en route*. A party of children from Anglesey had joined the train at Bangor and a mid-Wales contingent at Chester. The 'train-marshal', W.A. Jones, Head of Heyworth Street School, had been in Caernarvonshire since September 1939. The children leaving Pwllheli and the Lleyn peninsula were described as *'like a typical Welsh colony conversing with each other only in Welsh when they assembled at Chwilog'*. Just before boarding the 'Evacuee Special' they gave a rousing rendition of the Welsh National anthem.[9]

The final group to return in an offical party arrived on 30 November. These children, about 190 in all, had been living in various rural parts of Flintshire and Denbighshire. They were accompanied by 24 escorts, headed on this occasion by J.C. Aindow, Head of Priory RC School, Netherfield Road. Throughout the journey the WVS had established wayside canteens for the children and a meal was also ready for them on arrival. As with the children who had arrived back in Liverpool on the previous two days, all were taken from Lime Street by bus to a Dispersal Centre - either St James's School, Harrison Jones School, or St Anne's for the Liverpool children (those from Bootle, Litherland and Crosby were taken to St Matthew's Hall, the Town Hall or the Crosby Clinic). Here a team of nurses examined all the children, agreeing unanimously that they were in excellent condition - very well clad and well fed.

Many of the children had in fact come back with bags of farm produce for their families - not just eggs and butter but livestock as well! One child clutched a chicken, another a rabbit, there was a kitten amongst the luggage - and a ferret! It wasn't just the children who brought a little of the countryside home with them. Jessie Paisley, who'd been in charge of a class of evacuees in Silian, recalls:

> *When my time came to return to Liverpool, my hostess had let it be known that my father in Liverpool was suffering from a gastric ulcer, and the necessary diet at the time was difficult. So I was sent home staggering under the weight of a large case filled with eggs, chickens, and home-made butter from the local farms to help him.*[10]

On the final 'Special' one boy carried a sheepdog puppy 'almost as big as himself', another carried a dead rabbit and a third 'sported' a toy sten gun. Onlookers were amazed at what the children were bringing back with them - not least the number of books (including Welsh Bibles) and toys - Christmas shoppers in Liverpool were having great difficulty finding any toys at all. Almost all the girls carried dolls, many also had toy cradles, while the boys had hand-barrows and wooden engines - clearly the end-product of careful crafting by foster parents. In fact there were many signs that the Welsh householders continued to be anxious for the well-being of their charges; some foster parents actually travelled with the children so that they could hand them back in person to their mothers. One journeyed to Liverpool with his evacuee, met the child's parents and by mutual consent arranged to take the child back to Wales and keep him at his own expense. In fact, according to one newspaper report 'some of the children went back almost by the next train'. The most remarkable feature of the return of the Liverpool evacuees, it concluded, was the obvious lack of enthusiasm shown by the children over going back to their homes![11] The Rhyl Billeting Committee had to call a special meeting to discuss the fact that a number of evacuees were actually refusing to vacate their billets, declaring that they preferred living in the resort and did not want to return to the city.[12]

On 2 May 1945, the Government gave permission for Londoners also to leave the reception areas and travel home either in organised parties on special trains or independently with the aid of free travel vouchers. Circular 68/45, embodying London's Return Home Plan - a document of no fewer than 5,000 words! - was issued to reception authorities on 10 April and, as earlier with the Merseyside evacuees, surveys were made with regard to the numbers able to go back. Again, however, by the time official plans were ready to be put into operation, the majority of London evacuees had made their own way home. Whereas there were still 690 London evacuees in Wrexham in April 1945, when the special train finally left on 11 June the organised return home party numbered only 83, many having already left on VE Day.[13]

Back home in time to celebrate. Most Merseyside evacuees had returned by VE Day - here Thompson Street residents (Birkenhead) enjoy a VE party. (Photo courtesy Eric Jackson)

In many ways, the sheer administration of the return home, large scale as it was for some authorities, was often less a problem than the individual cases that the return home revealed. Some children had no house to return to, but there were others whose parents had been killed or whose families had been so ravaged by the war situation that their 'home' no longer had a place within it for a child.

Caernarvon Borough was faced with just such a case in February 1945. Private arrangements had been made the previous year for a child to remain in Caernarvon as her father was serving in the Merchant Navy and an older daughter who was trying to keep the home going couldn't look after a young child as she was out working. In February, however, the billetor informed Caernarvon authorities that she'd received no money since the billeting allowance had been stopped in November. Apparently the father had re-married, the older daughter had been turned out of the house and the stepmother had failed to keep up the agreed payments. C.F. Mott was requested to try and intervene as the Welsh householder had recently been widowed herself and couldn't afford the upkeep of the child who was, however, 'breaking her heart' at the thought of having to return to Liverpool.[14]

At the beginning of 1944 the British Legion reported that some 5,000 evacuated children had been deserted by their parents or families. Liverpool was proud to note, however, that 'hardly any' of these cases were from Merseyside. The previous December, when over 8,000 of the city's children had still been evacuated, less than 100 had not received letters or visits from parents for two months; sometimes other family members had been in touch, whittling the number of actual desertions right down to *no more than half a dozen real cases'.*[15]

The question of the future care of children left behind - for whatever reason - was a very difficult one, finally acknowledged by the Government with the appointment of the Curtis Committee in March 1945. At this point there were over 130,000 unaccompanied evacuee schoolchildren housed in reception areas across the country (in addition to 175,000 mothers with young children). A year later, on 31 March 1946, when the evacuation programme was deemed to be officially finished, there were still some 5,200 unaccompanied children in reception areas in England and Wales,[16] It was only with the passing of the Children Act of 1948 that such children were finally made the responsibility of the local authorities; until this time, they remained in the care of foster parents or special hostels. As at 16 June 1948 there were 34 young people (aged from 10 to 18) from Liverpool, who were still officially billeted, 13 through lack of accommodation, 21 who were orphans or came from broken homes.[17]

Where children had been orphaned by the war it was obvious that some arrangements would have to be made for their long-term care but sometimes adoption agreements were drawn up even though the children did have a home and family to return to. Gwenda McGarrity recalls: how *'two of the girls who came from poor homes in Birkenhead never came back; they remained with their hosts and made their lives in Llanfrothen.'* Bert Jones also remembers that *'we were the last to leave but one boy stayed behind. I think he was adopted by the people he lived with and he's there to this day - if he's still alive!'*

Similarly, Gwen Jones:

> *One child was taken in by a childless couple and they became so fond of her that they legally adopted her, paid for her education and sent her to College. She eventually became a teacher. She only returned to visit her parents on very few occasions.*

Some parents made the huge sacrifice of parting with their children because they could see that the life they'd been enjoying for the past few years offered much better prospects than their old one, the one to which they would otherwise be returning. Marjorie Baker's sister Margaret, terrified by the air raids, had been evacuated to a couple in the Welsh borders:

> *They didn't have any children because they had married late in life so of course they didn't want to let her go and they gave her things she couldn't have at home. When Mrs. W. asked if she could adopt Margaret my father thought she would have more opportunities and a better education, which she did get. My mother never forgot her, I don't think she realised at the time she wouldn't be able to see her again.*

There were other instances where foster parents wanted to adopt their evacuees but either the natural parents or the children themselves were very much against the idea. It was many years after the war before Margaret Jones discovered that her 'Aunt' Edie had wanted to adopt her but her father had declined - though Margaret did go and live with her eventually and became the next best thing to a 'real' daughter. George Crebbin had spent a happy two years in Abersoch when his mother began to suspect that his foster mother had plans to 'steal him' - and so he was promptly whisked home. Audrey Lowe really was involved in a kidnap attempt! She'd been an evacuee for three years and was due to be collected by her mother:

> *'Auntie' Dorothy had packed our things ... I remember being on the station with her and this soldier I called Uncle Bob and I believed we were going to Liverpool. I know now that she was actually leaving her husband with this soldier. And then my mum appeared, on the station with a bike. Now she must have cycled on this bike down the lanes from where I'd*

251

been living to the station. I don't know who told her where we'd gone but I remember her taking hold of my arm and being quite angry. So I really think that this Auntie Dorothy and Uncle Bob were kidnapping me in a way.[18]

Jean Cruickshank felt she'd had a lucky escape. The lady she was billeted with wanted to adopt her *'but wasn't a kind woman and when I was put into the Welsh school I hated it. My mother came to see me and was met by a flood of tears - so there was no chance of adoption after that.'* Frank Jagger by contrast, at the time was rather disappointed he wasn't adopted:

I was there [in Bala] almost two years. My Welsh was good and they wanted to adopt me. My parents took a dim view of this and repositioned me in a dump called Macclesfield. What a let-down. No more food in abundance, no more rides on horses. I survived, just.

By the end of the war, many of those who'd left the cities in 1939 were no longer children and could decide for themselves whether they wished to return or not. Albert Houghton whose life as an evacuee in Carmel was infinitely better than the life he'd left behind in Liverpool, became a local farmworker and didn't return until 1950; Leonard and Donald Parker had been evacuated from Liverpool to Llanfarian, near Aberystwyth. Leonard went home at the end of the war but his brother chose to stay. Donald got a job as gardener at Aberystwyth University and eventually became Senior Horticultural Technician in charge of the botanic gardens.[19] Cynthia Bullock, whose stepfather *'wrote to the people I was with and told them he didn't want me'* went into domestic service near Rhyl, aged 14, and never returned to Liverpool.

Sometimes there were romantic ties which kept evacuees from returning home. One of the masters evacuated to Holyhead with Alsop High School recalled that *'several senior pupils made attachments to local girls - two marriages at least resulted'.* Mrs Pritchard remembers that *'one evacuee teacher married the butcher at Clynnog and another from Carmel married a local boy'.* Mrs Redmund's cousin, a Welsh hillfarmer, married an evacuee who despite a town upbringing soon settled down to life as a farmer's wife and came to speak fluent Welsh. Mrs Schofield, evacuated to Cwm-y-Glo also recalls that *'one of our evacuees married a farm lad from the village and she is still there to this day. I believe she is a real Welsh lady now!'* Mimi Hatton, the schoolteacher from Kent who'd been in charge of a group of evacuees in Portmadoc, fell in love with the son of the household where she was billeted. Sadly, he died before they could be married but Mimi stayed on in Caernarvonshire to look after his mother, the lady who had given her a home during the war.[20] Another schoolteacher also found that evacuation was to change her life. In 1939 Norah Quaye was evacuated with Liverpool's Butler Street Infants School; she bumped into John Cox, her husband-to-be, one day when she was taking the children for a countryside ramble and he was in hot pursuit of a runaway pig!

For those evacuees who had to go home there were many tears shed when it came time to leave: some were tears of joy, others of sadness; some were shed by the children, others by their host families. If the initial evacuation had been a traumatic time for some, the thought of now having to return home after years of being away was equally traumatic for others. A poignant entry in the school logbook of Cwm-y-Glo evacuees, 23 April 1943, records that the *'Marsden children don't want to go home - George said he'd kill himself if he had to leave.'*[21] For many, ties had been made with Wales which never would be broken - some remained in regular contact with their 'foster parents' for the rest of their lives, some lost contact initially, only to renew it many years later. Even those who'd had an unhappy time as evacuees often returned at some stage, if only to lay the ghosts of the past. Yet, whatever emotions may have been felt on leaving, a whole new set must have been felt on actually arriving back home.

To many children 'home' of course was completely unrecognisable, as the home they had left behind had been completely demolished; many had to settle into a new district; familiar landmarks - churches, schools, cinemas - had also disappeared. Children who had been away in the quiet of the countryside for several years now had to readjust to town life. Audrey Lowe, returning to Birkenhead found that she hated the traffic and the noise of the town: *'I used to stand on the pavement for ages waiting for cars to go because they really frightened me.'* In fact there was a great deal of adjusting to do for all concerned. The lucky ones had managed to keep close and regular contact with home and sustained good relationships with their natural families as well as their foster parents. But some children had seen very little of their relatives and never did manage to re-establish strong family ties. Walter Hurst comments:

> *I was most anxious to return home but it took a long time to get used to being part of a normal family again and I never really managed to make a good relationship with my father.*

Similarly, Marjorie Lamb:

> *In retrospect when we did get home I was never really ever again very close to my mother, to leave at six years of age and return at ten was a big*

253

chunk out of my formative years. I could never get close to her ... For some reason I don't know why but my brother [also an evacuee] and I have never really been close either. It is as if those years of trauma created a hidden barrier.

Jean Cruickshank also felt like 'an outsider' when she returned:

We were away for five years and it was just not the same when we went back. We'd been a close family but I felt like an outsider and only now [sixty years on] feel as if I'm getting close to my sisters again.

George Crebbin found it took him a long time to get into the 'street scene' when he returned to Merseyside. He'd been billeted with a spinster who'd looked after him very well but hadn't let him play much with other children. So he'd become rather a loner and hadn't got many of the ball skills or team skills required for playing on the back streets! Many of the children, of course, had lost their scouse accents - some were now more used to speaking Welsh. Just as five years earlier these English 'ychafis' had been taunted in playgrounds all over North Wales, now they had to contend with taunts in their home playgrounds from the children who hadn't been away. As Ron Haworth puts it, it was a case of *'He's a Welshie - thump, thump, thump.'*

Alex Anderson comments about his return home that: *'The only thing I do recall was everyone, including my mother, accusing me of "talking posh".'* It must have been hard for parents and siblings, too, receiving back family members who'd become little strangers, with odd ways and, perhaps, different values. Margaret Jones remembers the case in Llanidloes of *'one little boy, coming from a slum area, who was placed with local gentry - with household staff - and after five years he was transported back to his large family all living in a bedsit.'*

Sometimes there were financial difficulties too when parents - or grandparents, where parents defaulted - found themselves presented with bills for unpaid billeting charges. Court orders were issued to those who were able to pay but had not done so, and the Liverpool authorities (and no doubt other evacuation authorities on Merseyside) took firm action. In a meeting of the City's Defence Committee on 28 February 1944, it was recorded that *'... every possible means has been adopted to induce these people to meet their obligations, but without success, and the committee are now requested to authorise their committal to prison in accordance with the judgement given by the Magistrate'.* On 3 December 1945 the Committee was presented with details of 396 persons who

254

were not complying with Court Orders against them for recovery of billeting charges. The Ministry of Health advised that if debts were under £5 no action should be taken and the local authority was given discretion to write off other amounts. In April 1946 the City Treasurer finally gave up the chase and wrote off 'irrecoverable' billeting fees amounting to £6,423/18/9d.[22]

Problems at this time were not confined to the child evacuees and their parents; even some of the adults who'd been evacuated found it hard to settle back to their former existence. Pam McNaught had spent much of the war with her mother, in a beautiful spot overlooking the Menai Strait. They finally returned to Wallasey in August 1945 and Pam remembers: *'Poor mother was terribly upset at returning, after having such a lovely life in Bangor - and her independence.'* Some hostesses also found it difficult to adjust to life without their wartime charges. Many had been acting as foster parents since the very start of the scheme. Some had looked after the same child for the duration, others had taken in a large number of different evacuees as the children came and went. Most had only an official letter of thanks to fill the void, although Mrs A. Matthias, a farmer's wife from Leeswood, who had looked after evacuees throughout the war, had the added honour of being selected as one of two 'evacuee hostesses' to represent North Wales in the Civil Defence parade in London on 10 June 1945.[23]

A few host families felt a little disgruntled that they hadn't been shown more gratitude - particularly from the parents of their evacuees. As early as 18 July 1942 the *Montgomeryshire Express* had reported how disillusioned Welshpool householders had become when parents 'just dropped in and took the children away' with no word of thanks.[24] Writing in 1960, E. Lloyd Jones, Head of Llanfairfechan Secondary School commented:

> *Most of the evacuee children came from homes where the conditions must have been appalling. They seemed to have no idea of personal hygiene or table manners. My wife and I can vouch for the truth of the above statement as we had altogether 3 evacuees, one of them for 2 years. Incidentally, the father of the last mentioned - a chargehand on the Liverpool docks - earned about twice as much as I did as a headmaster, yet the boy during the whole time he was with us did not receive a single present or any pocket money from his parents. We had a boy of our own about the same age and they were both treated alike. Yet I do not think we had one word of gratitude, either verbal or written, from the parents ... It was a general complaint here that the parents of these chidren showed not the least sign of gratitude for all that was done ...*[25]

255

Other householders viewed things differently. Mrs Doris Blackwell, then living in Rhosesmor (Flints), had taken in two Liverpool boys and a girl from London. She was all too pleased to have been of service: *'Our experience looking after evacuees'*, she says *'gave us great pleasure if only in the knowledge that we were helping to keep the children as safe as possible for their parents.'* When his mother died, John Ackerley was astonished to find amongst her treasured possessions the luggage labels that had been attached to the two little Merseyside evacuees who'd arrived on her doorstep in Prestatyn over fifty years earlier! Mrs Ackerley had clearly grown fond of the children but, like many other Welsh householders, had also been proud of the special part she'd been able to play during the war.

Certainly formal expressions of gratitude were sent from the evacuating authorities to all the councils who had organised reception arrangements for their evacuees. The following letter from Birkenhead for example was received in various parts of North Wales in February 1945:

> *Now that official evacuation is over the Birkenhead County Borough and the Education Committee desire to express their gratitude to the people of Wales for all they did for Birkenhead children throughout a long and anxious period.*
>
> *We would thank the Billeting Officers and the members of the Women's Voluntary Services whose difficulties we realised, without, we are afraid, being able to do all we would have liked to have solved them, the Directors of Education and the Welsh teachers, who so readily extended to our children the educational facilities which have given Wales its renown, and, above all, the foster parents who not only housed the children but extended to them a warmth of personal affection of which we had ever-recurring proofs.*
>
> *We wish to place our appreciation on record and it is our hope that the future lives of our children will be markedly influenced for good by their experience of country life and by the personal relationships which they have established during the years their home town went through the most trying period of its history.*
> *(Signed)................Mayor of Birkenhead*
> *......Chairman of Birkenhead Education Committee*

As for the evacuees themselves, most did eventually settle back home quite happily - but not all. Len Verdin had been evacuated from Liverpool to mid-Wales:

256

At the end of the war - two weeks after in fact - my mother came to fetch us. I went back to Liverpool and was there for two or three months and then I ran away from home. I wanted to come back [to Llanddewi] I couldn't settle in Liverpool. Going back there I had nothing ... I didn't have the farmwork. I got on the train at Lime Street and got as far as Shrewsbury and was met by a couple of policemen! - 'Your mother's looking for you - she'll be waiting at Lime Street Station.' I think my mother understood because she knew I didn't want to come away ... My brothers and sisters settled back straight away.[26]

Len, by the way, ended up joining the Army, marrying a Welsh girl and moving back to Llanddewi! Edna Griffiths lasted back in Liverpool a little bit longer. She had been 13 when first evacuated to the Wrexham area with Brae Street School, Kirkdale, in 1939:

When I was allowed to leave school at the age of 14, 'Aunty' Rose helped me to get a job in the Costing Office at the Steel Works and there I remained until the end of the war when I returned to Liverpool. But within three years I was back again, and I have stayed here ever since!

As the Birkenhead officials had hoped, even many of those who did happily re-adjust to life in the city found that they had been 'markedly influenced' both by country life and by the relationships they had forged during their time as evacuees. Many were left with a sense of what the Welsh call 'hiraeth' or longing - a longing to return to Wales, and over the years numerous evacuees have indeed made that return journey.

NOTES

[1] Portmadoc UDC letterbook 1942-44, letter to Mrs J.R. Roberts, 24 July 1944

[2] Holywell UDC, Mold UDC, Lleyn RDC, Council Minutes 24-28 July 1944; also *A Record of War Service - Wrexham RDC*. See Wallis, N. *Wales 1939-45* for full details of events in 1944.

[3] Flintshire Education Committee Minutes 1944-45, Higher Education Sub-Committee, 12 July 1944

[4] Although Wallasey had been an evacuation area in 1939, other parts of the Wirral had been designated for reception: West Kirby, Heswall, Neston and Irby had taken in evacuees from Liverpool and Wallasey, also Guernsey children following occupation of the Channel Isles.

[5] Birkenhead Education Committee Minutes, BC/IV/820

[6] See Penmaenmawr UDC File 'Evac Circs & Various Corresp.', Letter 7 Nov 1944

[7] See Notice to Householders Billeting Unaccompanied Children, Amlwch UDC Evac File 2(6), 1944-46

[8] See *A Record of War Service - Wrexham RDC*

[9] See *Liverpool Daily Post*, 30 November 1944

[10] Quoted in 'Homefront Heroes'

[11] *Liverpool Daily Post*, 30 November 1944

[12] *Liverpool Daily Post*, 13 December 1944

[13] Ibid.

[14] Letter to Mott, 21 Feb 1945, Caernarvon BC Evac Papers Box 2

[15] *Liverpool Daily Post*, 28 February 1944

[16] Titmuss, op.cit.pp.433-5; Liverpool Civil Defence Emergency Committee, 29 December 1944 reported that only 1200 were still evacuated, half of which were in Special Schools.

[17] Report of an evacuation official, cited in the *Liverpool Daily Post*, 16 June 1948.

[18] Quoted in *Our Evacuee* p.15

[19] See 'Homefront Heroes'

[20] Caerns XM/T/380

[21] Caerns EA9

[22] See Liverpool Emergency Defence Committee Minutes, February 1944, December1945, April 1946 (L'Pool RO, 352/MIN/DEF/11), cited in Julie Craine, *Evacuation from Liverpool*

[23] See *Clwyd at War 1939-45*, Clwyd Record Office, 1989

[24] Welshpool had taken in 2810 people to this date. (I'm most grateful to Margaret Stacey, Welshpool Library, for pointing out this newspaper article)

[25] Letter to P.E.Owen, 1 Nov 1960, PhD Thesis, appendix 32

[26] Quoted in 'Homefront Heroes' *Cambrian News* Supplement 1989

9- *Home Again to Wales*

For many Merseyside children, and some adults, being evacuated to North Wales had opened up a whole new way of life - creating a deep love of the countryside, a new circle of friends, even, in many cases, what amounted to a second 'family'. Especially for those who had enjoyed their time away, contact was naturally retained long after the war, through letters and visits (even up to the present day in some instances) - many children returned time and time again to their old billets for holidays. As the years passed, 'foster parents' were invited to their evacuees' weddings; evacuees had children of their own and took them to look at the place where mum or dad had safely seen out the war; now former evacuees are taking grandchildren to visit the sight of their 'evacuee experience'- be it happy or sad. Lilian Platt explains:

> *When I got married and had a family of my own I took them to see the place I was evacuated to. I have also taken my grandson there and spoke to a lady who remembered the evacuees and let us look around the school we had gone to, it was lovely. Croesor will always have a place in my heart, so will the Welsh people who opened up their homes to the evacuees.*

Similarly Alf Bryce writes:

> *Many years on I was driving through Prestatyn with my wife and three children and I said when we go around the next corner you'll see a huge carpet of bluebells! Alas it was a housing estate, but my love affair with North Wales is still burning.*

One person, evacuated to the tiny village of Llanaber, near Barmouth made a return visit, *'stood by the cobbled wall looking at the old childish scrawls, including her own "C.E.A. loves F.F.I" and wept for the lost years'.*[1]

Pam McNaught remembers her stay in Bangor so fondly that when the time comes she intends to have her ashes scattered on the Menai Strait!

Whilst many make a return pilgrimage to the Welsh hillsides to rekindle happy memories, some, sadly, go back in order to try and bury the past. Ron Organ had a fairly wretched time as an evacuee, made bearable only by his growing love of country life. Years later, it was the beauty of the Vale of Clwyd, not the warmth of the welcome he'd received as an evacuee, that drew him to return:

259

When I came back to live here I went round to see lots of people - to thank those who had been kind to me and confront those who had been cruel. The ones who'd been kind didn't realise they were - the ones who were cruel didn't care!

When Alex Anderson visited Criccieth in the 1990s, more than fifty years after he had stayed there as a very unhappy little boy, he found he experienced a mixed response - part of the town itself, the bit which had not been spoilt by recent development, 'felt like an old friend', yet Alex was very tempted 'to look in the local cemetery, seek out the grave of the good Dr D. [his 'foster father'] *and dance on it!*' Having thus purged himself of angry thoughts, he adds, 'In the end I contented myself with praying for the repose of his soul.' Marjorie Lamb also found a host of negative feelings surfacing in 1992 when she returned to the place of her evacuation:

I went back to Harlech this summer. The Hostel is now a private hotel. The owner allowed me into every room. The outside is identical, the inside has been modernised but not out of recognition as to how I remember it. Once again I re-lived the trauma of my evacuation years.

It was partly to help people who felt that they had indeed been traumatised by evacuation that the Evacuees Reunion Association was formed by James Roffey in 1998. Before this, there had of course been many 'evacuee reunions', ranging from small groups of ex-evacuees from one particular school getting together in the village which had given them a wartime home, to large-scale gatherings such as those organised at the time of various anniversaries connected with the Evacuation Scheme.

Alex Cross, who was himself evacuated from Birkenhead to Caergwrle, writes that *'One of my dreams has always been to have retrospective plaques situated in respective "home and away" schools, to remind youngsters of those strange days.'* In fact a number of such commemorative plaques have been exchanged. In April 1998, for example, Liverpool City Council sent a plaque and letter of congratulations to Carmel School, Caernarvonshire, on the occasion of its one hundredth anniversary. This was a move largely instigated by Don Aird, his brothers Stan and Ken and a group of other ex-evacuees from Aspen Grove School in Sefton Park, who had been evacuated to Carmel in 1939 and stayed in this little Welsh village for most of the war. The local children were delighted at the opportunity to hear firsthand about 'evacuation', now of course part of their history curriculum, and the headmistress was also very pleased to welcome them to the centenary celebrations, explaining: *'The evacuees have a very important place in our history and we wanted them to take part in this historic event.'*[2]

Former Liverpool evacuees from Aspen Grove meet up again to help their old school in Carmel (Caerns) celebrate its 100th anniversary. (Photo courtesy Don Aird)

Beaumaris Reunion - former Blue Coat evacuees meet up again in September 1989. (Photo courtesy Blue Coat Old Blues Association)

Jim Barrow and Bill Blakeborough relive their evacuee days at a Reunion at Llanidloes in 1989. (Photo courtesy Margaret Jones)

262

Former evacuees celebrate 'fifty years on' in Llanidloes, led by organisers of the reunion, Margaret Jones and Edith Woolfall. (Photo courtesy Margaret Jones)

Tony Lloyd (far left) organised a sponsored walk and service on 3 September 1989 to commemorate the 50th anniversary of the day that many Liverpool evacuees arrived in Ruthin. The sum of £4700 was raised for two Merseyside Children's hospitals. (Photo courtesy Tony Lloyd)

In the main entrance of Liverpool's Blue Coat School a similar plaque commemorates the days when its pupils were evacuated to Anglesey. The plaque was presented to the school in 1989 by the Mayor of Beaumaris whilst another, depicting the heraldic emblem of the school, was presented in turn to the Mayor by Revd Arthur Siddall, President of Liverpool Blue Coat Brotherly Society, as recognition of the hospitality that the Liverpool school had received in Beaumaris some fifty years earlier. More than 130 'Old Blues' had gathered in Beaumaris on this occasion, some from as far afield as Canada and Australia, to attend a reunion dinner and church service, and naturally to reminisce about their time spent on Anglesey as wartime evacuees.

The 50th anniversary of the outbreak of the war and, of course, of the start of evacuation, was celebrated by a number of other evacuee reunions in North Wales. One such 'Fifty Years On' trip brought together a group of former evacuees at the Rhos-y-Gwaliau Youth Hostel in Bala. Frank Jagger found it all 'quite a revelation':

> *One of the old teachers, a Miss Morris, fluent in Welsh, was asked how she felt about meeting her old pupils again. She answered, in Welsh, how disappointed she was when she saw how old and ugly we'd become!*

For all that, the group did present Miss Morris with an engraved silver tray, '1939-89'. Freda Beetson also attended the reunion; like Frank she had been evacuated with St Luke's School, Tranmere but she was billeted just outside Bala, in Llanderfel village. She recalls:

> *In 1989 we went back there with the rest of our School Evacuees, for a Re-union. We went in a coach with our name tags on our coats. It was a great day and all the memories flooded back.*

Labels were also worn by the group of evacuees who met together in Llanidloes in 1989 - some even went so far as to don clothing similar to what they'd been wearing when they first arrived in the town fifty years earlier! The event had been organised largely by Margaret Jones (a former Birkenhead evacuee who now lives in Llanidloes) her cousin and fellow-evacuee, Edith Woolfall, and a very dedicated fundraising committee. Margaret Jones describes the occasion:

> *In 1989 I organised a reunion in Llanidloes and managed to trace 73 ex-evacuees. We had a wonderful weekend. It was very emotional. One person came from Texas, one from Hong Kong and one from New*

Zealand. We met at the railway station and reenacted the walk to the Church Hall complete with our labels tied to our coats. The police stopped the traffic, sirens were wailing, ex-evacuees were breaking rank to touch walls of houses they had lived in so many years before. Elderly people were coming with old photos of children they had cared for but lost touch with. And the joy on the faces when they found each other will always stay with me. Many memories came flooding back but the overall message came from one of the many letters I received which said simply 'There'll always be a part of Llani in my heart.' ... After the event we had some money over and were able to make amends for any damage we may have done as children. (We evacuees were blamed for anything and everything!) Donations were made to six local charities connected with children, and a garden seat was presented to the Old People's Home which now houses some of those who opened their doors to we strange children of so long ago!

There was also a charity fund-raising theme behind the reunion held in Ruthin in 1989. This was organised by Tony Lloyd, a veteran charity walker, who had been evacuated to Ruthin with fellow pupils of Lister Drive School on the day war broke out:

On 3 September [1989] - a Sunday just as it was in 1939 - I arranged, with assistance from the North Wirral Rotary Club, a mass walk of those who had been evacuated or those with family connections to evacuees, as a Commemorative Charity Walk from Llanbedr over Moel Fammau into the market square of Ruthin where we were met by the Lord Mayor, having all attended a Commemorative Church Service in Llanbedr prior to the start of the Walk.

Over a hundred people took part, including a number of former Lister Drive School evacuees; more of their classmates attended a Charity night held on the Wirral a few months later, at which cheques totalling £4,000 were presented to Arrowe Park and Alder Hey hospitals, to purchase equipment for children suffering from cystic fibrosis.

Perhaps the most spactacular of the Golden Jubilee reunions, billed as 'Britain's Official Salute to the 1939 Evacuees' was that staged in Aberystwyth from 2 -15 September 1989. This two-week extravaganza, with sporting events, concerts, filmshows, exhibitions, Red Arrows display, fairs and children's entertainment - all rounded off with a spectacular firework show, was sponsored by the Welsh

Tourist Board, with contributions from local firms as well as from the 'evacuating authorities' - Liverpool City Council (who donated £5,000), and the Borough Councils of East Grinstead and Lewisham. As the official programme explained: *'former evacuees from Liverpool, Lewisham and East Grinstead wanted an appropriate way of saying "diolch" - thank you - to those Welsh "Mums and Dads" who, by taking them into their homes and hearts and sheltering them from the horrors of the War, helped save their lives'.* They felt that Aberystwyth's Bronglais Hospital (Special Care Baby Unit, Children's Ward and C.A.T.Scan Appeal) should be the main beneficiary of any money raised during the festivities.

Ron Haworth was one of 300 former evacuees who enjoyed the Aberystwyth Reunion. He had been evacuated from Holy Trinity School, Anfield, with his three brothers in September 1939, had gone back home, like so many others, before Christmas, but then returned to Devil's Bridge when his school was hit in the blitz - and he's been going back there regularly ever since. Talking of the 1989 reunion, he remembers:

> *They ran a train from Aberystwyth up to Devil's Bridge - you only had to pay 1939 prices for the journey and a hotel room if you wore 1939 clothing! ... At one point the Mayor of Aberystwyth and the Mayor of Liverpool stood up and asked for volunteers to sing 'In my Liverpool Home' - a group did get up to start with but somehow I ended up doing a solo! ... When I left Aberystwyth on the last Repatriation Train in 1945 the Station was packed with people and the singing was unbelievable. On this train was a girl called Dorothy. I met her again at the reunion - 'Hello Dorothy', I said, 'Hello, Ron' came the swift reply - we had no trouble at all recognising each other despite the interlude of fifty years!*

It was to commemorate not the beginning but the end of the war that former evacuees gathered in Oswestry in 1995. The Oswestry Heritage Centre had appealed for anyone who had been involved in the evacuation scheme - hosts as well as evacuees - to come forward with their memories in order that an exhibition could be mounted. The response was so good that the Centre ended up not only mounting an exhibition but also publishing a booklet, *Our Evacuees*, and organising an Evacuee Reunion. The actual reunion gathering was attended by the Mayor of Oswestry and also by the Mayor of Wirral, Walter Smith, himself a former evacuee. Frank Morris was one of those who made the return journey in 1995, having first travelled in 1940 (with his friends from Brassey Street School, Birkenhead) to Llanllyfni, just ouside Oswestry. *'A lot of people turned up for the reunion'*, he comments, *'and we were given a very warm welcome by the villagers.'*

266

Celebrations had of course also been held in London to celebrate the end of the Second World War, and a few former evacuees, wearing their distinctive badge (the luggage label) had been included in the Veterans Parade. As they passed down the Mall they were cheered by the thousands of spectators who lined the route, many of whom called out, 'I was an evacuee too!' Watching this occasion it became obvious to James Roffey that there was an urgent need for an Evacuees Reunion Association (ERA) to be formed and this was launched at the Imperial War Museum in March 1996. It now has members not only from throughout Britain but from all parts of the world.[3] Run as a registered charity it aims to help people contact their wartime friends and to exchange their memories of evacuation - good or bad - with others who are in a position to understand. It also meets a growing demand from schools and colleges for information about evacuation. Reunion meetings are held throughout the country - these are a lot of fun but are often therapeutic too, giving those who had a bad time as evacuees the chance to talk about experiences and emotions they had often bottled up all their lives. An ERA newsletter, *The Evacuee*, is also produced every month. In 1999 the ERA began to plan an event to take place on 3 September 1999 to mark the 60th anniversary of the start of the Government Evacuation Scheme. It had originally been intended simply as a

The memories live on - even in far off New Zealand! Former Merseyside evacuee Arthur Woods brings together 80 former British wartime evacuees for a weekend in Christchurch to celebrate the 60th anniversary of the Government's Scheme. (Photo courtesy Arthur Woods)

Government Evacuation Scheme. It had originally been intended simply as a gathering of members of the Evacuees Reunion Association (then numbering a little over 1000) but it became in fact an international event attended by some 6,000 people! The day began with a procession of evacuees from Horse Guards Parade to Westminster Abbey where a Service of Thanksgiving was conducted by the Dean of Westminster in the presence of the Duke and Duchess of Gloucester. In the afternoon, evacuees gathered at Westminster Central Hall for a presentation of 'The Story of Evacuation', told in words, pictures and music. Above all, it was intended that the day should symbolise what many felt had been lacking too long, namely the nation's recognition of its evacuees of the Second World War. In his Bidding, the Dean of Westminster must have echoed the feelings of many of those present when he said:

It is a time for mixed emotions: thanksgiving for welcomes received but bitterness at compulsory removal; joy at remembered kindness but anger when abuse is recalled; happy remembrance of friendships made but resentment of love denied; gratitude at the survival of many and sadness for those who died.

A Message of Thanks was delivered from the pulpit by ERA's General Secretary, James Roffey:

We who were the evacuated children of the Second World War wish to place on record our thanks to all those who cared for us during those difficult years. To the people who planned the evacuation, the teachers, helpers, nurses, billeting officers; to the train drivers signalmen, bus drivers, policemen, seamen and many others who helped us on our way. We thank all those in the reception areas, in this country and in Australia, America, Canada, New Zealand and South Africa. In particular we thank the foster parents who took the children of strangers into their homes and sometimes into their hearts.

Sadly not all evacuees were well cared for, some have bitter memories that will never fade. They find it hard, even impossible, to be associated with this message of thanks. But to the vast majority of people who did their best for us we extend our thanks. In doing so we pray that never again will the lives of so many children be disrupted.[4]

NOTES

[1] Quoted in *No Time to Wave Goodbye*, p.223

[2] Quoted in the *Liverpool Echo*, 11 July 1998

[3] In New Zealand, for example, where Arthur Woods (evacuated from Loraine St School to Devil's Bridge) organised a reunion in 1999 in Christchurch, NZ , which was attended by some 80 former evacuees now living in various parts of New Zealand.

[4] Reproduced in *The Evacuee,* September 1999. [Address of ERA: Goodbodys Mill, 17 Albert Rd., Retford, DN22 6JD]

10 - The Verdict

Since publication in 1950 of Richard Titmuss's official history of the government evacuation scheme, there have been numerous studies of the subject. Even while the war was still in progress, various groups attempted to assess the impact of evacuation and to use what was supposed to have been revealed about 'inner city' poverty to push for welfare legislation. The whole experience was in many ways a reverse of the 'slumming' experiments in the late nineteenth century. Then, middle-class pioneers had chosen to go and live amongst what they called the 'submerged tenth' in order to witness the impact of poverty first hand, and so supposedly discover a way of solving it. In 1939 rather than going to live with the poor, the middle classes found that the poor had come to live with them! At least this was the impression given in the first few weeks of the scheme. In fact, of course, whilst some evacuees did go from poor homes to middle-class 'palaces', many went from good homes to hovels, perhaps the majority went from one poor home to another. Yet those who felt their 'nice' houses had been invaded by something quite unacceptable were the people most able to get their views heard. They could, and did, demand that the government do something about this shocking urban poverty.

In this respect, as A.J.P. Taylor wrote, *'The Luftwaffe was a powerful missionary for the Welfare State.'*[1] Certainly in North Wales, as elsewhere, as the procedure for receiving and caring for evacuees developed so, too, did a new concept - that of state responsibility for many aspects of their welfare. Clothing schemes, school meals, residential hostels and nurseries and a growing pool of trained staff to administer the arrangements all indicated an approach which was taking Britain away from the old Poor Law mentality towards a new ideal of a Welfare State. Some see this as a direct result of the evacuation scheme; others argue that these developments were simply a natural progression from changes already underway in the 1930s.[2] Yet, whatever evacuation may have promoted for the future, it must be remembered that operation of the scheme itself, despite gradually becoming more sophisticated, did remain largely dependent on the goodwill of numerous individual householders.

If it is difficult to assess the true impact of evacuation on post-war welfare legislation, it is also difficult to make an evaluation of the after-effects of evacuation on any one particular district, given that the arrival of evacuees was just one aspect of a great upheaval caused by the war. In the case of North Wales, for example, could it be said that evacuation, as some Nationalists had feared, caused a decline in the use of the Welsh language? Who could say whether any threat to the language resulted from an immigration of English-speakers or to an emigration of Welsh war workers and soldiers to areas where they couldn't practise their native tongue? By and large it seems that evacuee children, far from eroding Welsh culture, were quickly assimilated into the Welsh way of life, even to the extent of becoming fluent in the language. As for the actual administration of the scheme in North Wales, whilst it is true that mistakes were made, what was an extremely complicated and difficult matter was on the whole handled well - certainly far better than might have been expected in the light of the woeful report on Welsh local government published in June 1939.[3]

Perhaps the most important impact to assess is the impact which evacuation had on the children themselves. In physical terms many of the children - 'dumplings' as one report dubbed them - did benefit from the fresh air and wholesome food of the countryside, also from the increased medical surveillance which resulted from the outcry over the first evacuation.[4] It had obviously been intended to carefully monitor the children as, only three weeks into the scheme, Liverpool headmistress M.M. Granger (of Prince Rupert Steers St School) noted in her logbook: *'Some classes were weighed and weights recorded as a matter of interest to test effect of new environment on the physical fitness of the children.'*[5] No doubt the virtual collapse of the first scheme put paid to this exercise, which was a great pity. Had all schools carried out such regular weighings whilst evacuation was in progress they would have discovered that by no means were all evacuees living off the fat of the land: as we've seen, some were very poorly fed indeed. Yet it would be wrong to see all instances where evacuees were under-fed as cases of deliberate ill-treatment. Much was made of the urban deprivation that was highlighted by evacuation. But many evacuees, adults and children old enough to notice such things, were appalled at the poverty and the primitive conditions they encountered in the countryside.

The question of the psychological effect of evacuation is altogether more difficult to assess. In March 1940, in the lull between the first evacuation scheme and the start of the second, Liverpool and District Child Guidance Clinic offered some thoughts on this matter. Whilst accepting that evacuation had certainly been beneficial in some cases, they felt that the real test would only come once the children returned home. Perhaps then, it continued, some unconscious resentment at being sent away might surface, some might encounter difficulties at having to leave behind new-found relationships, others at readjusting to life in the town. The Clinic concluded that it could certainly foresee an increase in

271

nervous and behavioural disorders amongst children as a result of the scheme.[6] Some psychiatrists, like John Bowlby, the British expert on separation anxiety, had, indeed, already voiced their concerns to the government. In 1940 Anna Freud also expressed the view that long-term separation of a child from its parents was detrimental.[7] But not all the experts agreed: Dame Josephine Barnes, for example, saw a move to the country as purely beneficial. As the evacuation scheme drew to a close a report was published in the *British Journal of Psychology* based on a study of 112 children mainly aged between eight and thirteen who had been referred to the Cambridge Child Guidance Clinic. The conclusions drawn were that the vast majority of evacuees had not needed psychological help and that those who needed help did so for reasons not connected with evacuation. Where children were exceptionally nervous or had shown signs of aggression or delinquency, the causes were the same whether they were evacuees or not - broken homes, lack of discipline or over-protective parents.[8] Yet it is now clear that some children were scarred, both mentally and physically, as a direct result of having been evacuated. Others may not have been psychologically disturbed as such but do claim to display certain character or behavioural traits which they feel are directly attributable to their participation in the scheme - even if only an aversion to packing or to filling-in a luggage label! Many more feel that they positively benefited from the whole experience.

Over and above all else, of course, it cannot be denied that with a few tragic exceptions, evacuation did save lives. But did Merseyside evacuees really receive a welcome in the hillsides? Was going to Wales a trip to Wonderland, as some reports claimed in 1939? Or was it a journey into Hell? In giving a final verdict on the evacuation scheme it is the evacuees themselves who must have the last word:

> *Looking back it was a good experience and although we were homesick we did settle to a certain extent and learned a lot about country life.*
> [Olive Murray]

> *Why the conspiracy of silence throughout the period of the whole evacuation years I will never understand. Perhaps it might not have been so bad if someone had just explained to us what was going on … I was never really ever again very close to my mother .. my brother and I have never really been close either. It is as if those years of trauma created a hidden barrier. I remained a shy child and suffered for it. It took me many years to regain my self confidence and have faith in myself.*
> [Marjorie Lamb]

Many things happened to us in that village [Llanderfel] and of course we were homesick, but in some ways it was quite an adventure, and I am glad I was there! [Freda Beetson]

I do think the evacuee children did benefit from experiencing a new way of life and in their social development, in coping with the unknown. The children I cared for were happy and well fed. Who knows what stress or deprivations they might have suffered had they remained in the city? [Helen Woodward] (former evacuee teacher)

... whilst a lot of good was done in the 'foster homes' and lives were saved etc, I am not sure that a good deal of harm was not done to children going away from the influence of their parents at a most important time of their lives - or must we say, 'C'est la Guerre' and hope for the best'? [Ronald Lascelles] (former Head of Newsham Boys', Liverpool) [9]

We had good and bad times, some evacuees enjoyed every minute and others like us had some very bad memories. But whatever experiences we had there is no doubt that being an evacuee had a lasting effect on my life! ... I vowed that if I had children I would never be parted from them no matter what happened. [Pauline] [10]

I didn't really think about it until I had grandchildren - then, when they were about five, the same age I was when I was evacuated, I wondered just how the parents could have done that - put their children on to trains and not know where they were going to be sent to. It must have been a terrible decision to have to make. [Margaret Jones]

In retrospect it must have been very difficult for couples to suddenly have other people's children foisted upon them without knowing anything about them. I suppose to them we may have appeared 'spoilt brats'. I do however look back on my time in Wrexham as an evacuee with fond memories ... One of the good things about the war and evacuation was how people rallied round and made the best of things. I for one am grateful for the time I spent in North Wales. [Rhona Parcell]

The children are the ones who got all the sympathy but to me, now a grandmother, it was the parents who went through it. Can you imagine, in a time when travel wasn't as it is now and Wales must have seemed like a foreign country, putting your child on a train not knowing where she was going or whose bed she would sleep in that night ... or when you would see her again. It doesn't bear thinking about. [Margaret Jones]

The best thing about being evacuated was the freedom from bombs etc. The worst was the breakdown in relationships at a very sensitive time. [Walter Hurst]

On the whole it was a good thing in a sense - with not having a mum we would have been moved from pillar to post, so being evacuated was the lesser of two evils; it taught us to appreciate the country as well ... it was a salvation of sorts for my sister and I. [Jean Marsh]

All in all it was a happy time for my brother and I. They were good people to live with, even if their lives were far more work than recreation. [Alan Tweedie]

Evacuation gave me religion, thrift and education! [Ron Haworth]

It was an enjoyable experience. It was just the factor of being away from your family that made it difficult. I learnt a lot of new things which I wouldn't have done otherwise. [Les Glover]

If anything it was better than being with my own family. I'm still in touch with my foster 'aunty' and 'uncle' (now in their eighties). They couldn't have been nicer. [Mrs Woods]

There was no way I would ever let my kids go away if there was a war. I had a horrid time in my second billet - the woman was very unkind ... I feel very bitter about the whole evacuation experience and my brother feels just the same. [Jean Cruickshank]

I was accepted into the home of a loving family whose names I will never forget. If I ever did win a million on the lottery I would try my damnedest to trace and repay them even though 60 years have gone by. [Edward Mandaluff]

Although I was only away a short time I feel as if I was permanently affected by evacuation. I felt very isolated and alienated, especially when our 'hosts' spoke Welsh. I've never been at all an outgoing person. [Mrs Jones]

274

I can identify certain character traits which have resulted from my evacuation. Although I was well looked after the lady wasn't keen on me playing with other children, so I had rather an isolated existence - perfectly happy - but now I realise it made me into a very 'individual' sort of person. I never acquired 'team skills' or 'ball skills' - I wasn't useless at sport at all but everything I did later was solitary - walking, cycling etc. ... So you make quite sure you give your own kids all the opportunities - and they've excelled at team sports! Would I have ever sent my children away - if it was to avoid bombing and the wiping out of a whole generation (which was as it was seen then) - I probably would on balance.
[George Crebbin]

When I look back now the Education Authority and officials must have had a very difficult task, transporting hundreds of children, arranging school places for all, and the kindness of the foster mums taking strange children into their homes and care. Although it was wartime with difficulties and shortages and terrible tragedies happening all over the world, people went to a lot of trouble on our behalf. [Mrs Roper] [11]

I have fond memories of being an evacuee ... and think that perhaps because of the experience I became more self reliant. [Joyce Triggs] [12]

I returned to live in Liverpool back to the existence that I had left - bugs, fleas, lice and rats ... Isn't it amazing how quickly children adapt. I did. Bethesda, however, remained my nirvana. I have never forgotten that idyllic period of my childhood. Every year I revisit my memories - my children and my grandchildren all have grown up with North Wales firmly implanted in their past. [Jim McHugh]

I have marvellous memories and I'm still in touch with the family. I can't thank them enough. The Welsh people could not have been kinder. My heart is still very much in Wales. [Barbara Wilson]

Considering that those people volunteered to take to their homes children from the cities - not knowing if they were scallywags - the folk of that generation deserved a very large pat on the back. [Ron Shaw]

Postscript -

What has emerged from this study of the Merseyside/North Wales experience of the government evacuation scheme is that it is, above all, a very human story. Many things have changed since 1939 - though the issue of how to best care for the vulnerable in our society remains a challenge. But what certainly has not changed is human nature. Half-listening to the TV recently the following comment caught my attention: *There are no suitable facilities here - no school, no medical centres, there isn't even a shop. We would welcome them if it was a suitable place.* Was this a programme about World War II evacuees, perhaps a documentary on those difficult days when village folk felt unable to cope with all the newcomers? Nothing of the sort. This was a news item, on 3 April 2000, and the speaker was a villager from Langford in Essex, giving her reaction to the arrival there of 30 asylum seekers! No - human nature doesn't change, and in passing a verdict on the wartime evacuation scheme perhaps we should ask ourselves; would we do better? How many of us have the capacity to warmly and unreservedly welcome strangers into our homes? Those who treated evacuees cruelly during the years 1939-45 should have been caught and punished; those who treated the children coldly deserve little respect, but the many who offered happy and loving homes - who gave evacuees a truly warm welcome in the Welsh hillsides - these were special people indeed.

NOTES

[1] A.J.P. Taylor, *English History 1914-45*, Oxford, 1965, p.45

[2] See Holman, op. cit, but see John Macnicol in Smith, H.(ed.)*British Society in the Second World War,* for a counter view.

[3] See Chapter 1

[4] One historian even refutes this, claiming evacuees did not show any marked improvement in health. See Harold Smith (ed.), *War and Social Change - British Society in World War II* (MUP, 1986), p.18

[5] Logbook entry, 21 September 1939 (Caerns RO, ref E.A.9)

[6] Reported in *Liverpool Daily Post,* 2 March 1940

[7] Anna Freud & Dorothy Burlingham, *Children in War-Time* (Methuen, 1940), cited in Ruth Inglis, *The Children's War*, p.154

[8] Drs Bannister and Ravden, 'The problem Child and his Environment', British Journal of Psychology, vol.xxiv, Jan. 1944, cited Holman, p.104

[9] Letter to P.E. Owen, 27 Sept 1960 (PhD thesis, appendix 33), Newsham school was evacuated to Llandudno Junction.

[10] Quoted in *Cambrian News* Supplement 1989

[11] Quoted in *Our Evacuee,* p.46

[12] Ibid. p.65

Bibliography

Primary Sources

Government Records
Only a specimen of files on evacuation have been retained at the Public Record Office. The following were consulted:Ministry of Health Records PRO HLG 900: /2 (Reception & Billeting 1938-45); /7 (Arrangements in Local Authorities Areas 1939-42); /8 (Camps for children); /11 (Complaints 1939-42); /16 (Hostel Accommodation). PRO MH 78 /148-52 Welsh Board of Health 1919-44 [Actual records of Welsh Board of Health have not survived] Home Office Records (Ministry of Home Security) PRO HO 186: /128 (Evacuation Scheme for England and Wales 1938-9); /131 (Evacuation of Government Departments 1939); /156 (Committee on Evacuation, meetings in event of air-raids 1938); /593 (Evacuation of dockside area of Bootle 1940-41); /116/640/29/9 (Public Information Leaflet No. 3 - 'Evacuation: Why and How'). See also PRO CAB (series 67 & 65), PRO INF 1, and Hodsoll Papers (E.J. Hodsoll, ARP Inspector General)

Local Records
Most of the local government archive material quoted in relation to North Wales relates to the old counties of Flintshire, Denbighshire, Anglesey, Caernarvonshire and Merionethshire and is housed at record offices in, respectively Hawarden, Ruthin, Llangefni, Caernarfon and Dolgellau. Additional material on Anglesey is held in Bangor (UCNW archive). Material relating to Liverpool, Birkenhead and Wallasey is located at Liverpool Record Office and at Birkenhead and Wallasey Central Libraries. Details relating to the experiences of a number of Merseyside evacuees is also housed at the Evacuation Archive of the University of Reading.

Material consulted for North Wales covers county council and district council records including minutes, correspondence and files on a variety of evacuation matters, as indicated below. See footnotes for more specific references. (A full list with all file reference numbers is too large for inclusion here but is available in G. Wallis, *North Wales: A Case Study of a Reception Area 1939-45* [unpublished MA thesis, University of Wales])

Anglesey - County Council: Minute Book 1936-44. Also wartime minutes for the following county committees: Education, Health, 'Scabies Order' 1942-44; Maternity & Child Welfare. District Councils: Minute Books and files on evacuation covering Beaumaris MB (housed at UCNW Bangor - series III/19-21, VI/255); Amlwch UDC; Holyhead UDC ; Llangefni UDC ; Menai Bridge UDC; Aethwy RDC; Twrcelyn RDC and Valley RDC.

Caernarvonshire - County Council: Minutes 1938-45 (excl.1939-40); ARP - Committee minutes, circulars etc.; Education Committee Minute Books (EM/1) 1939-45; School logbooks (various local schools in the ES/1 & EA/9, also Cym-y-Glo Evacuees Logbook, stock, clothing etc; Rowen Evacuees logbook 1941-43; Prince Rupert (Steers St) at Central School Caernarvon; Aspen Grove Junior (at Carmel) Logbook & Admission Summary, Gwyrfai 'A' Groeslon (Liverpool evacuees), M.M. Granger's Logbook, Minutes & 'Black file', Salisbury Council School (Senior Boys) evacuated to Garth, Bangor; Local Governing Body Minute Books, County Schools: Bangor, Bethesda, Bottwnog, John Bright, Portmadoc. District Councils: Minute Books, Letter Books and files on evacuation covering Bangor MB; Caernarvon Borough (especially Evacuation Papers DI/718 - a wealth of material including 2 pamphlets produced by Liverpool University: *Preliminary Report on the Problems of Evacuation* (1939) and *Our Wartime Guests - Opportunity or Menace?* (1940)); Conway Borough; Pwllheli Borough; Bethesda UDC; Betws-y-Coed UDC; Criccieth UDC; Llanfairfechan UDC; Penmaenmawr UDC; Portmadoc UDC; Gwyrfai UDC; Lleyn RDC; Nant Conway RDC; Ogwen RDC. Oral history material, including Mimi Hatton (XM/T/380)

Denbighshire - County Council: Minutes 1935-45; Education Committee 1939-45; local school logbooks; County Council Files on Evacuation (Files 1 to 37, Z1345-Z1352); Papers of Morris T. Williams (DD/DM/128/24); Colwyn Bay Council of Social Service - Executive Committee & General Meetings Minutes 1939-44 (DD/DM/121/1). District Councils: Minutes, Letter Books and files on evacuation covering Denbigh Borough; Ruthin Borough; Wrexham Borough; Ceiriog RDC; Wrexham RDC (including *Wrexham RDC - A Record of War Services* written by G. Vernon Price, Clerk of the Council, 1943); Edeyrnion RDC. Parish Councils: Minutes - Betws-yn-Rhos, Broughton, Llangollen

Flintshire - County Council: Minutes 1939-45 (FC/1/41-46); Education Committee 1939-45 (FC/2/40-45); Clerk's Department - Minutes, Correspondence etc on Evacuation Procedures 1939-45 (FC/4/250); Quarter Sessions Papers 1940. District Councils: Minutes, Letter Books and files on evacuation covering Flint Borough; Buckley UDC; Connah's Quay UDC; Holywell UDC; Mold UDC; Prestatyn UDC; Rhyl UDC; Hawarden RDC;

Holywell RDC; Overton RDC; St Asaph RDC
Merionethshire - County Council: Minutes 1938-41 (Z/CM/1/13-16); ARP
Committee 1938-40 (Z/CM/5/2); Civil Defence Committee 1939-49 (Z/CM/5/3
& Z/CM/1/19); Education Committee 1939-40 (A/1/6). District Councils:
Minutes, Letter Books and files on evacuation covering Bala UDC; Barmouth
UDC; Dolgellau UDC; Towyn UDC; Deudraeth RDC; Penllyn RDC. (See
Denbighshire for the transferred district of Edeyrnion RDC)
Merseyside - All of Liverpool's detailed papers relating to evacuation were
destroyed in the Blitz in 1941 but the printed and bound wartime records of the
council have survived. The following were consulted: City of Liverpool -
Proceedings of the Council (352/COU); Liverpool Civil Defence Emergency
Committee Minutes 1939-47 (352 MIN/DEF 1/1-11); 'Evacuation from
Liverpool during the great war 1939-45. Forms & Newspaper Cuttings Prepared
in the Library 1942' (HF 301 13 EVA). Birkenhead Civil Defence Emergency
Committee Minutes (B/025/1); Birkenhead Education Committee, Emergency
and Sub-Committee Minutes (series B/305-/308, B/313, BC/IV/820)

Newspapers and Periodicals
*Cefn Chronicle; Caernarvon and Denbigh Herald; Flintshire Observer;
Wrexham Advertiser and Star; Wrexham Leader; North Wales Chronicle; Rhyl
Journal; The Welsh Nationalist; Liverpool Daily Post and Echo* (including
special supplements *'Wales at War'* and *'Our War'* (1989), *Birkenhead News;
Birkenhead Advertiser; Wallasey News; Cambrian News* (plus 1989 supplement
*'Homefront Heroes'); The Liverpolitan, St Francis Xavier's College Magazine;
Cofio'r Cefn; Liverpool Collegiate School Magazine; Liverpool Blue Coat
Society Annual Report (1989)*

Unpublished
Edward Morgan Humphreys Mss. (UCNW X 15745-16028)
Blades, Bryan, *Welsh Rarebits: Memoirs of an Evacuated Teacher*
Craine, Julie, *Evacuation from Liverpool - A move that ultimately saved the lives
of thousands* (Edge Hill University College, BA 1999)
Sissons, John Norman, *Planning ARP in the City of Liverpool. A Study of
Politics and Administration* (University of Liverpool, M.Phil 1985)
Owen, P.E., *The Development of the Bilateral System of Education in
Caernarvonshire 1903 to date* (University of Wales, Ph.D 1961)
Wallis, Gillian, *North Wales: A Case Study of a Reception Area under the
Government Evacuation Scheme 1939-45* (University of Wales, MA 1979)

Secondary Sources

Aaron, R., 'A Modern Dispersion', University of Wales Guild of Graduates
    Annual, July 1940

Addison, P., *The Road to 1945*, Pimlico, 1975

Ayers, Pat, *Women at War*, Liver Press, 1988

Blasbery, Ken, *Children of the Blitz*, K.Blasbery

Boyce, Joan, *Pillowslips and Gasmasks*, Liver Press, 1989

Bryan, Tim, *Great Western Railways at War*, Patrick Stevens, 1995

Titmuss, R.M., *Problems of Social Policy*, HMSO, 1944

Boyd, W. (ed.), *Evacuation in Scotland*, (London), 1944

Calder, A., *The People's War*, Panther Books, 1971

Census of England and Wales, 1931,1951 (HMSO)

Clwyd Record Office, *Clwyd at War 1939-1945* (1989)

Crosby, Travis L., *The Impact of Civilian Evacuation in the Second World War*,
    Croom Helm, 1986

Davies, John, *A History of Wales*, Penguin, 1994

Dent, H.C., *Education in Transition*, (London),1944

Evacuees Reunion Association, *60th Anniversary of the Evacuation 1939-99*,
    ERU, 1999

Ferguson, S.M & Fitzgerald, H., *Studies in the Social Services*, 1952

Hansard, *House of Commons Debates* (vols. 270, 295, 338)

Healey, Peter (ed.) *The Liverpool Blue Coat Past and Present 1708-1995* (1996)

Holman, Bob, *The Evacuation: A Very British Revolution*, Lion Publishing, 1995

Fogarty, M.P., *Prospects of the Industrial Areas of Great Britain*, (London), 1945

Inglis, Ruth, *The Children's War*, Collins, 1989

Isaacs, S. (ed.) *The Cambridge Evacuation Survey*, Methuen, 1941

Gilbert, Martin, *A History of the Twentieth Century*, vol 1, HarperCollins, 1997

Griffiths, Doug (ed.), *With Oars and Sails: An Illustrated History of Rock Ferry
    High School 1925-1996*, Old Rockferians Assoc. 1997

Jackson, Carlton, *Who Will Take Our Children?*, Methuen 1985

Johnson, B.S. (ed.), *The Evacuees*, Gollancz, 1968

Johnson, Derek E., *Exodus of Children*, Pennyfarthing Publications

Jones, Audrey, *Farewell Manchester*, Didsbury Press, 1989

Jones, Ivor Wynne, *The Air War over Denbighshire and Flintshire 1939-45*

Jones, Reg Chambers, *Bless 'Em All*, Bridge Books, 1995

Leakey, J.H., *School Errant*, Queensgate Press, 1951

Le Gros Clark, F, & Toms, R.W., *Evacuation. Failure or Reform?* Fabian, 1940

Liverpool Daily Post & Echo, *Bombers Over Merseyside*, (1943), Scouse Press, 1983

Liverpool University (Social Science Dept), *Preliminary Report on Problems of Evacuation* (1939) and *Our Wartime Guests: Opportunity or Menace?* (1940) Liverpool UP

Liverpool Women at War: An Anthology of Personal Memories, Picton Press, 1991

Lindsay, J.A., *A History of the North Wales Slate Industry*, 1974

Longmate, N., *How We Lived Then*, Hutchinson, 1971

Manning, Leah, *A Life for Education*, Victor Gollancz, 1970

Marriner, Sheila, *The Economic and Social Development of Merseyside*, Croom Helm, 1982

Marwick, A., *Britain in the Century of Total War*, 1968

Massey, Victoria, *One Child's War*, BBC, 1978

Mowat, C.L., *Britain Between the Wars*, 1955

O'Brien, T.H., *Civil Defence*, HMSO, 1955

Oswestry Heritage Centre (ed. and pub.), *Our Evacuee*, 1995

Padley, R. & Cole, M., *Evacuation Survey*, (London) 1940

Parsons, Martin, *I'll Take That One*, Beckett Carlson, 1998

Parsons, Martin and Starnes, Penny, *The Evacuation - the true story*, DSM, 1999

Pelling, Henry, *Britain and the Second World War*, Collins/Fontana 1990

Perrett, Bryan, *Liverpool: A City at War*, Robert Hall, 1990

Place, G.W. (ed.), *Neston at War*, Burton & Neston History Society, 1999

Powys Montgomeryshire Federation of Women's Institutes (ed, and pub.), *Montgomeryshire Memories 1900-1960*, 1994

Rees, D. Ben, *Wales: The Cultural Heritage*, G.W. & A. Hesketh, 1981

Schweitzer, Pam (ed.), *Goodnight Children Everywhere*, Age Exchange Theatre Trust, 1990

Sheridan, Dorothy (ed.), *Wartime Women* (A Mass Observation Anthology), Heinemann 1990

Sinclair, James, *Welsh Scouse*, Sinclair Publishing, 1998

Smith, H. (ed.), *British Society in the Second World War*, Manchester UP, 1984

Stevenson, J., *British Society 1914-45*, Penguin, 1990

Strachey, St. Loe (Mrs), *Borrowed Children*, John Murray, 1940

Taylor, A.J.P. *England 1914-45*, OUP, 1965

Turner, E.S., *The Phoney War on the Home Front*, 1961

Waller and Vaughan Rees, *Blitz*, Optima, 1990

Waugh, Evelyn, *Put Out More Flags* (London), 1942

Wheeler-Bennett, J., *John Anderson - Viscount Waverley*, Macmillan 1962

Whittington-Egan, Richard, *The Great Liverpool Blitz*, Gallery Press, 1987

Whitworth, Rodney, *Merseyside at War*, Scouse Press, 1988

Wicks, Ben, *No Time to Wave Goodbye*, Bloomsbury, 1988

Williams, D., *Modern Wales*, 1977

Women's Group on Public Welfare, *Our Towns. A Close Up. A Study Made During 1939-42*, (Oxford), 1943

See pages 283-284 for a list of all former evacuees, and others, who kindly contributed their memories of evacuation.

NAME	EVACUATED TO	NAME	EVACUATED TO
Don Aird	Carmel	Walter Hurst	Harlech
Ken Aird	Carmel	Jean Hurst	Harlech
Stan Aird	Carmel	Eric Jackson	Oswestry
Betty Aindow (nee Lowe)	Shrewsbury	Frank Jagger	Bala
Catherine Allan	Ford	Bert Jones	Llanfarian
Alex Anderson	Criccieth	Anne Jones	Dolgellau
Bill Andrews	Pencader	Hugh Jones	Coedpoeth
Jim Barrow	Llanidloes	Margaret Jones	Llanidloes
Marjorie Baker	Oswestry	Trevor Jones	Oswestry area
Harold Beckett	Oswestry area	Edmund Jones	Montgomeryshire
Freda Beetson (nee Carruthers)	Llanderfel	Dorothy Kell (nee McKay)	Barmouth
		Ethel Kerry	Portmadoc
Elizabeth Belger	Cemaes Bay	Marjorie Lamb	Harlech
Beryl Bellier-Moudray	Machynlleth	George Lawson	
Dorothy Berry (Nickson)	Caernarvon	Hazel Lee	Prestatyn
Billy Blakeborough	Llanidloes	Joyce Light	Portmadoc
Bob Boyd	Llanegryn	Winifred Litten	Hawarden
Nora Boyd	Corwen	Tony Lloyd	Ruthin
Margaret Brent	Llanffestiniog	Harold Lyle	Carmel
Sarah Brumfitt (Clague)	Caergwrle	Mary Maher	Llanfairfechan
Joan Brumfitt	Rhosgadfan	Edward Mandaluff	Cefn Mawr
Alfred Bryce	Prestatyn	Archie Manser	Oswestry area
Cynthia Bullock	Gwernymynydd	Joan Marsh	Astley
Kathleen Burrows	Llaneliden	Jean McCarthy (nee Ogilvie)	Rhayader
Pat Byrne		Angela McDonald (nee (Pearson)	Pencraig
Eileen Byrne	Abergele		
Dave Carter	Deiniolen	Gwenda McGarrity	Llanfrothen
Ernest Carvell	Machynlleth	Don McKernan	Beaumaris
Elsie Carvell(nee Leyland)	Llwyngwril, and Rhostefain	Eddie McKernan	Beaumaris
Elsa Chatterton	Llanfrothen	Ken McGunigle	Carmel
David (Nick) Cheshire	Oswestry area	Honor McGrath	Anglesey & Bethesda
John Clayton	Anglesey	Jim McHugh	Bethesda
Hilda Cooper	Oswestry, Llanidloes	Pam McNaught(nee Heys)	Bangor
Les Cowle	Corwen	Jean Moeller	Denbigh
Doris Coxon	Rhos	Billy Moffit	Ruthin
Charles Crebbin	Meliden	Mary Morris	Bridgend
George Crebbin	Abersoch	Frank Morris	Queensferry & Oswestry
Pat Crick (Davies)	Welshpool area	Thomas Murphy	Barmouth
Alex Cross	Caergwrle	Olive Murray (nee Richards)	Newtown
Jean Cruickshank	Dolwyddelan	Gordon Nash	Oswestry
Sadie Dawson (nee Gaunt)	Fairbourne	Mr Nickson	Conway
G.M Dodd	Merioneth	Ron Organ	St Asaph
John Doyle	Gobowen & Montgomery	E. Olwen Owen	North Wales
Ron Edmondson	Penrhyndeudraeth	A.W. Otter	Towyn & Aberdovey
Sylvia Ellison	Ffestiniog & Llanidloes	Rhona Parcell	Wrexham
Dorothy Formston	Criccieth	George Parry	Overton, Sarn Bridge
Doreen French	Cheshire & North Wales	Lilian Platt	Braesor
Les Glover	Sarn Bach nr Abersoch	Phil Price	Marple, Hollinshey
Edna Griffiths (nee Kirby)	Pentre Broughton	Joan Price	Isle of Man
Stanley Griffiths	Marple Bridge	Jack Richardson	Llangurig
F.W Green	Broxwood	Sylvia Ripper (nee Clifford)	Abergwili
Enid Hardcastle		Mrs Runcie (nee Piercy)	North Wales
Ron Haworth	Devil's Bridge	Rita Sandford	Montgomery
Jean Hennity (nee Lyle)	Carmel	Mrs L Schofield	Cwm-y-glo
Roy Hill	Bangor	Ronnie Scholar	Carmel
Rita Holmes (nee Griffiths)	Buckley	Mrs D Shaw	Moss nr Wrexham
D.W Honey	Wrexham	Ron Shaw	Bethesda
	Mynydd Isa, Leeswood	Peter Sherlock	
May Hornby	Hanley	L.G. Smith	N.Wales
Ron Horner	Heswall	Mrs F.M Smith	Harlech
Maureen Horner (Woods)	Heswall	Miss L.G.Smith	North Wales
A.E. Houghton	Carmel	Walter Smith	
John Houston	Anglesey		
Frank Hughes	Carmel		
Mrs Hughes	Bala		

283

NAME	EVACUATED TO	NAME	EVACUATED TO
Kathleen Spriggs (nee Pickering)	Llanidloes	Stan Wallis	Bwlchtocyn
		Mrs E Watson	Aberystwyth
Jean Stanbury (Lucas)	Blaenau Ffestiniog	Dorothy Wharton	Wrexham
Helena Stenhouse	Portmadoc	Hilda Wilkes	Heswall & Oswestry area
Stan Sunners	Beaumaris	Bill Wilkinson	Beaumaris
Teddy Taylor	Beaumaris	Barbara Wilson (nee Hines)	Harlech
Christine Templeton	Barmouth		
Beryl Traynor (nee Carr)	Criccieth	Mrs Williams	Ruthin
Allan Tweedie	Cilmery	Mrs Woods	Shrewsbury
Peter Walker	Bangor	Arthur Woods	Aberystwyth
		Edith Woolfall	Llanidloes
		Clifford Wrightson	Montgomeryshire

Other contributors (hosts, officials, teachers, hostel matrons, etc):

John Ackerley, Vera Beecroft, Ralph Broster, Donald Broster, G.L.Bryant, John Byrne, Mrs M.Conway, John Cox, Mrs S. Davies, Lawrence Evans, Paul Gilbert, Beres Griffith, Mary Hughes, W.C Hanks, Jill Holmes, A.M. Jones, Gwen Jones (nee Ashton), Mrs E.M. Jones, John Manuel, Arthur Millard, S.M Milne, Dave Molyneux, Mrs H. Mowat (nee Jones), Barbara Norman, E. Olwen Owen, Mrs George Osborn, I.B Pierce (nee Morris), Mrs M. Pritchard, Mrs Redmund, Eifion Richards, Charles Roberts, Margaret Roberts, Sianw Roberts, Mrs N. Rushton, Glenys Thomas, Phyllis Williams, Howel Williams, Mrs Jessie Wynne; and former evacuated teachers: Bryan G. Blades, Ellen Baylis, Mrs M. Jones (nee Kirkup), T.H. King, Winifred Litten, Helen Woodward.

[With sincere apologies but many thanks to anyone who may have been accidentally omitted]

284

INDEX

Aber 120
Aberdaron 53
Aberdovey 102, 153
Abergele 99, 150, 188, 194, 200, 207, 228
Abersoch 67, 138, 251
Aberystwyth 27, 49, 72, 97, 131, 178, 195, 223, 229, 246, 252, 265
Abuse - *see* Ill-treatment
Abyssinia xi, 4
Accommodation - *see* Billeting; Overcrowding
Accommodation Surveys xvi, 1, 2, 15, 195
Ackerley, John 256
Addison, Lord 137
Adoption, of evacuees 252-4
Aethwy 12
Aindow, Betty 60
Aindow, J.C. 249
Air Raid Precautions (ARP)
Air raids - *see* Bombing
Air-raid shelters *(see also* Anderson shelters; Morrison shelters) 77, 78,177, 181, 185, 238
Aird, Don 105, 218, 260
Aird, Ken 81, 260
Aird, Stan 260
Aled RDC 147, 151*n*, 176
Alpha Drive School 138
Alsop High School 39, 88, 136, 252
Amlwch 2, 8*n*, 179*n*, 246*n*
Anderson, Alex 90, 97, 120, 145, 185, 224, 234, 254, 260
Anderson Committee xii, xv, 17
Anderson shelters x, 78, 176, 186, 189
Anderson, John x, xi, xii
Andrews, J.C. 129
Anfield 5, 159, 178, 266; Anfield cemetery 189
Anfield Road School 131, 138

Anglesey xiii, xviii, 7, 12, 32, 39, 44, 51, 96, 105, 116, 123, 149, 156, 180, 205, 206, 207, 223, 227, 229, 232, 233, 235, 237, 243, 259
Anti-Tuberculosis Service of Wales & Monmouth, Report of xvii, xviii, 14
Aspen Grove School 63, 68, 97, 113, 170*n*, 260
Asylum seekers 278

Baker, John Fleetwood 187
Baker, Marjorie 186, 251
Bala 32, 74, 100, 195, 198, 199*n*, 207, 252, 264
Baldwin, Stanley xi
Bands of Hope 158, 229
Bangor 49, 63, 109, 132, 151, 169, 178, 182, 191, 193, 202, 209, 222*n*, 228, 230, 237, 247, 255, 259
Bangor University 119, 169
Barmouth 72, 78, 101, 107, 138, 206, 219, 232, 259
Barnes, Josephine 272
Barrow, Jim 103, 217, 262
Bates, Percy 221
Baylis, Ellen 123, 158
BBC broadcasts; evacuees' 158, 159, 170, 212; from Liverpool 176; from Bangor 191
Beaumaris 12, 19, 44, 120, 124, 134, 136, 192, 193, 203, 209, 227*n*, 231, 232, 264
Bebington xv, 7
Beckett, Harold 127
Bed wetting 62, 86-91
Beddgelert 25
Bedding 9, 37, 52, 88, 195
Beetson, Freda 204, 264, 273
Belger, Elizabeth 205
Bellier-Moudray, Beryl 155

Bennett, June 97*n*

Berry, Dorothy 26, 41

Bethesda 109, 117*n*, 123, 151, 225, 227*n*, 233, 275

Bethesda & District Evangelical Council 151

Bethesda British School 113

Betws-y-Coed 119, 120, 174, 227*n*, 229

Billeting xv, 2, 36-53, 155, 165, 170, 172, 195, 203, 242; difficulties 10-11, 47, 170, 173-4, 175, 191-209; Tribunals 16, 37, 195-9

Billeting allowance 36, 174, 197, 236-7, 246; for sickness 95; fraud 199; parental contributions 74-5

Billeting officers 10*f.*, 36*f.*, 46-8, 68, 86, 88, 114, 129, 146, 179, 191, 195, 196, 198, 200, 203, 212; nature of work of 10, 37, 40 198-9, 201-3, 246

Billets 59, 69, 86-7; communal 206

Birkenhead Girls Secondary School 137, 205

Birkenhead Institute 127

Birkenhead xv, 12, 15, 17, 30, 31, 48, 49, 51, 58, 60, 72, 74, 143, 146, 178, 186, 204, 209, 253, 256; bombing in 175, 176, 181, 189, 192; Christmas arrangements 78; clothing schemes 109, 110; Education Committee 7, 75, 171, 177, 245, 256; evacuation plans 7-9, 17, 171, 178; evacuation rehearsals 17, 21; evacuation statistics 17, 30, 171; finances 78, 97*n*; health issue 51; return home plans 243, 245

Blackstock tenements 176

Blackwell, Doris 71, 256

Blades, Bryan G., 47, 62*n*, 63, 108*n*, 120*n*, 125*n*, 132, 134, 138*n*, 185, 228

Blakeborough, Billy 262

Blankets - *see* Bedding

Blasbery, Ken 136, 175, 185, 188

Blind evacuees 12, 15

Blitz - *see* Bombing

Blue Coat School (Liverpool) 12, 39, 124, 134, 136, 192, 231, 232, 264

Board of Education 11, 123, 201

Board of Trade 115

Bombing: effect on children 181-91, 273; expected casualties xii, 4-5; Merseyside 4, 92, 97, 169, 172-94, 200, 238, 239, 275; North Wales 231-2; 'V' bombs 242-3, 244; World War I ix

Bonner, J.D. 243,

Bontnewydd 153

Bootle xii, xv, 5, 21, 30, 57, 130, 135, 178, 188, 189, 248

Borthygest 207

Bowlby, John 272

Boy Scouts 41, 229

Boyce, Joan 205, 208

Boyd, Bob 65

Braddock, Bessie 84

Brae Street School 257

Braithwaite, H.E. 19*n*

Brassey Street School 266

Brecknock 32

Brent, Margaret 153

British Restaurants - *see* Food

Bromborough 67

Bronyfoel Council School 130

Brookes-Parry, W. 175

Brookfield School 178

Brooks, Miss 70

Broster, Ralph 217

Brumfitt, Joan 122, 140, 158
Brumfitt, Sarah 63
Bryce, Alfred 27, 129, 140, 192, 259
Buckley 17, 51, 64, 93*n*, 116, 237
Bulkeley, Williams 203
Bulkeley, Richard 124
Bullock, N. 139*n*, 142, 158*n*,
Butler Street Infants 253
Byrne, Eileen 188
Byrne, Pat 62

Cadet corps 230-1
Caergwrle 73, 233, 260
Caernarvon xv*n*, 8, 9, 25, 37, 41, 53,
        58, 66*n*, 75, 78, 93, 98, 101,
        108, 112, 121, 127*n*, 135, 170,
        221, 227*n*, 230, 238, 250
Caernarvon British School 117*n*, 139
Caernarvonshire xiii, xvii, xviii, 18,
        31, 51, 53, 72, 92, 94, 97, 111,
        113, 121, 142, 146, 169, 198,
        218, 226, 227, 230, 247
Caernarvonshire County Herb
Committee 119
Caernarvonshire Organiser of Infants'
        Schoolwork & Language 159
Calder High School 69, 75, 122
Callaghan, Jim 191
Calvinistic Methodism xviii, 146, 147,
        149
Camps: Harvest camps 221; Holiday
        129, 201; School camps 201
Carmel 68, 113, 159, 170*n*, 228, 252,
        260
Carneddi Infants School 117*n*
Carroll, Billy 98
Carter, Charles C. 141
Carvell, Elsie 41, 158
Carvell, Ernest 63, 67, 185
Catholics - *see* Roman Catholics
Catlow, Betty 215
Cattle market - *see* Reception arrangements

Cefn 139, 142
Cefn Mawr 233
Ceiriog RD 64*n*, 85
Cemaes Bay 205, 205*n*
Cerrig-y-Drudion 150*n*
Channel Islands evacuees 192, 244*n*
Chapel 108, 143-52; Chapel authorities
        123, 148
Chatterton, Elsa 27, 155, 204
Chelsea Polytechnic (medical
        gymnasts in Aberystwyth) 97
Cheshire 31, 247
Chester 15, 31, 247
Child Guidance work 226; Cambridge
        Clinic 272; Liverpool Clinic
        271
Chirk 64, 87, 148
Christ Church, Claughton 151
Christmas 56, 78, 79, 177-8, 181
Chrystal, George 50*n*
Churchill, Winston 177, 195
Chwilog 247
Cinema trips 78, 137, 232-3
Clarke, Joyce 131
Claughton Road Special School 206
Clint Road School 73
Clothing 22-4, 49, 53, 64, 106-115,225
Clynnog 203, 252
Cole Street School 72, 78, 98
Colomendy (*see also* Camps) 201
Colwyn Bay 12, 39, 109, 111, 242;
Council of Social Service 111
Communal meals - *see* Food
Condition of evacuees - *see* Clothing;
        Footwear; Health
Connah's Quay 17, 64, 114
Convents, *see* Religious houses
Conway 39, 114, 227*n*
Conway, HMS 192
Cooper, Hilda 28, 35, 46
CORB - *see* Overseas evacuation
Corwen 236

Cound 30

Country life (*see also* Food - country style) 62, 98-101, 119-22, 140-1, 222, 233-5, 272; and clothing 108; hazards (*see also* Deaths) 98-101; nature rambles 119-22

County Conferences (1939) 8, 15; (1940) 165, 172

Cox, John 100, 253

Coxon, Doris 44, 145, 215, 221-2

Crea, Eileen 106

Crebbin, Charles 25, 36, 43, 67, 590, 214, 222, 223, 224

Crebbin, George 251, 254, 275

Criccieth 14, 19, 93, 98, 120, 205, 223, 260

Crick, Pat 25, 28, 45, 61, 67, 220, 236

Croesor 259

Croft, George 32

Crosbie, J. (Miss) 132, 170, 212, 228, 229

Crosby xv, 4, 30, 32, 248

Cross, Alex 233, 260

Cruickshank, Jean 184, 252, 254, 274

Culture clash (*see also* National Conference for Safeguarding Welsh Culture) 56, 58-60, 196

Curtis Committee 250

Cym-y-Glo 97, 252

Czechoslovakia 4

David, A.A. (Bishop) 31

Davies, Clement xvii

Davies, Ellis (Miss) xiii

Davies, George A. 2n

Davies, J.C. 12

Davies, J. Iorwerth 216

Davies, S. (Mrs) 65

Davis, Janet 203

Dawson, Sadie 107, 153

de la Warr, Earl 171n

Deaths (of evacuees) 73, 97-9, 183

Dempsey, G.B. 7, 178n

Denbigh 39, 120, 170, 201, 227n, 228,

Denbighshire xviii, 9, 1, 15n, 17, 32, 37, 58, 116, 122, 128, 146, 148, 156, 165, 166, 247

Departure of evacuees (from Merseyside) 24-31

Deudraeth 14, 150n, 173-4, 178n, 195, 227n, 239

Deverell, Alderman 72

Devil's Bridge 266

Diamond-cutters (in Bangor) 191

Dingle 5, 49

Distribution of evacuees - *see* Reception arrangements

Dolgelley (Dolgellau) 102, 195

Domestic work - *see* Work

Dorothea Slate Quarry Company 114

Double shifts - *see* Education

Dovecot 188

Dovecot Estate 175

Dovedale Road School 78

Downey, Father 151

Doyle, Father 150

Doyle, John 27, 209, 219, 220

Doyle, Nellie 138

Dulwich Preparatory School 229

Duncalf, Edith 194

Dunkirk 87, 145, 172, 182, 191

Durning Road (shelter disaster) 177, 187

Dyserth 25

Edern 159

Edge Hill 53; Edge Hill Station 29

Edmondson, Ron 143

Education 11-13, 75, 115-43, 172, 274, 275; accommodation 12, 115, 172, 243; Catholic 149; double shifts 12, 77, 116-19, 122, 139; equipment 127; impact of

evacuation on 11, 137-40, 245;
    methods 139
Edwards, A.E. 193
Edwards, Betty 43
Eglwysbach 58
Eisteddfodau 157, 158, 159
Ellesmere Port xv
Elliot, Walter xvi, 3, 150, 169
Ellison, Norman 181, 189
Elsie, Canon 203
Emergency rations - see Food
Emmanuel School 110
Enuresis - see Bed wetting
ERA - see Evacuees Reunion
    Association
Evacuation (see also Private
    Evacuation; Trekking); 1939
    Ch 1; 1940 165-79; 1944 Ch
    8; and Munich crisis xiii-xv,
    154; Napoleonic wars x;
    numbers (1939) 8, 8n, 14-15,
    30, 37-9 (1940) 169, 170, 171,
    173-9; (1944) 242; principles
    of xii; priority classes xv;
    rehearsals 21, 22; Special
    Scheme 173, 175, 176n, 177,
    191; 'trickle' 178-9, 191;
    zoning xv, 7, 106, 176
Evacuees Reunion Association (ERA)
    260, 267
Evan Evans 148
Evans, Osborne J. 195
Everton 178, 184
Everton Terrace Spotters' School 137
Expectant mothers xv, 38, 40, 206

Fairbourne 107
Farmwork - see Work
Fazakerley 188n, 221
Fazakerley Cottage Homes 188n
Ferguson, Margaret 27, 29, 45
Ffair cyflogi ('Hiring fairs') 46

Ffestiniog 205
Fifth columnists 122, 151
Firewatching 190-1
Flint 37, 170
Flintshire xvi, 8, 15n, 17, 32, 51, 72,
    97, 108, 116, 157, 166, 237n,
    242, 247
Food (see also Ministry of Food) 9,
    40; British Restaurants 237-8;
    'country' food 62, 72, 102-4,
    140, 271; emergency rations
    10, 37, 39, 131, 194; gathering
    68, 104, 119-20, 235; lack of
    65, 104-5, 105n, 192, 215,
    216, 219, 224, 271; school
    meals 225, 237; supplies 9, 10,
    172, 237
Footwear 106, 108, 112-15
Formston, Dorothy 158, 205
Formstone, Mary 137
Forrester, Helen 22
Francis, J. (Sister) 124
Fraud - see also Racketeers 199, 202
French, Doreen 103, 144, 213
Freud, Anna 90, 272
Friary RC School 128
'Funk Express' 190

Gallantry, Joan 97n
Gautby Road School 73
Gerlan 59
Gibbon, I.G. xin
Gibson, A.M. 63, 66, 236
Girl Guides 41, 120, 229, 230
Glamorgan 32
Glover, Les 60, 67, 122, 155, 184, 274
Gobowen 219
Gondal, Maharajah of 109
Gordon, C.G.S. xiii
Granger, M.M. 110, 135, 271
Great Western Railway Company 30n
Grice, Mabel 97

Griffiths, Edna 71, 257
Griffiths, Nathan 101
Griffiths, R.T. 114*n*
Griffiths, Stanley 141
Griffiths, G.Wynne (Revd) 151
Hand, Eustace (Revd) 146
Harlech 35, 72, 78, 98, 206, 208, 262
Harne (or Hame?), Joyce 107
Harrison, Enid 127
Hatton, Mimi 139, 252
Hawarden 17, 64, 73, 149, 152
Hawarden Grammar School 125
Haworth, Ron 254, 266, 274
Head lice 50-3, 62, 65, 85*n*, 86, 275
Health (see also Bed wetting; Head
  lice; Ill-treatment; Impetigo; Ministry
  of Health; Scabies; Tuberculosis;
  Welfare; Welsh Board of Health):
  general planning 8-9, 13-14, 84-105,
  166-7, 169, 225, 226-7, 238, 246;
  hospital stays 98-9; immunisation 13,
  85; of evacuees 8, 14, 49-53, 166,
  246, 271-2; of locals 14, 53, 85, 101-
  2; sick bays (hostels) 14, 81, 91-2,
  93-4, 206, 227, 238
Hennity, Jean 94, 104, 216
Hensley, Cardinal 150
Herb collecting 119-20
Hereford 32
Heyworth Street School 247
Hill, Roy 141
Hindle, Francis 201
Hippodrome 191
Hirael Infants School 88*n*
Hiring fair (Ffair cyflogi) 46
Hoare, Samuel xiv
Hodsoll, John xi
Hodson, William (Father) 148
Hogan, Luke 84
Holly Lodge School 116
Holmes, Rita 35, 101, 137-8, 219, 232
Holt Hill Convent School 125, 149

Holy Cross School (L'Pool) 150
Holy Trinity School (Anfield) 178, 184,
  246, 266
Holyhead xvi, 40*n*, 85, 88, 136, 147,
  173, 174, 178, 198, 237, 252
Holywell 64, 93, 115, 227, 243
Home Office xi, xiv
Homesickness 60*ff,* 213, 272
Honey, D.W. 43, 71
Hope 73
Hornby, May 216
Horsburgh, Florence 201
Hospitality 71-2, 74, 273-5
Hostels (*see also* Health; Youth Hostels)
  208-9
Houghton, A.E. 68, 252
House of Commons' evacuation debate
  (Sept 1939) 53
Householders' Roll 169
Householders' Certificate 169
Houston, John 45, 86, 124, 153, 204,
  229
Howson, Miss 206
Hughes, Enid 13
Hughes, Glyn 98
Hughes, Iorys 192*n*
Hughes, Mrs 160, 219
Humphreys, Edward Morgan 18
Humphreys, E.O. 116*n*
Hunt's Cross Council School 110
Hurst, Walter 44, 98, 155, 208, 253,
  274
Huyton xv
Huyton Woods 189

Ifton Heath 42
Ill-treatment, of evacuees 89-90, 112,
  145-6, 171, 207-9, 212-25,
  271-2, 274
Immunisation - *see* Health
Impetigo 53, 86, 92, 207
Inland Revenue Department 118, 191

Isherwood, T.W. (Revd) 151
ITMA 191

Jackson, Eric 45, 61, 104
Jackson, E. (Mrs) 49
Jacob, Dorothy 111*n*
Jagger, Frank 29, 32, 68, 88, 181, 207, 252, 264
Jewish evacuees 151
Jones, Anne (Mrs) 35, 189, 274
Jones, A.M 40*n,* 88, 147, 173*n,* 178, 198
Jones, A.Reg. 178
Jones, Ernest (Dr) 247
Jones, E.Lloyd 255
Jones, Gwen 10, 19, 89, 92, 106-7, 251
Jones, *Gwladys* (Mrs) 237
Jones, Hugh 79, 144
Jones, J.E. 18
Jones, J.M.Parry 52*n,*
Jones, John Puw (Revd) 147
Jones, Laura 102-3, 192, 233
Jones, Lilian 134, 233
Jones, Margaret 94, 184, 251, 254, 264-5, 273, 274
Jones, Moya 144, 221
Jones, N. 52*n*
Jones, R.E. 100
Jones, W.A. 247
Jones, W.D. 235
Jones, William 16*n,* 166*n*
Joseph, Francis 203
Journeys 31, 35-6
Juvenile delinquency 218

Kell, Dorothy 78-9
Kelly, John (Revd) 18-19
Kerr, Madeline 57
Kerry, Ethel 59, 60, 128, 133, 156
Kerry, S.F. 79, 128
King, J. (Councillor) 72
Kirkup, Miss 68*n*

Labels - *see* Luggage labels
Laird Street Infants 98
Lamb, Marjorie 44, 98, 130, 138, 208, 219, 222, 253, 260, 272
Lane, Homer 139
Langford (Essex) 191
Large houses (used for evacuees) 69, 70-1, 106, 124, 202-7
Lascelles, Ronald 135, 273
Leakey, J.H. 229
Lee, Derek 97*n*
Leeswood 255
Letters home 72, 213-14
Levesley, Miss 107
Lewis, Saunders 18
Lewis's Department Store 9, 157
Light, Joyce 42, 72, 130, 190
Lime Street Station 31, 190. 247, 257
Lister Drive School 43, 265
Litten, Winifred 130, 135-6, 149
Liverpolitan, The 4
Liverpool: bombing
in 4, 174-6, 181*ff*; Child
Guidance Clinics 271;
Christmas arrangements 78,
178; clothing schemes 24, 109-
10, 112; Council support for
reunions 260, 266; Education
Committee xiii, 50*n,* 77, 127,
129, 171, 178, 218; Emergency
Committee 56*n,* 73, 75, 190;
evacuation plans xii, xv, 4-9, 15,
30, 165*ff,* 176; evacuation
rehearsals 21; evacuation
statistics 30, 50, 171, 176, 178;
finances 24, 75, 78, 85-6, 109,
123, 176, 254-5; health issues 9,
50, 52, 84, 86, 92, 166; morale
in 176; poverty in 22-3, 50, 52;
Public Assistance Committee
24, 109, 112, 115; receives
evacuees 244; records destroyed

199-200; return home plans 243*ff*; Welsh 'quarter' 157
Liverpool Collegiate School 63, 66, 117, 139, 182, 191, 214, 230, 236
Liverpool Institute 117, 139, 228
Liverpool University: Evacuation Surveys 85*n*, 88, 89, 111, 170; students help Council 200
Liverpool Victoria Friendly Society 191
Llanaber 79, 259
Llanasa 221
Llanberis 192
Llanddona 235
Llandegfan 109, 226*n*
Llandegla 43
Llanderfel 264, 273
Llandudno 19, 118, 135, 157, 191, 194, 225
Llandudno County School 118
Llandudno Cymrodorion Society 157
Llanfairclydogan 247
Llanfairfechan 53*n*, 117*n*, 148, 150*n*, 198, 207, 227*n*
Llanfairfechan Secondary School 255
Llanfrothen 251
Llangefni 8*n*, 179, 191
Llangollen 12, 196
Llangurig 103, 138
Llanidloes 10, 19, 92, 264-5
Llanllyfni 170*n*, 266
Llanrhaeadr 216
Llanrwst 52, 59, 103, 150, 192, 233
Llewelyn-Jones, W. 51*n*
Lleyn RD xviii*n*, 52, 150*n*, 227*n*, 243, 247
Lloyd, Tony 123, 155, 182, 265
Llwyngwril 123
Local War Instructions (LOWIN) 4, 21, 36
London University 191
Loraine Street School 267*n*

Lovat Scouts 141
Lowe, Audrey 251-2, 253
Lowe, Eric 97
Lowe, H.W. 8
Luggage labels 29, 30, 246, 256, 264, 267, 272
Lyle, Harold 104
Macdowall, J.L. (Miss) 200
Machynlleth 72
Magorian, Michelle 198
Maher, Mary 105
Malnutrition - *see* Food
Mandaluff, Edward 233, 274
Manning, Leah 7, 131
Manser, Archie 119, 140, 181, 221
Manod Slate Mines 191-2
Manuel, John 41
Maris Stella Council School 125
Martin, Arthur 203
Matthias, A. (Mrs) 255
Maxim, Hiriam ix
McCarthy, Jean 90, 183, 223
McDonald, Angela 154
McGarrity, Gwenda 25, 41, 250
McGrath, Honor 105, 222
McGunigle, Ken 86, 94, 103, 145, 159, 220, 222
McKernan, Don 136, 217
McKernan, Eddie 120, 136, 217
McHugh, Jim 49, 145, 274
McNaught, Pam 191, 237, 255, 259
Medicals - *see* Health
Meliden 214, 223
Mellanby, Kenneth 96
Menai Bridge 66*n*, 93, 150-1, 209, 227*n*
Mental Health Committees (*see also* Child Guidance; Psychiatric Social Workers) 226
Merionethshire xviii, 12, 17, 32, 72, 123, 146, 196, 203
Mersey Park· 182

Mersey Park School 26
Milk Marketing Board xvii
Minister of Education (*see also* de la Warr) 171
Ministry of Food 39, 172, 191
Ministry of Health (*see also* Elliot, Walter; Welsh Board of Health) xi, xiii, xv, 1, 3, 9, 11, 13, 14, 24, 50, 74, 84, 88, 109, 114, 165, 178, 201, 218, 242, 243
Moeller, Jean 116, 120, 127
Moffit, Billy 145, 209
Mold 235
Molyneux, Dave 244
Molyneux, G.W. 24, 112
Montgomery 178, 221
Montgomeryshire 32n, 62, 72, 97
Moore, Marie 207
Morfa Bychan 206
Morris, Bert (Mrs) 104, 168
Morris, Frank 132, 266
Morris, Miss 264
Morrison Junior School (Mossley Hill) 32, 78, 136
Morrison shelters 185
Mott, C.F. 4, 12, 15, 51, 78, 84, 87, 150, 171, 175, 250
Mowat, Hetty 104
Mulberry harbours 192
Munich crisis xii-xiv, 154
Murphy, Thomas 72, 103
Murray, Beryl 31
Murray, Olive 63, 272
Mussolini xi

Nant Conway 64, 102, 150n, 165n
Nash, Gordon 184
National Gallery 192
National Conference for Safeguarding Welsh Culture 154
Nature rambles - *see* Country life

Neale, A.S. 139
Neston 192n, 201
Netherfield Road School 170n,
Nevin and District Sunday School Union 159
New Brighton (Wirral) 119, 181
New Ferry 190
New Zealand 267
Newsham Boys' School 135, 273
Newtown 184
Nickson, Mr 39
Nits - *see* Head lice
Norris Green 188
North Wales (see also Bombing; Religion; Tuberculosis; Welsh language; Welsh Nationalists): character of area xvi-xviii; housing in xviii; local government in xviii, 271; population: ageing xvii, 95, falling xvii; unemployment in xvii
North East Coast Aircraft Company (NECACO) 192
NSPCC 112
Nursing Association 225

Oak Alyn Hall 207
Ogwen RD 151, 197
Old Mariners' Home, Egremont (Wallasey) 39
Oldershaw High School 125
Oldershaw Grammar School 125
Organ, Ron 33, 105, 112, 140, 217, 222, 223, 234, 259
Oswestry 33, 34, 73, 127, 184, 186, 266
Oswestry Heritage Centre 266
Otter, A.W. 192
Oulton High School 39
Our Lady's School (Birkenhead) 152
Overcrowding (*see also* Billeting) 191*ff*

Overseas evacuation 188, 188*n*, 268
Overton 48
Owen, Emyr 87*n*
Owen, Goronwy, MP 53, 58
Owen, Olwen 69
Owen, Wilfred 204

Pacifism xi
Paisley, Jessie 132, 248
Parcell, Rhona 63, 69, 122, 273
Parental contributions - *see* Billeting
    allowance
Parental visits - *see* Visits
Park Station (Birkenhead) 181
Parker, Donald 33, 252
Parry, George 100, 224
Parry, Roy 62
Pembroke 32
Penllyn RD xvii*n*, 17, 106*n*
Penmachno 12
Penmaenmawr xiii, 2*n*, 85, 87, 96, 97*n*,
    105, 117*n*, 120, 148, 205, 227*n*
Pennycuck, T. 200
Penrhyndeudreath 151
Penyffordd 98
'Phoney war' 48, Ch 3, 169, 172, 181
Plaques, commemorative 260, 264
Platt, Lilian 259
Platt, Major 194
Poison-gas warfare xi, 4, 5
Population of North Wales - *see* North
    Wales
Portdinorwic 88, 99, 109,
    196
Portmadoc 53, 92, 97*n*, 118, 124, 132,
    139, 148, 152, 177*n*, 196, 206,
    207, 208, 227*n*, 232, 236, 242,
    247, 252
Poulton Infants School 186
Poverty: in Liverpool 22-4, 49, 84*ff*,
    106, 113-14, 270-1, 275; in
    North Wales xvii-xviii, 59, 69,

104, 270-1
Powell, Lily 42, 147
Prenton 174
Prestatyn 36, 129, 192, 225, 256
Priestley, J.B. 22
Priests - *see* Roman Catholics
Prince Rupert (Steers St.) School 110,
    121*n*, 135, 170*n*, 271
Priory RC School (Netherfield Rd) 247
Pritchard, Robert Alun 201, 203
Pritchard R.A. (Mrs) 201
Private evacuation 31, 74, 157, 173,
    174, 184, 190
Privies (in billets) 86-7
Propaganda: 1939 2-5; 1940 169-70,
    176, 212
Psychiatric Social Worker 102, 226
Psychological effects of evacuation
    40*ff*, 90, 223, 271-2
Pwllheli 36, 39, 93, 114, 123, 150*n*,
    174, 237, 247
Pye, E.B. 73

Quarry Bank School 75
Quaye, Norah 253
Quinn, Vera 42, 71

Racketeers 202
Radnor 32
Raeder, Grand Admiral 174
Reading, Marchioness of xiv, 169
Reception arrangements 16, 36*ff*, 172;
    distribution of evacuees 39*ff*,
    172
Recreation (see also Boy Scouts,
    Cinema, Girl Guides, Urdd,
    Youth clubs) 227*ff*
Red Cross; (American) 114
Redmund, Mrs 48, 65, 236, 252
Reed, Meryl 188
Religion (see also Calvinistic
    Methodism; Roman Catholics,

Chapel) xviii, 8, 58, 143*ff*, 274; Jewish 151; Moslem 65-6
Religious Houses, used as billets 206
Requisitioned houses, use of 206-7
Return home (1939) 53, 56, 78*ff*; (1944) 244*ff*
Return to Wales (See also Reunions) 257, Ch 9
Reunions (*see also* Evacuees Reunion Association) Ch 9
Rhos Voluntary Helpers for Evacuees 108
Rhos-on-Sea 108
Rhos-y-Gwaliau 207, 264
Rhosesmor 71, 256
Rhostyllen 228
Rhydderch, Arthur Merfyn (Dr) 224-5
Rhyl 129, 194, 202, 238, 242, 248
Rhyl County School 117
Richards, H.M. xi
Richards, Gordon 73
Richardson, Jack 138
Rimmer, Sheila 31
Roberts, D.J. 166
Rock Ferry High School 53*n*, 79*n*, 118, 128, 134, 139
Rock Ferry Convent School 124
Roffey, James 260, 267, 268
Roman Catholics 8, 58, 145*ff*, 229, 244
Roper, Mrs 204, 275
Rowlands, Margaret 227
Rowlands, William 118*n*
Royal Welsh Fusiliers 230-1, 237
Royal visit (Merseyside, Nov. 1940) 176, 182
Rumours 73, 93
Runaways 208-9, 219, 256
Runcorn xv, 16, 37
Rushton, Nesta 59, 87
Ruthin 11, 13, 52, 85, 89, 182, 209, 265
Sabbatarianism (*see also* Culture

clash) 58-9, 144
Sacred Heart School 145, 152
Salford 75
Salisbury Street Infants School 132, 170, 228
Sandford, Rita 27, 43
Sarnbach 67
Saunders Roe Ltd 192, 193
Scabies 51, 86, 91*ff*
Schofield, L. (Mrs) 71
Schooling - *see* Education
Schools (*see also* Education; schools by name): host pre-evacuation meetings 7, 21; re-open in evacuation areas 77, 128, 170; used as distribution centres 116
Schools Inspectors xi, 118, 139*n*, 142, 158
Scotland Road 5, 41, 77
Scouts - *see* Boy Scouts
Seion Vestry Evacuee School (Criccieth) 120
Shakespeare Report 225-6, 228
Shanghai xi, xviii
Shaw, D. (Mrs) 105, 209, 215, 224, 275
Shaw, Ron 35, 143, 233
Shelter Welfare Departments (Merseyside) 187
Shelter rash - *see* Scabies
Shelters - *see* Air-raid shelters; Anderson shelters; Morrison shelters
Shennan, Ernest (Alderman) 191
Sherlock, Peter 44, 90, 144, 186
Shrewsbury 154
Sick Bays - *see* Health
Silian 132, 248
Simmonds, Oliver 5
Smith, Barbara 105, 188, 209, 216, 222, 224
Smith, F.M. (Mrs) 41

Smith, Frank 32
Smith, Walter 266
Social mismatching 68*ff*
Spain xi, 4, 7
St Asaph 41, 130
St Benedict's School 97
St Francis Xavier College 41, 79, 117
St Helen's 110
St John's Ambulance 41
St Joseph's Primary School 188
St Luke's School 32, 264
St Mary's Priory (Tithebarn Street) 84
St Oswald's School 99
St Saviour's School 141, 178
St Vincent's School 105, 148
St Werburgh's School 42, 147
Starkey, Dr 194
Summers, Dorothy ('Mrs Mop') 191

Tattersall, F.F. 124
Taylor, Jane x
TB - *see* Tuberculosis
Teachers (*see also* Welfare; teachers
        by name) 1, 7, 21, 25, 46, 60,
        77, 79, 108, 115-43, 212-13,
        217, 218, 227, 243; list of
        duties 134-5; new skills 142,
        (learn Welsh) 132; relations
        with locals 142, 143; use of
        trainees 134
Temple Road Central School 78
Teretski, Rabbi 151
Thomas, Elfed 142
Thomas, Glenys 153
Toc H 4
Toilets - *see* Privies
Tower Hill (Abergele) 99
Townsend, Carolyn 206
Towyn 66*n*, 78, 99, 177*n*, 179*n*
Transport 8, 12, 15
Traynor, Beryl 28, 45, 65, 187, 205
Treasury 13

Tregarth 49
Trekking 188-9
Tribunals - *see* Billeting
Triggs, Joyce 275
Trumbell, Dorothy 190
Tuberculosis (see also Anti-
        Tuberculosis Service Report)
        xvii-xviii, 14, 101
Tunstall, W. 184
Tweedie, Allan 274
Twrcelyn 66*n*, 227*n*
Ty'n-y-Maes 170*n*

Unemployment (*see also* Poverty): in
        Liverpool 22-3; in North
        Wales xvii
University of Wales Guild of Graduates
        85
Upper classes - *see* Large houses
Urdd Gobaith Cymru 230

Valley 227*n*
Verdin, Len 256-7
Vermin - *see* Head lice
Vestries - *see* Education; Chapel
        authorities
Visits (from parents etc) 63-8
Visit of King - *see* Royal visit
Visitors (*see also* Accommodation
        Surveys) 1,2

Wade, Beryl
Waen Fawr Cottage Hospital 94
Wales, North - *see* North Wales
Walker, Peter 230
Wallasey xv, 4, 7, 8, 12, 30, 32, 157,
        175, 176, 181, 184, 186, 244,
        255
Wallasey High School 125
Wallasey Grammar School 125
Wallis, Stan 138, 144
War, declaration of 31

War Office xi
War work - *see* Work
Waterhouse Inquiry 212
Watson, E. (Mrs) 26
Waugh, Evelyn 202
Weather 80-1
Welfare of evacuees (*see also* Billeting
    Officers; Clothing; Footwear;
    Health; Ill-treatment;
    Teachers) 17, 29-30, 97*ff*, 134,
    135, 212*ff*, 270*ff*; welfare
    committees 225, 227; welfare
    officers 64, 87, 152*n*, 225,
    227*ff*
Weller, Maureen 86, 145
Welsh language xviii, 1, 10, 13, 18, 33,
    38, 60, 68, 116, 131-2, 153-60,
    247, 254, 266, 274
Welsh Board of Health (*see also*
    Ministry of Health) 4, 14, 15, 93
    96*n*, 102, 149, 166, 226, 227
Welsh Nationalists 3, 18-19, 52, 154,
    157, 159, 160, 243
Welsh League of Youth 230
Welshpool 97*n*, 146, 255
Westmore, N. 77
Wharton, Dorothy 43, 63
Whelan, M.T. 100
Whitefield Road School 170*n*,
Whitegates Hostel (Ruthin) 89
Widnes 16, 37, 157
Wilkes, Hilda 209, 217
Wilkinson, Bill 44, 209, 231-2
Williams-Ellis, Clough (Mrs) 155,
    204-5
Williams, Menna Lloyd 227
Williams (Mrs) 63, 70, 91, 158
Wilson, Barbara 35, 42, 275
Window Cards 3
Winnicot, Donald 90
Wirral 32*n*, 64, 174, 244, 265, 266,
Women's Voluntary Service (WVS)
    xiii, 4, 9, 10, 16, 17*n*, 52, 66,
    75, 95, 108, 109, 110, 111,
    135, 169, 194, 195, 225, 228,
    237
Women's Institute (WI) 255
Women's Voluntary Aid Association 12
Woodlands School 74
Woods, Arthur 267
Woods, (Mrs) 274
Woodside Station (Birkenhead) 28, 30,
    63, 186
Woodward, Helen 77, 132, 139, 140,
    142, 156, 273
Woolfall, Edith 264
Wootton, Lord 9
Work: domestic 141, 220*ff*; farming
    xvii, 141, 220*ff*; war work
    119-20, 220*ff*
Wrexham xvii, 12, 14, 39, 43, 65, 66*n*,
    75, 84, 96, 104, 141, 144, 171,
    206, 238, 243, 246, 273
Wrexham Boys Grammar School 122
Wrightson, Clifford 97, 233
Wrightson, Elston 97
Wynne, Jessie 42, 130

'Ychafis' 92, 254
Young Farmers' Clubs 230
Youth clubs 230
Youth committees 230
Youth Hostels 42, 98, 207, 260

Zoning - *see* Evacuation

THETIS - The Admiralty Regrets –The Disaster in Liverpool Bay

by C.Warren & J.Benson

The definitive minute by minute account of this terrible tragedy in 1939 when 99 men lost their lives as HM Submarine *Thetis* undertook her first and only dive. With new photographs and documents as well as a new foreword by a survivors son Derek Arnold, and a new postscript by maritime historian David Roberts. Why didn't anyone cut open the submarine? Why was there no urgency in the Admiralty's rescue system? Did the Admiralty really regret?

ISBN 0 9521020 8 0   £9.50 + £1.50 p&p

HMS THETIS – Secrets and Scandal – aftermath of a disaster.

by David Roberts

The sinking of HMS *Thetis* cost 99 men their lives and is still today the worst submarine disaster in British History. This new book contains interviews with relatives of victims; sons, daughters, brothers, sisters and those very rare ladies, living widows. Also here are never before seen documents from the time; Offers of outside help, Secret Navy reports and even descriptions of bodies for identification. Why did the Official Inquiry blame nobody, explaining it away as 'an unfortunate sequence of events'? Why did the civil action on behalf of the widow's fail? Did the Admiralty cover it up? How much did Churchill know?

How were those left behind treated? A huge publicly subscribed disaster fund was collected for the relatives. How was this managed and distributed? Who got what and why? What ever happened to the money that was left?   ISBN 0 9521020 0 5   £8.99 + £1.50 p&p

'a book that shocks...tells the hidden story of those left behind' Sea Breezes.

LUSITANIA

by Colin Simpson - updated Merseyside Edition

THE definitive work on the real story surrounding this still mysterious ship.

On the 7th of May 1915 the Cunard vessel *Lusitania* was torpedoed by a German submarine off the Old Head of Kinsale on the south west coast of Ireland resulting in the loss of the vessel itself and 1,201 men, women and children. It also ultimately resulted in the United States entry to the First World War. More than eighty five years on the story of the *Lusitania* continues to be shrouded in mystery and suspicion. What was her real cargo? Why wasn't she protected? Why did she sink so quickly? Containing rare photographs from Germany and elsewhere; it is a truly intriguing and fascinating tale.   ISBN 0 9521020 6 4   £9.50 + £1.50 p&p

CAMMELL LAIRD - the golden years

by David Roberts. Foreword by Frank Field MP

Looks back at the world famous shipyard's history with particular focus upon the 1960s and 70s when Lairds were engaged in the building of Polaris Nuclear submarines. A unique look at the history of this yard that contains many photographs and references.

'Captures life in the prosperous years of the historic Birkenhead shipyard'- Liverpool Echo

'Puts into perspective...the strikes...the Polaris contract...and those who worked at the yard'- Sea Breezes

ISBN 0 9521020 2 1   £5.99 + £0.80 p&p

298

LIFE AT LAIRDS - Memories of working shipyard men

by David Roberts

When Cammell Lairds has gone and we are a generation or two down the line who will answer the questions 'What did they do there?' 'What was it like?' This book answers the questions. - Sea Breezes

A Piece of Social History – Liverpool Echo

Life at Lairds is a book of more than 120 pages about what life was like for the thousands of ordinary people that worked in the world famous Birkenhead shipyard. Contains many rare photographs of Lairds, it's ships and it's surroundings. ISBN 0 9521020 1 3   £6.99 + £1.50 p&p

FASTER THAN THE WIND - A History Guide of the Liverpool to Holyhead Telegraph.

by Frank Large

Take a journey along the one of most spectacular coastlines in Britain, the beautiful hills and countryside of North Wales and Wirral. On a clear day it is possible to see just how signals were sent along the coast to and from Liverpool. This book contains full details of the intriguing and little known sites of the substantial remains of the Liverpool to Holyhead Telegraph Stations. A second journey can then be taken into the fascinating workings of such a telegraph and those people involved in creating and using the signalling system and what life was really like living and working at the telegraph stations more than 100 years ago. ISBN 0 9521020 9 9 £8.95 + £1.50 p&p

IRON CLIPPER '*TAYLEUR*' – the White Star Line's 'First Titanic'

by H.F. Starkey

'Iron Clipper' is subtitled 'The First Titanic' for it tells the story of the first White Star liner to be lost on her maiden voyage. Built on the Upper Mersey at Warrington, the *'Tayleur'* tragedy of 1854 and the '*Titanic*' catastrophe of 1912 are disasters which have so much in common that the many coincidences make this factual book appear to be a work which is stranger than fiction.

ISBN 1 902964 00 4   £7.50+ £1.40 p&p

SCHOONER PORT - Two Centuries of Upper Mersey Sail

by H.F. Starkey

Schooner Port tells the story of the part Runcorn and navigation of the upper Mersey played in the Industrial Revolution and of the contribution of merchants, the shipbuilders, and the crews in making Britain 'The Workshop of the World'. Also recounted is something of the courage and tragedy, which was the lot of many flatmen and seamen who helped build British industry on the strength of the shipping fleet. ISBN 0 9521020 4 6   £8.95 + £1.50 p&p

'Recognised as the only authoritative work on this particular subject '- Sea Breezes

'Packed with hard facts and illustrated with some rare old photographs, this rare book should command a wide readership'. - Liverpool Echo

JUST NUISANCE AB - His full story

by Terry Sisson

The amazing but true story of the only dog that was officially enlisted into British Royal Navy, a Great Dane whose name was Nuisance, his official rank and name was AB Just Nuisance. Famed for his preference for the company of navy ratings (he wasn't too keen on Officers) in and around the famous World War II naval base of Simonstown, South Africa, Nuisance helped many a sailor rejoin his ship after a night on the town.

Today his own statue overlooking the bay off the Cape of Good Hope commemorates Just Nuisance AB. £7.50 + £1.20 p&p

THE GOLDEN WRECK - The tragedy of the *'Royal Charter'* by Alexander McKee

The effects of the hurricane of October 1849 were to shock the nation. 133 ships were sunk, 90 were badly damaged and almost 800 people lost their lives. More than half of those that perished were on one ship - *The Royal Charter*.

After two months at sea voyaging more than 12,000 miles from the Australian goldfields, disaster struck off Anglesey when she was just hours away from her home port of Liverpool.

Her story too is one of incredible bad luck...had she come to grief just yards away from the unforgiving rocks that destroyed her she would have grounded upon a stony beach where it is likely that most of those aboard would have been able to walk off.

Many of her passengers were returning home with the fruits of their labours - GOLD!

The worst shipwreck in Welsh history, this is the story of the *Royal Charter*...and her gold.

ISBN 1 9029640 2 0   £9.50 + 1.50 p&p

ALL AT SEA - **Merseyside Maritime Memories** - compiled by Ev Draper

Foreword by Linda McDermott -in association with BBC Radio Merseyside

Recollections of the men and women who sailed from and worked around the Mersey, for trade or defence, through two World Wars to the present day. ISBN 1 9029640 1 2 8 £5.99 + £1.25 p&p

VIDEOS

CAMMELL LAIRD - **Old Ships and Hardships** - the story of a shipyard.

After an extensive search for moving footage of this world famous shipyard at work a video of the history of this shipyard has at last been compiled. How Cammell Laird served the nation through two World Wars, building world famous vessels like the *Rodney, Hood, Mauritania, Ark Royal, Windsor Castle* and many more, up to the tragic day in 1993 when Lairds was shut down.

The story of the yard is also told through the voices of the men who worked at Lairds; Welders, cranedrivers, electricians and plumbers, they tell of the hardships of building ships in all weathers and the lighter moments that came from some of the 'characters' of the yard.

£14.99 including post and packaging in UK.

'ALL IN A DAYS WORK' Volumes I & II - a look at working lives on the River Mersey.

Just when you might have thought that the River Mersey was dead and buried the biggest surprise of all comes along. There is life in the old dog yet! The River Mersey is alive and well. Liverpool, Birkenhead, Tranmere, Eastham and Runcorn are still places that enjoy marine traffic and employ people working on the river. There are interviews with River Pilots, shipbuilders, shiprepairers, tugmen and dredgermen that show that the age-old crafts and seamanship itself are still as strong as they ever were. There is also archive footage of working life on the river.

Features Rock Boats, Mersey Ferries, the Bunker boats & crews on the Mersey, the Vessel Tracking System for river traffic, new vessels on the river, lockmasters and much more.

£14.99 including post and packaging in UK.

All videos are available in international formats for £17.99 + P&P £3.50.

Please state country/ format required.

To Order Books or Videos Direct Contact:-

Avid Publications, Garth Boulevard, Hr. Bebington, Wirral,Merseyside UK. CH63 5LS.

Tel / Fax 0151 645 2047

Look at the books and videos via the internet on

http://www.avidpublications.co.uk or   E-mail info@AvidPublications.co.uk

300